In the Meadows of Trimworth

a Kentish Country Diary

Chistmas 2019.
Love and Happy Christmas from Meewen ee al.
xxx

Richard Goodenough

For:—
Rebecca, Peter and
James.
Best wishes.
Richard

To Roz - and also the exuberant optimism of my young companions Jack, Arianna and Edward.

Acknowledgements

Among the many people who have given practical and professional support in writing this book, I would especially like to recognise the following. I am grateful to James Loudon of Olantigh and John Sunley of Godmersham who kindly gave me permission to gain access to their land. Bill Charlton and Roz have provided editorial assistance, resulting in far fewer errors than there would otherwise have been. Tim Ashenden of Mickle Print has patiently offered his professional skills and advice on layout, design and printing. All the illustrations and paintings are the work of the author, but I would like to thank the following for their permission to reproduce illustrations from their collections; Ediciones Patrimonio (Les Trés Riches Heures du Duc de Berry), pages 58, 153, 212, 236, The British Museum, page 22, The British Library, page 18, The National Monuments Records, page 136, I am also grateful to John Hills for providing the location map in the Introduction.

Finally, I am indebted to the rich heritage of landscape essayists, naturalists and diarists whose work has inspired me to recognise the extraordinary in the commonplace features of the natural world in these fields by the river. I hope, in turn, this book may encourage others to enjoy intimate and unforgettable encounters in their own special places.

Printed & Published by Mickle Print (Canterbury) Limited 2012
www.mickleprint.com

ISBN: 978-0-9559997-4-1

Front cover: *The Stour, Kitchen Meadow, Trimworth*

Introduction

During my working life as a geographer, I have developed a deeper understanding and appreciation of the natural and physical environment, and most recently the impact of human activity on these environments. Fifty years ago, Wooldridge and East, two great 'old school' geographers maintained that geography was, 'learnt through the soles of your boots.' Since then, the methods and skills of geographical studies have been impressively changed to meet new technologies and the solution of new problems, but the old axiom still retains some relevance. The 'soles of my boots' have certainly been the means by which I have collected and recorded many observations during my daily walks with Sam through the meadows in all weathers.

This journal is about the ecology of a small area, regularly visited. It has led to an intimate knowledge of everyday events in a beautiful, varied but unspectacular location. It reveals as much about the wonders of nature and an awareness of environmental change as the wilder, more spectacular designated sites for nature conservation. I'm not a trained ecologist, botanist, or biologist, so my daily discoveries do not carry the weight of expert views in these disciplines. This is not a scientific record, but a collection of observations, insights, questions and perspectives on the natural world, which have caught my attention during my daily walks. Throughout the year, countryside issues have arisen which have been reported in local and national media. Some have national, even global significance, but they frequently also have a local impact. These issues have found a place in this journal, often with a personal interpretation on their importance or relevance to the 'meadows by the river.'

Whilst an interest in the natural world is my main focus, I am sometimes diverted by a strong and parallel interest in local history. Consequently, at intervals there are items on the evolution of the rural landscapes in these meadows by the river, such as the origin of hedge banks, ancient woodlands, drainage ditches, field patterns and names, reclamation and clearance of woodland and marsh, and other natural and man-made elements of this valley in the chalk lands, all examined with reference to map and documentary sources. The geology and topography of this country represents the bones of the landscape and has inevitably influenced the characteristics of the 'flesh' which has developed upon them, and hence the flora and fauna of the habitats which emerge. In other words, it is difficult to understand and appreciate the present landscape without reference to the history that lies behind it and influences it so profoundly.

I have walked these paths often during the last 15 years, but over the last year or so I have observed, gathered and recorded information about small-scale changes and events in the natural world more carefully. I have looked with fresh eyes at places and objects in the natural world which I had long thought I knew. It has been a process of discovery and an illuminating experience of adventure, full of surprises, mysteries and wonders; I have become aware of the fragile, interconnected nature of these environments and their inhabitants. I feel as if I have engaged with this piece of country as a home that I share with plants and animals. Many of the places on my walks have become special through personal acquaintance, such as the place I first saw the kingfisher; the shallow riverbed on which my little grandson Edward and I sat to watch the river weeds moving in the current on a hot day in summer; the part of the wood where buzzards circle; the piece of meadow where the 'pilot lights' of glow-worms shine; the river bend where I know the biggest trout can be seen; the bank which will be covered in orchids in May; the dyke where snipe rise in their erratic flight; the field where I found a Neolithic flint arrowhead; the river path where we are almost daily escorted by wrens. These places are special to me because I have experienced events which have moved me and which I will never forget. They are nameless places far more significant to me than the more spectacular wilder locations. Hopefully, everyone will have their own joyful, intimate encounters with such special places.

The Lie of the Land

Trimworth and its surrounding fields lie within the Stour Valley, where the river has sliced through the chalk of the North Downs. It is a location with great historical and geographical significance. The house is located on a bench or river terrace, 30

The Downland landscapes have a rich archaeological heritage as well as providing shelter for the fertile river meadows of the Stour lying below.

metres above sea level, and 200 metres from the river. Across the river to the west the land rises up to Godmersham Downs reaching a height of 146 m in Kings Wood. To the east, a more gradual slope rises up to Trimworth Downs. Both downland landscapes have a rich archaeological heritage as well as providing shelter for the fertile river meadows lying below. The landscape in which we walk has been strongly influenced by geological structure. The underlying geology is Chalk, composed of marine sedimentary formations of the Cretaceous period, into which the River Stour has cut, breaching the North Downs escarpment. On the surface of the solid geology are superficial deposits of river gravels, silts and clay-with-flints, which have affected the landforms, soils and agricultural potential of the area. On the slopes of the downs run dry-valleys or coombes, formed during an extremely cold period when melt-water on frozen chalk eroded steep sided valleys.

These landforms have guided the movement of people and the location of settlements. Evidence lies in the rich archaeological heritage dating back to prehistoric environments 10,000 years ago, during which a slow transformation of a society that followed its food source to a more sedentary one concentrating on food production occurred. This brought about significant landscape transformation as woodland clearance quickened to allow cultivation and the domestication of sheep, cattle and goats. Bronze Age societies migrated into the south-east from the continent, bringing another wave of woodland clearance. Throughout this early history the Stour valley provided a trading route between the coast and the interior. Substantial finds have been uncovered only a few hundred metres from Trimworth, such as the Bronze Age hoard in a shallow pit consisting of 185 pieces of metal work, including rings, axe heads, spearheads and fragments of swords.

The River Stour would have been an important means of access inland as well as a source of fertile valley soils during the Iron Age. Forest clearance quickened with better implements and greater demand for timber products. Once again the area around Trimworth presents good evidence of this occupation in the form of settlement just below the crest of Trimworth Downs at about 100 m. Even more significant is the ancient system of fields on Godmersham Downs, clearly visible as shadow marks in the low evening sun. These have survived because they became abandoned at a later date in favour of heavier, more productive soils in the valleys below, leaving ancient fields undisturbed under the smooth, short turf of the chalk downs.

We can speculate on the country scene through which we walk as it would have looked during this period, just before the arrival of the Romans. Godmersham was probably established as a small community situated in the sheltered valley and farming the fertile soils of the valley floor and terraces. The river would have acted as a vital waterway, allowing trading of goods upstream and downstream. Heavy iron ploughs would have been used to cultivate the heavier soils to produce corn in enough quantity to trade and export. And overlooking the valley was the downland through which ran important route ways winding between small cultivated fields, woodland clearances and forests.

Following the Trails

With the unflagging companionship of Sam our black Labrador, and occasionally my wife Roz, I walk every morning between seven and eight, then again late afternoon, and if mood and weather suits, at dusk or even later on warm summer nights. It is a routine; grabbing an old coat, wellies, hat, gloves, camera, notebook and sometimes binoculars, then feeding Coco the horse and letting Sam go bounding ahead. We walk down through the garden, past the ponds and out of the field gate. In front of us the Stour Valley opens up, a broad valley crossed by drainage dykes, bounded on the east by the partly wooded terrace overlooking the floodplain, and to the west by the lower slopes of Godmersham Downs. In between, the tree-lined river meanders towards us from Ashford, crossing the floodplain on its way to Canterbury and the medieval port of Sandwich.

There are at least three routes, all shown on Fig1. Usually we cross Six Acre Meadow and Bridge Meadow to the river and then head upstream. At the end of the meadow our route narrows to a path running between the river on our right and Tye Wood to the left. We emerge into East Dane Meadow and follow the riverbank to the footbridge, crossing into Bilting Meadow and walking to the weir below Olantigh House. We retrace our steps back to Tye Wood and either follow the dyke through Six Acre Meadow back to the house or climb up the steep river

In front of us the Stour valley opens up, a broad valley crossed by drainage dykes.

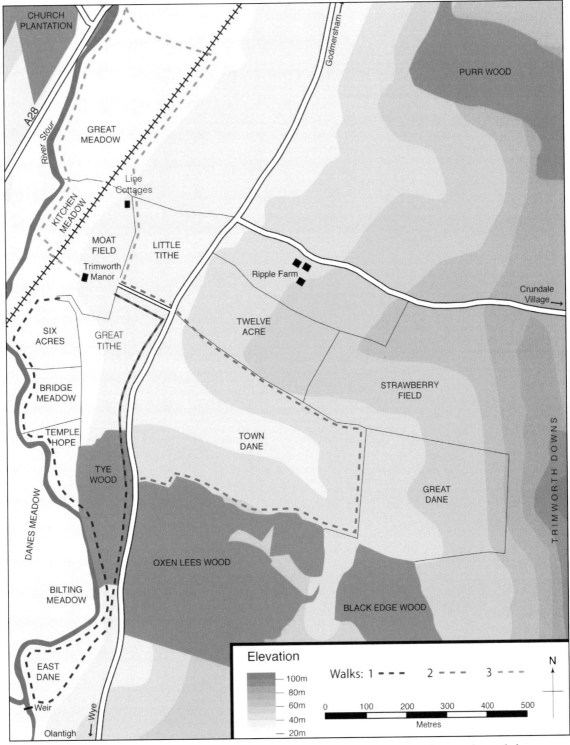

*Figure 1: The location of Trimworth and the routes followed. **The representation on this map of any track or path does not indicate the existence of the right of way.***

The route narrows to a path running between the river on our right and Tye Wood on the left.

We emerge into East Dane Meadow and follow the river bank to the footbridge at Olantigh.

. . . . returning through Tye Wood and Great Tithe field.

terrace, through Tye Wood and follow the hedge running beside Great Tithe field to
the top of our drive. It is about 3 km, and with head down, walking at a brisk pace,
the circuit can be done in 40 minutes, or an hour or more at a leisurely saunter
with frequent stops to observe, photograph, draw, rescue sheep, chat to a walker, or
snooze with Sam in the sun.

Sometimes we take an alternative, slightly longer and more challenging route by
walking eastwards up the slope of Town Dane Field on Trimworth Downs to the old
trigonometric point at 100 metres, with wonderful panoramas over the Stour valley
to Godmersham Downs. From here we cross the head of a dry-valley and return
along the margins of Black Edge Wood and Oxen Leas Wood, then we cross the
road into Tye Wood and return along the hedge line bordering Great Tithe Field to
the top of the drive. The third route takes us west from the house, under the railway
line and into Kitchen Meadow. Meeting the river we turn downstream through
Great Meadow towards Godmersham, pick up the ancient trackway back under the
railway and return past Line Cottages to Trimworth. Both the river walks follow the
parish boundary between Godmersham and Crundale, coinciding with the Anglo-
Saxon boundary charter of the year 824, in which Trimworth (Dreamwurthe), is
mentioned for the first time in written records.

Trimworth

We moved to Trimworth in 1995, a late 15th century Wealden hall house
surrounded by fields. There was no garden; sheep fields came right up to the
walls, brambles and nettles grew 2 metres high around much of the house. We
were starting a garden from scratch; a blank canvas, which was both exciting and

unnerving. We established a number of principles which would guide our overall design. Our location in a valley cut into chalk downland provided extensive views through and across the valley, as well as east to Trimworth Down and west to Godmersham Down. We wanted the garden to be part of this landscape, not cut off from it, so the idea of high hedges and small compartments or garden rooms was not part of the vision. Maintaining the spacious open character, using the slopes within the garden and creating vistas to the distant landscapes were our guiding principles. Another was the desire to garden with wildlife in mind. We felt it was possible to create an attractive garden for our enjoyment as well as create a haven for wildlife. We planted 250 metres of hedge using mixed native species to encourage butterflies, birds and wild flowers. Two garden ponds have been constructed, one fairly formal and planted with water lilies and other aquatic plants, the other unplanted and unlined, the water level fluctuating with the water table. Both have attracted a wide range of amphibians, insects and wild flowers. We covered walls and fences with climbers to add a vertical dimension to the garden and attract nesting birds, foraging and hibernating insects and small mammals. As far as possible, we use natural methods of pest control, on the grounds that however selective chemicals are claimed to be, they will almost always kill beneficial species, as well as those targeted.

We have made a garden out of fields, but no garden is forever, and no garden is ever finished. The garden is a process, not a product and we are aware that it could easily return to its former wilderness of long grass, nettles and brambles once again. Above all we feel that our garden is not isolated from the surrounding countryside; it is part of it, creating a different habitat with soft boundaries across which flora and fauna can move easily, including Sam, Roz and me.

January

January 1st

At the beginning of each month this journal will make reference to the Book of Hours, medieval illuminated manuscripts used throughout medieval Europe from 1250 to1550. Each book was divided into eight sections or 'hours' of the day, beginning with matins and ending in late evening with compline. Each hour contained prayers, psalms and activities appropriate to the needs, interests and economic status of the owner. Some were commissioned by the wealthy and were richly embellished and illuminated with lapis lazuli and gold leaf by the great artists of the day. They became less common when Henry VIII declared himself Head of the Church of England, because the Book of Hours was replaced by the Book of Common Prayer. From the 1560s, the Book of Hours was rarely used. But my foremost interest in these intimate treasures is that they show illustrations of the common monthly and seasonal activities in countryside and garden. A classic example is Les Très Riches Heures du Duc de Berry, painted in the early 15th century by the Limburg brothers for Jean de Berry. The pictures in the calendar section illustrate the agricultural life and labour of each month and are the most beautiful part of the manuscript, regarded as one of the greatest art treasures of Europe. Even the impact of the onset of the Little Ice Age has been detected in differences between early and later examples of these illustrations of agricultural scenes and activities.

Sparrows Bridge, a river crossing of great antiquity mentioned in an Anglo-Saxon charter of 824.

January is named after Janus, the Roman god of gates, doorways and beginnings. He is depicted as having two heads, one bearded and looking back to the past year, the other youthful and looking forward to the New Year. Since Roman times he has been used to symbolise change and transition, and was worshipped at the beginning of harvest time and planting. As the spirit of 'opening,' his name is an obvious choice for the first month of the year.

The garden temporarily emerges from recent frosts and snows with vegetation looking battered, limp and bruised. Mole workings are evident, rabbits have exposed roots with their scratchings and barked the stems of shrubs, a reminder that not all the mammal world has been hibernating. There is an air of neglect and melancholy about the garden, not helped by three days of fog without sight of the sky, let alone sun. We know, however, that this bleak, dismal prospect is a fleeting one because deep down, roots will be preparing for action, bulbs swelling beneath our feet. Memories of winter melancholy and long cold dreary days will melt away in the optimism of spring.

January 3rd

When we leave the house by the kitchen door, we are invariably met by the sudden soft sound of whirring wings as sparrows leave bird tables, feeders and gutters to congregate in the nearest hedge. We are pleased to have our colony of 10 to 20 pairs around the house. It is a permanent, resident flock: bustling, noisy and a gregarious. I counted 15 sparrows on a seed table today, including several males with their distinctive black bibs of various sizes, the bigger the bib, the higher the rank. When squabbles occur over food or the use of dust baths, the lower ranks with smaller bibs will give way. Sparrows dominate the birdfeeders with their aggressive behaviour, using deep conical bills to attack other birds as well as search out seed. The population of sparrows nationally seems to have stabilised after a decade of decline, for which no clear explanation has been provided. Recovery is greater in the rural areas of the South and East of England. At Trimworth, they congregate in small colonies in the roof space, under the eaves, but particularly in evergreen climbers on ivy-covered walls.

They are resilient little birds, able to tolerate climate change. They have lived amongst humans since the Ice Age, longer than any other wild bird, and have virtually colonised the whole world. Their spread has been associated with the emergence and spread of agriculture, but they have suffered a long spell of persecution. Under an Act of Parliament during the reign of Queen Elizabeth 1, payment of head money was given for sparrows, encouraging people to take heads to the local church in return for payment. This pest status continued through the 18th and 19th centuries when 'sparrow clubs' were formed to kill thousands of sparrows and steal eggs. Today the sparrow has few predators except cats, tawny owls and sparrowhawk, but attacks have not affected overall populations because they are prolific breeders, able to rear up to 4 broods a year with three eggs in each clutch. Failure of broods in suburbia is twice as likely as in rural areas, possibly because of fewer food sources and more cats.

The Anglo Saxon charter of 824 setting out the parish boundary of Godmersham.
(© British Library Board. All Rights Reserved. Stowe Charter 14 side 2)

A kilometre upstream from Trimworth is a small foot-bridge across the River Stour called 'Sparrows Bridge.' Today, it consists of two or three trunks nailed together by wooden boards, but it is a river crossing of great antiquity. The bridge is mentioned in an Anglo-Saxon charter of 824, which records the boundary of the parish of Godmersham by reference to trees, bends in the river, houses and bridges. It reads as follows, "First, from an ash North to Staettingforda: thence North by river to Dreamen wurthe, (Trimworth) in fish pool…. " Staettingforda is the name given to the present Sparrows Bridge and it is an interesting coincidence that the Anglo-Saxon word 'stetting' means sparrow. Not only has the name sparrow persisted through the centuries, but happily, the little bird also continues to thrive in good numbers in and around Trimworth.

January 5th

A mysterious, magical start to the day following a night of hard frost. The sky was the palest blue, but to the west across the valley, thick, drifting mist snagged the trees on Godmersham Down as if reluctant to be drawn out of the branches of the beech wood. As the sun rose, the grey mist reflected sky colours of pale ochre, slowly changing to rose pink. Constable wrote of Turner, "He seems to paint with tinted steam, so evanescent and so airy." This scene would have been a perfect subject for his work. As an amateur artist, the shape, perspective and colour of clouds and skies are a fascination and a challenge to me. How can this amazing visual experience involving shifting light and shade on clouds and landscape be fleetingly captured and compressed onto a two dimensional surface? Recently I completed ten watercolour sketches in a day to capture the changing effect of light on the river meadows; this morning I would have needed ten sketches in as many minutes to capture the translucent, diffused light and its shifting colours. In a few minutes the mists had cleared, and the bold, 'eyebrows' of the beech-covered downs were revealed once more.

It is 12th Night. In the Middle Ages, Christmas Day was just the beginning of a period of feasting and merrymaking lasting for 12 days and 12 nights, culminating on the 12th night of 5th January. This is the evening before Epiphany, the end of the medieval Christmas festivities. It is the night when Christmas decorations are removed. It was thought that tree spirits lived in greenery such as holly and ivy and it was important that they were given house room and safe haven for the harsh midwinter days. On the 12th night though, it was necessary to release these spirits back into the countryside, otherwise they would be mischievous and possibly cause crop failure.

January 6th

In the early morning half-light, I glimpsed the spread, barred tail of the sparrowhawk swooping menacingly around outbuildings and the birdfeeders. It took off to skim along a hedgerow, leaving behind a fearful garden bereft of sight or sound of birds. The river was in spate, grey-brown water thundering over the weir, rushing under the footbridge, gurgling and swirling through the alders. The meadows were soggy from heavy overnight rain and frost-thaw. The path between wood and river was almost impassable because of ankle-deep mud. In the skies above Tye Wood an aerial combat was in progress. Two buzzards gracefully circled, their 'mewing' calls carrying across the valley. A group of rooks was disputing the buzzards' territorial rights by making fast counter-attacks and harsh calls of 'kaaw,kaaaar.' This was no playful encounter, but a hostile offensive with outstretched talons. Their agitated wing beats contrasted with the languid, drifting flight of the unperturbed buzzards, and after a few minutes the restless rooks beat a direct path towards the lightening skies in the east above Oxen Leas Wood.

January 7th

Today is St Distaff's Day or Rock Day when women traditionally resumed their house work after the twelve days of Christmas. The distaff or spindle, sometimes known as a 'rock', was used as a medieval symbol of women's work, hence the term 'spinster', a legal term for an unmarried woman. The ritual of the day is illustrated in the poem by Robert Herrick (1591-1674) 'On St Distaff Day.'

> "Partly work and partly play
> You must on St Distaff Day:
> From the plough soon free your team:
> Then cane home and fother them:

Drifting mist snags in the trees, reluctant to be drawn out of the beech wood.

The river was in spate, grey-brown water thundering over the weir at Olantigh.

If the maids a-spinning go,
Burn the flax and fire the tow.
Bring in pails of water then,
Let the maids bewash the men.
Give St Distaff all the right:
Then bid Christmas sport good night,
And next morrow everyone,
To his own vocation."

So it was a day for getting women back to work, as Fitzherbert wrote in his, 'Book of Husbandry' in 1523, "it stoppeth a gap … It saveth a woman from being idle, and the product was needful." Incidentally men did not return to the plough until plough Monday on 11 January!

January 8th

Bands of rain and sleet driven by near gale-force winds drift horizontally down the valley. Sam sits expectantly by the back door. Roz and I look at each other. Who will capitulate? Certainly not Sam. At least the sky now has a structure to it, following days of gloomy fogs and mists. The 'Folkestone Ladies,' the local name given to the cumulus clouds resembling wigs worn by ladies of the 18th century, were drifting east over the skyline of Trimworth Down. Locals will expect stormy weather to follow. J.S. Collis in, "The Worm Forgives the Plough," writes about the way clouds stir the imagination, "… those creatures that are not alive: these buildings not made of brick: these domed and daring palaces in which there reigns no king: these vast foundries flaming without fire: these mountain ranges, upon which no feet may ever walk: these radiant prospects of a far country belonging to the paradise lost regions of the heart." There is little in nature which is more mysterious or fascinating than cloud formations, such as these brilliant, billowing white towers of the Folkestone Ladies drifting through the Straits of Dover.

After days of rain, the river runs fast and noisily, breaking its banks in places to flood the pastures. Lakes of grey water are studded with the white and black of black headed gulls, quarrelling noisily as they scavenge for scraps in the shallow water. Some appear to be tramping the ground on the spot, so-called 'foot paddling' to simulate the pattering of raindrops, luring the earthworms to the surface. Today they look uncomfortable as they all face into the wind to prevent their feathers being ruffled. This is the most common inland gull, hardly a seabird at all. Occasionally they will be joined by herring gulls with white heads and chest, grey backs and black wingtips. These noisy birds commonly visit inland tips, fields and reservoirs all year round. They should not be confused with the similar common gull, which despite its name is not at all common in inland areas unless wild weather drives it in from the coast, as has happened today.

January 9th

There was an early-morning encounter with a weasel. As we turned the corner around the house and entered the rose garden border, we noticed a rat-like movement, then stillness. Surprisingly the creature scurried closer and stopped, then sat up investigating us for at least 10 seconds. We saw its long, slim, muscled body with reddish-brown upper parts and white under parts, separated by a wavy line. It was motionless, alert, staring fiercely, then suddenly took off to the margins of the sunken garden, stopped, came back as if to playfully renew the acquaintance, finally scampering off towards the summerhouse, the haunt of rabbits, before slipping through a tiny hole no bigger than a 50p piece. It is our smallest carnivore, from the same family as the otter and stoat, but it is a fierce fighter with jaws built for power and leverage and long, sharp jagged teeth with four curving fangs. It administers a sharp bite to the neck of the prey, which may include voles, mice, even small rabbits and birds. With my grandson, little Jack reading about Peter Rabbit in Beatrix Potter's books, I wonder just how much he should know about this killing machine and the brutal realities of nature! (This troubling paradox of the glories and grimness of nature returns to engage my thoughts regularly throughout the year.)

The weasel ranges over a territory of 4 to 8 hectares in size depending on food supply, marking off its territory by emitting a strong-smelling secretion from anal scent glands. Its favourite habitat is a thick hedge or stone wall with crevices and interstices into which it can hide and hunt prey day and night. They have to eat about 25% of their body weight every day to avoid starvation, and when the population of voles and mice fluctuates, weasels will stop breeding, decreasing their population in turn. Young weasels are born early in the year; they are often capable of breeding during their first summer, unlike other carnivores, which usually don't breed until the second year. It is a short life span of only 1 to 2 years, often shortened by persecution by man, especially in areas where pheasant and partridge are being reared. We regard them as welcome, useful friends eating hundreds of mice in the year and keeping down the rabbit population.

The topography of this area has strongly influenced the movement of people and the location of settlements in the downland landscapes, and particularly in this valley of the River Stour. During Roman times this valley continued to be a natural corridor for soldiers and settlers moving into the interior. The whole valley has a rich archaeolgical heritage and there is certainly strong evidence for Roman activity on the terrace just upstream from Trimworth. Perhaps the most fascinating find near Trimworth was an Anglo-Saxon buckle of bronze, plated with silver and gold, and inlaid with garnets. The central spine of the buckle is a golden fish whose body is decorated with fine gold wire. The fish was an early Christian symbol and its use here may be a deliberate reference to Christianity. In this respect, the dating of the buckle to the early seventh century is significant, because in 597 a Christian mission led by St Augustine landed in Kent to convert pagan Anglo-Saxons. The Crundale buckle may therefore be an indication of conversion to Christianity and the indirect social and economic changes which this brought about. The buckle was found in a man's grave together with a garnet-inlaid copper alloy buckle and an iron

Anglo-Saxon buckle of bronze, plated with silver and gold, and inlaid with garnets found near Trimworth (© Trustees of the British Museum)

sword with decorated pommel, all purchased by the British Museum and on display in room 41. During the Anglo-Saxon period the landscape around Trimworth was transformed by the open field system. More settlements were established over the period between 450 and 1066, during which time England became a land of villages.

It is Plough Sunday when the beginning of the agricultural year was celebrated by a plough being taken to the village church and blessed. This was the ceremony of 'ploughlode.' In our village of Crundale, the tradition was for ploughboys to lead horses around the farm, collecting donations of eggs, meat and cheese which they took to the local inns to be cooked. Plough Sunday reflects a time when farming festivals drove the calendar. It seems odd to us that ploughing started as late as January, because today the ploughs are in the fields almost as soon as harvesting is finished. In times past the stubble had a use in feeding and fattening up chickens and geese in preparation for Michaelmas, an important feast day. It was also felt that the action of frost would help to break down the soil after a January ploughing, ready for sowing in March. The fabric of life centred round the seasons and the farming year, and despite the hardship, this farmers' prayer, used on Palm Sunday would have expressed a widely held sentiment of gratitude for the value of life in farming communities.

> "Let the wealthy and the great.
> Roll in Splendour and State,
> I envy them not, I declare it.
> I eat my own lamb,
> My chicken and ham,
> I shear my own fleece, and I wear it.
> I have lawns, I have bowers,
> I have fruit, I have flowers,
> The lark is my morning alarmer.
> So jolly boys now,
> Here's God speed to the plough,
> Long life and success to the farmer." (Anon. circa 1890)

The morning peace was shattered by the horrible sound of destruction along the railway embankment. Screaming chainsaws were being used to clear-cut trees and shrubs which came within 10 metres of the railway track. It was carnage in the name of vegetation management and the justification was 'leaves on the line.' Healthy trees up to 20 metres high were being cut, branches stripped and fed into huge, powerful chippers. I was powerless to intervene; it was Railtrack land and Railtrack business, despite the enormous visual and wildlife impact this destruction would have on the landscape. By the end of the day over 400 'trunks,' measuring 2 metres in length and more than 20cms in diameter were piled up along the edge of our river field. We will use some; the rest will go to Godmersham Park when the field is dry enough to get them out without serious rutting. There is some consolation. Network Rail has joined with local authorities in Kent to fund a Kent Free Trees scheme! They state how committed they are to the environment and have 'actively supported the planting of over 50,000 trees throughout Kent.' It is a neat move. They can salve their uneasy conscience by diverting attention away from ill-considered impacts of woodland destruction, focusing instead on their role in the enrichment of landscape and biodiversity, however measured.

January 11th

The first Monday after 12th night is Plough Monday, a more entertaining, fun filled, money raising day than Plough Sunday with its greater ceremonial significance. It is the turn of the ploughmen to blacken their faces, mark the end of Christmas festivities and make some money at a difficult time of the year. Ploughs were decorated and pulled through the villages in an attempt to extort money from wealthy landowners. Penalties for non-payment could be the removal of the front doorstep by the plough, or the ploughing of a furrow across the offender's lawn! The custom goes back to the 15th century, when the aim was to raise money for the church in order to keep the 'plough light' burning. After the Reformation in 1538, the ceremonies became more associated with personal gain for farm workers than assisting the church. Many of these activities continue today, particularly in eastern England and consist mainly of Molly dancing, a form of Morris dance. There are also Mummers plays: folk plays performed in the streets, in house-to-house visits and in public houses, all accompanied by the vigorous rattling of money boxes.

January 12th

In the winter-sown wheat fields redwing are roaming. They tend to roost together in large numbers in the thick hedges, leaving roosts early in the morning to range over the open fields. They are mobile birds and if poor weather sets in, they will move on in flocks of 10 to 200 birds to find better weather conditions. Today they flitted along hedgerows in search of hawthorn and holly berries, and although rarely seen in gardens, they will visit in harsh weather, stripping berries from cotoneaster and rowan. A buzzard circles lazily in the cold air high above the Bilting Meadow, closely and silently watched by a crow in flight. The closer the buzzard circles to Tye Wood, the more concerned was the crow. Reinforcements were called up from the wood and the buzzard slowly retreated towards Olantigh. The silent aerial confrontation to defend territory was over – for now. In the paddock, jolly jackdaws rise gleefully in noisy packs to tumble and roll in the sky, then swoop down to forage for seed under the birdfeeders, displacing a flock of chaffinch.

Cool grey, warm grey, neutral grey, slate grey – or just grey, there is little other colour to be seen in the landscape today. The alders along the river are an exception. Male catkins are like small dark-brown chippolatas hanging in clusters of three to four catkins. In a month or so they will grow longer and swell, changing to deep red. The female flowers are cone shaped and deep brown. They have released their seeds, and those that remain are much sought after by goldfinches who tease out the tiny seeds leaving empty cones on the tree well into spring. These clumps of alder give a dense deep- red/purple glow to the riverbank, rather similar to the winter twigs of the limes along the drive. This tree, which a few months ago gave us green /

gold light and scented blossom is now stripped of leaves to reveal graceful arching branches and long, deep-red buds. It is from the lime trees that the nocturnal tawny owl is heard but rarely seen, unless caught in the beam of headlights flying on soft, silent wings. We hear its quavering call almost nightly as it marks out its territory in preparation for nesting and breeding in February.

January 13th

It is St Hillary's feast day and a day which has gained a reputation as being one of the coldest days in the year. Many Frost Fairs were held around this date, notably on the Thames at a time when the river was broader, shallower and flowing more slowly. From 1400 to the 19th century, there were 24 winters when the Thames was frozen over, the last being in 1844, when an elephant was led across the river below Blackfriars Bridge.

Despite today's cold and damp, our mood has been raised by the continued appearance in the garden of clumps of the earliest of our daffodils, the diminutive Narcissus Cedric Morris. The Latin name for the daffodil is Narcissus, named after the beautiful youth of classical mythology who fell in love with his own reflection in a pool – then fell into the pool and drowned! Narcissi sprang from the place where he died. In reality, this wonderful little variety shows its beautiful face at the cusp of the year, beating the first snowdrops and aconites. Its shallow, golden miniature trumpet is shaded with emerald green where the outer petals meet the short stems. When bathed in winter sunshine it is a real heart warmer, a moment described as, 'not the start of spring, but more the end of lifelessness.' The little Narcissus was named by Beth Chatto after Sir Cedric Morris, the artist, plant collector, plant breeder and well-connected gardener. It was collected (quite improperly in current practice) 50 years ago from a rocky ledge in Northern Spain and has never again been found in the wild. On his 90th birthday Beth Chatto took her great friend and mentor a pot full of narcissi Cedric Morris, because it had disappeared from his own garden!

January 14th

The red kite has been sighted around Crundale. We have seen it soaring effortlessly over Warren Wood and Oxen Leas, staying in the air for long periods with hardly a beat of its wings. It is a distinctive bird with a deep forked tail and chestnut red colour. Its huge wingspan of nearly two metres is larger than a buzzard's making it more graceful in flight. The location of their nesting site around Crundale is uncertain; they build large, flat, untidy nests of sticks almost exclusively in hardwood trees such as oaks, but we have not seen their nests. It is likely that the birds we see are exploring over a wide territory beyond their normal breeding and nesting range. We will see more of them in March or April as they prepare for the nesting season. The red kite has successfully returned from a point of virtual extinction. For centuries it has been regarded as a threat to expanding agriculture and has been persecuted, most recently by gamekeepers of large country estates. Only in mid-Wales did they continue to survive. Despite threats from egg collectors and poisoning, their numbers have increased and their distribution broadened.

It is estimated that in southern England in 2008 there were between 400 and 500 breeding pairs, largely as a result of a programme of reintroduction of birds to new locations by the Nature Conservancy Council (now Natural England) and the RSPB.

Over a period of five years, more than 90 birds were brought from Spain and introduced into the Chilterns AONB, where they were placed in pens on the Oxon/ Bucks border, then released into the wild. Other re-introductions have been placed in the East Midlands and Yorkshire, north-east England, Scotland and Wales. The success of these projects raises the prospect of the reintroduction of other native animals which have become extinct. Britain, like a number of other countries, is legally obliged to consider the restoration of native species to their former range. Natural England has a regulating role in this area, following strict international guidelines. In the last 20 years ,the red kite, corncrake, osprey, great bustard, large blue butterfly and pool frogs have all been successfully reintroduced, and there are plans to extend this to include hen harriers, white tailed eagles and shorthaired bumblebees. There is sometimes local opposition on financial and conservation grounds, as in the planned reintroduction of white eagles to Norfolk, which met with strong opposition from landowners, farmers and birders and where the scheme has now been dropped. More successful is the programme to reintroduce the great bustard, the world's heaviest flying bird, to Salisbury Plain. European Union funding of £1.8 million has been awarded to run the project which began six years ago with chicks from Russia being the first to successfully mate in the UK since 1832.

January 15th

Our stretch of the river valley and its meadows runs south-west to north-east, which means prevailing winds from the south-west are funnelled through the valley. Sited on a terrace above the valley, the house and gardens of Trimworth are exposed to these winds. We could provide protection with windbreaks of trees and tall hedges, but prefer the open aspect which allows us to watch the arrival of weather as it sweeps down through the valley. Curtains of rain drift by in various tones of grey; mists and clouds provide dramatic effect against a backdrop of the downs. Today Sam is eager to walk, but it is a grey day with cold wind and a scattering of icy showers from a low cloud base which obscures the downs. This is a monochrome landscape, except for the dull green, bruised and flattened pasture emerging from under the blanket of snow. At the entrance to Tye Wood a buzzard sits motionless in a sycamore, patiently looking down on rabbit tracks and contemplating a warm meal. They are scavengers, and the cold weather has provided struggling prey, and some fresh corpses. The buzzard looks well fed, but kestrels, seeking small prey hidden under snow look miserable and tatty, hunched on posts and poles.

After a long spell of snow and temperatures below freezing, there are signs of a thaw. The crisp white powdery snow is now grey and stained with sheep droppings and mud. There are sounds of running water everywhere. The focus of the news media shifts from the dislocation of transport and shortage of sand and grit, to burst pipes and potholed roads, flooding and fog. We followed the intermittent footprints of fox through the woods and into the meadow, occasionally seeing droppings left on molehills, the tops of grass tussocks and occasionally on paths through the wood. The droppings are grey/ white, indicating the large number of bones in the fox's diet. Like other mammals, the fox has a strong sense of smell and uses scent to mark its territory. This scent marking is particularly pronounced from fox urine, used to mark boundaries of its territory or as a signal to the opposite sex in the mating season. Flocks of pigeons are feeding on young brassicas in fields. There are fieldfares, our winter visitor from Scandinavia, searching for hips and other hedge fruits, chattering as they search. They are attractive members of the thrush family with chestnut / brown, grey and ochre colouring. They fly along hedge lines with plump bodies that seem too bulky for their wings.

The first new moon of the year offers little competing light to the stars which flicker brightly from clear skies.

Warm air circulating over frosty ground usually results in fog. 'Cold, dull and overcast with stratus cloud base very low at 150 metres, visibility poor in mist and drizzle,' is the forecast usually associated with this weather situation. Forecasters use the term 'anti-cyclonic gloom', as much a description of the mood of the population as it is a meteorological event, because it can persist for days on end. This sombre day was enlightened by crowds of cheerful, chirpy long-tailed tits flying between the weeping willows and following us along the riverbank. They have become more numerous partly because winters are, on average, milder than they were 25 years ago, allowing them to survive the winter and breed in larger numbers in the spring. Also, the long-tailed tit has migrated from hedgerows and woodlands into our gardens where it has learnt to feed from tables and feeders. It is a sociable bird, travelling in family parties, and passing on the knowledge of this increasingly reliable food source for the winter.

This is the old Twelfth Night, the traditional date for wassailing, which was celebrated on 17th January before Britain changed from the Julian calendar to the Gregorian calendar in 1752. The traditional greeting of 'wassail,' (waes haeil) meaning ' be whole or healthy,' is said to derive from a toast given by the daughter of the Saxon leader Hengist to the British King Vortigern. As a result, the King became enchanted by her beauty and her generous welcome and the two were quickly married, a union between a pagan girl and a Christian King arising from 'a wassail.' Thus, the Christian custom of wassailing was born in which festive toasts of cider and ale were drunk from wassail cups. Edward Hasted in his 'History and Topographical Survey of the County of Kent, 1799' describes how, "a number of young men with a most hideous noise run into the orchards, and encircle each tree." These young men were the 'apple howlers' whose intent was to stimulate the tree and wake it from the dormancy of winter to produce growth and plenty for the spring. The custom is still practised today in parts of Somerset with the wassail bowl being paraded, trees being blessed with mugs of cider, lots of singing and gunshots, cider-soaked bread being left in branches, and other strange actions to encourage the trees to become productive.

My research into early written records at the Centre for Kentish Studies and the Canterbury Cathedral Archives, has revealed a great deal of fascinating information about Trimworth and the surrounding fields. One of the great early sources is the Anglo-Saxon land charter. These land charters referred to the estates of individuals or monastic institutions. Hundreds of land charters survive from the late seventh century onwards giving insights into an obscure and distant period of our history. These set out the boundaries of estates, right down to a single tree, a bank, the line of an old hedge, a bend in the river, or an old building. The estate boundary of greatest relevance to Trimworth dates from the year 824, in which Trimworth Manor appears for the first time in written record. The original parchment document, held in the Manuscript Room of the British Library, is fragile but legible, and records the proceedings of the court to resolve a dispute over land between Archbishop Wulfred and Beornwulf, King of the Mercians. On the reverse of this document is set out the boundary markings of the Godmersham estate, beginning as follows. "First, from an ash, north to Staeting Ford: thence north by river to dreamen wurthe (Trimworth), in fish pool: thence east straight by southward of Broad Lea: so south of Purr Wood by Pit Lea to Winchelcombe......"

Equipped with a 1 to 25,000 OS map, it has been possible for us to identify and follow the route of this estate boundary in the fields. Scrambling over hedges, traversing deep woods, following narrow paths blocked with brambles, walking up on high ridges with magnificent views of the country around, was a wonderful way for us to gain a true and detailed knowledge of the countryside around Trimworth, establishing a link with landscape features which existed over 1100 years ago. In practice, the task was not so straightforward. It was a slow process with constant cross-referencing between map and field. Often we used old maps as a follow-up to provide some clues. For example, the tithe map will show boundaries older than those which survive today, and will record field names which have long since passed out of use. A vital clue in the work is often the parish boundary, which generally coincides with the charter boundary for much of its length. In the end, the exercise of combining the written document with the fieldwork was rewarding and fascinating. As WG Hoskins, the great landscape historian so aptly puts it, "once the charter is solved, one has the intellectual satisfaction akin to that of a mathematician who has solved a long and difficult equation." (The Making of the English Landscape.)

January 19th

The world warmed by about 0.6°C in the 20th century, with each year except one being warmer than the previous year. If carbon dioxide levels could be magically stabilised to the present levels, the world would still probably warm by another half a degree centigrade. The overwhelming evidence for global warming (a subject which this journal will raise in a number of contexts) is that it is real and man-made. If this is true, how will global warming, with its milder winters affect hibernation? The ecosystem is a very delicate chain, easily disturbed by changes in seasonal temperatures. Hedgehogs, dormice and bats are among many species which hide themselves away with frost triggering their torpid state. Their bodies retract, keeping essential elements of their metabolism going at the lowest level in order to survive before being aroused by warmth. Milder winters could bring them out of hibernation prematurely when food sources are still scarce, causing them to lose weight and become stressed. Dormice now hibernate 5½ weeks less on average than they did 20 years ago. The breeding cycles of birds, reptiles and rodents are all undergoing change. Great tits are laying eggs a week earlier, and red kites 10 to 11 days earlier than nine years ago. Hedgehogs are now frequently seen walking around in February, which used to be a rare occurrence.

In addition to changes in hibernation, global warming is also affecting the timing and distance of bird migrations. A warming climate could push the breeding ranges of birds considerably further to the north, making some migrations longer. This added distance may constitute a threat to some birds, especially those unable to 'refuel' on the way. High winds and atmospheric instability associated with global warming could also affect the ability of birds to complete long migrations. Another problem may affect those birds which to decide to overwinter in a warming Britain. A subpopulation of blackcap warblers, for example has begun wintering in England instead of the Mediterranean. This decision to 'tough it out' here could put them into competition with resident species for available food supplies. Of course, nothing in the natural world ever stays the same, and unless the changes are very sudden or drastic then it is likely that species will be able to adapt. Hibernation was a process which evolved to deal with a cooling climate and so it is reasonable to expect adaptation over time to a warming climate, unless the human impact causes the rate of change to become too rapid. As Charles Darwin observed, "It is not the strongest species that survive, nor the most intelligent, but the ones most responsive to change."

It is St Agnes Eve, commemorating Agnes, a 13-year-old Christian girl who was martyred in 304 A.D. because of her beliefs. She became the patron saint of virgins, betrothed couples and gardeners, and is often depicted holding a lamb. On St Agnes Eve, following a day of fasting, young single women went to bed in silence, walking backwards and reciting:

January 20th

> "Fair St Agnes, play thy part and send to me my own sweetheart,
> Not in his best, nor worst array, but in his apparel for every day,
> That I tomorrow may him ken, from among all other men."

The story has created one of the richest literary and artistic themes in history. Keats's long poem of 42 stanzas, written in 1819, opens and closes with descriptions of a frozen winter night affecting animals outside, and humans inside.

> "St Agnes' Eve -Ah, bitter chill it was!
> The owl, for all his feathers, was a-cold:
> The hare limp'd trembling through the frozen grass,
> And silent was the flock in woolly fold:
> Numb were the Beadsman's fingers while he told
> His rosary, and while his frosted breath,
> Like pious incense from a censer old…"

Tennyson was influenced by Keats's description of this saintly story and responded with a poem on St Agnes' Eve which also uses images to depict a frozen winter's night. Such poetry inspired Pre-Raphaelite art as in William Holman Hunt's portrait of St Agnes, painted in 1857. John Everett Millais painted a sentimental scene of a girl holding a candle, gazing through an open window onto moonlit snow covering the outbuildings and the garden.

The day started badly, rabbits had attacked the stems of all the climbing roses on the arches and around the base of trees. They have never stripped rose stems before. Apple trees, even mature ones have been barked all round the trunk, the depth of snow making it easier for them to reach above the protective netting. I suppose all the gnawing was the only thing separating these little creatures from starvation in what has been an extremely harsh winter. On the river meadow, crows were playing at being shot; diving headlong, cascading and twisting downwards and just having fun. Others were playing at aerial bombing of buzzards. Even the heron occasionally becomes a target as it flaps slowly and rhythmically along the river course. Later in the day, starlings gathered on the tops of ash trees to engage in music and movement, singing and preening, chattering and whistling. The sound builds up to a pitch, then switches off; some birds leave their perches, others fly in. This is euphemistically called a 'murmuration', but there's nothing soft or subdued about the sound from this gathering.

We collected armfuls of twigs and small branches from below the upswept branches on the smooth grey trunks of ash, the best of all firewood. Along the field margins, a few half-closed daisies and dandelions are showing; celandine will follow shortly. In the drive, spikes of leaves from bulbs are bursting through; snowdrops emerging and cyclamen beginning to flower. Teasels around the pond are standing erect and prickly, the perch of small birds although seeds have long gone. Many have germinated below the dead spikes as neat green rosettes on the grass. A robin high on a wind vane nonchalantly surveys the competition on the bird table below, ready to assert its superiority. He welcomes us with a burst of song which will reach full-force in spring as it seeks to attract a mate and defend its territory.

Our gardens owe much to the Victorian plant hunters who risked life and limb to bring back exotic plants from around the world. Their legacy lives on in the plants that we now consider to be quintessentially English. For example, the British plant explorer Charles Maries left England for Shanghai in 1877 and found Hamamelis mollis in the Lusham Mountains, returning with seed in 1879. Plants were grafted from the original and the species was eventually awarded Garden of Merit status by the RHS in 1922. Since then this Chinese witch hazel has become a delightful flowering shrub in the dark days of December to February. The blooms, which grow directly from the branches, are spidery, bright yellow and very fragrant. It is growing at Trimworth in a lawned area containing a number of specimen trees such as acers, cornus and ginko. Another treasure in the cold gardens of winter is Viburnum bodnantense (Dawn), with its clusters of rose pink sweetly scented blooms, flowering from January to March and responding quickly to any milder periods during that time. We grow it as a hedge plant where the flower and bronze leaves stand out in the bare hedges. Both plants make a cheery sight on this gloomy January day, but nearby is a dismal, depressing sight.

Our fully grown horse chestnut is showing worrying signs of a phenomenon affecting trees, initially in south-east England, but increasing its distribution markedly since

2001. This is bleeding canker, spread by the fungal pathogen Pseudomonas syringae which in 2007 affected 80% of horse chestnut trees surveyed by the Forestry Commission in south-east England. The main trunk of our tree is affected by deep gashes with liquid ooze discharging from the cracked bark. In a few years, it is likely that the bleeding areas will coalesce to encircle the whole trunk, leading to crown death and eventually destruction of this much loved feature of our garden and the British landscape. Death of one life form invariably brings life to another, and so we see the gelatinous ear-shaped fruiting bodies of the edible Jew's ear mushroom clustering in diseased patches of the tree. Lifting the diseased bark reveals beetles which have lived and reproduced under the weakened, dying and dead bark of the tree, their shallow feeding tracks etched in the decaying wood. These beetles and other insects such as woodlice and millipedes are being extracted from crevices by woodpeckers. The softwood of the main trunk is peppered with beak marks and holes. This is likely to be the greater spotted, commonly seen on our birdfeeders nearby. They probe the crevices in the bark using their long sticky tongues to extract insects and beetles before taking off on a bouncing flight with wing feathers folded against the body between wing flaps. Its relative, the green woodpecker, is more of a ground feeder, surviving on a diet of ants on the lawn and returning each day to excavate ant hills.

As I write, a lacewing lands on the paper and moves slowly over the surface, its long antennae twitching from a small grey head. Other lacewings are emerging on windows, walls and curtains throughout the house. Their transparent wings are incredibly delicate, crisscrossed with tiny green veins and although the head is small it has strong mandibles for chewing. The life-cycle of the lacewing goes through the stages of egg, larvae, pupa and adult. They are predatory as both adults and larvae, feeding on aphids and other insects by sucking juices from the insect and rather gruesomely covering itself with the drained bodies of its victims. Some species are reared and sold commercially to gardeners as a biological control agent. In the spring, they will court by emitting a low-frequency sound produced by vibrating the abdomen. Males and females take turns in 'tremulating' as an essential prerequisite to mating. They are most commonly seen from May until August. In the winter, many enter houses and other shelters to hibernate, and the one crossing my notepaper has obviously been aroused from hibernation by morning sun through the windows during this spell of warmer weather.

January 23rd

How have they and other insects survived the winter, especially those outside in freezing temperatures? Quite often they will cluster together for warmth and use their collective body heat to keep warm. Ladybirds and honeybees use this method, while ants go below the frost line in large numbers. Other insects go into a state of torpor or temporary sleep to survive drops in temperature, coming out of this state as the weather warms. Sometimes a longer state of suspension known as diapause occurs, allowing the insect to synchronise temperature changes with stages in its life cycle. Some butterflies will spend the winter as a chrysalis and then emerge as a

The spidery, bright-yellow fragrant blooms of witch hazel.

Death of one life form, as in this horse chestnut, invariably brings life to another.

butterfly as the weather warms. Many insects survive by evacuating as much water as possible and packing their tissues with a sugary anti-freeze molecule called glycerol. This gives the insect super-cooling ability, allowing it to survive well below freezing temperatures until warm weather returns, when glycerol levels will drop. The winter moth pupa for example can survive temperatures of -30°C. Nymphs of dragonflies and mayflies survive below the ice of ponds, feeding actively, growing and emerging as adults in early spring. The biggest problems generally occur in situations where temperatures fluctuate, causing some insects to become active, like our lacewings, and leaving them vulnerable when temperatures suddenly drop again.

Seeking shelter from a blustery south-west wind, we walked along the eastern edge of Oxen Leas wood. A flock of tits followed us along the woodland margins; soon they will be pairing up and looking for nesting opportunities. Fat, fluffed-up pigeons sat moodily in branches, crows took off and were carried far across the fields on the following gusts with hardly a wing beat, before tumbling around and landing to strut and scavenge in the winter-sown wheat. Then a half-noticed quick movement and the suspicious flick of a bushy tail as one, then two grey squirrels appeared close to the thick, untidy winter 'drey' which they had built in the lower branches of a beech. We had observed their presence here in the autumn, but now the milder weather had roused these confident little bounders from sleep, and they were searching for hidden stores of fungi, leaves, shoots, and beech mast. They chatted as they chased one other, perhaps a prelude to mating in which the female squirrels will leads suitors in a merry dance of amazing agility through the upper branches of the tree, eventually being mated by the leading male.

The grey squirrel was introduced into Britain from North America in 1876 to satisfy a Victorian penchant for novelty. Since then its numbers have increased dramatically, but despite the obvious charm of this most commonly seen British mammal, its spread has contributed to the catastrophic decline of the native red squirrel. They cannot co-exist because the grey squirrel is stronger, bigger, more long-lived and can forage over much wider areas. Even more significant is that the red squirrel is susceptible to the fatal parapox virus, first noticed in East Anglia in 1984. The grey seems to be unaffected by this virus, leading to high population densities in broadleaved woodland. So what are the chances of our charming, irresistible native red squirrel returning to challenge the dominance of the little grey villain? There is some evidence that they are beginning the long march back from exile. As well as Scotland, there are strongholds south of the border in Merseyside, Anglesey, and particularly Cornwall, where the removal of grey squirrels has started on a voluntary basis on four estates. The replacement red squirrels will come from local wildlife centres which have been breeding them over the last 10 year years, a scheme backed by the Red Squirrel Survival Trust. According to the Forestry Commission, survival will depend upon the design and management of coniferous forests, their preferred habitat, but the prospect of England's isolated red squirrel populations joining up in the near future looks remote.

To the north and south of our fields are the managed parklands of Godmersham Park and Olantigh House, through which flows the River Stour, overlooked by river terraces and dry tributary valleys cut into the chalk. Both the neighbouring estates of Olantigh and Godmersham have enrolled their land into an Environmental Stewardship Scheme, delivered by Natural England on behalf of DEFRA, which offers payments to farmers for effective land management to protect and enhance the environment and its wildlife. Nearly 6.5 million hectares, that is nearly 70% of England's farmland, are in such 'agri-environment' schemes of which 5.5 million hectares are in the Environmental Stewardship Scheme. In 2003 we enrolled the land of Trimworth into the scheme, thereby creating a protected corridor of floodplain running for about 5km in which the conservation of wildlife, (biodiversity) is a major objective. The scheme also ensures the land is well-managed and retains its traditional landscape quality, including the protection of historical features and the natural resources of the river and its valley.

Our involvement over the last seven or eight years has provided additional habitat for a range of species through the construction of a new pond. We have also encouraged otters along this part of the River Stour through the provision of an otter holt. Two broad bays have been constructed along the river to create protected areas of shallow water for fish and breeding wetland birds. These bays have been fenced off from the field and protected from all human interference. On the floodplain, the numbers of sheep and cattle are regulated to maintain the sward height throughout the growing season, and restrict stocking densities to no more than 0.6 livestock units per hectare from May to July. This has minimised damage to flowering plants. There are also restrictions on tillage and the use of pesticides to encourage ground nesting birds. A shaw has been constructed along an ancient boundary between Godmersham and Crundale, reinforcing its historical significance. It is planted with weeping willow and hawthorn and acts as a wildlife corridor running from the river, across the floodplain and up to the railway embankment. We have further plans for hedgerow management, tree planting and protection of in-field trees on grassland, the use of beetle banks, the use of nectar-rich flower mixtures and the selective cutting of nettle banks .Most importantly we are keen to encourage educational use of these habitats by young people, something we have been involved in for several years. The scheme has allowed us to cooperate with our neighbours up and downstream to provide environmental management through this whole section of the valley and enhance its reputation as a designated Site of Special Interest for Nature Conservation.

January 26th

Drawing back the curtains in a rarely used bedroom this morning revealed a cluster of 20 or 30 ladybirds seeking to minimise heat loss and survive through the winter in a dormant state before becoming active and finding food, probably aphids. Occasionally they will be tempted out of dormancy by warm sun in January or February, resuming their over-wintering state when the cold weather returns. It is thought that hibernating ladybirds release pheromones to 'call' each other to hibernate in the same place. Not all of them over-winter in houses; some use leaf litter, tree bark crevices, low herbage and grass tussocks. I had uncovered the ten-spot variety, all red with black spots, the variety which most commonly over-winters in buildings.

Potential predators of the ladybirds can be repulsed by a toxic, distasteful yellow liquid which ladybirds emit, but they still have many enemies such as swifts and swallows, which are immune to the chemicals. Some wasps and flies will lay their eggs on the ladybird larvae, and they will feed on their host and kill the ladybird. The biggest threat, however, is the newest and most invasive ladybird, the Harlequin, introduced into North America in 1988 as a biological control agent, then invading Europe and arriving in Britain in 2004. Animated maps (www.harlequin- survey. org) show the spread of the beetle across the UK from its original point of arrival in south east England in 2004 through to its extensive distribution in August 2010. The rate of spread is dramatic, widespread and unprecedented. It is a voracious feeder of aphids, scale insects and lacewings- in other words a generalist feeder, not specific like our native ladybird. It is sometimes known as the Multicoloured Asian ladybird, and in America the Halloween ladybird, because it often gathers in houses at that time of the year. It has a very variable appearance and is quite difficult to distinguish from our native ladybirds, so it is unwise to squash suspects because we may be destroying our native species. The most common UK form is orange with 15 to 21 black spots, or black with two or four orange or red spots. If it is small, less than 5 mm (fifth of an inch), it is definitely not the Harlequin.

January 27th

There was a mild sense of optimism in the air as we set out for Trimworth Downs; a distinct but probably premature feeling of a seasonal shift, as if the weak sun was not quite able to rouse the earth from its languid sleep. We walked to the top of the downs, across the disturbed ground on the site of an old Iron Age settlement and into Warren Wood. Pigeons clattered out of the trees. The whirring wings of partridge and pheasant took them through the wood before drifting down the contours and fields into the valley bottom. We followed, past the old manor house of Crundale and up the valley side to the ridge- line between two dry-valleys cut into the chalk of the North Downs. From our vantage point the countryside looked washed and clean with trim hedges and fields of winter wheat like verdant, well-mown lawns making a patchwork with ploughed fields in tones and textures of corduroy, except where ploughing had brought chalk to the surface. Distant sounds of cockerel and quarrelling dogs rose up from the dry-valley below through which rattled a toy-sized trailer and tractor. Below us a kestrel glided down the hedge lines, revealing its black-spotted chestnut upper parts, grey tail with black bar; a change from the usual view looking up to its spotted buff-coloured underparts.

Across the valley were the margins of ancient woodlands, some of which are now semi-natural, combining native trees with some replanting. The indicators of ancient woodland are evident: sinuous boundary lines, woodland boundaries made up of earth banks, and old place names. Vineys Wood, originally 'deffinegh,' comes from the Old English meaning enclosure. Marriage Wood lies on the boundary of Wye and Crundale, the name derived from 'gemaere,' meaning boundary ridge. Church wood is near a church which predates the Norman Conquest and is on the site of a Roman building. Many of these old woods owe their location to the heavy clay-with-flint deposits, which cap the chalk and make cultivation difficult.

We returned through the churchyard to a chorus of blackbird song coming from the church tower. It was liquid gold, melodious, mellow, varied and interspersed with the odd chuckle and cackle. William Henley, the 19th century British poet was impressed:

> "The nightingale has a lyre of gold,
> The lark's a clarion call,
> And the blackbird plays but boxwood flute,
> But I love him best of all."

And overhead, the purest, palest blue sky with the soft edges of white cirro-cumulus clouds arranging themselves into bands and ripples, like gentle ocean waves approaching the shore.

From the study window I saw the sudden movement of a long, slender, red-brown animal emerging from the base of the hornbeam hedge. It scanned the garden with **January 28th** quick movements of its head and disappeared back under the hedge. Moments later, it reappeared and bounded across the front lawn into an old dried-up farm pond, checking for areas where rabbits had burrowed out shallow daytime shelters in the long grass. I thought it was a weasel, but the black tail tip confirmed it was a stoat, the stoat also being slightly larger. We have seen them occupying rabbit burrows in the bank along the field dyke, especially near the woodland margins, where they can watch rabbit activity from the cover of their occupied burrows, or from the woods.

The margins of ancient woodland are often marked by old earth banks

In recent snow, tracks of stoat were visible in this area showing the bounding nature of the animal with the impression of its body and tail also left in the snow.

They are sinuous, fast movers, vaulting over the ground after rabbits and administering a shark bite to the neck when the quarry is petrified and exhausted. The stoat's eyesight does not have the resolution of a human, and it uses scent to relentlessly follow a trail and hunt over areas of up to 5000 square metres or more. Their night vision is good, making them effective night-time hunters. In the 1950s, when rabbit populations declined because of myxomatosis, the stoat population declined also, but they survived by eating small birds, eggs, earthworms and carrion. Eventually their population recovered to make them one of the most common carnivorous mammals today. They are still trapped by some gamekeepers who accuse them of killing gamebirds, despite their preference for rabbits and mice. In the winter, particularly in the northern extent of their range, the stoat will turn completely white except for its black tail tip. This response to nature was the subject of a wonderful book which fascinated my children in the 1970s called, 'The Strange Story of Slim the Stoat,' written by the naturalist, RD Hunter. Slim turned white prematurely, becoming a conspicuous target for hawks and owls in the brown winter landscape, until the snow arrived and gave him a white 'ermine' camouflage. The changing colour is determined by temperature and length of daylight. In their more southerly range, stoats will still produce a winter pelt of a chestnut colour, similar to the summer coat, but thicker. Like weasels we welcome the presence of these successful predators which help to keep our rabbit, rat and mice populations down.

January 29th

We left the house in flurries of snow and hail carried in a biting wind, and a sky rapidly shifting in colour between tones of grey, yellow ochre and cobalt blue. This is real weather as opposed to the monotonous grey stillness of recent anti-cyclonic gloom. Overnight temperatures had fallen to -6°C. How do birds, faced with the prospect of 14 hours of darkness and freezing temperatures survive these nights? The answer is that many of the small birds like goldcrest, robins, coal tits and wrens do not. Others survive by fluffing up feathers, placing their heads in their scapular feathers and huddling with other individuals. Roof spaces in houses and old buildings become vital roosting places. Other birds look for crevices and cavities in tree trunks or squeeze into spaces behind loose bark. Our sparrows are clustered in the ivy clinging thickly to the walls of the house. Birds will adjust their metabolic rate when temperature variations occur; energy taken in as food being turned into heat to maintain body temperatures. However, in these freezing temperatures a bird can still lose a fifth of its body weight during one cold winter night. The previously harsh winters of 1962 and 1963 were probably the events that had the greatest impact on wildlife survival in living memory. This is why bird tables and feeders are essential to the survival of birds, especially those which do not have a cache of stored food, like crows.

Conversely, the big freeze can actually benefit many creatures and plants surviving beneath the ice on ponds because oxygen levels can rise. The conventional wisdom about breaking the ice during cold spells to allow oxygen into the pond is now felt to be unnecessary because oxygen diffuses very slowly into still water, moving through only two millimetres in a day. So in a pond with a depth of 50 cm, it would take eight months for oxygen to diffuse to the bottom of the pond. Underwater plants or algae are the oxygen providers. Even in the coldest weather they will continue to photosynthesise and produce oxygen, especially in shallow ponds where light can easily reach the plants.

I woke to the sound of frantic scratchings coming from the roof space over our bedroom. It was probably starlings or sparrows using their feet to fluff up the insulation and nestle together to conserve body temperatures. It was 3.00am and moonlight was streaming in through the mullioned windows of the old Jacobean porch, patterning the wide floorboards in rectangles of soft light. I looked over the moonlit font on the front lawn towards the sculptural silhouettes of the Scots pines with their gaunt broken branches, then, on up to the downs covered by the dark blanket of Warren Wood above which the moon shone through a misty veil of cirrus. The silver surface of the ponds, the black earth of empty beds and dark shadows cast by trees and hedges on frosted lawns created an ethereal, delicate beauty. The sunken garden was a tranquil centrepiece with the geometry of the dark box contrasting with the seams of gleaming white flint in the boundary walls. Even the grey foliage of the lavender was bright with a reflective glow, and the weeping silver pear looked magical. In this light, our garden creation has surpassed all our expectations. This is the best light to see the garden structures: monochrome, mysterious and beautiful, made distinctive by the frost, especially when coinciding with a full moon. Vita Sackville-West talked about her garden in moonlight, "drinking deep nocturnal silences… Only with nightfall can I stand apart and view the shaping patterns of my way."

January 30th

As we walked upstream, two cormorants flew low overhead one behind the other, necks outstretched, heads held up, and wings beating briskly. Further upstream, where the riverside path along the margins of Tye Wood opens up into East Dane Meadow, the river flows slowly through thick reeds and ground vegetation with stretches of boggy mud. This is the location where we often 'put up' snipe which

January 31st

frequently feed along the river edge. Today, a group of three common snipe (known as a 'wisp') rose noisily and zig-zagged across Bilting Meadow before flying high and circling towards Godmersham. On the ground they are slightly furtive birds in their movement, skulking through the muddy stretches and pushing their long straight bills into the mud to detect worms and insects. They often feed in a group of two or three (known as a 'walk'), but they are not gregarious and are not easily seen because of their camouflage. Their mottled brown backs and buff stripes blend into the dry stalks of the reeds, but in the sunshine the stripes look straw yellow, even golden. This meadow is a perfect nesting site for snipe because it is an unimproved conservation meadow with limited access where snipe can nest in well-hidden locations, usually in shallow hollows in the long grass. Two years ago shallow 'scrapes' were constructed in this meadow. They become flooded in the winter, providing additional feeding sites and reed cover for water birds.

The word snipe derives from the Old English word 'snite,' meaning a long thin object, a description of their long straight bills. Their name is commemorated in the village of Snitterfield near Stratford-upon-Avon, which in the Domesday Book is referred to as Snitefield. Very similar in habit and appearance is the Jack Snipe, which is smaller, more secretive and even less likely to be seen. It has very similar markings but a low and undulating flight when disturbed. The Jack Snipe is a migrant, arriving in September or November from Northern Europe and leaving in February or March. On its departure the common snipe is left behind to perform spectacular aerial mating displays with fast dives, reaching speeds of up to 80 kilometres an hour and producing the notorious 'drumming' sound from the vibration of tail feathers held out almost at right angles to the bird's body.

Trimworth and its surrounding fields have an entry in the Domesday Book as one of the 11 manors in the Wye Hundred. The Domesday Book is a unique survey of the disposition of wealth and power after the Norman Conquest. Trimworth in 1085 was held from the King by Hamo the Sheriff, steward of the Royal Court, and consisted of 'land for eight ploughs, a church, seven slaves, a mill at nine shillings and 60 eels, 20 acres of meadow, woodland for 30 pigs, 16 villagers with 15 smallholders have 10 ploughs.' The reference to slaves is a clear indication that Norman England was a slaveholding society. The value of Trimworth was recorded as £14 in 1086; it was just a small hamlet, a collection of buildings, despite the fact that its importance was indicated by having a church and a mill. We are still investigating the position of the church, probably a manorial chapel, through map and archaeological surveys.

The Domesday Book also provides information on the economic geography of the area around Trimworth including woodlands, recorded in terms of the number of swine paid to the lord for the 'right of pannage.' Many estates owned swine pastures in the Weald despite being located some distance away. These pastures were called 'dens' or 'denes' and were connected to the villages by drove ways. Meadows and pastures were also recorded, usually in acres, and the annual value of fisheries was generally assessed in terms of eels. Mills were recorded by number and occasionally by annual amount rendered from milling activity. Vineyards were recorded in 'arpents' of vine, an arpent being a term imported from France amounting to 100 square perches. The Domesday Book is a complex return of resources from the land and its division between the King and the lord to whom he granted them. It is a very rich source for understanding the origins and subsequent development of Trimworth and the surrounding lands in which this journal is set.

February

February, the primrose month, the Latin word 'februum' meaning cleansing or purification, when worshippers washed away the stains of the previous year and prepared themselves for the year ahead. In the Book of Hours, the rural occupations depicted for the month usually involve keeping warm and chopping wood. 'Les Trés Riches Heures du Duc de Berry depicts a group of peasants in front of a roaring fire, skirts and coats drawn up to feel the warmth. Outside in a snow-covered landscape sheep are feeding in pens; a group of hooded crows eat seeds scattered in the snow, and beyond, woodsmen chop down trees from coppiced plantations. This is currently a very appropriate activity at Trimworth. Ash wood from the earlier woodland clearance of the railway embankment is piled up in 2 metre lengths to be sawn and stacked along the barn wall for open fires. It is the best wood for burning as the conclusion to this traditional poem suggests:

> "But ash logs, all smooth grey,
> Burn them green or old:
> Buy up all that come your way,
> They're worth their weight in gold."

There is more activity along the river as mallards continue to pair up in preparation for nesting, using leaves and grasses in locations near water. Each year we find two or three nesting sites along our river stretch and sometimes another in our garden by the bottom pond. The population of these birds is closely linked to food supply and where extra food is regularly given to these ducks, as around many urban ponds, artificially large numbers can result. They are the best-known and most recognised of ducks, resident breeders as well as migrants, overwintering here from Northern Europe, and all making the familiar 'quaark' or 'quoork' call and dabbling around near the water surface. The most striking feature is the beautiful metallic green head of the male or drake in contrast to the more subdued brown and buff markings of the hen duck.

It is Candlemas day, marking the midpoint of winter, halfway between the shortest day and the spring equinox. It is also celebrated as the day Jesus was presented in the temple, 40 days after his birth, prompting the recognition of the child as the Messiah to lighten the world. For this reason, candles would be lit and processed around the church. The association of this day with birth and renewal is highlighted by snowdrop leaves beginning to pierce the frozen ground.

> "The snowdrop in purest white array
> First rears her head on Candlemas Day."

It is a flower connected with hope and purity, growing in shady places under the hedgerows and trees. We planted hundreds down the drive and under the birches where they flower like patches of left-over snow amongst the dead leaves. In some rural counties, snowdrops were ceremoniously used to cleanse the houses, being carried from room to room around the house as a sign of purification, but in Sussex, dairymen thought that picked snowdrops meant that the milk would be thin and colourless.

Candlemas Day like many other festivals also has its association with weather lore, often illustrating the precarious balance between winter and spring

> "If Candlemas be fair and bright,
> Winter will have another flight.
> If Candlemas be shower and rain,
> Winter is gone and will not come again."

Another popular verse encourages farmers to recognise that winter is still only halfway through and that anybody with less than half their feed left could have problems later in the year.

> "A farmer should on Candlemas Day have half his corn and half is hay."

Some farmers in Dartmoor still refuse to start 'Candlemas fodder' until 3rd February. Another ancient Candlemas ritual (unlikely to be observed at Trimworth), is to circumnavigate the garden in a clockwise direction at dawn, saying "…this is the quickening of the year, tuber, root and seed quicken into the coming of the light and the growing of the year."

The bare branches of trees and shrubs allow us to recognise their different outlines and profiles, and more specifically the nature of buds beginning to form. The small grey male catkins of the hazel have now expanded to become brown and gold lambs' tails. The dense clusters of Traveller's Joy have persisted through the winter and cover the hedges like a dusting of snow. Also visible on the trunks and branches

February 3rd

of trees are various forms of lichen which, like mosses and algae, are non- parasitic plant-like organisms that colonise tree bark as well as rocks, walls and roof tops. The lichen is not a sign of disease. It does not harm the trees on which it grows. It is especially prolific on the less vigorous trees and sometimes is unjustly blamed for the poor condition of the tree. Lichens in the woods reveal different forms and

Lichens and mosses are prolific in their different forms and colours.

colours, most commonly crusty patches of grey to green. These are the crustose lichens, others are more leaf-like lobe structures (foliose) and some look like small grey tangled branches (fruticose).

Nearly all the lichens in Oxen Leas and Tye Wood are on the side of the tree facing the prevailing wind and rain. They prefer the damper sites because they need moisture to grow and reproduce, but require few other nutrients. Many beech trees have gold and orange crusts, chestnuts exhibit grey crustose forms with orange centres to the lobes. Most of the ageing elderberry bushes along the dyke are covered in green/yellow crusts, the crack willows along the river are lime green on the windward side, and on hazels are bunches of small tree-like grey growths. All these lichens grow at slow but variable rates ranging from 1 mm to 1 cm a year. Lichenometry refers to a method which attempts to date the surface on which lichens grow, using a series of photographs to work out the rate of growth. From the size of the lichen it is possible to estimate how long it has been there. Stonehenge has a collection of 80 different lichens, many of them surviving on the sarsen stones for thousands of years like miniature, self-maintaining gardens. In the absence of roots, lichens absorb water and minerals from rainwater and the atmosphere over their entire surface area. For this reason, they require clean air and water, making the lichen a good indicator of air quality. As air quality improves, lichen species are re-colonising places from which they disappeared at the start of the Industrial Revolution.

Living in chalk country brings with it the pleasures and graceful beauty of rolling hills, scarplands, hidden wooded hollows and dry-valleys. For farmers and gardeners, there is also the need to cope with an abundance of flint, which litters the fields and gardens, breaking ploughshares and bending forks. Flint comes from the Upper Chalk strata where it occurs in thin bands or seams. As the chalk surface erodes and is lowered, these extremely hard black and dark grey stones of various shapes and sizes are left near the surface. Ploughing also brings them to the surface of the fields. Flint is almost pure silica, originating from the infiltration of silica-rich water, which becomes trapped in its movement through the chalk and eventually becomes crystalline. It is the impurities which give the different colours. When broken, flints appear almost blue; thin pieces are almost translucent, many are stained brown by iron absorbed in the water. Occasionally fossils of sea creatures such as sea urchins, sponges and shells are embedded in the flint. The construction of garden borders and beds using a pick axe rather than border fork has resulted in the excavation of tons of flint which lie in discrete piles around the garden, serving as an overwintering habitat for wildlife.

The practice of shaping or 'knapping' the flint has become a skilled and distinctive process in the preparation of building stones in Kent and other chalkland areas. Churches, walls and domestic buildings show the use of flint of different colours and

Contrasts in the use of flint on external walls of Crundale church.

shapes, some rounded and collected from riverbeds and beaches, some shaped to give a flat surface and arranged in intricate patterns, some used as bands between layers of brick or rag stone to give attractive chequer-work patterns. They all form a distinctive part of the vernacular architecture of chalk country. There are many examples of fine flint work in the churches of East Kent, but none better than our own church of Crundale described in detail by Albert Lancefield in his 'History of a Downland Church.' The external flint work is superbly knapped using small flints with hardly any mortar, probably the work of Roger de Crundale, the King's Master Mason of the late 13th century. The quality of this work is highlighted in the contrast between the skilled flint knapping on one side of the chancel wall and the use of irregular flints and rubble on adjoining walls, characteristic of the Norman period.

February 5th

'February fill dyke, be it black or white,' illustrates the wet and unpredictable nature of weather in February. Farmers are busy with livestock, especially lambs. The ewes are becoming heavy with unborn lambs and need good feeding, as counselled by Thomas Tusser, an East Anglian farmer best known for his instructional publication 'Five Hundred Points of Good Husbandry' written in 1557. (He was also author of the proverb, 'a fool and his money are soon parted'!)

> "Serve rye straw out first, then wheat straw, and pease,
> Then oat straw, then barley, then hay, if you please:
> But serve them with hay, while the straw stover (stack) last,
> Then love they no straw, they had rather to fast."

Days are getting longer and new growth is appearing along the base of hedgerows and in the woods. Dark green spikes of wild arum lily are widespread in the woods, ditches and shady hedges. The fern-like leaves of cow parsley are appearing as low-growing rosettes, and in the drive and garden, spikes of daffodils and snowdrops emerge alongside winter aconite, which has naturalised widely. The six golden sepals of the aconite appear before the glossy leaves and make a wonderful early spring complement to the snowdrops. They are known as 'choirboys' in Suffolk because of the ruffs that surround the flowers. Walking in nearby Purr Wood, we found a strange evergreen plant which we identified as butcher's broom, fairly common in well-drained chalky soils of woods, copses and hedgerows. It is a member of the lily family, but curiously has a tough woody structure bearing sharply pointed dark green leaves. Tiny green and white flowers are visible, giving the whole bushy plant an attractive appearance. These flowers, if fertilised will become small round red berries in autumn and remain on the plant through much of the winter. The name of the plant is derived from the use of its abrasive leaves to clean butchers' chopping blocks. Not surprisingly, the plant was known in the past as 'knee holly,' or 'Jew's Myrtle,' because it is said to have composed the Crown of Thorns.

Snowdrops emerge alongside the golden sepals of aconite which have naturalised widely.

Flocks of geese and swans fly daily along the valley, their rhythmic wing beats announcing their arrival. Running ahead of us along the river Sam disturbs the grey heron from its motionless, aristocratic pose in the water and it takes off with powerful, slow, deep wing beats. Occasionally we see the snow-white little egret, which has been a solitary visitor in our stretch of the valley for a few years. It feeds in shallow water near the weir using its long black beak to stab creatures which have been disturbed by the shuffling of its yellow feet in the mud. The little egret has responded to climate change by shifting further north, making this once-exotic little rarity a fairly common, but very pretty sight.

At about 8 am, the calm of a pearl grey downland day was broken by the sound of gunshot and the slapping of pigeons wings as they took off in their hundreds from a field of young rape seed. Shortly after, a large flock of Canada geese flew low overhead in formation towards Godmersham, followed again by gunfire and then, minutes later, the sad sight of disorientated survivors flying aimlessly in different directions. I later learned that these geese, grazing in a field by Purr Wood, were shot in full view of bewildered and distressed families living in houses nearby. Some birds lying in these 'killing fields' were shot but not yet dead.

This provoked a storm of correspondence locally, not on grounds of legality, but in terms of conduct and neighbourliness. Supporters of these field sports would probably dismiss these comments as those of 'townies,' unsympathetic to countryside living and the right of people to follow these legally approved recreational activities. But people living in the vicinity of these scenes of destruction also have a right, which is to enjoy these animals and birds in their living state, not shot to pieces. As Richard Mabey claims, "Rights – especially those that determine the fates of living things – cannot be claimed unilaterally." ('A Brush With Nature'). I find the rearing of birds like pheasant and partridge which are then released into the wild and shot, to be unpleasant and not my idea of sport. I'm not comfortable with the conditions under which these caged birds are kept, or the fate of un-retrieved, injured birds. And can the number of birds killed in these shoots all be taken for food? If the number of birds released into the wild is sustainable in the local area, and shooters are judicious and considerate in their attitude to local people, then I would find the activity more acceptable. Indeed, where landscape conservation is carried out on some of our well-managed shooting land there is a significant complementary benefit to other wildlife and the quality of habitats in which they live.

The wind shifts to the north-east, temperatures drop, and the white stuff returns, just enough to whiten one side of the freshly formed molehills, making little mountains out of molehills. Every now and again we are given a reminder that Kent, like my home county of Norfolk, is a peninsula open to inclement weather from three points of the compass. In Tye Wood the granular snow falls on dry leaves, making a soft hiss. This snow is an indication of very low temperatures because the crystals do not stick together and the resulting snow is fine, hard and powdery with a simple structure to the snowflake. Snow in the woods brings

Striking tonal contrasts and reflected light from the snow opens up the wood, creating space.

striking contrast between dark trunks and white ground reminding me of an Ansel Adams photograph. Reflected light from the snow seems to give a lighter appearance to the wood than usual and has the effect of opening up the wood, creating space. A pheasant appears looking colourful and overdressed, patrolling in a dignified procession of one. Dark, shapeless rags of broken cloud brush over the downs, leaving a dusty white covering. Sam and I turn into the wind and head for home through a curtain of snow, now falling more thickly; larger wetter flakes as temperatures rise to near freezing. Back in the garden, birds are clamouring over the feeders and bird tables. The spotted woodpecker dominates. Moorhens fret and strut around the edge of the activity like embarrassed guests at the party. More pheasants swagger along the hedge line. The garden has become a safe haven for reared pheasants from the keepered shoots of neighbouring estates.

'Biodiversity' is a commonly used but frequently misunderstood term which has often led to a gap of understanding between policymakers and ordinary people. I've been encouraged by a recent DEFRA (Department for Environment, Food and Rural Affairs) publication which defines biodiversity as "the diversity of individual species, the genetic diversity within the species, and the range of ecosystems that support them." To illustrate the unambiguous nature of this definition they take a number of biodiversity indicators in order to measure the gains and losses in biodiversity in the UK over the long term (20 or 30 year period), and also the short-term change since 2000. The publication represents an indication of the state of biodiversity in the UK in 2010 and is produced in a pocket-sized book, obtainable free of charge from DEFRA. It is highly recommended, very readable and clearly illustrated, challenging some of the popularly held views reported in the media about habitat diversity. For example, within arable fields, contrary to popular belief, there has actually been an increase in the richness of plant species since 1990. Bird populations are considered a good indicator of the broad state of wildlife and the countryside because they occupy a variety of habitats and tend to be near the top of the food chain. The research shows that the population of woodland birds fell by 23% between 1973 and 2002, but then rose to 14% below the 1970 level by the year 2008. Bats have undergone severe declines historically, but since 2000 have increased by 20%. In 2008 the percentage of rivers of good biological quality in England was 72%, up from 63% in 1990.

Of course there are many indications of serious environmental concern, such as continued declines in plant diversity in woodland, grassland and boundary habitats, a fall in the number of breeding farmland birds, and an increase in invasive species, but it is by no means a comprehensive picture of declining quality. In fact, the overall assessment of all 33 measures shows that 15 indicate improvement since 2000 and nine measures show improvement over the longer term. However, in a climate of financial uncertainty there is concern that funding for agri-environment schemes and public-sector funding for priority habitats will be put in jeopardy. As well as recognising the economic and social value of biodiversity, there is a need for initiatives which reward protection of the environment and penalise harm.

February 10th

Rarely do we cancel a morning walk because of bad weather, but today we came very close. Strong, bitter north-east winds brought snow flurries over the downs, and through the valley. Already sub-zero, the wind-chill dropped temperatures by another 5° or more. Nevertheless, with tails tucked in, we followed the dyke to Tye Wood and our resolution was rewarded by the sight of a buzzard perching on a branch above the dyke on the sheltered south-west side of the wood. We stopped and watched from about 15 metres. His trouser feathers ruffled in the wind, the dark and pale brown feathers, dark wingtips and barred tail were strikingly clear. His hunting tactic is to sit motionless on a perch for long periods before swooping onto the prey, which may be rabbits or other small mammals, or carrion. This is his favourite perch along the woodland fringes, hunting over open farmland. He watched us cautiously, eyes heavily browed and staring, then flew with erratic, heavy wing beats through the upper branches of the wood before catching the force of the wind and sailing freely over the tree tops towards Olantigh, tail fanned like a hand of cards and wings wide. Further along the river there was another surprise. Two campers were brushing snow off their tents and preparing to continue a long-distance walk along the Stour Valley.

On our return through the wood, we were accompanied by a playful group of long-tailed tits flying ahead of us; waiting, teasing, then flying on. They seemed to appreciate our company. How do they view us in their world? On our walks we look for sights, smells, sounds of other animals; do they know our smell and habits? We are frequent and regular movers through this habitat; do the birds know us and look out for us and react to our presence as we respond to theirs? Do these creatures regard us as a threat in their habitat, or a benign presence?

Snow returns silently at night. The early-morning light begins to reveal fields of freshly fallen snow and tree branches laden to breaking point. Sam and I wander around the garden with its snow covered ponds, and enter a field of pristine snow – perfect and undisturbed, like being the first on the beach after the tide has receded. Sam runs around with his nose in the snow like a plough, gulping great mouthfuls. The fields and woods are silent – not a bird in sight or even a bird call. There is no silence like the silence of a wood under deep snow. Even the tits which chase us playfully along the woodland edge are nowhere to be seen. Returning, we trace our outward footprints along the dyke. I'm almost offended to see our marks in the fresh snow, as if we had violated this immaculate wonderland of white.

There is an increase in activity in Tye Wood. Last night we heard the sounds of foxes calling. This is not unusual, we hear them all year round, but it is the mating season and as well as the usual barks and yelps we are hearing the occasional bloodcurdling scream, probably the result of vixen being approached by a dog fox in preparation for mating. January or February is normally the mating season when young foxes disperse from their natal areas and begin to find and follow females. In early February, the vixen will be looking around for suitable places to give birth, frequently occupying the earths of other animals, such as old badger setts or large rabbit warrens. The mating season is only a few weeks and pregnancy lasts about fifty days with the birth of 4 to 5 cubs occurring in March or April. Sam is well aware of this activity and chases eagerly around the woods, returning with a strong smell of fox which can stay on his coat for days.

Today we also saw a badger dropping down the steep terrace in Tye Wood towards the area of badger setts, which this month will be the scene of great activity. Badgers do not hibernate, but can go into a state of torpor during the kind of very cold or snowy weather which we have been experiencing recently. In a state of torpor, they will metabolise fat reserves accumulated during the summer and autumn months. Body temperatures fall and allow for greater economy of fat reserves. When they become more active in warmer winter weather, their territorial range is a fraction of their spring and summer ranges, which can be 20 to 50 hectares. Like foxes, the badger is another scent marker and will leave his scents along the boundaries of this territory. Males will regularly patrol these margins during the mating season, with fierce fights possible if they encounter another boar. The majority of badgers will mate between February and May and reproduction involves the unusual phenomenon of delayed implantation, when the embryo doesn't implant in the womb and begin growing until the winter months. Most of the 1 to 5 cubs will be born between January and March, the majority being born in February. This gives the cubs time to eat, grow and put on fat for the winter months ahead, but sadly, up to half of the badger cubs are expected to die before reaching adulthood.

The industrious but destructive little diggers are back, creating tunnels, chamber systems, and of course molehills. In early English they were known as 'mouldy warp' from the North European 'muld varp,' where 'muld' is soil and 'varp' means throw, hence 'soil throwers'. In recent frosts and snow they have retreated deeper underground, but now with warmer temperatures and softer soil, full of juicy earthworms, they have begun cleaning the burrows and runs which they used last year by pushing up heaps of rich brown, finely-worked soil – the best possible base for home-made potting compost. In a sense I have encouraged them, digging in tons of well- rotted garden manure full of earthworms and creating a mole heaven – and a gardener's hell. Parts of flower beds collapse like mineshafts, roots of plants are left hanging in space, unsightly heaps of soil appear daily on lawns, mowers suck up heaps of soil or veer off along runs connecting molehills. Moles in the field are acceptable, but in the garden they are not welcome, and I have to confess to occasionally using traps, but I always feel that the success of capture is annulled by the sad sight of the little dark brown, silky coat, pink snout and big white hands. They are solitary creatures, fiercely protective of their territory and with a sensitive snout and an incredible sense of touch from little hairs on the body. With these sensors the mole can detect temperature changes, vibrations, changes in air pressure, imperceptible movements of air, and, of course, the presence of worms which they can paralyse by using toxins contained in their saliva.

Not far away from the 'Maginot Line' of molehills is an area of lawn sloping down to the pond, which is always riddled with small holes, like Gruyere cheese. These are the holes of a small burrowing creature which I have never seen. It could be a vole, bank vole, field mouse or wood mouse. The only way to identify it is through its habitat. I've ruled out the field vole, because its habitat is mainly open and grassy, usually nesting above the ground in tufted grassy areas. It could possibly be a bank vole because they often nest in underground burrows, but are probably less common in gardens, preferring the edges of deciduous woodland or the base of hedges. They can also be seen in daylight, so I would be surprised if I had failed to notice any sign of these little creatures, although they are very timid and fast moving. My guess is that the culprit is a field mouse, because they nest wherever there is cover and warmth, usually below ground, but also in hedgerows. Their holes in the ground, lead to a complicated system of burrows, which are used by consecutive generations. They share their nest with three or four other individuals and will begin breeding in March. They are nocturnal, omnivorous and provide a vital food source for owls and other carnivorous animals and birds, leaving enough surviving to aerate my lawns.

This evening, the sky had stunningly beautiful pastel hues of pinks, blues and yellows, a feature known as nacreous, or 'mother-of-pearl' clouds which commonly form in February. They form very high in the sky, between 10 to 20 miles up, far higher than the height at which clouds normally form. They are composed of extremely fine ice crystals at temperatures of -85°C. This evening, just as the sun disappeared over the horizon of Godmersham Downs, these amazing rainbow-like colours appeared as sunlight passed through tiny ice crystals in the stratosphere. February is the month with the most impressive night skies and a new moon which is closer to the earth this month than at any time until the harvest moon in September. As the sky gets darker, the prominent constellation of Orion is among the first to become visible, setting in the south west, his distinctive belt pointing downwards to Sirius, the brightest star in the sky.

At Trimworth the builders are busy removing old Kent peg-tiles from an area where the battens have rotted, causing the tiles to slip and fall. The name peg-tile derives from the way tiles were fixed to battens using square oak pegs driven into round holes in the tile. The tile industry has existed in Kent since the 12th century when tiles were made on-site by travelling tile makers using locally dug clay. Chalky clays produce a light brown tile, whereas clay rich in iron oxides produced orange-brown tiles. Alec Clifton Taylor describes them evocatively as "these gently billowing eiderdowns of mellow terracotta, which offer an experience of colour and texture of quite exceptional richness." A Royal Charter of Edward IV, dated 1477, stated the tile size should be 6½" wide and 10½" deep, and this remains the British standard for plain clay tiles, but for some reason, the Kent tile was 9" x 6" up until the late 19th century, when they became standardised, so modern tiles cannot be used on old buildings. In 1891, there were 150 brick and tile makers in Kent, and by 1938 only 64 existed. The last known manufacturer at Staplehurst ceased production in the 1960s. These old tiles are a very marketable commodity because in the 1987 hurricane up to 50 timber framed barns were destroyed, leading to a revival in the manufacture of hand-made plain clay tiles. The frequent theft of tiles from remote unprotected buildings is an indication of their rising market value.

Taking off the damaged wood and plaster back to the timbers of the house has revealed more about the structure of this old medieval Wealden hall-house. The end of the tie beam marking the boundary between the hall and the high end of the house was clearly visible, elaborately carved on the 'high status' side. The 500 year-old oak posts looked good for another 500 years. Alterations to the old structure showed that materials had been salvaged from other houses for a partial rebuild, or to increase the size of the house. Watching the work in progress reminded me of the charming phrase by T.E. Hume, "…old houses were scaffolding once with workmen whistling." As the work progressed, I noticed, tucked away in the loft space, various fragile wafer-like circular constructions varying in size from a golf ball to a large tennis ball. These were wasp nests, the small ones probably being failed 'queens nests' built in spring by emerging queens around mid-April. The nests are made out of chewed wood and wasp saliva, usually straw coloured with swirl shapes around them. When the first brood of worker wasps hatch, they will begin adding to the nest. The queen will stay in the nest and continue to lay more eggs and so the nest grows. By late summer, the nest could contain up to 10,000 individuals and measure 30 cm across. The cold weather will have killed off all the workers and the males, with only the queen surviving by hibernating, often in a small hibernation cell the size of a golf ball.

Today is Collop Monday, a movable feast but traditionally the Monday before Shrove Tuesday and an ancient festival day since medieval times. The word 'collop' means slices of meat, especially bacon, which were eaten along with other perishable foods before Lent. In other words, it was the last 'blowout' before the enforced abstinence of Lent and described by one 17th-century cleric as a chance for people to 'ballast their bellies with meat'!

February 15th

Down the drive and under groups of trees in the garden, daffodils, the Lenten lily, a symbol of spring and friendship, are beginning to show. The name is derived from 'affodel,' the 'd' being added as 'de'affodel became merged. It is from the genus Narcissus, the words daffodil and Narcissus being synonymous. There are probably over 100 species, but several thousand registered hybrids, the classification being based on differences between the perianth (petals) and the corona (cup). They will form clumps of colour, dancing and tossing in the boisterous breezes of spring but some modern plant breeders in their quest for spectacular blooms have produced heads which are so heavy they will snap in the wind. The hardened leaf tips of snowdrops have pushed through the frozen soil and are now in full bloom, a celebrated symbol of early spring. They are a native of continental Europe, probably being introduced here in the 16th century. Their slender white pendulous bell-shaped flowers held on slender stalks are appearing as clumps under trees or drifts of snow-white flowers on cool slopes. Also catching the eye are spring-flowering cyclamen, part of the primrose family, but with no obvious affinity. Under the trees, their upswept petals of pink and purple are pirouetting on slender stalks growing from dark-green marbled leaves. These are all very welcome glimpses of fragile beauty in a bleak and wintry landscape.

February 16th

Today the weather has reverted to a more normal 'Atlantic type' – milder with some rain at times, but the last two days have shown just how diverse are the short-term fluctuations in our weather. Yesterday at 8.00 am we had temperatures of -2°C with frosted grasses crunching underfoot, clean boots and bright sun. In the afternoon the air became still with heavy overcast skies. By 6pm the temperature had dropped and flakes of snow were beginning to cover the ground, but by 10pm it had disappeared in a rapid snow-melt. This morning it was raining heavily, paths were deep in mud, and temperatures had risen to 6°C. Such is the variety of our weather, which occupies our thoughts and conversations so regularly. This afternoon my mood is being affected by a flat, grey sheet of stratus cloud from which drizzle is steadily falling. There is no depth or variety of shape or tone in the sky, just a concrete-grey, oppressive, miserable layer of stratus nebulosus. The cloudspotter Gavin Pretor-Pinney describes it as stagnant dishwater, "it feels as if God's decided to cut his fuel bills and install a fluorescent strip." Perhaps my mood will lift if the cloud changes to stratus-fractus; at least the grey will be ragged with the attraction of changing outlines and visible lumps of grey. Rapidly changing weather conditions can also play a crucial role in the behaviour and survival of birds at this time of year. Research has confirmed how short-term variations in temperature and rainfall affect feeding frequency, nestling growth and nest survival of birds.

February 18th

In the corner of my eye I was aware of a disturbance in an outbuilding and saw through the window a large bird flapping on the inside trying to get out. It was clearly a raptor, and a closer look revealed a juvenile sparrowhawk which had obviously followed a small bird through the open door into the building. Roz, wearing thick gloves, caught the bird at the window, and held it while I photographed it. It was warm brown and speckled grey on its upper parts and light grey with brown speckles on its under parts and a distinctive barred tail. This was a female, easily distinguished from the larger bluish grey male. Two features were striking, firstly, the large, staring, unblinking bright yellow eyes with black pupils, and secondly the very long, slender middle toe, which closed around Roz's fingers without leaving a gap (and drawing blood!). We released it into the garden to pursue the small bird population. This all reminded me of a previous sparrowhawk experience, and so I checked our five-year garden diary. Exactly two years ago we recorded the sighting of a sparrowhawk on its flight of terror through the garden and made the following entry on 18 February. "Sparrowhawk on patrol again – no bird activity or birdsong. Seems to lurk near the bothy birdfeeders and swoop on tits and sparrows."

To what extent are they a threat to the survival of small birds? It is a contentious issue with feelings running high on both sides of arguments that are often expressed with more emotion than evidence. Myth and reality become entangled to confuse the issue. The sparrowhawk often attracts the label of an evil trespasser whilst songbirds are seen as innocent victims. The 'wild' is felt to have entered the safety and comfort of the garden and many find the conflict distasteful and distressing; an unwelcome reminder that the killing and consumption of one organism by another is a characteristic of our natural world.

A juvenile sparrowhawk with its staring, unblinking, bright-yellow eyes.

A recent study by the British Trust for Ornithology found that there was no link between the flourishing numbers of birds of prey (including the sparrowhawk) and small bird species, with the exception of the tree sparrow, bullfinch and reed bunting. The report concluded:

"Whilst a small number of associations may suggest significant negative effects between predator and prey species, for the majority of the songbird species examined there is no evidence that increases in avian predators… are associated with large-scale population declines."

Furthermore, when the population of sparrowhawk declined because of organo-chlorine use, there was no corresponding increase in songbirds, and if predators did reduce the number of small birds drastically they would starve themselves. It is human interference and more significantly, changes in agricultural practices and the availability of food sources which are the most likely causes of small bird declines.

A bright frosty day with birds throwing their little voices into the air. Chirps from chaffinch, squeaks and whistles from tits, flowing melodies from wrens and robins. Groups of raucous rooks are beating their bounds between fields and roosts; jackdaws are pairing up on the fences and rooftops or hopping around the paddock

February 19th

in search of spilt food; green woodpeckers are either hammering the dead alders along the dyke (how do their brains endure this thrashing) or stabbing the soft ground for ants as the frost retreats across the lawn with the rising sun. Disturbed, they take off with quick wing beats on their bouncing, undulating flight, laughing their 'yaffle'call and displaying their green and yellow plumage, bright redcaps and black moustache.(How fortunate that this spectacular bird managed to cross the land bridge between Britain and the continent before melting ice raised the sea level to form the English Channel).

Rabbits have been active again overnight, like little JCBs in the border, scratching up soil to expose roots of plants to their munching molars. The garden looks like a war zone, but it is a battle I can never win. They come from the railway embankment and the field banks of Trimworth Down, enjoying apartment accommodation in the field dykes where they pop in and out of burrows like targets on a shooting range. I cannot bring myself to shoot them, and they now seem largely unaffected by the ravages of the awful myxomatosis disease. A young local farmworker uses his ferrets to work the hedge and ditch line. Watching him work with fine purse nets, I realise ferreting is not just a matter of throwing a ferret down a hole and hoping for a rabbit to emerge. It is a real skill which has been practised for centuries; a method of rabbit control which is an effective, selective, ecologically safe and humane solution.

Long before written calendars, the progress of months and seasons was measured by the phases of the moon. A full moon occurs every 29 days, giving an average of one every month. Different cultures, such as the Native Americans, named the various full moons according to events occurring in their natural world at that time. The full moon for February is known as the Snow or Ice Moon since the heaviest snow usually falls in this month. Some refer to this moon as the Hunger Moon, since harsh weather conditions led to difficulties in hunting and gathering food supplies. We are most familiar with the moon that comes closest to our autumn equinox, the Harvest Moon of September, followed in October by the Hunters Moon.

We know the gravitational pull of the moon affects tides of the oceans, and it is increasingly thought that the lunar cycle influences animal and human behaviour also. We have much to learn and understand about this kind of biorhythm. Lister Kaye in his book "At the Water's Edge," describes how the female badger's pituitary gland secretes fewer hormones during full moon, so no mating occurs. Mating peaks on the darkest night of the lunar cycle, around the new moon phase, perhaps to prevent attack from predators (although observations also suggest that amphibians, frogs, toads and newts synchronise their mating activity around the full moon phase).

Two areas of activity which continue to be partly guided by the phase of the moon are gardening and farming, the theory being that just as the moon exerts a pull on the tides of the oceans, it also affects movement of moisture in the earth. Those who garden by the moon claim higher yields and healthier crops by planting during a waxing moon, whereas in a waning moon foliage is at rest and the suitable activity is pruning and weeding. When the moon is in ascending phase, that is the orbit is higher than the night before, this is considered to be a good time to take cuttings and harvest crops. During the descending phase, composting, harvesting of root crops and transplanting are the recommended activities. Have we lost our way because we are now out of touch with the biorhythms that controlled our lives long ago? What could we gain by reconnecting more closely with these natural forces?

'February fill dyke' is an apt description of the condition of the drainage system in the river meadows around us. Dykes are full to overflowing; patches of water are quickly coalescing in the meadows and watery furrows shine in the fields. With more heavy rain forecast for most of the week the rising river level, already bank-full, will add to the extent of flooding between Olantigh and Godmersham. We walk through the woods on the terrace overlooking this soggy, squelchy scene. Heavy raindrops splatter on wet leaves and on the exposed margins of hollows where old trees have been uprooted to leave root bowls 5 feet deep. Fine sand and clay was being washed away to reveal flints. These are good locations to find fossils and possibly archaeological objects on a site with a record of rich finds, such as the third century Roman cremation urn associated with later Saxon burials located just half a kilometre south of Trimworth Manor. The most prolific site is the terrace on which we stand, overlooking the Stour on the edge of Tye Wood. It is like a walk over history. At this site in 1703 a skull was found by a walker and later a human skeleton. Nearby was a child's skeleton with a little red pot. The site was excavated by a local rector and a grave dug into the chalk was found containing three urns. There were later excavations in the 18th century, which are all well documented. This wooded terrace lies about 10 to 20 m above the floodplain of the River Stour, which throughout history has afforded a dry site for settlement as well as easy access to the river and its fertile valley. It is on this same terrace, a little further downstream, that Trimworth is situated.

Sustained rainfall and further snowmelt has exceeded the capacity of the river channel, and so the river meadows from Olantigh to Godmersham are completely under water. Our focus on the bird world shifts from songbirds of hedge, wood and garden to water birds, such as cormorant, mallard, geese and flocks of gulls, many of which are looking for fish left stranded in shallow water in the fields. In this middle stretch of the catchment area of the Stour, the flooding problem is intensified by the meeting of five main tributaries of the River Stour which drain clay headwaters. Over the years, the floodplain has been further modified by urban centres like Ashford, striving to meet its target of doubling its population in the next 20 years, and requiring new development sites on floodplains. Future management will have to provide more flood storage schemes, better management of run-off, and better awareness of flood risk constraints in relation to new developments.

The Environment Agency has provided an excellent evaluation of the flood risk on its website. This allows one to put in a postcode which brings up a map showing neighbourhood areas that are at risk. The flood plain around Trimworth is at 'significant' risk, meaning that there is a one in 75 chance that flooding will occur every year. This risk is likely to be heightened by global warming trends, bringing more frequent and intense storms and causing more widespread regular flooding. Another trend is the increasing likelihood of more winter rain events and consequently more flood events. How prophetic were our forebears in siting housing and settlement well above the flood plain, making them safe from all but floods of biblical proportions.

The river, now bank-full, spreads across the water meadows below Godmersham Downs.

The strong south-west wind brings a 'marine roar' through the branches of tall beeches.

The bare tops of coppiced chestnut and hazel rattled in the strong south-west wind and there was a marine roar through the branches of the tall beeches. Millions of leaves were being driven across the open woodland glades. The long-term prospect of wetter, windier weather is bad news for the majestic, top-heavy, shallow-rooted beeches in Juniper and Marriage Woods. They have been made more vulnerable by the fragmentation of large woodlands, which leaves them as small exposed copses or shelter-belts separating arable fields. Juniper Wood was full of moss-covered rotting trunks of beech, casualties from previous storms, most recently 1987 and 1990. Although dead, they are still a vital component of the woodland ecosystem, covered with lichens and mosses, attracting birds and insects. The bright green mosses, growing over dead stumps or at the shaded base of healthy trees are features of the wood. They are harmless, epiphytic, but not parasitic plants which take up moisture from the ground. Their high moisture-retentive capacity allows them to stay green and fresh, even in drought conditions. Another shade and shape of green, especially in heavily shaded areas of this woodland, is the iris foetidissima, the architectural evergreen native to Britain. It is also known as 'stinking iris' because the leaves have an unpleasant sickly smell when crushed, but its real attraction is the display of bright orange seeds which appear in autumn after the grey purple flowers have faded. Threading through the trees at the woodland edge was the wonderful old perennial, Traveller's Joy or Old Man's Beard, its long, grey, hairy seed heads held in dense clusters, glowing softly golden against the setting sun.

I have become impressed by the quality and volume of observations on the natural world which have been made by village clergy in the past. They were able to combine their theological studies with a deep interest in natural history, expressed perhaps in compiling lists and drawing wild flowers or making detailed observations of bird and animal behaviour, and in some cases making real scientific advances with studies of fossils, geological structures, birds and insects. Their work usually dates from the time when the vicar had a small number of parishioners and a less arduous workload than clergy today. They also had the advantage of a long association with a particular location, perhaps being born and dying in the parish which they served. Here in Crundale, the Filmer family were Lords of the Manor of Trimworth for over 200 years, and had the right to appoint the incumbent at Crundale church. During this time there were several Filmer vicars, giving a long and strong association between family and parish, and a continuity of interest in the natural history of Crundale.

The 19th century was the heyday of the English parson-naturalist and perhaps the most notable of all was Gilbert White who had a long association with the parish of Selbourne in Hampshire and developed an intimate knowledge of the locality, leading to the publication of, "The Natural History of Selbourne," in 1789. His style was precise, perceptive, detailed, personal and evocative, bringing nature writing to a new level. He was committed to the importance of field observation and the need to restrict observation to a small area, on the grounds that "the more confined your observation, the more perfect will be your remarks." He kept meticulous records of observations on plants, birds and other creatures, daily accounts of the weather, observations about leafing and flowering, and the arrival and departure of birds. He shared this information with nationally recognised scientists like Joseph Banks, and with relatives, through copious correspondence. "More than any other single book it has shaped our everyday view of relations between man and nature." This from arguably Britain's greatest living nature writer, Richard Mabey.

I engage with Gilbert White because of his love of the particular and local, one of the reasons why I have become absorbed in this project involving meadows by the river in Crundale. Gilbert White's Selbourne, has become my ' secret, private parish inside each one of us.'

February 27th

Roz and I took our grandson, little Jack, for a walk along the river with Sam. Eager to expand his knowledge, interest and love of the natural world, Roz and I showered him with fascinating information on footprints, habitats, bugs and bird calls. After about 10 minutes came a little pleading voice –" Grandad, can we just walk?" He had become saturated with our intensive educational bombardment and just wanted to wander, throw sticks in the river, kick molehills, chase Sam and do anything else to sidestep the well-meaning aspirations of obsessive grandparents.

March

March 1st

March, named Martius by the Romans after the God of Mars, was referred to by the Anglo-Saxons as 'Hyld monath', meaning the loud or strong month and regarded as the month of many weathers. Jim White from our neighbouring farm at Hunt Street, described it as a 'treacherous month'. He remembers cultivating in March with no shirt, it was so warm, and then lambing in a blizzard a few weeks later. He warned gardeners to curb their enthusiasm to plant seeds too early by quoting a rhyme by Thomas Tusser, the 16th Century English poet and farmer:

Les Très Riches Heures shows a rustic scene of ploughing and planting against a backdrop of the Chateaux Lusignan.

"White peason, both good for the pot and the purse
By sowing too timely, prove often the worse:
Because they be tender and hateth the cold,
Prove March 'ere ye sow them, for being too bold."

In the illuminated manuscripts of the Book of Hours, the occupations shown in the country are digging or breaking the ground and sowing. Les Très Riches Heures shows a rustic scene of ploughing and planting against a backdrop of the Chateau Lusignan, one of his favourite residences. An old bearded peasant stoops over the handles of a plough, one hand controlling the oxen, the other guiding the plough. His bare knees show through the holes in his tights. He is using a wooden-wheeled plough, but the plough-share is wrought iron. The furrows show that the plough had a moveable mould board, allowing it to work across the field turning one furrow on top of the other and forming a path for the oxen to follow. The fixed mould board could only turn the furrow in one direction and was therefore worked around the field. In the field beyond, a peasant is putting seed from a sack into a seed box for broadcasting whilst to the left vines are being pruned. With our warmer climate this activity is now best suited to January or February, an example of how these wonderfully produced scenes of rural activity illustrate evidence of a changing climate. They also indicate how farm equipment such as bill hooks, ploughs, scythes and pitchforks remained almost unchanged for centuries until the late 19th century.

March 2nd

In recent years, national monitoring schemes have raised concerns about the state of British breeding woodland birds, generating such depressing headlines in the national press as 'A tailspin of decline' and 'A route to extinction.' The British Trust for Ornithology and the Royal Society for the Protection of Birds have made a specific survey of broadleaved and mixed woodland habitats which looks at long-term trends in breeding bird populations since the 1960s. This is the Repeat Woodland Bird Survey (2006) conducted at 400 woodland sites over a three year period and is the first attempt to link UK woodland bird populations to environmental data. Declines of greater than 25% were recorded in eight of the 34 species studied, including the garden warbler, lesser spotted woodpecker and wood warbler. The starling, although not strictly a woodland bird, was abundant in earlier surveys and was virtually absent in 2005, probably the result of the intensification of management practices on agricultural land. There is some good news; the survey shows that 11 species including the blackcap, blue-tit, chaffinch, greater spotted woodpecker, robin and wren all recorded an increase although national and regional patterns of change are varied and complex.

What explanations can be found for the decline of these woodland birds? Most long-distance migrants are in decline suggesting problems in habitats outside the UK, particularly for those migrant woodland species which spend part of the year in Africa. Studies in West Africa point to problems of habitat degradation such as desertification, the intensification of agriculture and other land-use changes. In our own woodland habitats, increased predation has been a factor, particularly in relation to the grey squirrel which is thought to affect nests and nesting success in some species. Another driver of decline has been an increase in deer browsing, particularly by the small muntjac deer, which causes large-scale structural changes to low-level vegetation and undergrowth, a prime habitat for nightingale and garden warblers. Changes in woodland structure, such as increasing age may also be a factor, although there appears to be no relationship between declining species and the amount of standing dead trees compared to fallen deadwood. Forest management is responding to these changes. There are programmes to enhance the understory by more woodland thinning of the type we have experienced here in Tye Wood, Black Edge and Oxen Leas. There is greater provision of wider forest rides, better deer management, more coppicing and replanting. Another enduring uncertainty is climate change and the way the natural world will respond to rising temperatures, such as the timing of leafing of trees, and the emergence of insects and other food sources. More research is required on the way wildlife is responding to such changes in 'nature's calendar.'

A postscript to this concern over the state of woodland breeding birds is provided by the UK Biodiversity Indicators published by DEFRA in 2010, which regards bird populations as a good indicator of the broad state of the environment because they tend to be near the top of the food chain. Their results, which include data from 2008, show that since 2000, woodland bird populations have shown a 7% increase (but the population index still remains 14% below the 1970 level).

I often contemplate how these fields around Trimworth might have been occupied and used in the past. One of the great documentary sources of information to assist in this speculation is the Inquisition Post-mortem which provides information about the estate on the death of the tenant following which an Inquisition was set up to establish what lands were held and who should succeed to them. Under the feudal system which followed the Norman Conquest, the King held all the land, but granted some land to his followers and supporters in return for success on the field of battle or notable domestic service. They were the 'tenants in chief', managing the lands as an important social and economic unit. In the early 14th century, the Trimworth estate appeared to be flourishing with over 300 acres, mainly arable and pasture, 40 acres of 'bosci amput'(coppice), a watermill (probably located just below the present house on leat run off the River Stour), and a church. The 1343 entry notes that the Manor continued to hold the 'advowson' of the church of Crundale. This term is significant because it bestowed the legal right of the Lord of the Manor to nominate a person to hold ecclesiastical office.

By the middle of the 14th century a significant change in the estate had occurred. The extent had fallen to 100 acres, possibly due to the ravages of the Black Death and the consequent shortage of labour. Falling levels of population at such times were clearly reflected in the extent of land abandonment and the amount of scrubland and woodland. The document, dated 1367, reads, "40 acres are worth only twopence per acre, because they cannot be sold unless well tilled and manured." Further deterioration occurred at the hands of Ingelram de Courcy, whose tenure was followed by scandal and disgrace on the grounds that he "adhered to the Kings adversary in France before all others as his natural and superior Lord." In other words, he was a traitor and was required to forfeit the Manor. The extent of his neglect is shown in the records for 1367 by such phrases as "The Manor of Trimworth contains diverse ruinous buildings of no net value which cannot be repaired or maintained from year to year without help from the issues from the Manor. Twenty one acres of wood are of no value because they were all felled when the Manor was in the hands of Ingram Lord of Courcy, and they cannot be felled or turned to profit within ten years of that time."

Such records provide fascinating insights of parish life, early house occupancy and the use of land on the estate. It has been possible to trace the changing fortunes of the house and its estate and speculate on the causes of these changes. Treason, disease, famine, war, have all been part of the story, bringing the estate at various times to dereliction and decay. At other times powerful landlords have worked to produce a flourishing estate with large farms playing a vital role in the evolving economic life of these riverside communities.

March 4th

From the dead trees along the railway embankment came an early morning sound of a green woodpecker 'drumming' the dead trees, either the sign of the bird establishing its springtime territory or the beginning of a successful search for wood boring insects which the bird finds by guiding its long tongue into insect galleries. The territorial call in spring is a distinctive full-throated laughing 'kleu-kleu-kleu-kleu,' accelerating at the end. During courtship it is sometimes possible to observe the male flying in a spiral around trees, with a female beneath showing her excitement by spreading out wings, fanning the tail and swaying head from side to side. The activity in the trees this morning may possibly be signs of nesting. It can take a pair 10 to 30 days to excavate a nest hole in the trunk of a tree.

The green woodpecker is also a frequent visitor to lawns as well as trees, exposing ants' nests by using its long sticky tongue to hoover up the insects. The green colour of these birds is thought to be an adaptation to ground-living habitats, such as grasses and lawns. Even with snow cover the bird will still find feeding sites on lawns, their locations marked by bare earth hollows in the snow. Its colourful relative the greater spotted woodpecker is a frequent visitor to birdfeeders here. It is a striking, almost exotic site with its bright red under-tail. Its contact call is a sharp, loud 'tchick.' We rarely see the much smaller lesser spotted woodpecker, although February and March is the most likely time to see them because branches are bare and its drumming activity is more active. They frequent the tops of trees searching for insects in smaller branches.

In the garden, blackbirds are pairing up and beginning to sing, a sign that the male has found attractive territory. They will fly fast, low and noisily across the garden into dense cover. A little later we will see courtship behaviour, consisting of quick, oblique runs across lawns, making head- bowing movements with beak open. Meanwhile, the female will perch quietly nearby provocatively flicking up its tail. Our large collection of moorhens is also becoming aggressively territorial at this time as they begin to put together untidy rafts of twigs in the reeds around the bottom pond. We frequently see running battles and squabbles all over the garden and paddock leading down to the ponds.

The capricious nature of weather at this time of the year can be a curse. Warm sun begins to open blossoms, buds and shoots, and then a vicious, sudden frost turns them all crisp and brown. John Clare's poem, 'February – the thaw,' describes one moment when the shepherd is seen, "by warm banks over his work to bend, chattering to a passing friend," and then later, with the return of snow and frost, "shepherds bend along, crouching to the whizzing storms," or "shuffling through the sinking snows, blowing his fingers as he goes." Today the promise of spring is stronger, but like an unreliable firework it will fizz with promise, splutter unreliably before hopefully bursting into life.

March 5th

The main objective of our winter gardening is using plants to activate all the senses. Colour comes from the red and green stems of dogwood, emerging hyacinths and daffodils, the variegated leaf colours of eleagnus and choisya, bark colours and textures, particularly the various betula. Smell is provided by Christmas box, winter honeysuckle, viburnum bodnantense (Dawn) and flowering hazel. At this time of year the enterprising gardener is able to turn adversity into virtue and, like the weather, take pleasures with the pain as Vita Sackville West observes in her poem 'The Garden', written in 1946.

> "Still may you with your frozen fingers, cut
> Treasures of Winter, if you planted well:
> The Winter-sweet against a sheltering wall,
> Waxen, Chinese and drooping bell:
> Strange in its colour, almond in its smell:
> And the witch hazel, Hamamelis mollis,
> That comes before its leaf on naked bough,
> Torn ribbons frayed, of yellow and maroon,
> And sharp of scent in frosty English air..."

Forecasters will talk about a day when 'temperatures really struggled' as a bitter wind keeps temperatures below 7°C all day, but there are still heartening sights and sounds of the pulse of spring. Along the dykes, silvery catkins of the pussy willow are showing like silver buttons, and the golden tassels of hazel catkins are releasing their lemon pollen to the wind. The bird world is getting 'edgy.' Jackdaws are grouping up, making friendly gestures and walking with a swagger. They are intelligent, amusing, sociable birds whose activities are entrenched in literature and folklore. For years they have tried to nest in our chimneys by dropping large twigs until they've become wedged, then building a rough platform. They are poor nests and we occasionally have nest and bird falling through the chimney stack and emerging into the living room. Now they nest as a large group in the roof space over the bothy. Wrens are whirling around the house, ducks circle frantically overhead in pairs, rooks haggle, magpies chatter and in contrast, the ever present buzzard spirals lazily in wide circles above Tye Wood.

Long-tailed tits are not common visitors to bird tables, but today a handsome pair is feeding together displaying their distinctive pink, white and black plumage and long tails – the 'flying teaspoons.' They are very vulnerable to cold weather, often huddling together in groups of five or six to conserve warmth. I hope they will build their delicate lichen-studded, feather-lined nests nearby. Each nest can account for over 2000 journeys. They are great travellers, extending up to a 30 mile range despite being the lightest of the tits. Below the feeders and under the yew trees a flock of 15 or 20 greenfinches are feeding and quarrelling. It is good to see them in such numbers after recent scares of a 20% reduction in numbers because of the virulent infectious disease caused by the Trichomonas parasite.

We are beginning to see barn owls around the nest box in Six Acre Meadow or perching in hedges along the road. By early spring, pairs are beginning to spend more time together around the intended nest site. The male will spend time hunting, then presenting food to his mate or leaving it in the nest cavity. It is heartening to contemplate that these early signs will hopefully develop into another exciting year of barn owl observation from the riverbank.

Little Jack was impressed to know that the solitary oak standing near the river in East Dane Meadow was older than his grandad. 'How much older,' he wanted to know. Ring counts were impossible, so we followed the other traditional method for estimating the age of trees which is to measure the girth of the tree approximately 5 foot from the ground. The rule is that one inch of girth represents a year of growth (although this varies according to site, situation and soil). On this basis, the 14 foot girth dates the tree back to the middle of the 19th century, when it was probably planted with others in the deer park of Olantigh. A hundred and fifty years is not particularly old for an oak, 400 years is not uncommon, but 'our tree' is still impressive with its grey fissured trunk covered in lichens and mosses, the spreading branches producing a large domed crown visible from a great distance. The tree provides shade and shelter for livestock, firewood for campers, swinging

We gazed up into the twisted, gnarled, knobbly branches of the venerable oak.

fun for children and a rubbing post for sheep. In recognition of its venerable status, Jack and I hugged the trunk and gazed up into its twisted, gnarled, knobbly branches.

A few hundred metres away stands another magnificent tree with a very different origin, history and appearance, creating an equally distinctive skyline. This is the Wellingtonia or Sequoia giganteum introduced into Britain by the plant hunter William Lobb in about 1854. They were loved by the Victorians because of their impressive size, growing up to 100 feet and living for over 3000 years. This one at Olantigh was planted as a single specimen, although they have been planted in groves or avenues leading to stately homes, and in churchyards. The naming of the tree caused an international dispute between Britain and America. Named after the Duke of Wellington who died in 1852, America objected and wanted it named after the first President of the USA, General Washington. The dispute was resolved by naming it Sequoia giganteum because of its similarity to the Californian Redwood, Sequoia sempervirens. The name Sequoia commemorates the famous Cherokee Indian of that name who invented the Cherokee language. With its pointed crown, the Olantigh sequoia stands high above the surrounding oaks, ash, and sycamore, visible for miles up and down the valley.

Sequoia giganteum at Olantigh, visible for miles along the valley.

In the darkness of a March dawn, the birds are making their voices heard. A dunnock or hedge sparrow has chosen a high perch on the barn and sings a fast, short, thin, but sweet song, a little more subdued than the wren's loud, vigorous,

March 8th

cheerful collection of trills, rattles and clicks, producing over 50 notes in about five seconds. The robin joins in from the summerhouse roof, sending a high drawn-out plaintive sound with a run of fast clear notes. When it is disturbed we hear its ticking alarm call, like a clock being wound up. The rich repertoire of the blackbird with its long, liquid notes is fluting across the garden. They are scuttling around in pairs, young males projecting their melodies to attract a mate or announcing to the world that they have found their summer territory. Clucking alarm calls tell others to 'keep off my patch.' Gradually, the thin reed of sound begun by the dunnock becomes woven into a rich tapestry of sound featuring the chirps and chatters of sparrows, the short repetitive tumbling song of the chaffinch and the see-sawing, mechanical notes and trills of the blue tit. And sounding supreme over this chorus are the vigorous, varied cascading notes of the song thrush, repeated in triplicate like a virtuoso flute player warming up for the full sonata. The sounds wash around us: the sounds which promise spring as the skies lighten over Trimworth Down.

The sounds make up a combination of bird calls and bird song. The call is specific and sends information – a warning, an alarm, a call for help, all expressed in a simple vocabulary. The song is generally more elaborate and varied, projecting the singer's feelings and moods in high-pitched, high-frequency sound which travels through the clear, cool morning air. It is used to defend territory or attract a mate. Evidence suggests that birds are born with a basic ability and vocabulary to sing, but much of the song is learned from the baby bird's own father. (It is normally the male bird which sings). If songbirds are raised away from their own kind they will often adopt the songs of other species within earshot, and if they are raised in isolation, will only develop an incomplete version of the song of their species. Some are good mimics. The starling has the ability to mimic other birds, (as well as the sound of machines, wolf whistles and car alarms!). There is still much to learn about the language of birds. This morning, I'm convinced that they not only give pleasure, but also gain pleasure from singing, so 'Hail to thee blithe spirit.'

March 9th

The weather map today is simple. A great anticyclone is plonked over central England with virtually no isobars. To the west, unbroken sunshine, to the east, especially the east coast, a grey cloud of unfathomable depth is being blown in off the North Sea by an icy wind. These systems are difficult to shift, so the prospect of anything other than relentless, grey, anti-cyclonic gloom is not good for the rest of the week.

The appearance of dead rabbits, squashed game-birds and badgers is sadly a common sight in the country roads around us. Early spring foraging and courtship rituals seem to leave birds and mammals oblivious to danger and unaware of the presence of approaching cars. With the presence of road kill comes the clever, adaptable, carrion crow, perching on posts and in treetops and quietly observing the roads, woods and pastures, especially after game shoots, when they attack injured birds with their thick blunt bills. In a group they are fearless, like a gang of furtive adolescents, and will drop onto pigeons or small mammals and see off larger birds like buzzards or heron. An outcome of this increased bird activity around house and garden is that in the heat of the chase birds are often confused by the reflection of skies or trees in patio windows and will fly into the windows suffering concussion or serious internal injury. This behaviour is particularly noticeable in the breeding season, but even in winter, small birds like robins that hold winter territory can also suffer in this way. At this time of year we also notice the strange habit of birds, particularly tits, picking at the putty in window frames or the lime mortar between bricks. Perhaps it is the linseed oil that attracts them, or other minerals which supplement their diet.

For weeks I have been absorbed by the writings of William Cobbett, whose traveller's tales are a valuable source of economic and social history, following on from the great travel journals of Celia Fiennes and Daniel Defoe, both of whom recorded detailed observations of Kent. William Cobbett was born in 1763, son of a yeoman farmer, who travelled on horseback through England just before the railways spread their network and changed the face of the country. Cobbett fled to the United States after 'blowing the whistle' on military corruption in the army, returning in 1800 to become a champion of traditional rural society at the time of its imminent transformation by the industrial revolution. He was a grass-roots radical, a supporter of labourers' rights, and his observations reveal a love of the countryside and a dislike of towns. The town of Sandwich is described "as villainous a hole that one would wish to see, surrounded by some of the great lands in the world". Deal has even less to commend it, being "a villainous place of filthy looking people, everything seems upon the perish". These observations are recorded in a ride he took on September 1823, from Dover to the Isle of Thanet, then on to Canterbury, Faversham, Maidstone, Tonbridge, passing through the Weald of Kent to London (the Great Wen). He describes the sheep farming of Romney Marsh, the importance of hops around Canterbury and Maidstone, giving details of yields and returns. Highest praise is recorded for fruit. "The fruit in Kent is more select than Herefordshire where it is raised for cider, while in Kent it is raised for sale in its fruit state….The orchards are beautiful indeed, kept in the neatest order, and indeed all belonging to them excels anything of the kind to be seen in Normandy, as to apples I never saw any so good in France as those in Kent".

Just as Cobbett wrote on the eve of the Industrial Revolution, Charles Igglesden's travel journals in 1939 were followed by another phase of conflict and turmoil on a scale which was impossible to envisage, making his snapshot of Kent even more endearing and significant. His 'Saunters through Kent with Pen and Pencil' is a delightful set of volumes written with a sympathetic and perceptive eye and illustrated with superb pen and ink drawings. Igglesden's motive for this work is conveyed in the preface of the first volume. "My idea in writing this saunter through Kent is to preserve a picture of our countryside as it appeared at the beginning of the century. As years roll by, changes are inevitable with the appearance of villages and towns, of our lanes and other rural scenery and customs". There's a wonderful description of the Downs overlooking the Stour around Trimworth. "It is one of the most thinly populated parts of Kent, and therein lies its charm. The pastures and wooded slopes are alluring in their peacefulness and rural simplicity, dotted with a solitary homestead here and there, wide links to join up with villages, or rather hamlets, still sleeping and undisturbed by the turmoil of the busy world… Here on the top of the Downs or down in the valleys you will find peace"

Male catkins of hazel are adding a touch of gold to the woodland edge. The dark sausage-like catkins of autumn have been transformed into golden pendants stuffed with pollen. The hazel produces these flowers so that pollen can be shed before the leaves appear, allowing the pollen to spread widely in the wind and to be intercepted

March 10th

by the female flowers. The male flowers along the underside of the branches of our ancient yew have become yellow and are also shedding clouds of pollen. There is a sensuous feeling of pleasure and impending delight in the air. Daffodils, primroses, snowdrops, hazel catkins and pollen; it is a combined optimistic evocation of early spring; a feeling echoed in a beautifully expressed love poem by an unknown writer in the Song of Solomon.

Male catkins of hazel are adding a touch of gold to the woodland edge.

"Arise, my love, my fair one, and come
    away:
for now the winter is past, the rain is over
    and gone.
The flowers appear on the earth:
the time of singing has come,
and the voice of the turtledove is heard in
    our land.
The fig tree puts forth its figs,
and the vines are in blossom:
they give forth fragrance.
Arise, my love, my fair one, and come
    away."

March 12th

After heavy overnight rain the weir is a white-water torrent. Fast moving lines of foam below the weir mark the direction of the current as it surges onto the outside bank of each river meander, undercutting the banks. Large lumps of meadow grass attached to blocks of rich silty soil slip into the water, leaving a fresh face of soil vulnerable to the relentless river force. Young crack willows planted along the bank now tip awkwardly towards the river, their roots insecure and exposed. Bank-fall is almost a daily occurrence. The changing shape of a river channel, normally noticed over a period of many years, can easily be observed here in less than a decade. As the day progresses, the river level rises, the banks are breached and flood waters rise in the meadow.

Blocks of meadow grass slip into the water leaving a fresh face of soil exposed to the relentless force of the river.

Later in the day, floodwaters recede to leave a depressing sight of litter marking the high-water mark of the flood. At such times, we collect bin loads of rubbish including plastic and glass bottles, polystyrene, wooden pallets and white goods. The woodland margins adjacent to the road have become an easy disposal site from cars as they pass through this ancient wood. Illegal tipping is an all too common sight in the country lanes nearby. Society insists on 'the right to roam' but surely rights must come with responsibilities. Our river valleys have become dumping grounds, exposing wildlife and farm animals to danger. 'Respect, protect, enjoy' may sound a simplistic motto for a countryside code, but the words are certainly appropriate in relation to these river meadows.

March 13th

Trees have a conversation dictated by the wind as its energies pass by pine needle, leaf, twig, branch and trunk. In their soft moods the trees sigh and breathe. These are the sounds of stillness when the wood seems to expand in size and take in distant sounds like the drone of a tractor, a passing train, the hum of faraway traffic, as well as nearby birdsong, scratchings and scamperings in the forest litter. One is conscious of one's own presence in this small, intimate setting. In the forceful, energetic mood of the wind in the woods today, branches clatter, crash, creak and groan. I thought of John Muir, the 19th century advocate of wilderness preservation in America who climbed to the top of a 100' Douglas Fir to experience first-hand the force and beauty of a fierce Sierra Nevada wind storm. He remained tied to his lofty perch for hours with branches swaying violently. "Every tree was excited, bowing to the roaring storm, waving, swirling, tossing their branches in glorious enthusiasm." ('The Mountains of California', 1894).Sam and I did not share Muir's need to get so close to the elements and experience their untamed power; we tumbled out of the wildness of the woods like leaves before a wind and headed for the safety of the open meadow.

We followed fallow deer footprints along muddy riverside paths. Slender prints of the doe could be distinguished from the longer prints of the buck and much smaller prints of fawns which were probably born last spring in May or June. We were seeing the prints of a small herd of between four and six deer in their favourite habitat of mixed woodland with clearings, and adjoining pasture for open grazing, whilst being near enough to the wood for cover. Here they eat grass, fresh shoots of trees and brambles, fungi and bark. There are signs of the barking of young trees; occasionally the incisors leave furrows in the trunk surface. The most likely time to see them is at dawn or dusk because during the day they will be resting to ruminate.

March 14th

The first comprehensive survey of the flora of the county of Kent was published in 1899, the next one being undertaken in 1982 by E. Philp, ('An Atlas of the County of Kent.') He vowed never to get involved in another, but fortunately he did, and the result is 'The New Atlas of Kent Flora,' published by the Kent Field Club in 2010. This latest survey makes use of global positioning systems (GPS) to give a more accurate picture of plant distributions. The county was divided into 58 x 10 km squares, and then each 10 km^2 was divided into 25 tetrads each being 2 km^2. Looking at the spatial distribution of individual plants for the county, the controlling influence of geology appears paramount. This is not surprising because different rocks produce different soils which support different plants. The great diversity of geology, together with a long tidal coastline and many rivers, has presented a wide variety of plant species in the county.

Some plants show significant gains since 1982, such as the Guernsey fleabane from the daisy family, first recorded in Kent in 1985 but spreading rapidly, especially on bare and waste places, old walls and pavement cracks. Common scurvy grass has spread from its original salt marsh location on the coast, especially at Dungeness, along main and minor roads which have been treated with salt. However, the overall results for the county show a disturbing loss in numbers of records, the main reason being a loss of habitat through urban growth and development in its many forms, and also the intensification of agriculture. With the population of Kent growing by 10,000 between 2008 and 2009, (largely through migration), the future of native wild flower habitats continues to be under threat.

The primrose is now appearing under trees and in damp patches of hedgerows, ditches, banks and forest floors. Prima rosa–'first rose' – frequently flowers as early as

Prima rosa, 'the first rose', is appearing in hedgerows, ditches, banks and forest floors.

Deep yellow flowers of the cowslip grow in nodding clusters on long stalks.

February in southern England, but much later in the north.(The Orcadian name for them is May flower.) A close look at the flower reveals that some plants bear 'pin' flowers, where the capita of the style is prominent, like a pinhead; or 'thrum' flowers, where the anthers form a ring around the style halfway down the flower tube. It was Darwin who first explained the reason for this arrangement. When an insect visits the pin flower, pollen gets stuck on the insect's proboscis which it then wipes on the stigma of the thrum-eyed flower. This fertilisation can only take place between pin and thrum flowers, or vice versa, and is an example of cross pollination. Numerous cultivars have been produced for garden planting giving pink and red-flowered primroses, but it is the wild primrose in its natural setting which makes it one of the most loved spring flowers. Also flowering in damp hedgerows and ditches is the cousin of the primrose, the cowslip, its deep yellow flowers growing in nodding clusters on long stalks.

March 15th

More welcome visitors arrive at the peanut party. A flock of delicate, bouncy, colourful goldfinches flies between the peanuts and the old cardoon seed heads by the bothy. They are a strikingly beautiful sight with their bright red faces and yellow wing patches. Their silvery, tinkling, twittering chatter accompanies these gregarious little flocks, appropriately called a charm, 'a blended noise, as of birds.' The little bird has been time-honoured since appearing with the Madonna in Raphael's Renaissance painting. The red face of the little bird was considered to represent blood when the bird removed a thorn from the face of Christ. Then for centuries it was caged because of its attractive appearance and song. They love thistles, their Latin name is Carduelis carduelis, which means thistle, twice. Teasels around the bottom pond are now acting as a feeding station having been a favourite winter feature. The seeds are at the base of long tubes, protected by sharp bristles and only the greenfinch (and crossbill) can reach and extract them with their sharp conical bills.The food store for many birds has been given a much needed boost in this wet, milder weather by the appearance of worm casts in gardens and fields. Working near the surface the worm is breaking down partly decomposed organic material and then excreting nutrient-rich worm casts. Nothing could be more enticing and nutritious to the robin, blackbird, or song thrush than a worm, spotted by eager eyes in the early morning light, and pulled from the soil with their strong beaks.

March is a month of shifting seasons, slipping into and out of winter before spring finally and assuredly announces its arrival. Today, there are glimpses of better things to come. Ladybirds are on the lookout for early aphids; and partners. A honeybee is seen stumbling across the flowers of heather and a solitary queen bee bumbles and drones methodically from flower to flower on heathers and hazel catkins. Now they can be seen skimming low over the rough grass in search of nest sites. Some will nest underground in abandoned burrows of rodents such as mice and bank voles, others will look for dense piles of leaf-litter or grass. Once located, the nest will be stuffed with pollen and nectar and then the queen will lay eggs and incubate them, shivering her flight muscles to produce warmth.

We live in a small country blessed with a rich variety of wildlife, but we all have different perceptions of how our natural world has changed over the years. The younger generation will feel this is the way things have always been, but older generations will be working to a different baseline, and will be aware of changes in biodiversity. Perhaps we are conscious of seeing fewer butterflies swarming over chalk downlands or fewer moths caught in the headlight beam of cars on summer nights or fewer hares and cornflowers in the fields or the sight and sound of skylarks becoming less common. These changes have been a concern of Natural England, which has recently produced an authoritative survey to demonstrate that this variety of wildlife is under pressure from human activities as never before, resulting in species extinction. Change in species population is a natural consequence of environmental change and technological advance, but over the last 200 years, 492 species have been lost, the losses being greatest in butterflies (24%) and amphibians (22%). The report shows how regions have been affected by the loss of different species, some charismatic, others lesser known. Loss of species in the east of England includes the red squirrel, great bustard, dainty damselfly and marsh fritillary butterfly. In the south-east, losses include the greater horseshoe bat, blue stag beetle, orange-spotted emerald dragonfly, the bumblebee 'bombus pomorum', and crested cow wheat.

What has happened to cause such a widespread and rapid decline in species of plants and animals? Sea level rise is impacting on many coastal habitats through erosion and saltwater inundation. Fragmentation of habitat has restricted the range over which some species can operate resulting in remnant or isolated sites which become more vulnerable to climate change. Since the Second World War, intensification of agricultural management including the use of pesticides and insecticides has had a profound impact. There are fewer mixed farms and more crop specialisation over large areas, able to respond to demands for greater food security. As England's climate warms it is likely that intensive arable management will spread further northwards and westwards, causing further reduction in habitat diversity. Other factors causing concern include decline in the numbers of long-distance migrants visiting the UK, or illegal killing of predators perceived to threaten livestock and game, or the invasive nature of some non-native species.

Both plant and animal species have their own intrinsic value, and to over-exploit or damage our environment in ways that lead to their loss is simply wrong and a failure in our duty of care to nature. Dr Helen Phillips, the Chief Executive of Natural England, writes "Each species has a role and, like the rivets on an aeroplane, the overall structure of the environment is weakened each time a single species is lost. We seem to have endless capacity to get engaged about rainforests, but this (report) reminds us that conservation begins at home."

March 17th

Walking north along the river to Godmersham Bridge we were greeted by the 'caawing' of dozens of rooks in the woods by Godmersham church. In the autumn, their roosts were disturbed by tree thinning and underbrush clearance but the rookery has become re-established with 30 to 40 bulky nests, each one an untidy tangle of twigs propped in braches of the tallest trees. This is breeding time, with family squabbles and the thieving of sticks from neighbouring nests. The noise of their clamouring in the treetops is a common feature of our villages and woodlands.

The rook is a member of the Corvidae family, C. frugilegus, Latin for 'food gathering'. It is very similar to the carrion crow, but slightly smaller and with black feathers which have a blueish purple sheen in sunlight. The rook also has shaggier feathers around the legs, and a distinctive bone-coloured patch of skin around the base of its beak. They are more difficult to distinguish in the air, although it used to be said that 'if you see a flock of crows they are rooks, and if you see a solitary rook

The clamouring noise of rooks in the treetops is a common feature of our villages and woodlands.

it is a crow'. Generally, the end of the rooks wings are spread, more like fingers in flight. Both are intelligent birds, and an Aesop fable written 2000 years ago tells of a crow bringing stones to raise the water level in a pitcher so that it could reach the liquid and quench its thirst. A recent study has successfully replicated this, using rooks, and the same research team also showed that corvids could select the correct tool to extract food from a horizontal tube.

Now the rooks are gathering in the fields, commuting between their feeding and roosting areas. Always gregarious, they are often seen feeding in mixed flocks with jackdaws. We are pleased they have remained in their colony at Godmersham because country folklore states that abandonment of the rookeries will bring bad fortune to the family that owns the land.

In Tye Wood and Oxen Leas very few trees were showing any sign of leaf burst, and virtually no spring flowers were on show. I would have expected blackthorn to be in flower by now, but it will be a week or more before it flowers. Studies suggest that springtime in the UK is starting on average 11 days earlier than 30 years ago, so is this cold spring going to break a trend of earlier spring arrivals?

March 18th

The science of phenology is the recording of natural, regularly occurring events, which allows us to demonstrate how climate change is affecting wildlife habitats. The science has a long history; Robert Marsham was Britain's first phenologist and started recording his 'Indications of Spring' as early as 1736. In 1875 British phenology took a major leap forward when the Royal Meteorological Society established a national record. In 2010, a major study was produced by the Centre for Ecology and Hydrology in Cambridge and the Woodland Trust which compiled 25,000 records of spring trends for 726 species of plants, animals, insects, and birds, across land, sea and freshwater habitats. These have been analysed to reach conclusions on the timing of events in the life-cycle, such as flowering of plants, leaf burst on trees, migration habits of birds, and the first appearance of bumblebees, frogspawn and butterflies. Results show that more than 80% of the trends between 1975 and 2005 indicated earlier seasonal events, and that change has accelerated in recent years. Is spring becoming the new summer?

These changes have biological implications. Some animals and insects will benefit from a long period of hibernation because if they are woken earlier by mild winter days, they will expend energy searching for food that isn't there. Animals and birds also time their reproduction to coincide with periods when food is abundant. If changes result in not enough food being available, this could have negative consequences for their offspring. Phenology has been described as 'the canary in the cage', indicating that the nature of climate change could have profound consequences for the complex web of life. If spring is arriving earlier, the resilience of our ecosystems will be put to the test. The UK phenology network of volunteer observers, and the recent research it has produced, is a key benchmark in understanding the processes in order to make projections of future changes.

March 19th

We have been accused of antisocial behaviour by a neighbour because we refuse to have our stretch of river 'stun fished.' This fishing uses electricity to stun fish and is used as a common scientific method to sample fish populations to determine species composition. It does no permanent damage to the fish if performed correctly. They return to their natural state in minutes and can be released unharmed back to the river. We have no objection to the method, but are opposed to its use to select out coarse fish, leaving only salmonid species (salmon, trout) in the river for sport fishing. In our quarter mile stretch we have pike, chub, roach and other species, including trout, and this is the way we wish to keep it -in its natural state. Where stun fishing has been done on neighbouring estates of Godmersham and Olantigh, the catch in terms of biodiversity is very poor. As a regular angler recently warned, "We need coarse fish in our rivers, they give us a good indication of the quality of river water. If they are removed, trout alone would not give us a full picture of the state of the river." It appears that coarse fish have not over-wintered well this year, probably because of the long spells of high water and flooding.

March 20th

We have reached an important milestone in the calendar and, for many, the best day of the year because it is the vernal equinox, symbolic of changing seasons. Even though the day is grey and cold, the sun will still cross the equator heading north and our days will lengthen and warm. This certainty is enough to raise the spirits: we have shifted seasons. The equinox has Christian significance also, because Easter always falls on the first Sunday after the first full moon following the vernal equinox. Many other cultures celebrate this day: the Iranian calendar begins its New Year on the vernal equinox.

Farmers respond and the countryside fills with the sights and sounds of springtime farming activity. Lambing is in full swing and although new-born lambs can cope with cold and dry weather, the present wet and cold weather is a real threat to their survival. On our walks, we now watch for ewes which have left the flock to find a quiet location in which to lamb, letting the shepherd know if we suspect problems. Seed drilling is also in progress, together with muck spreading, fertilising and the ploughing of game cover. We are told there is a good prospect of high prices being fetched for linseed, so this useful 'break crop' is likely to feature in the fields around us, bringing a wonderful powder blue colour contrast to the golden corn and the vivid yellow of rape this summer.

As the garden comes to life, the casualties of the hard winter become apparent. Several small trees of bay and border shrubs have not made it, and more will be revealed as the growing season unfolds in response to warmer temperatures and lengthening days. I was delighted to see the long dark- green leaves of the common spotted orchid growing on south-facing grassy banks in the garden and displaying the characteristic dense, purple blotches on each leaf. Soon the flower spike will emerge which will hold the summer spires of pink and purple flowers.

A day of contrasts, beginning with a biting east wind bringing low-level, featureless grey cloud. By mid-morning the cloud base had lifted to reveal a diffuse and hazy sun breaking through to give brightness and warmth, and the milieu of the countryside shifted from winter to spring. It was as if the arrival of the vernal equinox had flicked a switch and the countryside responded with a flurry of activity. Hedgerows were now full of fussing birds, a quarrelling cloud of sparrows chased from house to hedge, chaffinches cart -wheeled in pairs, groups of tits whizzed around the feeders, starlings whirred and whistled from chimney pots displaying their smart glossy black feathers with iridescent streaks of purple and green, and a conspiracy of crows watched from the tops of the ash. 'A thousand blended notes' of birdsong joined this celebration of spring. The afternoon warmth lulled one into a sense that the temperature graph was on an upward trend, but we are not complacent, for frosts and even snow may return. Nevertheless, the sights and smells and sounds of spring raised the spirits and energy levels. We could smell the arrival of spring as we worked the dark, damp earth and tidied neglected borders, then rested on sunny banks to smell the scent of new- mown grass after the first cut of the year. Along the river, swarms of small flies emerged into the warm sunlight and a cob swan pluffed out its plumage, arched its wings and patrolled protectively alongside the female pen. Three pairs of mallards circled high overhead before clumsily crash- landing in the river and pursuing each other through the reeds. On the pond, the first sighting of a newt nosing the surface of the water before flicking its tail and heading for the safety of darker, deeper water.

March 21st

During an early-morning walk onto Trimworth Down I saw two hares on a young wheat crop. I was standing against the dark background of the wood so there was

March 22nd

no silhouette to reveal my presence. They were sitting still, looking at each other, and then began a headlong chase down into the dry-valley, rising up the far side and disappearing into the safety of a hedge line. Their speed was awesome; probably 60 km an hour or more, bodies close to the ground, ears flat along backs, legs scissoring then stretching out. The hare is a creature of mythology and folklore across many cultures– 'the hare in the moon'; its African origin as a 'trickster'; Brer rabbit and Uncle Remus; March madness; the tortoise and the hare. As well as being Britain's fastest mammals, two other aspects of their behaviour are well known. First, they 'go mad' in March; and secondly males rear up on their hind legs and 'box' each other with flailing paws to gain supremacy in the competition for mates. In fact, 'madness' is no more a feature of March than any other of the months in their long breeding season from January to September. Furthermore, boxing does not represent competition between two bucks for a doe, but is more likely to be an interaction between the sexes, whereby the female tries to prevent the male from mating.

March 23rd

The forest floor is greening up with blades of bluebells, and in other areas dog's mercury grows as a dense carpet, excluding all competitors. This widespread woodland plant is from the spurge family and is especially common in dry alkaline areas where its dense and rapid growth can shade out other light-demanding plants. It has poisonous foliage which can cause enteritis in cows and lead to the production of slimy yellow milk. The prefix 'dog' is often given to wild flowers that are lacking in scent or other qualities – hence dog violet, dog rose etc. In the past the plant has been called 'boggart's posy' by country folk (a boggart being a malevolent household fairy or goblin).However, it is one of the first fresh greens of a woodland in spring with its hairy oval leaves and inconspicuous spikes of tiny green flowers forming in March and April. Along the edge of the wood and in shady hedges and ditches, lords and ladies are throwing up large bright green arrow-shaped leaves, sometimes spotted purple. The flower head will become enveloped in a large green hood. This plant was called 'cuckoo pint' in Culpeper's 16th century herbal, and also goes under local names of willy lily, parson and clerk, Adam and Eve, Jack in the pulpit, Jack of the green and other, more sexually evocative names. It is one of the more toxic plants, producing poisonous foliage and berries, but the root can provide edible starch, which was used to stiffen Elizabethan lace ruffs, and is also a substitute for arrowroot. In East Anglia, the blades of sickles were traditionally coated in arrowroot juice to keep them sharp through the harvest.

March 24th

Today, a countryside encounter of a unique kind. Three men were observed wandering around the margins of the river meadow a long way from any public footpath, and clearly lost. One was carrying a large wooden box, which turned out to be a beautiful hand-made pinhole camera. Another had state-of-the-art photographic gear and the third, dressed in a pinstripe suit was carrying a life-sized plastic swan. They were a group of artists and their bizarre story was that they were undertaking a reconnaissance trek in preparation for a filmed journey in a swan-

A Pythonesque picture of eccentricity, madness, humour and originality which only the English character can display so effectively.

shaped pedalo between Swan Lake in Hastings and the Olympic Site in Hackney. It was difficult to see how Trimworth featured on this route, or how the drainage system would allow them to cover it without some long-distance portage. However, they were pointed in roughly the right direction and headed off on this very English odyssey, a Pythonesque picture of eccentricity, madness, humour and originality which only the English character can display so well.

Lords and ladies are throwing up large bright green arrow shaped leaves, sometimes spotted purple.

The flower head will become enveloped in a large green hood.

Pools and ribbons of shallow water called 'scrapes' have been constructed to attract wading birds.

March 25th

It is Lady Day, one of the Quarter Days, the others being Midsummer Day (24th June), Michaelmas (29thSeptember), and Christmas Day, when the annual contracts between tenant farmers and landowners came to an end. Farming families who were changing farms would travel from the old to the new farm on Lady Day. It was also the day that the Hearth Tax became due. This tax was introduced in 1662 to help with serious financial problems facing the government of Charles II, and was repealed in 1689. Each liable householder had to pay one shilling for each hearth within their property.

Along the path between Tye Wood and the river I heard two distinctive sounds of spring. From the wood came the call of a chiff-chaff. It is a little early for this summer visitor which usually arrives from the Mediterranean and North Africa in late March or early April. Perhaps it is one of the increasing number of overwintering chiff-chaff. Trying to locate the call, I played hide and seek through the woods to get a sighting of this nondescript, tiny insectivorous bird. It has an onomatopoeic name derived from its simple 'chiff-chaff' song and there are vernacular variations of 'chip chop' and 'choice and cheep'. The great naturalist and ornithologist Gilbert White was one of the first people to use the song to distinguish it from the wood warbler and willow warbler, both very similar in appearance.

High up on the branches of a riverside alder was a yellow hammer, very yellow, and likely to be an adult male. He was holding his head high, constantly flicking his tail with the effort of singing 'a-little-bit-of bread-and-no-cheese', one of the common sounds of summer. The farming practice of autumn-sown crops and loss of winter stubble has affected populations of this charismatic little bird and it has been placed on the red list of conservation concern.

In Bilting Meadow, the resident skylarks are now becoming active, although their song is still subdued. They are probably choosing ground nesting sites in preparation for breeding from April onwards. The nests will be slight hollows in the ground, lined with leaves, grasses and hair. Their short, shallow, frantic flights this morning were intended to lead us away from these favoured sites. Soon we will enjoy the loud, continuous, liquid chirrups of these 'minstrels of heaven' as they soar and dive high above the meadows. Bilting Meadow has been designated a Conservation Area by Natural England to encourage ground nesting birds like skylarks whose populations are in decline because the growing practice of autumn-sown wheat deprives these birds of winter stubble and nesting habitats. There is no public access to the meadow apart from along a footpath on which dogs are required to be kept on leads. In this meadow, pools and ribbons of shallow water called 'scrapes' have been constructed which dry out slowly during spring and summer. As the water retreats, the warmer margins attract invertebrates and breeding birds. We have seen lapwing recently and the yellow wagtail is another regular visitor. In winter the shallow water attracts wading birds such as snipe and possibly teal and wigeon. The scrapes are in a large meadow so the landscape character is unchanged and the edges grade gradually into the water with no unnatural mounds created by spoil from the excavation. In many farmland areas, traditional ponds have become shaded, silted up or filled in, so the provision of these scrapes creates a broader diversity of habitats for birds, mammals and invertebrates in these river meadows.

Hovering over the emerging nettles along the riverside was the first sighting this year of the peacock butterfly, a harbinger of coming spring. The peacock hibernates through the winter and can even be seen in cold late-winter months but usually emerging in early spring. It is probably the longest-lived butterfly, many living to see their 11th month. The common stinging nettle is its primary food source. Eggs are laid in clusters on the underside of young nettle leaves, and it is here that they will spread webs over the growing tips of the nettles on which they feed, stripping each leaf bare. As long ago as the 17th-century this butterfly was called the 'peacocks eye.' Its survival and widening distribution is probably due to gradually warming temperatures, despite suffering temporary setbacks in periods of minor climatic deterioration. Long may this nomadic butterfly range widely across our countryside with its message of coming spring.

Sallow or pussy willows are now dramatically recognisable with their large, bright yellow catkins which glow golden as the evening sun catches the pollen. They have been described as 'pointillist globes of shimmering yellow'. How attractive to a bumblebee, sailing by on a cold wind in a largely dead landscape to find these great golden mushrooms of colour, rich in nectar. These are the male flowers and will be pollinated by the bumblebees, as will the female trees with their silky green catkins which explode in May, liberating white cottony seeds. This year there will be no shortage of pussy willow, traditionally used in Palm Sunday church processions. They are sometimes used to decorate churches in the absence of palm leaves, the

The first sighting of the peacock butterfly, a harbinger of spring.

Bright yellow catkins of the sallow or pussy willow catch the evening sunlight like globes of shimmering gold.

willow symbolising grief as illustrated in Psalm 137.

"By the rivers of Babylon we sat down and wept when we remembered Zion. There on the willow trees we hung up our harps."

Back in the garden, I witnessed a spectacular, synchronised flight by a pair of pied wagtails, with the following bird displaying amazing reactions to mimic the lightning changes in speed and direction of the leader, and with no variation in the short distance between them.

March 28th

At 1am on the last Sunday before Easter Day our clocks go forward one hour as we go into British Summer Time and we have the gift of an extra hour of light at the end of the day. This is an hour when colour, scent, birdsong, and our spirits, are given a welcome boost. The panorama of life is opening up, but unfortunately the weather appears to be closing in. A return to colder temperatures and the prospect of snow is forecast, hopefully the last farewell gesture of winter. Just when we thought the seasons had shifted, March is having its last laugh as 'the month of many weathers.'

March 29th

For over 30 years, the Royal Society for the Protection of Birds has conducted one of the world's largest wildlife surveys, the 'Big Garden Bird Watch'. In 2012 more than 600,000 people recorded over 9 million birds, covering 73 species across nearly ,000 gardens. It provides the best evidence for fluctuations in species populations in gardens and indicates how species have been affected by the winter weather. It was tight at the top, but the house sparrow just pipped the starling and blue tit as the number one bird in both the country and in Kent. As expected, the smallest birds were most affected, particularly coal tit and gold crest. Long-tailed tits flew into the top 10 for the first time, suggesting their greater familiarity with the use of garden feeders and bird tables.

The weather was also responsible for more sightings of countryside birds like fieldfares, redwing, bullfinches and yellow hammer in our gardens. Blackcaps are also becoming more visible as a result of familiarity with feeders. Sadly, sparrow and starling numbers continue to decline, by 17% and 14% respectively in the last five years. Nevertheless, the house sparrow remains in top spot, followed by the blackbird and starling. Long-term changes over a period of 20 years reveal that the house sparrow has declined by over 62%, with the robin recording the next largest decline. Not surprisingly, the greatest percentage gains go to the wood pigeon and collared dove.

The drop in water levels in the dykes bordering the river meadows has revealed the outlets of field drains. Their presence explains why floodwaters recede so rapidly from the water meadows, quickly allowing sheep back onto the pastures. The under -drainage of the fields along the River Stour is a long and interesting story. Early drains were simply trenches cut across the fields and filled with brushwood, hedge trimmings and faggots before being backfilled with soil. In the mid-19th century, these brushwood drains were replaced by tile pipes made in the county brickyards. A tax was levied on all bricks and pipes, although at a later date agricultural enterprises were excused this tax, but only if each pipe was clearly marked with the word DRAIN. Pipes varied in size and shape, some were horseshoe -shaped with the open side placed over a plate at the bottom of the trench. Some were in the form of tapered terracotta pipes which fitted into one another. In all cases, water filtered through the soil and then through the porous pipes before running into the drainage ditches. A wide variety of tools was used for the very arduous work of cutting the ditches. Imagine the labour required to dig closely spaced channels across heavy clay soil. In the early 20th century, the use of tractor power and larger cement or plastic pipes has made the operation easier, leaving only the heaviest clay soils in poorly drained condition. The improving technology of under-draining has resulted in a regional change in cropping patterns and increases in levels of productivity on pastures with higher stocking levels for sheep and cattle. In turn, these changes have had an environmental impact on the wildlife and habitats of the riverside meadows.

Along the river banks where floodwaters have receded is the cheery sight of the glossy yellow stars of lesser celandine, the spring messenger, which will eventually grow into extensive patches of golden yellow. These are abundant flowers of early spring, their shining brilliant yellow colours displayed in damp woods, shady banks, or as here, alongside watercourses. The heart-shaped leaves are on long stalks and the solitary flowers have between 8 to 12 petals forming a bright yellow star. Not surprisingly, the plant has attractive vernacular names such as 'goldy knob' and 'golden guineas,' and in France they are known as 'bouton d'or.' Wordsworth considered it to be his favourite flower. This year, they are flowering a little late. In 2001, the average date of flowering in the UK was the 15th March: in 2009 it was the 3rd March. This year the earlier flowering trend has been reversed by two or three weeks, making its long-awaited appearance even more welcome.

March 30th

In the woods, another carpet layer is showing vigorous growth. The fresh green leaves of the common nettle will soon become a tall perennial with stinging hairs, and yet its healing cures are legendary. Roman soldiers beat themselves with nettles to cure rheumatic joints. It has culinary virtues; nettle tea is regarded as an effective spring tonic, and John Murrell, a 17th century herbalist wrote of its virtues;

"If they'd eat nettles in March
And mugwort in May
So many fine maidens
Wouldn't go to the clay."

Although much despised as a common stinging nettle, the plant has an essential role in the life-cycle of many moths and butterflies, and as a breeding ground for ladybirds and lacewings. Butterflies look for new leaves, so some of our nettle patches will be cut back in June, providing new leaves for our winged visitors by July.

March 31st

Heavy overnight rain continues well into the morning. The field drains have come into use again. The river runs fast, brown and frothy, and the sound of the weir at Olantigh becomes a low roar. The inevitable flotsam races by: wood, polystyrene blocks, plastics of all kinds, and the occasional sign. Today, a large red board had lodged against the bank reading 'Pedestrian Crossing.' The most memorable notice to float by was a temporary sign for a new residential development upstream, which read 'River Close,' obviously too close! Maybe another example of planners and developers failing to heed the advice of environmental agencies not to build on floodplains.

Sights, sounds and smells of fox are common experiences in countryside and garden. The female will be giving birth to cubs at this time and rarely leaves the den, so it is left to the male to search for food. Foxes adapt readily to new environments and so are regarded as a successful invasive species, especially in cities and suburbs. We recently saw a fox neatly evading people and traffic on the South Bank in London. His food intake is not obtained by countryside cunning, but by being streetwise on the location of food bins at the back of restaurants and hotels. Today, during the playing of national anthems before the Calcutta Cup at Twickenham, 'Volpes twickenamus 'slipped from under the grandstand and crossed the pitch, ignoring the pre-match ceremonies and the cheers of 80,000 spectators. If only the England backs had been able to replicate the neat footwork of the fox as he dodged and feinted around the ground staff it would have been an even more entertaining game!

When the fox first appeared in urban gardens it was considered an 'exotic 'rural visitor, almost fashionable, and to be encouraged by putting out food. Attitudes have changed; they are now seen as vermin, a nuisance, no longer fed so now they scavenge. Foxes in the countryside are sentimentally seen as red, bushy-tailed attractions, but in the city they are regarded as mangy and malnourished. In fact, urban foxes are probably no more or less healthy than rural foxes. Their lives are certainly much shorter, many being killed on roads in their first year as they search for food. Culls are not a solution, because within days, new foxes will move into the vacated territory. "A better response would be to accept these intrusions into our comfort zones as a kind of tithe, a voluntary sacrifice for the privilege of living on a planet rich with life." (Richard Mabey, 'A Brush With Nature.')

April

The sound of new born lambs is a sign of April, but on this foul day of strong westerly winds bringing rain and hail, their arrival is untimely. We have reversed out of spring momentarily. The name April is derived from the Latin word 'aperire', meaning 'to open' and in the leafless wood, the newly opened star-like flowers of wood anemones sway on long, slender stems. It is one of the earliest spring flowers and is generally confined to sites of ancient woodland. Surprisingly, even the delicate wood sorrel can survive the blustery wind and rain. Its five white petals veined with lilac are held on slender stalks above soft bright-green leaves resembling those of shamrock. It has long been known as Alleluia in remembrance of the Resurrection. Equally delicate are the small, pale, yellow-green flowers of the moschatel flowering in large colonies along the moist woodland edge and giving a faint smell of musk. The arrangement of flowers is amazing. The flower head is cube-shaped with a flower on each of the side faces and another on top – hence its alternative names of Townhall clock or five-faced bishop. It is also known as Good Friday flower because it generally blooms in early April. Under dry hedges cow parsley is flourishing, together with herb robert, primrose, lords and ladies, and the occasional yellow blaze of a dandelion. Most exciting is the welcome splash of blue from the early dog violet forming large patches of unscented flower. On hands and knees we search for the sweet unmistakable scent of the sweet violet flowering either in dark violet or even more strongly scented, in white, used by the Victorians for the production of fragrances and perfumes. The flower even has a reputation for calming horses, hence the use of Parma violets in buttonholes of riders and hunters.

After moving to Trimworth in 1995 we renovated an old outbuilding known as the bothy, originally basic accommodation for gardeners or farm workers, which has become a studio upstairs and garden/tool-shed below. We put an owl box in the gable end facing west. The next day jackdaws moved in and have been there ever since. We are entertained almost daily by these beguiling, comical and intelligent rogues. Today in the strong westerly wind, nest building was in progress. One jackdaw was struggling in flight, his airworthiness being adversely affected by a huge beak full of straw, pheasant feathers and horsehair. Approaches to the nest on a strong, erratic downwind caused him to overshoot, so with rapid wing beats he tried to hover unsteadily above the opening, waiting for a lull in the upwind before making ungraceful lunges at the entrance and losing half his payload in the process. There is a strong social unity in the jackdaw colony and I'm sure his chums, observing all this from nearby field maples, were as amused as I was by this ten minute performance.

News today of another member of the Corvid family under the heading, 'As the crow flies,' which documents the spread eastwards of the raven. Through most of the 20th century it was confined to the Celtic fringe, having been persecuted by Victorian gamekeepers. The recent advance of the raven from the moors of the English lowlands has been described as 'one of the most remarkable British wildlife phenomenon of the last 20 years.' By 2005 they had reached Sussex and last year, they were nesting in the White Cliffs of Dover.

Rising average temperatures and longer daylight hours bring daily changes in leaf emergence and the visual impact on the landscape is dramatic. Hedges are greening as hawthorn shoots break. The long, narrow buds of beech are bursting, especially on woodland margins where sunlight is stronger. Fat green buds of sycamore, narrow leaves of the elder and iridescent green shoots of hornbeam are all splitting. Most dramatic of all are the orange/brown bud scales of the horse chestnut which are peeling back to reveal large oval leaflets concealing the flower clusters which will eventually form the decorative candelabras of white and pink.

Walking back across Little Tithe Field from the wood there are frequent reminders of just how low winter temperatures had dropped. Lumps of chalk thrown up by autumn ploughing have been weathered by a freeze/thaw process and become shattered into piles of chalk rubble as if hit by a sledgehammer. Flints of all shapes and sizes litter the surface and amongst the broken chalk fragments are pieces of belemnite, fossils of life forms that emerged in a warm tropical ocean 100 million years ago. Today we headed home into a rain-laden icy wind, trampling on the tropical origins of our local geology.

The delicate flowers of moschatel (or town hall clock) have colonised the moist woodland edge giving a faint smell of musk.

Orange-brown bud scales of the horse chestnut are peeling back to reveal oval leaflets and flower clusters.

The study of old maps in local archive collections has provided a rich source of information and insight into the landscape and social history of the meadows and fields around Trimworth. As a prominent landholding over the centuries, Trimworth is also featured frequently on estate maps drawn for the purpose of recording details of the extent and use of the estate at the point of change of ownership. Some of these early maps (the first one for Trimworth being 1680), give opportunities for cartographers to record features of local importance and also to indulge their creative content with flamboyant drawing, shading and use of colour.

First editions of Ordnance Survey at 1 inch, 6 inch and 25 inches to the mile were carried out throughout the 19th century, the 25-inch map setting new standards of accuracy. Fields and their boundaries were accurately represented with each field numbered, and acreages given. Tithe maps, and their accompanying field books, from the early 19th century are available for the whole of Kent and give details of ownership, field names, state of cultivation, crops planted, acreage and rent payable. These allow an accurate representation of the agricultural economy of each parish. I've also been able to source maps and plans for public schemes affecting these meadows by the river. The arrival of the railway through the valley in 1850 required alterations to the river course and drainage ditches, all of which are documented on maps and accompanying indentures. Of even greater interest have been the maps of drainage and water management, showing complex networks of banks and ditches for the water meadows. They have left physical traces on the landscape and are an archaeological and historical resource, evidence of vital farming resources of the early 18th century.

Finally, reference must be made to two national land surveys, one in 1910 (so important that it was called the 'New Domesday' of land), and secondly the Farm Survey of 1941, prompted by the need to increase production to feed the country during time of war. Both give excellent insights into land ownership, tenancy, farm techniques, land management and even the competence of the farmer. The 1901 survey gives a four-page description of Trimworth Manor Farm, which had an income of £326 from sporting activities, £120 from the sale of timber and an annual overall value of £3500. By 1941 the farm was being run by Sir Edward Hardy and a summary of the enterprise by the Ministry of Agriculture reads "This farm was taken over by Mr Hardy last Michaelmas, all ploughing and winter cropping has been done. Although the farm is not yet clean it must be considered an 'A' class farm."

I am intrigued by these maps for their content, cartographic methods and skills of the map mapmaker. They also give an indication of the context of the time they were drawn. Taken together, they provide an excellent picture of the continuity of land-use and landscape change in these meadows by the river, from the early estate maps of the 17th century to the Ordnance Survey maps of the 21st century.

April 6th

With a warming sun comes the hesitant emergence of colourful floral displays, such as the sky-blue field speedwell, the bracts of lime green wood spurge, the ubiquitous red and white dead nettle and the deep blue of ground ivy or ale hoof, so named because it was used for flavouring beer. In the Book of Hours, April is appropriately depicted as a flowery month with images of couples picking flowers, courting and making music. Nature revives; fields, woods and flowers seem to celebrate this rejuvenation. In the words of the prince and poet Charles d'Orleans:

"Le temps a laissé son manteaux	Time has shed its cloak
De vent, de froidure et de pluie,	Of wind, rain and cold,
Et s'est vestue de broderie,	To assume the embroidery,
De soleil rayant, cler et beau."	Of the sun shining, bright and beautiful.

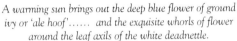

A warming sun brings out the deep blue flower of ground ivy or 'ale hoof'...... and the exquisite whorls of flower around the leaf axils of the white deadnettle.

I'm reminded of the wonderful tapestries of the Lady and the Unicorn, woven in wool and silk in 15th century Flanders, each panel decorated with a background of 'millefleurs,' literally a thousand flowers. The work is not some imaginary representation of the countryside. It is probably what people actually saw and experienced in the fields and meadows at the time.

Why are so many spring flowers yellow in colour? One theory is that yellow is a conspicuous colour which will attract the pollinators such as queen bumblebees. It is certainly a colour which fascinated the contemporary sculptor Anish Kapoor, who used yellow as a centrepiece in his exhibition at the Royal Academy in 2009.

His huge installation, 'Yellow', is a panel of 6 square metres which occupies one's whole field of vision. At the centre, a great belly recedes into the wall, 'more than yellow.' It plays with our perceptions, draws us in, and has a deep rooted effect on us, like being drawn in to warmth and sunshine, or the centre of a yellow flower. Perhaps the attraction of spring yellow for the pollinators in the natural world has the same attraction for us as well.

Blackthorn, another herald of spring is in blossom along hedgerows. From across the fields it appears like a pile of snow, a bank of froth or a cloud at ground level. Close-up, the white honey-scented clusters of flowers, with their conspicuous orange/red anthers, cover the leafless branches, (hence blackthorn.) It is rarely a tree, usually part of a hedge or

Blackthorn, another herald of spring, is in blossom along hedgerows.

April 7th

thicket, but what a welcome springtime sight, especially for the bees, beetles, moths and butterflies, including the unusual brown hairstreak butterfly. It is an invaluable source of nectar following on from the sallow willow and preceding the appearance of hawthorn. Blackthorn blossom also recalls the frequent and unwelcome event of a 'blackthorn winter,' a reminder that the weather can quickly slip back to subzero temperatures, strong winds and the possibility of 'blackthorn blossom blizzards.' At the other end of the year the attraction of blackthorn is the harvest of blue/black plums known as sloes, picked after the first frost and enjoyed by us as sloe gin; a rich, warming, reward for being torn to bits by the vicious, long, sharp thorns.

April 8th

A glorious spring morning, so Sam and I turned away from the river and headed upslope towards the sun and Trimworth Down. Pheasants burst out from the base of hedgerows squawking in alarm, wings whirring. In complete contrast, the exquisite lark ascending, pouring out its unbroken musical stream of song. It is a song which has earned its place in literature and music, described as 'heavenly sunshine translated into sound,' or 'the flawless expression of pure serenity.' As we walked through tussocks of grass above the cultivated fields, the skylarks became more excited and vigorous, parachuting down from several hundred metres and nestling in the grass. We were clearly unwelcome in their nesting territory at breeding time and retreated back to the open fields, reluctant to create any more problems for this threatened little bird whose population halved in the 1990s. Between 1972 and 1996 the RSPB estimate that skylarks declined by 75% and are still declining, resulting in their 'red listing' as a bird of conservation concern. Changes in farming practice and intensification of agriculture are the main causes. For example, the switch from spring to autumn-sown cereals results in taller, thicker vegetation growth, less suitable as a habitat for breeding chicks. Additionally, the loss of winter stubble leaves fields without weed-seeds for winter feeding. The welcome introduction of environmentally-friendly farming practices, such as leaving unplanted plots in cultivated areas will hopefully help to turn around the fortunes of this inspirational little icon of spring and summer.

As the day warmed the insects swarmed, and butterflies basked in the sun on dry paths, wings open, absorbing the warmth and sensing the air for scents, winds and nectar. I watched a pair of peacock butterflies supercharged with solar energy, circling and spiralling to 100 metres then plummeting joyfully downwards, one mimicking the other in flight as if joined by an invisible thread. Then, emerging from the woodland edge into the field, a greenish white butterfly landed in the grass, wings closed like a pale green leaf. This was the brimstone, one of the first butterflies to emerge in spring, although a new and much larger generation will appear in July or August. We will see them frequently patrolling this woodland margin. I lay full length and closely watched it open its wings to the sun, twitching the long proboscis which will draw life-giving nectar. This was the female, distinguished by its colour from the sulphur-yellow male.

These springtime encounters bring home to me the personal joy of this nature journal and the opportunity to recognise objects that I had probably seen before, but never really observed, registered and stored in my mind. I have become more sensitive to aspects of the natural world and its complex, fragile and interconnected ecosystems. It is a privilege to perceive and enjoy the richness of the rhythms of nature and rural life observed in these river meadows.

The high pressure deepens, drifts further east, and brings continuous warm sun. The palette of green is spreading across the countryside and there is buoyancy in the air. It has been an exciting day, beginning with the first sighting of the kingfisher as it flashed downstream like a brilliant electric-blue dart over the shimmering water. Its intense colour comes not from any pigment in the feathers, but from the actual structure of the feathers which create a scattering of light at the blue end of the spectrum – the so-called Tyndall effect. In a few seconds it was gone, leaving us with an intimate sense of pleasure and a little disbelief. Reading back through our five-year diary, on 1st April 2007 I noted the first sighting of the kingfisher followed a day later by several sightings along the river towards Godmersham. The sightings continued, becoming almost a daily occurrence. The following year there were fewer sightings, a trend which has continued each year since; and yet every day I walk the riverside I am excited by the prospect of seeing this shy bird which is now 'amber listed' because of general concern over its conservation status. Sadly, they are vulnerable to harsh winters, but even in milder temperatures only half the fledglings survive more than a week or two, and then only a quarter survive to breed the following year. Few birds live longer than one breeding season. Flooding has resulted in destruction of nests and disruption of habitats, and since the kingfisher is high up the food chain, it is vulnerable to the build-up of chemicals from agricultural run-off and industrial pollution.

In the garden later that morning, we heard the distinctive call of the cuckoo, great symbol and envoy of spring, proclaimed by the traditional English round that 'Summer is iccumen in, lhude sing cuccu!' The parasitic nesting habit of the cuckoo does, however, arouse mixed feelings. The ever-watchful female lays eggs in the nests of other birds, especially dunnocks, meadow pipits and reed warblers, usually pushing out some of the smaller eggs from the host's clutch before laying her own, which will have similar markings to the eggs of the host birds. Then begins one of the gruesome acts of nature as the newly hatched baby cuckoos shove all the other eggs out of the nest, and if the host chicks have hatched, they go overboard as well.

Regardless of our feelings about this extraordinary behavioural evolution, it is the song of the bird we really respond to because it is an enigmatic bird, often heard, rarely seen, so it was a moment of sheer joy to spot this bluish-grey bird perched at the top of the ash in Six Acre Meadow, wings characteristically drooped. I was surprised by its size, sleek body and long tail, looking like a kestrel as it took off towards the wood. The ephemeral nature of the cuckoo was suggested by Wordsworth in his poem, 'To the Cuckoo,' in which he described it as a "wandering voice". Lister Kaye describes how the cuckoo "will float pairs of muted minims into

Taking off on a low flight with legs dangling, the moorhen leaves a nest containing six light-brown speckled eggs.

Along stream edges, marshes and ditches the large golden-yellow flower of the marsh marigold is visible.

the air like audible smoke rings, notes that seem to hang there, directionless…." Thomas Hardy echoes my sentiments today: "This is the weather the cuckoo likes, and so do I."

This memorable day of bird observations was not yet over. We rescued a dunnock from the kitchen, got buzzed by a chirping crowd of ten sparrows heedlessly careering around the house, saw a moorhen leaving its nest by the edge of the conservation pond, nervously twitching its tail before taking off on a low flight with legs dangling. The nest contained six light-brown speckled eggs.

April 10th

Along stream edges, marshes and ditches, the large golden yellow flower of the marsh marigold is clearly visible. In partial shade it is a luxuriant plant with large kidney-shaped leaves, bluntly serrated at the margins, and with a waxy texture. It is one of the earliest wild flowers to show, surviving frosts and rain and often flowering well into June. It is a great pond plant, attracting bees and bumblebees and providing cover for pond life, such as frogs. Also along moist places is the first appearance of milkmaid, also known as ladies smock or cuckoo flower, traditionally flowering as the cuckoo arrives. It is associated with damp meadows, a habitat now frequently being 'improved' for intensive livestock or arable, making this beautiful little flower less abundant. The mauve white flower, along with garlic mustard, is the host plant of the delicate orange-tip butterfly which we are beginning to see in gardens and fields. The orange-tip deposits its eggs at the base of flower heads and the emerging caterpillars will feed on the tender seeds contained in the flower. The timing of egg laying is crucial because if the seed has developed beyond its tender condition the caterpillar will be deprived of its primary food source.

Late in the afternoon, we walked along a remote, ancient, flinty track near Crundale church. It is an intimate, peaceful landscape through which the alignment of old trackways has remained unaltered for over 1000 years. Here we came across a strange and uncommon plant growing among bluebells on a mossy bank below some hazel saplings. It had no leaves or chlorophyll, just a white, downy stem rising up from the moss, with pale pink flowers covering one side of the spike. This is the toothwort, a member of the broomrape family, flowering from April to May, often in large clusters under hazel coppice, on which it is parasitic. It is especially common on chalk soils and is remarkably persistent, often flowering in the same location for over 100 years.

In September 1912 a Mr Trull was picking apples in Huxtable when he heard a rumble beneath him. Looking down, he saw an enormous pit had opened up, and his ladder was resting on a single tree root. He climbed cautiously down to safety. More recently, John Waller of Chartham recounts how he felt some resistance to the plough as he crossed the valley field. Looking back, he was alarmed to see his plough shares on the edge of a pit which had opened up in the 'solid' ground. These, and other hazardous experiences of farmworkers in chalk downlands, were usually the result of collapsing deneholes or chalk wells which were underground structures consisting of small chalk caves entered by a vertical shaft about 1 metre in diameter.

The process of sinking deneholes has a long history and there are many theories about their original function including druids temples, flint mines, grain stores and animal traps. The most likely is as a source of chalk to be spread on fields, a process known as marling or chalking. Pliny wrote about its use in England in 70 A.D. Norman leases contained covenants requiring its use, and in 1570 the historian Lambarde wrote about "sundry artificial caves or holes in the earth, whereof some have 10, some 15 and some 20 fathoms in depth at the mouth, narrow like a tunnel of a chimney or passage of a well…. these were in former times digged, as well for the use of chalk towards building as for to marle their arable lands therewith." Camden's Britannica in 1637 referred to pits of great depth in the Faversham area, each with a narrow mouth and spacious chamber beneath. The use of chalk will sweeten or neutralise acid soils and assist drainage on heavy clay soils, so their distribution is therefore associated with those parishes which required chalk for these purposes. Even on chalk soils, leaching by rainfall could wash out calcium which could be replaced with fresh applications of chalk obtained by hauling up rope and bucket from depths of up to 12 metres. With the introduction of new methods of soil improvement and fertilizing in the 20th century, no new chalk holes have been dug.

A few hundred metres from Trimworth on the margins of Oxen Leas Wood is a large depression, probably a denehole, supporting the idea that they were often marginal or boundary features which did not disrupt activities on cultivated land. In more recent years, field enlargement by hedge and woodland clearance has often exposed these features and required their infilling and obliteration from the landscape.

The wren is a busy little bird at the moment, bursting with spring song and bustling with activity. It is one of our most common breeding birds and has become a friendly companion for me along the footpath separating the river from Tye Wood, where this larger-than-life little character has taken up some unusual nesting sites. Alders, ash and willow branches hang low over the river at this point and have accumulated debris brought down in flood. These thick collections of reed, grass and twigs, caught up in the lower branches present the wrens with nesting sites, nesting material and a copious source of insects and spiders at the water's edge. They also indicate that high water has reached well over 1 m above normal flow.

April 11th

The strange, uncommon toothwort has no leaves or chlorophyll, just a downy
white stem with pale pink flowers.

On the sexually mixed up ash, male flowers are
spectacular globular bunches of purple ...

... female flowers have a filigree of purple, then pale green.

Horsetail is a living fossil with light-brown stems
topped by a cone-like spore-producing structure.

Along the riverside in Six Acre Meadow, the ash is the most common tree and is
displaying fascinating changes in spring growth almost daily. It is a sexually mixed-
up tree. Some trees are all male, others female and some are male with a few female
branches, producing a variety of foliage and flowers on the same tree. Male flowers
are spectacular globular bunches of purple, turning to dark red buds, and then
slender yellow anthers begin to appear. The female flowers have a filigree of purple
then pale green, and will go on to produce bunches of dry seeds known as keys.
These have been on the trees all winter and will soon fall.

For the past few days, April appeared to have borrowed a few days from May. Today we are paying the price with a day borrowed from February. The wind has shifted to the north-east, bringing strong cold winds, a temperature drop of over 10° and the odd drenching from bands of scudding, low-level, formless cloud. Tye Wood is wrapped around with a soaking cloud.

Sadly, the moorhen nest has been plundered of its six eggs, probably by a fox, but I'm confident this successful little survivor will produce another clutch or two. They have a habit of choosing unwise nesting sites. Last year, they nested in a raised circular pond in our sunken garden. The adults could easily fly or run from this nest when alarmed, but the red-beaked black-legged chicks were confined to the sunken garden and several perished there. For years a nest has appeared on the top of a half-submerged post in the dyke, usually floating away when the water level rises, only to be rebuilt again on the same post a little later. They are strongly territorial and we have seen ferocious fights, but they have many appealing habits and have cleverly adapted to environments that have been altered by human activity.

This evening we visited our spot by the river in Kitchen Meadow. It is where the field narrows to a point as the river and railway intersect. The water is shallow and bubbles noisily over stones and gravels. The banks are full of bushes and trees, and the birdsong is prolific. We have two old chairs where we sit, look, listen and dream. This is the spot where four years ago, kingfishers nested in the muddy bank opposite our viewpoint. We had sightings nearly every day. This little haven of peace, solitude and beauty provides us with some of our most contemplative, magical moments at Trimworth. Wordsworth wrote about a similar place in his poem 'The Recluse', in which he described his place of beauty and repose as, "….a blended holiness of earth and sky."

Under each sallow willow along the dyke lies a golden green carpet of catkins, like yellow mustard dust, which has fallen from the trees as the fresh green leaves begin to appear. Walking close to the dyke releases a strong minty smell from leaves of the water mint, crushed underfoot. This highly aromatic plant is widespread along watercourses and damp ground, producing an attractive flower of lilac/purple in July. On the river, a pair of tufted ducks quietly feed from the mud of the shallows before rising in flight to display their white stripe across the back of the wing. Mallards are more common here and have adapted readily to disturbed and man-made environments. 'Dabbling' is a good word to describe their feeding habits. Many have begun courtship rituals of bill dipping, mock preening, water flicking and other unusual postures. They take off quickly from the water with fast wing beats, quacking anxiously and chasing each other in wide circles above the meadow.

We have a living fossil which has become a problem spreading in the wetter areas of Kitchen Meadow by the river. Horsetail has been around for over 100 million years, spreading its spores in the wind. In spring, fertile light-brown stems appear with a cone-like spore-producing structure at the end of each stem. In summer, upright fir-tree like shoots appear growing up to 60 cms. The plant is virtually impossible to dig out because of its deep underground rhizomes and it cannot be eradicated by herbicides designed to kill seed plants. It is small comfort that it can be used to scour metal plates and mugs because of the abrasive silicates present in its stem, hence its alternative name of 'scouring rush.' Maybe we'll just have to live with this pernicious relict, and wonder at its survival from the Paleozoic past.

April 15th

Early yesterday morning, we met three young campers in East Dane pasture. They were agreeable young lads from a local school, going on to further education at the end of the academic year. It was a lovely morning and the location of their campsite by the river was idyllic. I didn't know whether they had permission to camp, but that was not my business and I was gratified to see young people enjoying the countryside. I wished them well. Today they had gone, leaving a litter of paper, plastic, cans, bottles, a metal barbecue grill, all in a field with 50 sheep. There were two fire pits full of burnt wood, bricks, (taken from an old boundary wall nearby) and an upturned foil tray containing rotting food. Did they know that they were behaving irresponsibly? If they did, why did three pleasant, seemingly well-educated lads behave in this way? If they didn't, how had they reached this stage in life with such disregard for the natural environment? I cleaned up and left the site with feelings of frustration and disappointment.

In small clearings of the still leafless wood, white carpets of wood anemone are in flower.

The 'wind flower', derived from the Greek anemoi, has no petals, but five or six sepals often tinged with pink.

Spirits were raised returning through Oxen Leas Wood. In small clearings, white carpets of wood anemone were in flower, made more attractive by the contrast with a bare, almost leafless wood. In fact, the flowers have no petals, but five or six sepals, sometimes tinged with pink. Its other name is 'wind flower' derived from the Greek 'Anemoi,' the wind gods, who sent anemonies in the early spring days as the herald of their coming. It is sometimes referred to as a 'woodland ghost' because it is also found in meadows or hedge banks, denoting the site of vanished woodland. It is a short- lived joy, because once the tree canopy forms, the plants wither and fall.

April 16th

I've been walking with little Jack, my grandson of just six years. He's a joy to be with, but Jack and bird watching are incompatible. He's at his happiest whacking everything with a big stick: nettles, thistles, cow parsley. All break and bend to the lusty blows of his sycamore sword. Moveable objects have to be hurled into the river. He likes looking for beetles in wood piles, but has to poke things into action with his 'sticky.' Not yet the behaviour of a budding naturalist, but I'll continue to find opportunities to nourish that vital lifeline of natural curiosity for the benefit of Jack - and the natural world.

Within a mile of Trimworth, there are several areas of woodland which have ancient origins, such as Purr Wood. The word 'pur' is probably a derivation of clean or pure, referring to its undisturbed nature. Even closer is Tye Wood and Oxen Leas Wood, whose outlines remain virtually the same as recorded on estate maps of Trimworth in 1680. Changes have been minimal, adding or subtracting a few metres. Where the wood has been enlarged, the old boundary can often be seen as an earthwork. If part of the wood has been grubbed out, the old boundary is often visible as a hedgerow across open fields. I am fascinated by the small-scale changes to the rural landscape which can be monitored by the use of maps or documentary sources, such as Anglo-Saxon charters, tithe and enclosure maps.

It is quite probable that some of these irreplaceable remnant landscapes represent a link with the original post-glacial wildwood. Their survival is probably due to the fact that the land was not useful for anything else: too steep or stony or wet, as in the clay-with-flints, which caps the chalk of the downs. They often exist in the inaccessible far corners of parishes away from villages. Rarely are they on floodplains or terraces, which would have been more profitable as a meadow. The shapes of these small ancient woodlands have much in common. The boundaries are often sinuous, frequently changing direction, reflecting the attempts of piecemeal clearance to extend the cultivated area. A straight boundary is likely to be for a wood planted later than 1700. Within some woods, such as Tye Wood, recent clearance and management are evident in the straight rows of trees, or coppicing, the latter resulting in spectacular displays of primrose and wood anemone. These plants flourish in the alternating years of shade and light. They often indicate an ancient woodland, as does dog's mercury, oxlip, woodland hawthorn and service tree, although caution is needed here; it is safer to use these indicator plants as a group of species rather than a single plant.

The survival of these remnants of the original vast forest cover is vital for their landscape value as well as their rich biodiversity. They are often small, fragmented sites, a situation exacerbated by the increase in wood-letting, where woods are broken up into smaller multiple ownerships. This practice can result in greater fragmentation and difficulty in achieving comprehensive woodland management. I hope the Woodland Trust and Natural England and other guardians of these ancient treasures will remain vigilant.

April 18th

Shades of spring green adorn the woods with the luminous green of beech, the golden green of lime, pink-tinged sycamore and new, fresh, green buds on oaks. The edge of Tye Wood slopes gently down to the river path, a boundary scuffed up by rabbits. Over the sun-baked path can be seen a cloud of hovering flies with darting flights, emitting a high-pitched whine. They appear to float on the air and hover like hummingbirds. These agile insects bear a strong resemblance to a bee, but closer

Shades of spring green adorn the woods such as the luminous green of beech, the golden green of lime, and the pink-tinged green of sycamore.

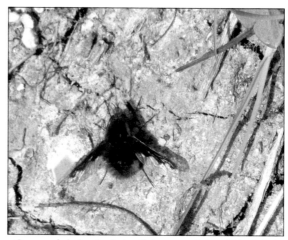

Over sun-baked paths the bee fly hovers, emitting a high-pitched whine and displaying a long, rigid proboscis to probe for nectar.

observation reveals spindly, fly-like legs and an extraordinarily long, rigid proboscis held out in front to probe nectar from flowers. These are bee flies, appearing in the first days of spring and feeding on nectar. Their larvae are predators of the true wasp or bee larva. When the bee is out in search of pollen, the fly drops eggs into the tunnel and the larvae which emerge will feed on food meant for the bees. Later, the larva changes its form and becomes carnivorous, attacking the bee larvae itself. Another nasty little story of the unsentimental workings of the natural world!

April 19th

In golden evening sunlight at the end of a warm day, sitting on the telegraph lines crossing the field, was our first swallow, like an official messenger of the arrival of spring and looking in good shape after its 9000 km flight from South Africa. As we watched I thought about its journey, beginning in South Africa, crossing the forests of the Congo, the semi-arid Sahel, 1000 km of Saharan desert, the Atlas Mountains, over France and the Channel to our shores. My mind is full of questions. How did they develop the instinct to migrate? How do they know when to migrate? How do they find their way? Do they recognise landscapes; do they use a sense of smell or the heavenly bodies to navigate?

In the 18th century Gilbert White was obsessed in resolving the problem about whether swallows migrated or stayed. For 30 years he struggled with the problem. His biographer Richard Mabey has a lingering thought that White was reluctant to accept that swallows, swifts and sand martins ever left his village for foreign parts, because they preferred to stay with him over winter! However, the amazing story of this little bird's flight was confirmed when John Masefield, a solicitor in Cheadle, Cheshire slipped a numbered aluminium ring onto the leg of a swallow chick. Eighteen months later, a letter dated December 1912 was sent by an hotelier in Natal, South Africa to the editor of the journal 'British Birds,' saying he had found the numbered label on a swallow captured on a farm near the Natal. Thus, it was revealed that swallows breeding in Britain undertook a 9000 km journey down the length of the African continent.

The swallow is a regular and very welcome visitor to our barns, using the same nests year after year. (Some records show that swallows have occupied the same nests for up to 50 years.) Soon we will hear trills and chirps as they skim low over the ponds, feeding on the wing and chasing each other at speed. For now though, a quiet period of adjustment and contemplation, following a hazardous four-week journey covering great distances at speeds of 30 to 40 km an hour. The decline in the European swallow population has led to its amber listing as a species of conservation concern. There are several reasons: climate change in the wintering and breeding grounds, reduction of nest sites due to changes in farming practice, farm-barn conversions, and the ever expanding hazardous environment of the Sahara through desertification. Our swallow will have to cope with a more immediate local problem. Wrens have been using some of the swallows' nests for roosting during the winter and seem to be happily installed for the breeding season with large lumps of moss attached to the swallow's nests. This tiny, larger-than-life character is unlikely to surrender his accommodation willingly!

(I wrote about the arrival of our swallows to my old friend Phil Kane, living near Lassen Volcanic Park in California, for which he has written a definitive guide. His reply was classic. "So the Goodenoughs' swallows have come back from a 6000 mile trip to South Africa, and the Kanes' hummingbirds have come back from the 6000 mile trip from Costa Rica. None of this beautiful cycle has anything to do with human beings. I find this quite uplifting. The sooner human beings get out of here the better.")

Along the woodland edge are the warmer white petals of wild cherry, the ancestor of our sweet garden cherry.

April 20th

Dotted around our paddock and garden are remnant, rotting stumps of cherry trees from an old orchard. Some are a metre in diameter and must have been magnificent 15-metre trees, very different from the scattered orchards of Kent which now currently graft on to dwarf rootstock. At Burnt House Farm in Chartham, a 15-metre tall, tapering ladder still leans against the barn wall, long since abandoned by skilled cherry pickers working under large canopies of these orchards. As the sun strengthens, the chalky white blackthorn blossom is joined by wild cherry, the ancestor of sweet garden cherries. The warm white petals surround long stamens and gold-tipped anthers, and there is a touch of pink from opening buds and sepals. They occupy the woodland edge, seeding and suckering their roots and providing a short-lived but stunning sight before wind blows the blossom from the trees in drifts to cover the ground like snow. The sight and smell brings a beautiful springtime experience to treasure. A E Housman eloquently celebrated its charm:

> "Loveliest of trees, the cherry now
> Is hung with blossom along the bough,
> And stands about the woodland ride
> Wearing white for Eastertide.
>
> Now, of my three score years and ten,
> Twenty will not come again,
> And take from seventy springs a score,
> It only leaves me fifty more.
>
> And since to look at things in bloom
> Fifty springs are little room,
> About the woodlands I will go
> To see the cherry hung with snow."

Another creative image of the springtime spectacle is provided by Samuel Palmer's 'A Shoreham Garden,' painted in 1829. It is an enigmatic picture in which a cherry tree is central to the picture, dominating the woman in red who passes dreamily by. Palmer has effectively used the tree as the portrait, upstaging the figure. The tree is 'hung' with blossom, but Palmer's interpretation of the word is very different from Housman's. There are no individual delicate blossoms; the painting has blossom like cascades of pinky white foam or overflowing cumulus cloud. Palmer's son wrote of spring as, "clothing the innumerable orchards with clotted blossom."

April 21st

When the river runs at flood level, a low branch of riverside ash traps passing grass, reeds and twigs. With the return to normal river flow, this collection is left as a flat bed of dry material well above the river and is frequently used as a perch by birds. The surface of this perch is covered with the tiny shells of freshwater molluscs, bi-valves, gasteropods and seeds, which wrens and robins, living in the woodland edge, have obtained from the muddy river banks exposed at low water levels. The molluscs represent leftovers from the feasts of little birds.

My knowledge of the local rural environment has been shaped and enriched by conversation with those who have lived and worked in the area for generations. For example, our neighbour, Ted Hope was the shepherd at Trimworth when it was a large, busy working farm of 200 hectares. He was a source of information on changes in the rural economy and landscape, and on his role as a highly-skilled performer and teacher at sheepdog trials. Sadly he died, taking a wealth of unrecorded knowledge with him. The farm scene was also delightfully told by Gladys Pegden who lived nearby at Little Olantigh, frequently visiting her uncle at Trimworth, who was recorded in the 1901 Census as having nine children ranging in age from 1 to 20. Gladys remembers the great fire at Olantigh in 1903 when her father dragged furniture from the house. She remembers corn being taken from the farm to markets in Faversham by horse-drawn carts decorated with brasses, ribbons and bells. She listened for the bells as wagons returned down White Hill at the end of the day. Farm workers were paid 18 shillings a week, many not returning from the First World War. Gladys picked potatoes, ran around the fields to keep the birds away, looked after stock, and walked to school in Wye. She remembers the high moments of the year, such as salting down the pigs for winter, the festivities of Cherry Sunday and the exploits of the Irish working on the railway. Saturday was pay-day for the Irish, and all women were kept indoors! Joan Hartley recounted her time as a member of the Land Army billeted at Trimworth. She was 17 and it was her first time away from home. Regular food parcels from home were joyously received and Saturday evening dances at Wye Village Hall eagerly awaited. The girls were paid monthly. One hot day, Joan fell asleep turning the hay and had two hours' pay stopped. All meals were taken in the living room of Trimworth. She remembers the two front rooms which were out of bounds, except for those who were courting! These and many other oral histories have provided me with stirring reminiscences of a long-gone lifestyle.

It is St George's Day, which has been celebrated as a feast day and a national holiday from the early 15th century. But despite being the patron saint of England (and also patron of rocky and dangerous coastlines, the mentally ill, places liable to flood, chivalrous knights and soldiers), his popularity has waned. Today he is regarded as an obscure figure with little direct connection to this country. St George's Day is usually the day when we wander through Kitchen Meadow in search of St George's mushrooms, which thrive along the riverside pastures in fairly short grass. It is one of the few good edible fungi to be found in spring, distinguished by its white, closely-spaced gills, creamy white cap, and a flowery odour. Confusingly, some inedible species with a similar appearance are to be found in spring, but it is the 'mealy' odour and the white, as opposed to brown or cream cap, which makes St Georges mushroom distinctive. There were none in sight today, probably because we have had no rain for nearly 3 weeks, but they can appear any time from now until early June.

April 23rd

The fresh smell of spring accompanies a surge of activity in countryside and garden. It was as if all the elements of spring had been distilled into one composite image of scenes, scents and sounds, like a symphony of spring. Lister Kaye describes the moment as "nature, shaking out her skirts after a coma of her own for six long months." Edward Thomas describes the arrival of spring as being "lusty, fragrant, many-coloured, many-voiced, fair to see... she is fresh, she is bold, sweet in her motion and in her tranquillity: and there is a soft down upon her lip as there is a silken edge to the young leaves of the beeches."

April 24th

The river was running crystal-clear. Fresh lime-green weeds were shifting and drifting in the current; I watched trout moving below Olantigh bank, reminding me of Betjemans autobiographical verse, "When trout waved lazy in the clear chalk streams, Glory was in me..." And the orange-tip butterfly appeared above the dykes in the meadow, the more reclusive female looking for cuckoo flower, garlic mustard or cow parsley to lay its eggs. While many British butterflies have become less common in recent years, the orange-tip is actually increasing its range into northern

Fresh lime-green weeds were shifting and drifting in the currents of the crystal-clear river.

Unseasonably warm temperatures have encouraged the common lizard to build up body heat by basking on stones and grasses around the pond.

Scotland, one of the beneficial impacts of global warming. It will soon be time to look out for the bluish green caterpillars covered with small black dots which will be laid on the cuckoo flower and garlic mustard.

Swallows dart from barn to stable; tits, dunnock, jackdaw, and so many other birds have paired up; there is activity in nest boxes and ivies. Orchestrating all this activity with hours of singing from the top of the field maple is the song thrush. We gardened most of the day to the accompaniment of its loud, melodious song. At a distance we mistook it for its relative the mistle thrush (the mistletoe eater), but having listened to the song, observed its flight and compared its colour we knew it to be the song thrush, establishing its territory before finding a mate and nesting. It was a joy to see and hear, especially considering its red alert status as a garden songbird whose numbers are declining seriously because of loss of hedges, wet ditches and permanent pasture. In addition to the short, varied, repetitive sound of the song thrush was the loud, pure, melodious blackbird and plaintive, earnest phrases of the robin, garrulous chirps of sparrows, and various other trills and flutes, all blended into one great stream of song.

There are 'dragons' in our garden; in fact, they are so prolific that we have been chosen by the Kent Reptile and Amphibian Group (KRAG) as the most reptile and amphibian-friendly garden in Kent. To encourage reptiles and amphibians we have created damp areas around fish-free ponds for breeding, provided basking places in rock piles, straw bales and compost heaps, and built log piles for hibernation. During the past week of unseasonably warm temperatures, the 'herpetofauna' have been conspicuous in and around the garden. Common lizards are basking on dry stones in the stream course running into the top pond and in the hot soil of the raised beds, often flattening their bodies to get full exposure to the warm sun. Basking allows the lizard to build up heat which can be retained when the surrounding temperature changes – a characteristic known as thermo-regulation. The common lizard is a quick mover over land and is also a good swimmer. They have beautiful green brown markings with spots, lines and flecks, and a distinctly pointed snout. These lizards came out of hibernation in March and will be mating in April and May before giving birth to up to 10 young, born in an egg sac that either breaks during birth to release a lizard, or breaks soon after birth. This characteristic of giving birth to eggs or live young is known as 'viviparious'- most lizards will lay eggs only.

Our most common reptile is the grass snake, the largest indigenous reptile in the UK, reaching lengths of 1 m or more, but non-venomous and harmless. It frequents the water, feeding almost exclusively on amphibians, and we occasionally see them swimming strongly across the ponds. There are places where we can expect to find them basking in the sun displaying green, olive green and brown colours with a distinctive light yellow collar. A pile of old fence posts in the field, and compost heaps are their favourite haunts. We see adders basking on bare earth banks, or on piles of wood and stone along the hedge-line near the bottom pond, displaying the distinctive zig-zag pattern running lengthwise along the body and tail. They emerge in early spring from hibernation, and then become active on warm days, with males looking for females and occasionally performing a 'dance of the adders' to drive off competitors. The meadow will be the source of its main diet of voles and other rodents, frogs, newts and even young ground nesting birds. We see them less frequently now, and wonder if this is associated with less frequent sightings of frogs and toads. Maybe the loss of food sources is the reason for the widespread reduction in adder numbers nationwide losses being confirmed by surveys undertaken over a six-year period by the National Amphibian and Reptile Recording returns. Historically, they have always been at risk from persecution by people who kill them because they are venomous, although under the Wildlife and Countryside Act of 1981 it is illegal to kill or harm them.

April 26th

'Dent-de-lion' is the French derivation of our dandelion, the name referring to the downward pointing teeth on the edge of the leaves. The flower gives a golden edge to the lanes in which high hedges channel seed dispersal along clearly defined paths. The plant has many uses such as in making wine, roasting roots as a substitute for coffee and as a diuretic (hence its alternative name of pissen lit). And which child has not played the game of dandelion clock as they blow the seeds from the blowball? The vivid, golden-yellow flower contrasts with brilliant little white flowers of greater stitchwort with which it shares the roadside verge.

Under the developing leaf canopy in the woods, red campion and yellow archangel mingles amongst the dense smoke-blue carpets of bluebells, one of the most memorable spectacles of the botanical world and a sign of ancient woodland, thriving where the sun reaches the forest floor. In Elizabethan times their bulbs produced the starch to stiffen collars and ruffs while the flower stalks exuded a glue to bind books and fix feathers on arrows. There are now several different types of bluebell in the United Kingdom, including the Spanish variety and other hybrids. The easiest way to tell the difference is in the pollen colour. If it is creamy white, it is a native, and any other colour such as pale green or blue is definitely not a native. The flowers of the native curl over and nod at the top of the stalk, so most of the flowers hang from one side of the stem and also have a stronger, sweeter smell. The need to protect the threatened native species has been recognised in the Wildlife and Countryside Act, which makes the removal of native bluebell bulbs a criminal offence.

The beech increasingly draws our attention. The dull brown buds of March have been swelling with the warmth of the sun, changing colour to bronze and red just before they burst. They have now reached their springtime glory with young emerald green leaves, a perfect match for the bluebells below. Sunlight filtering through these young leaves is one of the joys of an English spring. On the edge of Oxen Leas Wood it is possible to gaze at the blue carpet under its green canopy, then swing round to a field of brilliant golden rape shimmering on the slopes of Trimworth Down; complementary colours of blue and gold which artists, notably van Gogh, have exploited so effectively. Within a few weeks, much of the countryside around the chalk downs will be draped in golden rape which, since the 1970s has attracted guaranteed prices for farmers and now covers over a quarter of a million

The brilliant white star-shaped flowers of greater stitchwort form a dense covering under hedgerows and woodland edges (above left). Under the developing leaf canopy, red campion and yellow archangel mingles amongst the dense smoke-blue carpets of bluebells (left & above right.)

Much of the countryside around the chalk downs is draped in golden rape.

hectares nationally.(There is a strong smell of subsidy in the air!) Even Linnaus in 1740 recognised the useful soil improving qualities of this crop and its vital role in improving the yields of cereals which follow. A little later in the year, another trend in agricultural economics will turn the countryside a delicate shade of blue as farmers take advantage of good guaranteed prices for linseed.

April 27th

The migration of millions of birds to and from our shores is one of the enduring wonders of the natural world. They arrive from Africa, from across the Atlantic and from Eurasia, each bird facing the daunting prospect of maintaining its food reserves, navigating hazardous environments and adverse weather conditions, as well as human obstacles. These 'spring-bringers' constitute a stirring expression of the arrival of a new season; and we take it all for granted. But experts are at pains to identify a dramatic fall in the number of cuckoos, nightingales and turtle doves. Their slow disappearance has been recognised for several years, but there is now evidence to support the sad and catastrophic fall in our cherished spring visitors, although the exact reasons are far from clear. According to Dr Danae Sheehan of the RSPB, numbers of migrant birds from Africa have been declining since 1995: turtledoves by 71%, nightingale by 53% and cuckoos by 44%. The causes of loss are many and varied, making it difficult to pinpoint the most significant factor, and therefore respond to the problem. Changing agricultural practices in the UK may be affecting the breeding success of spring-time arrivals; there is destruction of natural habitats through population growth and development in places where they overwinter; climate change is another factor because it affects the timing of breeding cycles. The arrival of new chicks is no longer synchronised with the best period when food, especially insects, is available. There are also declines in some insect numbers; for example, cuckoos thrive on large moths whose numbers have dropped significantly in recent years. As if natural problems are not enough, there is a human factor associated with the slaughter of birds flying to and from Africa and passing over or landing on, Mediterranean islands such as Malta or Cyprus. This 'sport' is against EU law, but the birds are still being shot in their hundreds of thousands. In Britain we have a deep and complex relationship with these birds, which is woven into our culture. We are passionate and possessive about them, associating their return every year with the arrival of spring and warmth. We are now hearing the two-note call of the first cuckoo of spring, but we must not assume that we will be hearing its call in 10 years' time.

Researchers at the British Trust for Ornithology have achieved a significant scientific breakthrough using micro-technology to follow the track of migrant birds and find out why certain species are in decline. Minute tracking devices weighing less than a gramme, called geo-locators, have been fitted to birds and can transmit data for analysis. Of 20 geo-locators fitted to nightingales in 2009, seven were recaptured, all in a similar location in Norfolk. The loggers had recorded the migrating track of one nightingale after it left Norfolk on 25 July, travelling through France and Spain, crossing the Mediterranean to Morocco, where it had a three-week resting period. The little bird continued down the West Coast of Africa where it overwintered, returning to Britain in April. The geo-locator has confirmed the amazing accuracy with which birds relocate to sites in Britain: in one case being recaptured only 50 metres from where it was originally tagged. The device also reveals amazing feats of endurance, such as the journey of a cuckoo tracked in April 2011 crossing the Sahara and recording a distance of 400 km in four hours, an average speed of nearly 100 km/h – and all this with no shade, no food, no rest. With the growth of such information, our understanding of this wonderful natural phenomenon will increase. Sadly, we have become accustomed to loss in the natural world, but decline of these 'aerial streams' and the loss of spring- bringers in these meadows by the river in April is something I find unthinkable. Ted Hughes, that 'guardian spirit of the land and language,' understood the importance of this amazing natural phenomenon when he declared, "They made it again… Which means the globe is still working."

April 28th

Out early with Sam on a still, misty morning with a thin veil of cirrus under a pale blue sky. The heavy dew outlined the shape of spiders' webs, giving a silver grey sheen to the meadow grass, gradually turning golden with the rising, warming sun. To the accompaniment of our ever present song thrush we reached the river, still easily within sound of its insistent call nearly a kilometre away. Lots of quick, quiet movement on the river as fish broke the surface momentarily then disappeared, sending slowly moving concentric ripples across the surface of the water. Over Bilting meadow there was a dramatic aerial display by a flock of pigeon-sized, but distinctly distinctively black and white birds. For ten minutes I watched as these lapwings skimmed the fields, swept high into the air, then dropped as if shot, before wheeling away and gaining height. This exhilarating performance gave a flickering black-and-white effect to the sky; noticeable also were the rounded wing tips, or frying-pan wings as they are known. Mewing calls ('pee-wit') were part of their tumbling, exuberant display, all part of the primary springtime process of attracting a mate. Returning across the meadow, we saw several pairs flying high and direct, a one-note call urgently announcing their arrival to the aerobatic flock now foraging in the field. It is some years since we saw closely packed flocks of lapwing feeding in the fields. Egg survival and hatching success have been greatly affected by predation and changing agricultural practices.

April 29

We continue to see snipe taking off from the muddy edges of the river where they feed on invertebrates. John Clare described them as "lovers of swamps", where security pervades, "using their bills of rude unseemly length" to drill and delve. In 1768 Gilbert White noted how "in breeding time, snipes play over the moors piping and humming: they always hum as they are descending… Some suspect it is made by their wings." 250 years later, researchers at the University of Manchester using high-speed video confirmed White's suspicions that it is the tail feather acting like a flag that causes the noise.

There is frantic nesting activity in the garden. Wrens are building several mossy nests in barns and outbuildings before choosing one which will be used to lay eggs. One pair has chosen to coat an old swallow's nest in the barn with a mossy covering. Robins already have young to feed and will soon be building new nests for the next brood. Blackbirds are darting in and out of thickening hedges with beaks full of mud to line their nests. Starlings are constantly flying to roof eaves with food-filled beaks, each arrival being greeted by a 'churring' chorus of hungry nestlings.

At the end of our downland walk we reached Tye Wood at dusk to a forest full of birdsong. Walking through the deep blue carpet of bluebells dotted with colonies of bright pink campion, we reached the river. Evening comes; the fields are still – a moment captured perfectly by Matthew Arnold in part of his poem 'Bacchanalia'.

> "The business of the day is done,
> The last belated gleaner gone.
> And from the thyme upon the height,
> And from the elder-blossom white
> And pale dog-roses in the hedge,
> And from the mint-plant in the sedge,
> In puffs of balm the night-air blows
> The perfume which the day forgoes.
> And on the pure horizon far,
> See, pulsing with the first-born star,
> The liquid sky above the hill!
> The evening comes, the field is still."

April 30th

Cow parsley brings back childhood memories of country lanes in Norfolk bordered by winding ribbons of frothy white flower billowing and blowing freely on long stalks and spilling itself along the roadside and hedges. It is also known as Queen Anne's lace, probably after St Anne, mother of the virgin. Philip Larkin in his poem 'Cut Grass' writes about "lost lanes of Queen Anne's lace", like a "high builded cloud moving at summer's pace." Lace is a good description of the flower head. It is like a delicate, white effervescent umbrella, slightly scented. Monty Don expresses his rapture by saying, "I do not believe that there is a more beautiful sight on the planet… Why bother to garden when the countryside can do these things so much better than we can?" I hope the brutal hedge flails will stay away from the verges long enough for us to enjoy the long swathes of its simple beauty.

A passage in Michael Boulter's book, 'Darwin's Garden,' describes a eureka moment for Darwin as he travelled along the country lanes to Downe House. Darwin describes it as one of the happiest moments in his life, immersed in beautiful sunlight in this quiet green landscape. He spotted a patch of hedge parsley (a close relative of cow parsley, and a member of the same carrot family) with an unfamiliar flower colour. He questioned how a different species could appear in a different environment. Was this how a new species was created by moving to a new territory? How did the migration occur? I find the idea that the humble hedge parsley had generated such far-reaching evolutionary thoughts very heartening.

May

"May is defiant, it breaks free like a half trained puppy, running away from the North wind and rain, ducking sleet squalls and raising its shout for the sun and the springing grass." This description of the arrival of May by Lister-Kaye has a distinctly high-latitude feel of the Scottish glen through which he walked for 30 years. Here in the river meadows at Trimworth we have just enjoyed the warmest, sunniest and driest April for decades with less than 1 mm of rain during the month. This is good for displays of spring flowers and blossom, but is creating very serious problems of river flow and reservoir levels, affecting farmers, growers, gardeners and wildlife.

May Day is related to the Celtic Festival of Beltane, marking the beginning of the pastoral summer season and celebrated with the lighting of bonfires on mountains and hills, and the hanging of May boughs in the doors and windows of houses. Maypoles were cut from tall, straight trees and decorated with foliage, flowers and coloured ribbons. There was dancing, eating, tug-of-war and a great deal of earthy good humour. The May Queen was crowned and it was common to elect a May King known as the Green Man or Jack-a-Green.

In the calendar of the Book of Hours, the month of May is depicted as a time of leisure, relaxation, courting, music making, gathering of wild flowers and green branches, weaving of floral garlands and dancing around the maypole. In 'Les Très Riches Heures,' the month of May is illustrated by a colourful pageant celebrating the 'joli mois de Mai' in which people wear green garments, the 'livrée de Mai.' A group of riders passes through a forest, there is a distant view of the chateaux and in the foreground the hawthorn is in blossom. May is also the month when the religious focus is on Mary, who is associated with the beginning of new, fresh life and the start of summer. Statues of Mary were traditionally crowned with flowers, and many flowers make reference to Mary through the use of the word 'lady', such as lady's smock, lady's slipper, lady's mantle, lady's bed-straw (on which Mary supposedly gave birth), lady's candle (mullien) and lady's thimble (harebell).

For us, it was a day to celebrate the fresh iridescent green beauty of a fine May morning in which the volume of birdsong reached new heights. We felt an intensity of beauty on this special day of spring, as if the natural world had taken us to the edge of something so profound that it was difficult to express it in words.

Today is International Dawn Chorus Day, an annual celebration of the world's oldest wake-up call which reaches its peak at this time of year as the songs of our resident bird species are joined by those of returning summer visitors, such as the nightingale. This is also the time when birds are busy establishing territory and breeding. It is territorial warfare conducted through music. Although they continue to sing long after dawn, songs seem to travel further in the still air of early morning. Later in the day their energies are diverted from singing, to finding food and building nests.

Nick Aitchison, Education Officer for Norfolk Wildlife Trust, expresses a unique birder's view on the sounds of spring and the language of songbirds. 'Fruity, rich and happy' is not a description of a bottle of red wine, but the song of the blackcap. The mistle thrush is 'like an opera singer who is getting a bit old and drifts into dementia halfway through her song '. The blackbird 'stops, quite suddenly, as if someone has grabbed her neck,' while the wren is described as 'very Italian, like Verdi, loud and boisterous'. The great tit is 'metronomic, seesawing, loud and distinctive,' while robins sound like 'water rushing over stones – a bit sad, yet you want more'. However described, the sounds lift the spirits and give a sense of release and freedom from the traumas of the modern world.

The weather does a time-travel and returns to March. Four little swallows are huddled together on the telephone wire in a gusty north wind driving sheets of rain. Their body language suggests melancholy, dejection and disappointment. A cartoon caption could read, 'Is this our welcome after 9000 kms of anxiety and adversity. Never again.'

Today, the Guardian Country Diary returns to the subject of the dawn chorus which the correspondent, Mark Cocker considers an inappropriate term because it doesn't occur at dawn and is certainly not a chorus. He describes the timing as "the moment when the night sky and the landscape first start to separate from one another." What a wonderful way to express this enchanting event! He goes on to suggest that the birds across the country take their cue to sing at different times as the dawn and the waves of music spread across the country. "Given that birdsong is the energy derived from sunlight and from landscape (soil, vegetation, insects, etc) expressed simply as sound, you should think of those blackbirds as perhaps the self- delighting voice of Britain itself, musing on spring."

Leaf emergence of oak and ash produces no clear consensus to support the great weather lore of precipitation. Even before bud-burst, caterpillars are dangling from the branches and other insects are ready to munch the soft foliage before the leaves harden to the deeper green of summer. We must wait to see whether the outcome is a summer splash, a soak, or both. Other May-time predictions on the rhythms and patterns of weather include 'a swarm of bees in May is worth a load of hay,' and 'mist in May, heat in June, makes harvest come right soon.' These familiar regional rhymes rarely have any basis in scientific reasoning. They are right too often for us to ignore, and wrong too often for us to rely upon.

Later in the day I entered Tye Wood to aerial cries of terror, and watched a panic-stricken bird pursued by a buzzard which was streaking through the trees in a combination of power, elegance and tenacity. The buzzard lunged, grabbed the bird in its talons, and then veered sharply on seeing me, releasing the struggling bird which slammed into the nettles at my feet. The fledgling mistlethrush struggled to move, then it eyes clouded over and closed. I picked it up carefully, felt its warmth and saw the talon wounds in its chest, pumping blood. Another life and death struggle of beauty and awe in which nature, red in tooth and claw, goes about its natural business.

May 5th

An ostensibly simple little poem by William Browning symbolises the character of the romantic bliss of an English rural spring. In 'Home Thoughts from Abroad,' Browning is cast in the role of a homesick traveller during his self-imposed exile in Italy. As the British Empire grew, many more citizens left England to move abroad. For these people, Browning sought to maintain a connection with England by describing a typical springtime scene with birdsong and blossom. One wonders whether Browning missed such scenes enough to move back, or whether he felt these magical moments of nature were best appreciated from abroad.

"Oh to be in England
Now that April's there,
And whoever wakes in England
Sees, some morning, unaware,
That the lowest boughs and the brushwood sheaf
Round the elm-tree bowl are in tiny leaf,
While the chaffinch sings on the orchard bough
In England – now!

And after April, when May follows,
And the whitethroat builds, and all the swallows!
Hark! where my blossomed pear-tree in the hedge
Leans to the field and scatters on the clover
Blossoms and dew drops – at the bent spray's edge –
That's the wise thrush: he sings the song twice over,
Lest you should think he could never recapture
The first fine careless rapture!
And though the fields look rough with hoary dew,
All will be gay when noontide wakes anew
The buttercups, the little children's dower
-Far brighter than this gaudy melon-flower."

May 6th

Deer are not uncommon in our deciduous woods overlooking the Stour Valley. Like most fallow deer in England they were introduced by the Normans in the 10th century, and during medieval times many deer parks were established. Escapees from these deer parks are now thriving in the mature broadleaved woodlands, such as Kings Wood, where today I saw seven deer cautiously approach the road. They stood, statuesque, poised, with ears flicking and noses in the air until they registered my presence and, with a sudden spasm, quickly disappeared amongst the understory of the beech woods and the bluebell carpet. It was one of those unforgettable, brief but timeless encounters with the natural world. We have observed these fallow deer in Oxen Leas and Black Edge Wood; followed their footprints along the edge of Great Tithe Field and found black, shiny and freshly deposited droppings on the footpath. The footprints of the fallow deer are narrow and longer than those of the red deer and the pad imprint is large and clear.

In and around the bottom pond, ragged robin and red campion have seeded profusely and yellow flag irises are in flower. As we walked around the margins of the pond, frogs plopped into the water and disappeared beneath the algae. Then we saw a snake-like movement across the water, followed by vigourous writhing in the algae before the head of a grass snake appeared, its mouth open and holding what appeared to be a small frog or nymph. It swam smoothly to the edge, head held high, then rested on the bank and slowly consumed its meal before disappearing sinuously into the reeds at the water's edge.

May 7th

Yesterday was a day of exhilarating observations; today began with a distressing sight. In the river field at Godmersham close to the A28 we came across a wide scatter of pure white feathers and large chunks a swan lying below overhead electrical cables. In the sky above, three bewildered swans circled the scene of devastation. Several years ago this was an all too frequent occurrence, and so we contacted a wayleave officer of the power company who arranged for the installation of deflectors on cables, making them more visible. This has been fairly effective, but breeding time always seems to heighten the level of activity with flights of swans between lakes and ponds through the river valley, increasing the risk from this major cause of swan mortality. Clear statistics are not easy to obtain because bird remains are often scavenged before cause of death can be recorded, but research suggests that the use of reflective markers on lines is not necessarily enough to prevent deaths. The reason is that some birds have 'blind spots 'in their field of vision when tilting their heads downward in flight to look for foraging and nesting sites. This

As we walked around the pond, frogs plopped into the water and disappeared beneath the algae.

A mute swan majestically cruises the river.

is confirmed by vision experts at the Centre for Ornithology at the University of Birmingham who concluded that because of this vision vulnerability, other means of decoying birds away from power lines are required at points where collision rates are high. We have become accustomed to the almost daily sight of mute swans majestically cruising the river. They often stay in their territories all year round with the cob and pen usually mating for life and frequently returning to the same breeding sites from the wintering areas where flocks gather. The sad sight of the stricken swan reminds us not to take these stately creatures for granted. Although swans have few natural enemies, pollution of freshwater areas remains a threat, as does the careless dispersal of nylon fishing line and the now illegal use of lead-shot weights. Swans have established themselves in our culture through music, literature and visual arts, most often in the ancient belief that a swan's singing prowess was heightened as death approaches, giving rise to the idea of the swansong or final performance. Despite Pliny the Elder refuting this idea in 77 A.D., it has continued to appear in the artistic works of Aesop, Chaucer, Shakespeare and many others.

May 8th

On dead wood covering parts of the forest floor, the formation of fruiting bodies of bracket fungus has been stimulated by rising temperature, humidity and light. Most frequent are the attractively named, but inedible coriolis versicolour, a fairly common bracket fungus with the upper surface showing concentric zones of creamy, rusty-coloured growth. In fading evening light we watched a flight of 20 to 30 swallows on the wing over the pastures adjoining the river in Bridge Meadow. They had collected together near water to find a good supply of small insects before returning to their roosts in roofs and lofts of old farm buildings nearby. Their spectacular flight was exhilarating to watch as they flew fast, close and low, swooping for insects and demonstrating impressive speed, agility and manoeuvrability. They are the modern jet fighter of the bird world, with their sleek scimitar wings and long forked tails.

We returned to the house to experience a different flying performance. Maybugs were out of control in the light evening breeze, crashing into people, trees and buildings like drunken drones. These early summer night fliers are beetles belonging to the same family as scarab or dung beetles. Colloquially known as billy-witch in East Anglia, the mayfly or cockchafer frequently crashes into lighted windows on warm evenings. Although buzzing noisily and getting stuck in clothing they are harmless, with no bite or sting. The fat white grubs which they lay in soil can attack roots of grasses and cereals, but cultivation of borders and plots will usually keep plant loss to a minimum.

May 9th

Hoverflies, lacewings, earwigs, small beetles and other predatory bugs are everywhere in the garden and they are all very welcome. They are the enemies of the aphid and we encourage them by planting alyssum (a good source of nectar and pollen and loved by hover flies), cosmos and solidago species, all of which encourage these voracious little predators to their pollen and nectar. We encourage them to overwinter with us by providing log pits, compost heaps and water sources. We rarely use any pesticides to wipe out the aphids on the grounds that they destroy the food source of our friendly predators causing them to leave us for pastures new. Ladybirds are also numerous at the moment, but the sighting of our native five-spot ladybird is becoming rare, partly because of the arrival of the invasive Harlequin, introduced from East Asia into North America and Europe to keep down aphids and scale insects. They are voracious feeders and reproduce continually from spring to autumn giving rapidly increasing populations to the detriment of indigenous predators.

Ladybirds are numerous, but the sighting of our seven-spot ladybird is becoming rare because of the arrival of the invasive Harlequin.

There is a generally held view that native plants in gardens attract most wildlife, and yet this axiom of good gardening is not supported by any real evidence. How do we find out which plants the bugs prefer? A controlled experiment undertaken by the Plant for Bugs project at the RHS will hopefully provide the answer. They are using plots of identical size to grow plants of three different levels of nativeness. Some are fully native, such as common box, broom, honeysuckle, English bluebell, purple loosestrife, scabious, betony and guelder rose. Others are part of the wider northern temperate flora, so-called near natives, such as the Spanish bluebell, cottage pink, musk mallow, Christmas box. The final group is composed of exotics, remote both geographically and taxonomically from our native plants. Sets of plants have been planted in two different locations at Wisley to overcome the problem that differences in plots may be caused by chance. Entomologists are observing flying insects such as bees and butterflies, trapping slugs and ground beetles and sucking leaf dwelling insects off the foliage with suction samplers. In 2010 they observed more than 2500 flying insects, including seven species of bumblebee, 12 species of butterfly and more than 8000 invertebrates. The experiment is being reported regularly on the RHS website and results will be published in 2013, giving us evidence from a controlled experiment to answer the question of whether 'native is best' for wildlife.

May 10th

A cold night, down to 4°C, followed by a misty morning slowly brightening with the rising sun. The trees in leaf form a tapestry of greens. The buds of April, have become the leaf burst of May – a vibrant metamorphosis from brown to green. It reminds me of the Impressionists who were acutely aware of the effects of subtle contrasts obtained by mixing shades of green, blue and yellow, using cobalt green, viridian, ultramarine, cadmium yellow, lemon yellow and yellow ochre. Van Gogh creatively depicted dark thickets of evergreen, lime green poplars dappled with deep shadows, pools of sunlight falling on the 'soubois.' Across the meadow towards Tye

Wood I see silhouettes of trees and foliage of different hues and textures, creating a panorama of subtle colour harmonies and contrasts in the cool, misty, early-morning light.

Inside the wood, closer inspection of the emerging leaves reveals a fascinating variation. The early leaves of lime are tinged bronze/red, becoming translucent green with sunlight. Sycamore shows a similar leaf colour with long clusters of yellow/green flower. But nothing compares with the flower spikes of the horse chestnut. Candelabras of flower rise from hand-like leaves. Not all the flower on the spikes open at once, so the flowering period is prolonged; and once the flower is pollinated its colour changes from red-pink to yellow, a message to bees not to bother with it. The burnished brown of young oak leaves gives the tree an olive/bronze glow in contrast to the fresh green of beech. Along the river the alder is one of the latest to leaf. Now its strikingly rounded hazel-like leaves are emerging on the same twigs as the female catkins which have remained on the tree long after tiny winged seeds have been shed. Also late to emerge is the sexually confused ash with some trees all male, some all-female, some male with a few female branches, some branches being male one year, female the next. The jet black buds have opened to reveal long pinnate leaves with 3 to 7 pairs of leaflets. The keys remain on the tree, having shed seed last autumn.

An injunction issued by King Henry in 1536, required that, "the curate of every parish church shall keep one book or register, which book you shall, every Sunday, take forth and in the presence of churchwardens write or record in the same all weddings, christenings and burials made the whole week before." These records make it possible to trace back the history of a family in the parish community. In addition to these vital statistics, parish records contain fascinating information which has been deposited by previous rectors or churchwardens. My search in the Canterbury Cathedral Archives revealed lots of examples of documents, letters and notes concerning the land and people of the parish of Crundale. For example, a lease of 1695 gives details of all the parsonages, glebe lands, barns, stables, outhouses and buildings, together with the crops growing on the glebe land. A 1700 record gives the calculation of the value of woodland and the production of open land, with calculations projected forward for the next 100 years. The setting up of local charities to support the poor in the parish is documented (many of which the present members of the Parochial Church Council still have to administer). For example, when the Rev Richard Foster died in 1729, not only did he leave a priceless rectorial library, which still exists today as a single collection, he also left property in the parish to be sold and the money invested for the poor children to be taught to read and repeat the church catechism. The will of the Rev Francis Filmer, who owned Trimworth Manor, bequeathed the sum of £19- 19 shillings, to be divided at Christmas "amongst the most infirm and aged parishioners of that parish, preference being given to those who have been most exemplary for their sober, industrious and virtuous habits and those who being in like manner exemplary, have large families." In 1828 the records contain an intriguing letter to the rector from Edward Knight, brother of Jane Austen, of Godmersham Park about the trees in the churchyard. An opinion from Lincoln's Inn had been sought, which declared that churchwardens were entitled to bits that fell from trees, and trees that had died, but that they might not replace the trees because the soil in which they grew did not belong to the churchwardens! These and many more examples reveal fascinating insights of English village life and the role of the church in rural communities such as ours.

The view across the meadow is a panorama of subtle colour harmonies and contrasts in the cool misty early-morning light.

In a recent study on the comparative biodiversity of rivers, streams, ditches and ponds in lowland Britain, it was found that at the regional level, ponds contributed most to biodiversity, supporting considerably more species, more unique species and more scarce species, than any other freshwater body. This research has been confirmed by wildlife trusts and conservation organisations and yet ponds continue to be threatened by human activity. They are polluted by agricultural chemicals, depleted by land drainage schemes, swallowed up by enlargements of the cultivated area, or completely neglected and serve as rubbish holes. Probably three-quarters of our ponds have been lost since the Second World War. New excavations cannot re-create the loss of an ancient pond, although aquatic plants and animals do move quickly to occupy newly constructed ponds as we are well aware at Trimworth.

We have two ponds, both created in 2003. The first is lined and varies in depth from a few centimetres to more than a metre and is stocked with native waterside plants, but no fish, apart from those which have become established naturally, such as sticklebacks. Within weeks of completing the pond we began to observe a good range of aquatic species. It has been the most significant feature in our attempts to garden with wildlife in mind. The second pond is our conservation pond and is completely unmanaged. It lies below the first, at the level of a drainage dyke which feeds into the river. It has no liner, simply being dug out of the chalk and left without further interference. The water depth fluctuates with the changing level of the water table: in summer, almost drying out, and in winter disappearing into the flood waters of the surrounding fields.

Today, I spent some quiet moments observing damselflies, water boatmen, pond skaters and newts. Damselflies, the daintier cousins of the dragonfly, flutter lightly around the ponds, joining together and mating in flight. We saw the common blue, possibly the azure damselfly, less stunning than the banded demoiselle with its flashing metallic blue/green colour. Soon, the females will dip their abdomen below the water to insert eggs into incisions made in the stems of pond plants. They belong to the insect 'odonata,' meaning toothed-jaws, so not surprisingly they are regarded along with dragonflies as the raptors of the insect world: beautiful, graceful, but voracious hunters. They will remain as larvae for 2 to 3 years, feeding on tiny underwater creatures before emerging from the water onto a stem or reed and leaving their larval case, or exuvia, as adults. They can now be seen drying out and hardening their wings before living a life lasting only a few weeks.

Further into the woods the garlic smell is intense and overpowering when leaves of ransoms (above) or garlic mustard are crushed.

Fish are rising in response to the mayfly, which coincides with the appearance of hawthorn blossom or mayflower.

The flower of the yellow archangel is orchid-like with two-lipped whorls attracting insects into its cosy pouch.

Water boatmen are sculling upside down across the ponds, propelled by two long legs which paddle like oars. I watch them resting on the water, waiting for a movement or vibration on the surface, looking to sink their feeding tube into some unsuspecting prey and inject a toxic saliva. Newts drift to the surface and hang just below the water level, scooping up dead or dying insects, then wiggle off down to the depths.

Wild flowers are abundant in the nearby dykes. Unscented bright red flowers of red campion stand out on the shaded bank, the five petals so indented that at first glance there appear to be ten petals. Bumble-bees bite through the prominent calyx to obtain the nectar. Nearby is herb robert with its bright pink flower giving off an unpleasant acrid scent when crushed, typical of the geranium. On the edge of the cultivated fields is common fumitory, its old name 'earth smoke' describes the hazy effect of its fern-like leaves en masse. Burdock is another shade lover, sending up its great heart shaped leaves and sticky seed heads which reputedly inspired the inventor of Velcro fastening. Garlic mustard or Jack- by- the- hedge is scattered widely along the dykes, its erect stalks and fresh green leaves, attracting the orange-tip butterfly. The flowers are insignificant, but the garlic smell of the plant when crushed is quite distinctive. Further into the woods the garlic smell is much more pungent and overpowering when leaves and stems of ransons are crushed. Cattle have a compulsive liking for this allium with its starry white flower heads. Although it does not cause illness in cattle, the strong garlic smell taints the milk and can make it unfit for consumption. Elsewhere in the ditches and banks, hemlock competes with cow parsley, the more complex flower head of hemlock probably not appearing until June. The butter-coloured flower of the yellow archangel is dotted among bluebells in the wood. Named after Archangel Michael it is an exotic, orchid-like flower, in which two lipped whorls attract insects into its cosy pouch. It is a member of the mint family, the leaves giving off a distinctive smell when crushed.

The presence of anglers coincides with the appearance of the mayfly, and this evening we observed the subtle relationship between fishermen, fly and fish on our river. For days we have noticed signs of fish rising; chomping, swishing and sipping the surface, leaving bubbles and slowly expanding rings of disturbed water. They have been rising in response to the mayfly, so-called because it coincides with the appearance of hawthorn blossom or mayflower. What a strange life cycle. Eggs of the mayfly are laid underwater and sink to the bottom. Eventually, the nymph emerges and exists in this stage for months or even years before rising to the surface and casting off its nymphal skin. At this stage they are prey to fish, especially trout. Mayflies are unique among winged insects because they will moult again into adult mayflies whose primary function is reproduction. This adult life span is short, sometimes only a few hours, or perhaps a day – hence the term 'one day fly,' (the French 'éphéremè'). Having mated, the male dies; the female lays eggs in the water and then dies too. Despite their ephemeral existence, mayflies are amongst the oldest winged insects in existence, dating back over 300 million years. They are also great indicators of the state of the river, being sensitive to areas of polluted freshwater. One of the unforgettable sights of spring is when hundreds of mayfly hatch at once, filling the air above the water with dancing, fluttering flies, particularly spectacular this evening against the golden light of the setting sun.

National Moth Night is a celebration of moths and moth recording, and each year the event is associated with a particular theme. This year it is collaborating with the Bat Conservation Trust. Bats and moths share a close relationship. Both are under pressure from changes in the countryside with the bat now protected under law. We have pipistrelle hibernating in our roof space at Trimworth, in an ancient yew tree and in bat boxes around the house. They are Britain's commonest bat weighing about 5 g, less than a one-pound coin. We also see serotine, one of Britain's largest bats appearing early evening in good light, its broad wings giving a characteristic flapping, yet highly manoeuvrable flight with short glides and steep descents. The predator/prey relationship between bats and moths is a fascinating one. Bats echolocate by producing ultrasonic sounds, then detect the echoes that return from solid objects such as night-flying insects. But moths have their own defence mechanism. Extremely acute hearing allows them to detect the fluttering signal produced by the wings of hunting bats. They can judge the direction of the bats approach and change their flight pattern or fall out of the sky in steep spirals. Despite these escape tactics, bats are very capable fliers and are probably ahead of the moths in this evolutionary 'arms race.'

Moths are closely related to butterflies and come in a huge range of shapes, colours and sizes. We see probably 60 species of butterfly in the UK, but there are over 2000 species of moth, making them one of the most diverse animal groups on the planet. They play a prominent role as pollinators, and are an essential part of the food chain for birds, bats and mammals. The decline of some bird populations is probably directly related to the drop in moth numbers. The purpose of the National Moth recording scheme is to provide an accurate assessment of their conservation status. Sixty-two moths have become extinct in the UK during the 20th century, the total number decreasing by a third since 1960 because of habitat loss, light pollution and warming temperatures. Raising their profile through the National Moth Night will hopefully stimulate interest and lead to further conservation initiatives.

Today, the parishioners of Crundale and Godmersham gathered at Crundale church to relive the ancient festival of Rogation, from the Latin rogare, 'to ask'. The custom originated in Saxon times, possibly in response to natural disasters and was certainly undertaken in Crundale in the 16th century, because a record in the old Parish Book for the year 1593 reads "Paid at the court at Canterbury, November 26, for not going the perambulation – three shillings and sixpence." This heavy fine suggests that the perambulation was not something to be overlooked! The excuse may have had something to do with substantial building work which we know was being undertaken at Crundale at that time.

Rogation traditionally involved beating the bounds of the parish to bless fields and stock. Along the route various important landmarks such as streams, ponds and trees were also blessed. The festival had a practical purpose, because in the days before Ordnance Survey maps the boundary demarcation between parishes was not precise, especially where there were open field systems. The inexact nature of the Crundale boundary is indicated in a description of the bounds of the parish which reads "On an oak in a shave next a field called Pedless. So to Purwood, the mark in the wood hedge being a lump of stones. Under the hedge which parts Pedless from Purwood, to the stile, in the wood hedge leading to Godmersham. The bounds over the stile are marked by a ditch, taking in a little of the wood, which belongs to Mr Browning, where mark on an ashen stud in the further corner of the wood....where we marked for the last time on a Dowl a little above the stile in Banky Field hedge." During the procession boys were often bumped on prominent marks or boundary stones and even rolled into ditches and ponds, so they never forgot where the boundaries were! Today we began with a few prayers, sang some hymns (unaccompanied) and set off for a two-hour walk in warm sunshine and cool north wind, returning to the church invigorated and with a renewed appreciation of our glorious landscape and its community.

Monday mornings never used to be this good. At last the wind has shifted to a warmer quarter and the air was swarming with gnats and midges, forming little grey clouds drifting over the water surface. The St Mark's fly, so-called because the adults usually emerge around St Mark's Day on 25 April, swarms along the woodland edge and over the grassland, its legs dangling down looking black and menacing, but actually quite harmless. In fact, they seem to lead a piteous life, acting as a prolific source of protein for a large number of predators, getting stuck in spiders' webs or found floating in their hundreds on ponds. It's a wonder any survive to breed, and yet Mark Cocker finds a mesmeric beauty in their collective movements. "Follow the trajectory of a single insect among its kind, and you see that it inscribes slowly twisting loops and zigzags through the still air. There is a form of organised chaos to the shape of these clouds, because each fly spirals steadily through the leisured column of its neighbours, until it reaches the outer edge of the group. Here it twists calmly to regain the inner sanctum of mid swarm. Then slowly it arrives back at the outer perimeter again and repeats its inward turning motion. By this elastic system, the swarm is always mutating."

May 18th

Along the dyke, yellow flags have quickly spread their rhizomes. The bright yellow flowers make an eye-catching sight rising above sword shaped leaves. It is the only species of iris native to Europe, growing in damp habitats of slowly flowing and stagnant waterways. On tops of sunny banks the bed-straws, both crosswort and ladies bed-straw, are widespread. As the name suggests, they were used in stuffing mattresses in the Middle Ages. The plant also contains renin, an enzyme which curdles milk and was used in cheese production, or as a colouring in Double Gloucester. Its attraction for me is the intense honey scent, particularly noticeable in warm weather- a great nectar source for bees. Hedges are bustling with bird activity and there is much tail twitching and wing flicking. At this time of May I feel that the natural world is racing away from me on a tide of intense, luminous green, and I'm struggling to keep up.

In late May around the time of the Chelsea Flower Show it has become good practice to cut back some garden shrubs to produce bushy, more compact plants which will then flower more profusely in the summer. This practice is known as

May 19th

the 'Chelsea Chop.' At Trimworth, the 'chop' came unexpectedly early, and with unwelcome consequences. Returning from our morning walk I was distracted by bird activity around a nest box along the dyke and inadvertently forgot to shut the field gate. An hour later, the shepherd called to say there were 50 sheep enjoying the lush and varied vegetation of our garden. Some shrubs and trees had been pruned to the height that a sheep can reach, others were hoovered off at ground level. What the rabbits had missed, the sheep found and completed the job. Such are the delights of gardening in a rural setting.

May 20th

May is the 'crown of the year.' Light, length of day and temperatures all combine to expand the greening, blossoming world, filled with birdsong. The countryside scenery has shifted again. Along road and river, hawthorn is proclaiming its exuberant message of the impending arrival of summer. Blossom is breaking in waves along hedgerows, its creamy white flowers set against a smoky grey and pale blue sky. There is a wonderful combination of cow parsley and hawthorn blossom which moves Monty Don to exclaim "Eat your heart out, white gardeners everywhere: May time and may blossom do it better than you will ever know how!" Hawthorn has been a boundary marker for centuries. Some solitary, stunted, windblown trees mark ancient boundaries; unbroken lines of hawthorn stretch for miles, often the result of the enclosure of open fields in the 18th and 19th centuries. Not surprisingly,

Hawthorn is proclaiming its exuberant message of the arrival of summer with blossom breaking in waves along the hedgerow.

it is the agricultural hedge of choice, being fast growing, producing a thick and thorny protective barrier, tolerant of any soil and drainage condition and producing essential cover and winter food for birds.

The mystical cult of the hawthorn has pre-Christian origins associated with fairies and protection from evil spirits. These sentiments were easily translated into Christian legends, such as the hawthorn tree being linked to the crown of thorns and the famous Glastonbury hawthorn which flowered in spring and in midwinter, bursting from the staff of Joseph of Arimathea. Sex and fertility are suggested in some May Day celebrations, and its association with death and bad luck makes its blossom unwelcome indoors as a decoration in church. May blossom is also portentous, as in the Scottish farmers' belief that 'Harvest follows thirteen weeks after whitethorn scents the air.' The phrase 'N'er cast a clout till May is out' is thought to refer to the blossom, not the month, and 'Here we go gathering nuts in May' is probably a corruption of 'Here we go gathering knots (or blossoms) of May.' What is certain is that the sight of hawthorn draped in snowy blossom is emblematic of the freshness and beauty of my favourite month of May, and a sign that spring is growing up to become summer.

The Young People's Environment Day at Trimworth once again brings 20 eager young naturalists aged 7 to 12 to explore our garden, ponds, fields and river. It is our affirmation of involving young people in garden and environmental issues, (as well as dramatically reducing the average age of the membership of the Godmersham and Crundale Gardeners Association for at least a day)! The Kentish Stour Countryside team begin the day by introducing the subject of food chains, wildlife corridors and habitats, followed by a riverside walk culminating in the Great Duck Race. We return to Trimworth for pond dipping and the hunt for garden mini-beasts and bugs. Warm temperatures and continuous sunshine stimulated a great deal of activity in the various habitats, all observed and recorded by 20 pairs of eager young eyes, before the flora and fauna of garden and ponds returned to their peaceful and undisturbed environments for another year.

There were some notable sightings around the pond. Female and male common newts were prolific with their orange bellies, olive green bodies and wavy crests running from head to tail. The crests of the male wiggle provocatively in the water, wafting secretions to seek out the female. We associate the newt with standing water like ponds and ditches, but they are actually the most terrestrial of our amphibians, leaving ponds when breeding is over in late July and living in grass, deciduous woodland, bogs and gardens, where they feed on insects, worms and slugs. They emerge from hibernation in February or March and return to

The Young People's Environment Day brings eager young naturalists to Trimworth for pond dipping and the hunt for countryside mini-beasts and bugs.

the ponds for breeding, the female laying up to 400 eggs on broad-leaved aquatic plants. They exist in the pond as free-swimming creatures, hunting for insect larvae near the water surface and gliding gracefully to the depths. Warm weather has stimulated dragonfly activity with nymphs leaving the water and climbing stems of reeds and other pond plants. Many dragonflies had already emerged from their cases, and were clinging to plants for a few hours to dry and harden their wings in preparation for flight. We counted over 30 empty larval cases (or exuviae) which can be used by biologists as an important way to identify species and even their sex. Floating on the water surface was one of the largest and fastest-flying British dragonflies, the Emperor. It was a female with a bright green thorax and had fallen into the water before its wings had become fully ready for flight. We lifted it out, examined its transparent patterned wings and placed it in the sunshine to recover. These creatures are some of the most primitive groups of freshwater insects, with fossil records dating back to the Carboniferous era, about 300 million years ago. Forty years ago there were 42 breeding species in the UK, three of which are now extinct. As I examined this fascinating insect I hoped it would not be our generation that witnessed any further declines of this beautiful creature.

May 22nd

Cloudless skies, high temperatures and light winds have brought butterflies to the gardens in search of newly-opened nectar-rich flowers. Holly blue is a delightful small, pale-blue butterfly which is easy to spot and identify because the underside of its wing is also blue. Flying over the pond in strong sunlight, it appears silvery blue in the reflected light of the water. This is likely to be one of the first brood. When they become adults and have mated, they lay their eggs on ivy plants then overwinter as chrysalis, emerging in spring to mate and lay eggs on holly. Populations fluctuate, but they appear to be abundant this year. Also prolific is the orange-tip, frequently seen flying along hedges and in gardens. Honesty and garlic mustard is in flower, and the orange-tip female will lay eggs on the underside of flower buds. The males have a specific role in warning off predators and it is difficult to believe that such an attractive, fragile little butterfly is likely to eat another of its own species. On the nettles by the willow dyke, a withered leaf took off and then returned to the same spot. This butterfly had the appearance of a beaten up tortoiseshell, but the ragged edges of the wings had a symmetry which identified it as a comma, so called because of the small white mark in the shape of a comma on the underside of the wing. They are frequently found on the sunny side of woodland margins, visiting gardens to search out nectar sources. The comma is one of the few species whose increase in number and distribution is likely to be linked to global warming. It has recently been seen in Scotland, the first sighting there since the 1870s.

May 23rd

In the space of 10 minutes, I counted eight visits by great tits to the nesting box on the bothy, each visit bringing a beak full of insects. No wonder birdsong declines when eggs hatch. With 5 to 11 eggs to incubate and small beaks to fill, this is no time to stand around singing. From hedgerows and nesting boxes comes the solitary sound of urgent wheezing, rasping, rustling and other hungry demands from small birds.

Another scenery shift is taking place along the hedgerow. The white may blossom of hawthorn is turning pink and the white component of the landscape is now being provided by the elderberry with its headily fragrant creamy-white blossom. A tree is often defined as a woody perennial plant which attains a stature of 6 metres or more. Hawthorn just about qualifies, but elderberry fails on this definition, as does dogwood. The poor elder has gained a rather malevolent reputation as the wood of the Cross and has become an emblem of trouble and sorrow.

The bright-green thorax of a female Emperor, one of the largest and fastest British dragonflies.

> "Bour tree, bour tree, crooked, wrong,
> Never straight and never strong,
> Never bush and never tree,
> Since our Lord was nailed on thee."

But there are pleasurable associations also, such as the use of the flower for making champagne and the berries for making wine. English summer begins with elderflower and ends with elderberries. Clare's lines in 'The Shepherd's Calendar' suggest a fondness for the shrub.

Another scenery shift along the hedgerow with the headily fragrant creamy- white blossom of elderberry.

> "The sunbeams on the hedges lie,
> The south wind murmurs summer soft:
> The maids hang out white clothes to dry,
> Around the elder-skirted croft."

As a boy I searched for straight branches of the elder to make pop- guns. The pith was removed to make a hollow cylindrical barrel and a piece of pine was shaped as a plunger. The ammunition was provided by acorns which could be fired at least 25 yards. Sadly, the plant has gained a reputation for its toxicity which can cause a build-up of cyanide, so children are discouraged from handling the wood to make such toys. So, no pop guns, no conkers, no fun.

We rarely miss the Chelsea Flower Show. It is a fixed date in our minds and calendars, as significant as many other portents of summer. But Chelsea is the

May 25th

antithesis of the real world garden. At Chelsea, celebrity garden designers with their stupendous budgets create theatrical and dramatic simulations of Provence, Tuscany and other exotic locations a world away from our own modest, personalised and less controlled garden creations. Nevertheless, in our own gardens and at Chelsea we find many common expressions of the British love of the garden. In both, we are trying to simulate the natural and at the same time spending a fortune trying to keep it under some degree of control. Even Vita Sackville West talked about 'fine carelessness' in her garden at Sissinghurst and although she was happy for roses to romp away with gay abandon, this carefree, easy-going attitude was matched by careful, subtle and systematic pruning.

In the spring of 2004, plans were being drawn up for the construction of a sunken garden at Trimworth measuring 10m x 5 m and a depth of 1 m. This required a considerable amount of earthmoving and alteration of the garden to the north of the house. It has always been conjectured that a domestic chapel, first mentioned in the Domesday Monachorum was located to the side of the house. Hasted in his topographical survey of the County in 1797 says of Trimworth Manor: "it had formerly a domestic chapel belonging to it some of the walls of which are still standing." Charles Igglesden's saunter through Kent in 1939 noted that "Mr James Hodgson who at present lives there has found some flint foundations in an adjoining field." Adding to the speculation is a map of 1680 showing an isolated building in the area where the sunken garden was planned, so before starting any earthworks to construct the sunken garden, we felt it was necessary to conduct a geophysical survey to ensure that construction would not disturb any old structural remains such as foundations, floors or demolition rubble that might exist below the ground. Very few archaeological sites reveal themselves fully in aerial photographs or in landforms, so it is sometimes necessary to use geophysical prospecting techniques to explore invisible features of the buried site. The use of resistivity surveys at Trimworth would be expected to find any human artefacts by measuring the resistance of the subsoil to the passage of an electric current, the latter detecting variation in the subsoil's magnetic characteristics. A 20 m grid was laid out and probes were pushed into the ground at measured intervals and readings taken to show variations in resistance. The current passes easily through damp soil, but drier, compact material, such as the buried wall or rubble, creates high resistance.

The outcome of the survey was that features of interest could be clearly identified, possibly relating to structural remains and one possibly representing a former ditch. The northern corner of the garden gave the highest resistance readings, indicating building remains which continue beyond the property border into an adjoining field. They appear to form two distinct linear shapes at right angles and may represent walls or discrete areas of rubble. The low-resistance area nearby may indicate the presence of the silted up former ditch, and could represent a former boundary. Further surveys will be needed to extend the search into the adjoining field. This could take the form of exploratory trenching to determine the nature of these features of interest, but we are presently reassured that no human artefacts were identified in the location of our planned sunken garden, which now exists as an unusual and attractive garden feature.

May 26th

Along the river and dykes, wild roses (or dog roses) are arching outward and downwards over the water, their silky pink white flowers subtly reflected in the dark water beneath. This is the unofficial English rose and is one of a number of sub-species, including the field rose which has white flowers, and the sweet briar, smelling of apples when crushed. A little further upstream there are extensive patches of yellow iris or yellow flag, the flower standing out clearly on the leafless stem. It is like a garden iris without the beard, but displaying the typical form of three veined outer petals (the falls), three inner petals (the standards) and three stigmas. The flowering period is long because they flower in sequence and when the flower is gone, large three-sided seedpods dominate well into the autumn. Clear blue flowers of the water forget-me-not line the edges of still water, the large root systems growing thickly into deeper water. (Its name is said to derive from German folklore in which a knight fell into the river whilst collecting the flower for his lover. Before he drowned, he threw her the flowers saying, 'vergisz mein nicht'). Along the riverbank clusters of pinky-white bells grow above the hairy pale-green leaves of common comfrey whilst towering above, to a height of 2 metres, is the white-flowered umbellifer called hemlock, a plant linked with the devil, witchcraft and the fatal draught which poisoned Socrates. Its stem is purple-spotted and the delicate white flowers attract a host of insects, such as leafhoppers, shield bugs, chafers and bees. It is highly toxic and produces drowsiness and paralysis in cattle when eaten in the field. Toxicity is reduced when the plant is dried, so hemlock in hay is therefore harmless. Another toxic plant coming into flower now in the fields is ragwort with its attractive clusters of yellow flowers, but this attraction is lost on farmers and horse owners because the plant can cause severe liver damage and death if eaten by animals. The Ragwort Control Act of 2003 makes landowners responsible by law for controlling the plant. Its total eradication would be sadly missed by the black and yellow caterpillars of the little cinnabar moth, which later in the year will strip the foliage bare.

Today is Oak Apple Day and declared as a national holiday in 1660 to commemorate the restoration of the English monarchy. People wore oak apples and sprigs of oak leaves to celebrate the occasion when in 1651, the future Charles II of England escaped the Roundheads by hiding in an oak tree in Shropshire. Today, the oak is in the news for reasons of concern rather than celebration. Just as oak buds have burst and the fresh green leaves give the burnished olive tint to the woodlands, we are confronted with the threat of a disease which may decimate this native tree which has been an intrinsic part of our history and culture. Acute oak decline (AOD) is a result of the bacteria which causes trees to 'bleed' black fluid, killing them within five years.(Dutch elm disease killed 25 million trees in Britain from its outbreak in 1967.) This bacterium is so virulent that the destruction of oak forests could be even more widespread and devastating. The Forestry Commission has identified 55 affected sites in southern England and the Woodland Heritage warns of 'a frightening disease with potential to cause destruction on a massive scale.' The method by which the disease spreads, whether by air, animals or humans, is not known, but with oak accounting for 16% of our woodland, the depletion of this quintessential native tree will have a huge impact on our culture, history and the future of our British landscape.

May 27th

In the early evening light we headed for Yockletts Bank, 23 hectares of ancient woodland on a chalk escarpment with a clay capping. It is a Site of Special Scientific Interest, managed by the Kent Wildlife Trust and is famous for its orchids. The diversity of species is related to the wide variety of calcareous habitats within the site, including short grass of the downs, glades and woodland edges. The slope supports mixed woodland of ash, hornbeam and beech with a hazel understory, and regular coppicing maintains the biodiversity of the woodland plants, especially orchids. It faces south-west and this evening was bathed in rich golden evening sunlight filtering through the beech leaves, like radiant green lanterns of light.

Identification of orchids is not always easy because many species interbreed and produce natural hybrids with characteristics of both parents, and in these cases identification may require inspired guesswork! In the mid-19th century Charles Darwin wrote a book entitled 'The Various Contrivances by which Orchids are Fertilised by Insects,' and the topic of pollination has become one of the most enigmatic and fascinating aspects of the orchid world. While an insect is attempting to reach the nectar, it comes into contact with a sticky pads joined to the pollinia

Wild roses or dog roses are arching outwards and downwards over the water, their silky pink-white flowers subtly reflected in the dark water beneath.

The wood was bathed in rich golden evening sunlight filtering through the beech leaves like radiant green lanterns of light.

Orchids, the 'royalty' of the plant world.
A common twayblade with its inconspicuous yellow-green
flower spike and twin rounded leaves at the base of the stem.
(above left)
The early purple with its conspicuous black-spotted leaves.
(above right)
Lady orchid displaying coloured pink and white flowers and
dark hood, resembling the shape of a ladies dress. (right)

(a mass of pollen grains). When the insect moves, the pollinia attach themselves and the insect then makes contact with the next flower visited. An even more elaborate evolution has occurred in some species such as the bee orchid, fly orchid and early spotted orchid, where the flower mimics the female of a certain insect using scent or some tactile means. The male insects are deceived by this and visit the flower causing pollen to be attached. During our one-hour walk through Yockletts we discovered six species of orchid. Most prolific was the common twayblade with its inconspicuous yellow-green flowers and twin rounded leaves at the base of the single stem. Also common was the early purple orchid, its glossy green black spotted leaves which have been showing since January, but now a spike of purple flower rises above the rosette, standing proudly above the dog's mercury. Strongly associated with East Kent is the lady orchid which we found in small groups in woodland clearings. The flowers on long stout stems resemble the shape of a ladies dress, coloured pink and white with a dark hood. The cylindrical spikes of the common spotted orchid flower were also abundant as groups in open woodland, the blunt ended leaves closely marked with dark spots. Finally, on shady banks, especially under beech, we saw the distinctive, creamy white flower of the white helleborene, also known as the 'poached egg orchid' from the yellow spot hidden at the base of the lip of the flower.

This short walk in the serene and radiant evening light of the woodland brought home the fascinating, breath-taking attraction of these 'royalties' of the plant world, whose assortment of species, colour and morphology will continue to change throughout the spring and summer months.

There are some documentary sources which are accessible, easy-to-use, and which reveal a real understanding of the changing rural community and major life-events affecting the households. One of these sources is the census, taken every 10 years since 1801, with the exception of 1941. An examination of the census returns for Trimworth shows fascinating changes in the agricultural and domestic labour force, the area under cultivation and characteristics of the farm economy. In 1851, the household at Trimworth consisted of 12 people, including two young house servants and four farm servants. The farm was 250 acres in size and employed nine labourers and three boys. By 1871 the farm had grown to 366 acres, employing 13 men and six boys. The tenant was a widower of 37, with his children aged 5, 6,7,8,9, 11, 12 and 13. Not surprisingly, the household also contained a governess, two servants and a housemaid! By 1881 the farm had grown by well over 50% to 570 acres employing 27 men and three boys, but the residents of Trimworth had fallen to only two local unmarried brothers and a female domestic servant. From 1891, the population of Crundale records a substantial population decline, particularly female, probably a response to better employment opportunities in urban areas at the time. In 1851, half of the country's population resided in cities. By 1901 this figure had risen to ¾, largely as a result of rural depopulation.

June

The arrival of June coincides with warm weather and the longest daylight hours of the year, bringing roses and honeysuckle to flower. The Book of Hours for June features images of mowing or haymaking using scythes with long open blades. In Les Très Riches Heures, peasants are seen moving across the meadow in unison, with the Hotel de Nesle, the Dukes Parisian residence, in the background. Two women are shown raking up the hay with pitchforks. This was arduous work, beginning when the dew had dried and working until noon, sleeping through the heat of the day, and continuing on to dew fall. Maintaining a constant pace and a sense of balance and rhythm, a good worker could cut nearly an acre of hay in a day. The scythe is an implement at least as old as the Roman era and became one of the countryman's most valued tools, remaining supreme until the arrival of the mechanical mower in the 1850s. Even then it was still frequently used to open up the headland for the mechanical reaper. Odd corners, edges of fields and wild patches allowed the prudent yeoman to harvest a few extra yards with his scythe. The illuminations of the Falstoff Master, produced in 1450, shows the tools for sharpening scythes. Using a wooden handle called a 'straike' or 'strickle' smeared with sand, the blade was stroked to give a sharp edge (the word straik means to strike). The keenness of the edge required depended on the crop being harvested; soft sand for hay and sharp sand for corn. Mutton-fat was carried in a horn, the sand in a drawstring bag.

Warmer weather has led to an increase in activity around the ponds, particularly dragonflies energised by warmer weather, allowing their wing muscles to become more effective. Larger dragonflies require a temperature of over 25°C, hence they bask in the morning sun, occasionally whirring their wings to generate heat. By the afternoon, they begin hunting over the water, swooping and darting with amazing speed and agility. From a standing start they can cover 15 metres in one second and reach speeds of 60 kph. Their wings, delicate in appearance but with the strength of steel, can beat 50 times a second. They are formidable hunters as their names suggest: chasers, darters, hawkers, all cruising and gliding over their patch, seeking their prey by sight. Their compound eyes are made up of 30,000 facets, each one producing an image. The front and hind wings beat alternately, not together as in most insects, giving them greater agility and flight control, switching rapidly from forward to sideways motion. Today I watched the bright blue male Emperor, the bulkiest of our British dragonflies, whirring across the pond at speed in its short life of only a few weeks. As it settled on the blades of water iris I could observe its striking deep blue and black-lined abdomen and green thorax before it skimmed off a few centimetres above the water in search of mosquitoes, midges, moths and butterflies, any of which can be detected at a distance of up to 10 metres and plucked out of the air in flight. This is the beginning of an exciting period of activity involving these fearsome but beautiful predators, together with the fluttering forms of the delicate damselfly.

The last full moon of late May is appropriately known as 'the flower moon' and accordingly the road verges and hedgerows are full of the colour of wild flowers.

The pale-blue, purple-tinged flowers of bugle carried in whorls around the stem have attracted fritillary butterflies but are now fading, leaving an attractive dark leaved spike. Scarlet petals of common poppy are scattered along field margins and the verges are still full of campions and field scabious, whose name is derived from 'scabiosa herba', the herb for scabies. The hedgerows are spectacular. Field maple is producing new pinky maroon leaves contrasting with the already established, shiny dark-green foliage. Common spindleberry bears tiny green flowers which will be followed later by outrageous shiny pink and orange fruits. Dogwood is producing sparkling white flowers in small rosettes, but the queen of the hedgerow in early June is the elderflower with its huge clusters of creamy-white flowers so dense that the green leaves can hardly be seen. They have a highly aromatic smell and flavour, producing refreshing cordials when steeped in concentrated sugar solution, so the flavour is infused into the syrup. Also creamy white, but fading now, is the wayfaring tree, the name being given by the 16th century botanist John Gerard to this viburnum which is so common along the chalky lanes of southern Britain. The hawthorn show is over for the time being, the blossom now turning brown and looking and smelling unattractive, but the fruits have yet to make their stunning visual impact, to the delight of the bird population. The guelder rose, another viburnum, is also prominent in hedges with its unusual white flowers arranged in an outer ring of creamy-white blossom. The flowers are sterile, but they attract insects which then find nectar on an inner ring of small greeny-white flowers. Struggling up through the roadside hedges with its tenacious tendrils is the tufted vetch, which will eventually reach the top of the hedge to display its blueish-purple flowers, as many as forty individual flowers on each spike.

June 4th

You will know by now that Sam, our black Labrador, is with me on nearly all my walks and shares my love of the meadows by the river. A walk without Sam is like having a garden without flowers. We have a mutual accord, based on attachment, affection and understanding, but he has one characteristic that puzzles me. During our walks of about three or four kilometres, he zigzags across the fields with his nose down to the ground ('nose down dog'), picking up smells and lifting his leg, not once but many times. Another sniff, another carefully calculated drop, leaving a message for a rabbit, answering a message from the fox, setting down a challenge for the badgers. How much has he got in his tank, and how does he calculate its contents so carefully that by the time we reach the field gate on our return, the tank is empty? (Today's walk was strangely short of observations of the natural world, hence my preoccupation with the impressive muscular control of Sam's bladder.)

June 5th

Sadly, the most likely sighting of a badger in the countryside is likely to be a squashed one by the roadside where an estimated 45,000 are killed each year. So I was exhilarated by the sight of the familiar black-and-white striped face watching me as I turned into our drive. I was less overjoyed to see him trundle off down our drive towards the garden in which a badger and a JCB would have much in common. Their staple diet is earthworms and they can eat up to 200 worms a night requiring a major excavation. If worms are in short supply, bulbs, vegetables and fruit are equally acceptable. They are unlikely to make their home, or sett, in the garden, but they will establish a territory around their sett, which may well include gardens with plentiful food sources. I prefer to watch the delightful sociable family activities under the cover of darkness in such natural settings as Tye Wood, where dozens of large entrances and exits have been excavated into the well-drained chalk, leaving rubble and discarded bedding of grass, straw, or hay at the large openings. Most of the holes are riddled with roots of trees, making collapse of tunnels less likely. Apparently some setts are over 100 years old, and so are the paths they take through their territory. Despite my fear of garden excavation I am attracted to this amiable character, so endearingly portrayed in the 'Wind in the Willows.' 'That most ancient of British beasts' scuttled off down the drive and I wished him a long life free from persecution, killing and culling.

June 6th

Our evening walk was magical. It had been a warm, humid day, and to the west over Godmersham Downs were towering ranks of cumulus cloud, building to cumulo-nimbus through which sunlight broke in broad golden shafts. To the east, solid lead-blue skies formed a dramatic backdrop to the sunlit trees and downs. Mutterings of thunder rolled and rattled gently around the skies. The landscape forms were watery, pastel shades painted 'wet in wet'. There were no sharp lines just soft, unfocused outlines. The air was breathless, motionless, silent and heavy with humidity. One of those evenings to sit outside late into the night, gazing at candles burning with a steady, unflickering flame.

Here in Kent we are fortunate to have a wonderful collection of personal travels and county histories to provide an evocative portrayal of the communities and changing environments of Kent. Most notable is Hasted's 'History and Topographical Survey of the County of Kent', published in 1799. This is a major work, comprising 7000 pages; his manuscript notes ran to a hundred volumes. The work covers every hundred and parish and was compiled and written entirely by Hasted himself from field observation and a vast range of archival sources. It is more than a history because it includes many contemporary maps, as well as topographical descriptions of the state of the county. The period in which it was written was one of unprecedented change, with the population practically doubling between 1750 and 1801. Hasted captures this and many other changes and portrays the characteristics of regional diversity within the county in the late 18th and early 19th century.

The parish of Crundale merits 13 pages in Hasted, which he initially describes as "a small parish containing within it not more than 24 houses". His landscape description is not heartening, being "exceedingly cold", "exceedingly barren", with a "wild and dreary appearance". His descriptions of many parishes refer to wildness and remoteness, one of the overriding characteristics of much of Kent at the time. There is a fascinating reference to Trimworth in which he notes "the old mansion has been moated around....it had formerly a domestic chapel belonging to it, some of the walls of which are still standing." The importance of Trimworth in past times is recognised by the statement in Hasted that "it was formally of such eminent account, that the parish was called by that name... Crundale is frequently referred to as lying in Tremworth." Hasted's work received pejorative comments from contemporaries, who described him as' hasty',' careless', 'lacking critical ability', but his reputation grew to the point where his work became greatly admired, certainly not for the nature of his prose which was rather dull, but for the enormous diligence in producing one of the finest county histories ever written. "His laborious history of Kent took up more than 40 years, during the whole of which he spared neither pain nor expense to bring it to majority." These are the words of Hasted himself, which he instructed his executor to use for his obituary!

The barn owl is back, and we are overjoyed. We had very few sightings last year, and virtually none during the winter, but tonight at about 10.00pm, after watching for nearly 10 minutes we saw the white, silent shape ghosting low over the fields and up into an alder near the owl box by the river. Moments later he silently flew to the box. We heard claws scrape on the wooden platform below the entrance, then the faint rasping squeaks of hungry chicks. Within seconds, he departed on another sortie, a spine tingling sight as he flew towards us, a silent flutter of wings, then a glide over the pasture. Owls have very large wings to support a light body so they can fly slowly and hover in only the lightest rising air. This low flight speed enhances their hunting ability, giving them time to locate prey on the ground below. Quiet flight is aided by very soft flight feathers which are covered in tiny hairs, helping to deaden the sound of air through the wings, enabling them to detect sounds of small mammals below. These attributes of flight are supplemented by highly light-sensitive eyes which are also sensitive to movement. We always keep perfectly still as we wait because they can detect the slightest movement, but a motionless figure even at close quarters will probably not be observed.

Two years ago the barn owl was a regular visitor to Trimworth meadows. We would watch it from the house sweeping through Moat Field a few minutes either side of 8.00pm. Then one evening, returning late at night along the A28 through Bilting we saw a white shape lying in the road. It was probably 'our' owl killed by a passing vehicle, possibly visually impaired by sudden exposure to car headlights, and sucked into the path of passing vehicles.

Strong, gusty west winds provoked an irritable mood as I surveyed a bashed and bruised garden with broken rose stems, collapsed peonies and flattened poppies, but geniality returned with the stimulus and excitement of observations in the natural world. Pied wagtails are nesting near the barn, and from the wild flower bank above the pond I watched them in a high-speed playful chase around the garden, occasionally resting at the water's edge and frantically wagging their tails. They have a restless lifestyle of continuous movement, with tail bobbing and fast airborne sorties to catch insects with amazing agility. Their twittering song of varied call-notes is often punctuated by a lively 'tchizzick'or an abrupt alarm call of 'tchick'. They are delightful, slender, smartly marked black-and-white birds which have the habit of roosting in large numbers throughout the year, especially between August and March when resident and migrant groups roost together. (Michael Seago reports

Banded demoiselle flutter around the ponds and streams like iridescent metallic strips. This male displays dark blue bands across the wings.

a group of over 5000 birds nesting in a Kentish reed bed in September.) In previous years we have seen yellow wagtails, summer visitors, nesting in the long grass by the railway bridge. They love shallow, fast moving water and the small insects which abound there, but numbers are declining because of loss of suitable habitat and they have not been seen around here for several years.

As I watched the antics of the pied wagtails, in the corner of my eye I was conscious of a flash of dark blue and green over the pond. Two banded demoiselles, the largest of our native damselflies with wingspans of 70 mm, were spiralling and fluttering together in bright sunlight like iridescent metallic strips. They are frequent visitors to slow flowing streams, and especially ponds with muddy bottoms, making a welcome sight because they are very sensitive to pollution and their presence is an indicator of good water quality. These were both males with dark blue bands across the wings. At this time of year males compete on the wing for breeding territories and will perform a special flight display for visiting females, often dipping to touch the water gently at an egg-laying site, which it will then defend from other males for hours if necessary.

And then later in the day, another unforgettable, mesmeric moment as we passed through the field gate into the garden. A kingfisher flew up from the edge of the top pond, rose steeply and veered off along the dyke through the meadow. I was entranced and stood grinning in amazement and disbelief. Magical!

June 9th

It looked like a buzzard flying over the meadow towards Tye Wood, except it had an unusual tail shape and its legs were dangling below its body. Through the binoculars we confirmed it was a buzzard trailing a large dead bird the size of buzzard's breakfast. It was being closely followed by very angry rooks, which must have just settled on their perch to relish a tasty morsel, when it quickly vanished in a buzzard's grasp and disappeared off towards the depths of the wood. With slow, laboured wing beats, the buzzard reached the safety of the wood undeterred by the noisy aggressive behaviour of the hostile, hungry rooks.

The foliage in the wood has lost its fresh lime-green tint for darker tones of green, causing more shade to be cast on the forest floor. Bluebells have faded but there is plenty of colour along the forest edge. Scrambling, trailing stems of bittersweet are showing leaves resembling a potato and masses of bright purple, star-like flowers each with a cone of yellow anthers. This is also known as woody nightshade, a less poisonous form of deadly nightshade, leaving only a bitter taste followed by a sweet aftertaste. A similar blueish-purple colour is carried in whorls on the tall stems of wild clary with their jagged, toothed leaves similar to sage but less aromatic. Some of the flowers are probably cleistogamous, which means they are self-pollinating, setting seeds without opening. Colonies of red campion still dot the forest floor, and along the meadow ditches is meadowsweet and ragged robin, a member of the pink family and distinguished by its shredded pink petals.

A cold breezy day with fair-weather cumulus scudding across the skies and creating fast moving patches of shadow racing over the surface of the downs. Field tracks and hedgerows were spotted with the purple of common mallow and the powder blue of field scabious. In the corn fields the scarlet petals of the common poppy stood as survivors of weed-killer sprays and along the field edge, the large, white, flat flower heads of oxeye daisy formed a mosaic of colour with ragged robin, bladder campion and red campion. Buttercups were everywhere on the rough pasture of the downs, the name replacing descriptive local names of goldweed and soldiers' buttons during the 19th century. We passed piles of recently logged pines from Black Edge and Oxen Leas Wood, smelling strongly of resin seeping from the 30 year old trunks. These systematic clearances are an important aspect of woodland management, maintaining a diversity of habitat by giving patches of light and space. Many plants flourish in years of light, but they also need years of shade to suppress tall grasses and other plants that would overwhelm them. Our return home was more arduous than we had wished. There was no headland between the metre high crop of rape and the hedge line of Ripple Farm. We waded through shoulder height nettles, sow thistles, tufted grasses, couch and dock– all bound together by tenacious strands of cleaver or goose grass snagging the feet. Our high -stepping, burdensome, laborious progress left behind clouds of pollen, and feelings that this walk was best reserved for the winter.

In the late evening I was perched on an anglers bench near the owl box, hoping for a glimpse of the white night-owl returning from its hunting patrol, silently

A cold breezy day with fair-weather cumulus scudding across the skies creating fast-moving shadows racing over the surface of the downs.

"In the cornfields, scarlet petals of the common poppy and cornsow thistle stood as survivors of weed-killer sprays."

gliding the hedgerows and quartering the meadows in search of mice and voles. Instead, I watched the now familiar sight of a kestrel, 'wind- hovering' or 'kiting' in search of similar prey. It is unique among falcons in its ability to hover, facing into the wind, tail spread, head perfectly still and tilted downwards. High-speed video photography by the Raptor Foundation has shown that the head will move less than 8 mm during wind-hovering, enabling it to catch 10 to 15 times as much food as when searching 'in- flight'. Furthermore, the kestrel can see well into the ultraviolet spectrum, creating a problem for the field vole, which marks its trail with urine, a substance which reflects ultraviolet light. Despite this evolutionary setback the field vole remains one of the two most common rodents in the countryside, which is just as well because a kestrel requires at least two every day to maintain its body weight.

Systematic woodland clearances are an important part of management, maintaining a diversity of habitat by creating patches of light and space.

Another food rodent for the kestrel is the water vole, which has suffered serious decline to the point of being an endangered species. Once common on all waterways in the UK it is regarded by the Environment Agency as the fastest declining mammal, and almost non-existent in Devon and Cornwall. There are recent signs that improvements in water quality have helped its recovery, aided by effective control of its main predator, the mink. Our most common rodent in the garden at Trimworth is the bank vole, making its habitat in holes scattered liberally in the dry grassland and hedge banks. These little creatures with small eyes and ears and blunt noses have red-brown fur on their backs and creamy stomachs. I do nothing to control this amiable little rodent. His behaviour and diet are no problem to me or my garden.

Whenever the conservation pond is approached at this time of year there is frantic scuttling of moorhen chicks across the surface of the water. They occasionally duck below the surface of the thick algae, which has developed in the strong sunlight, leaving half submerged heads, adopting the 'I can't see you see, so you can't see me', approach. They are a daily feature of life at Trimworth, often leaving the pond and walking into the paddock, several chicks obediently scampering after an adult in single file. The moorhen is from the same family as the coot, their twitchy nervous behaviour leading to the name 'skitty coot'. They are not moor birds at all; the name is a corruption of 'mere hen'. We have already seen one batch of six eggs this year, and there will probably be two or more broods. Survival rates are low for several reasons. Newly-hatched chicks are nidifugous, covered in down, active shortly after

June 12th

(left) *Low evening sunlight on the slopes of Godmersham downs reveals archaeological evidence of old ploughing marks called lynchets or terraces.*

(below) *The aerial photograph of Godmersham Park shows glimpses of an Iron Age field system which has survived despite centuries of more recent ploughing.* (Copyright NMR ©)

hatching, and quickly leaving the nest, as opposed to songbirds which are nidicolous, born naked, blind and helpless but remaining in the nest for weeks. Moorhen chicks often fall prey to the fox or get separated from parents. The first two chicks have the best chance of survival being big enough to challenge later arrivals for food. Another risk element is the hastily-built, poorly-constructed, badly-sited nests, usually just a rough platform or raft, which is easily visible and accessible to predators. Those which survive rapidly develop red and yellow beaks and lose their grey brown feathers for the black plumage of adults. They are unusual birds in that the offspring of one brood will often help to raise the next, but their outward timidity can easily switch to aggression because they are acutely territorial. They are often seen fighting each other, spilling over flower bed, onto the lawn and into the ponds, where they attempt to push each other underwater. We find them fascinating neighbours, and would miss their 'curruck' call, and their twitchy, nervous, jerky movement.

The low evening sunlight on the slopes of Godmersham Downs emphasises the irregularities in the ground surface by highlighting bumps and filling the hollows with shadow. In this light, a series of lines following the contours around the slope of the downs becomes clearly visible. They mark the position of lynchets, formed as a result of ploughing on slopes. The movement of soil down-slope forms a boundary edge, whilst below, soil movement, trampling and rain-wash undercut the slope. They are common on the chalk downland and can remain grassed over for many years as cultural formations, some dating back to medieval times and beyond. Near these lynchets in Godmersham Park are remains of an extensive field system which dates back to the Iron Age. These are rectangular plots about 60 m x 30 m. The ancient fields have survived despite centuries of more recent ploughing because they are laid out on smooth, short turf on the dry chalk soils and also because the fields were abandoned at a later date in favour of heavier, more productive soils in the valley below. They are clearly visible on aerial photographs. Aerial surveys show where crops growing over buried features develop at a different rate from those nearby because of the different moisture-retaining properties. In some cases, soil marks can be observed where the land has been ploughed, causing building fragments to be brought to the surface, giving variations in colour. All of these marks are most likely to be revealed during the near-drought conditions we are currently experiencing.

In a letter to Thomas Pennant, dated 1769, Gilbert White gives a timeless reflection of the countryside on a summer evening. His 'Naturalist's Summer Evening Walk' contains delightful and stirring observations, suggesting a symbiotic relationship between man and nature. His contribution to the realm of the natural world is historic, and this poem illustrates why he has gained such a prominent position in our national consciousness.

"When day declining sheds a milder gleam,
What time the may-fly haunts the pool or stream:
When the still owl skims round the grassy mead,
What time the timorous hare limps forth to feed:
Then be the time to steal adown the vale,
And listen to the vagrant cuckoo's tale:
To hear the clamorous curlew call his mate,
Or the soft quail his tender pain relate:

To see the swallow sweep the dark'ning plain.
Belated, to support her infant train:
To mark the swift in rapid giddy ring.
Dash round the steeple, unsubdu'd of wing:
Amusive birds! – say where your hid retreat
When the frost rages and the tempests beat:
Whence your return, by such nice instinct led
When spring, soft season, lifts her bloomy head?
Such baffled searches, mock man's prying pride,
The God of Nature is your secret guide!

While deep'ning shades obscure the face of day,
To yonder bench, leaf-shelter'd, let us stray,
Till blended objects fail the swimming sight,
And all the fading landscape sinks in night:
To hear the drowsy dor come brushing by
With buzzing wing, or the shrill cricket cry:
To see the feeding bat glance through the wood:

To catch the distant falling of the flood:
While o'er the cliff the awakened churn-owl hung
Through the still gloom protracts his chattering song:
While high in air, and pois'd upon his wings,
Unseen, the soft enamour'd woodlark sings:
These Nature's works, the curious mind employ,
Inspire a soothing melancholy joy:
As fancy warms, a pleasing kind of pain
Steals o'er the cheek, and thrills the creeping vein!
Each rural sight, each sound, each smell combine:
The tinkling sheep-bell, or the breath of kine:
The new-mown hay that scents the swelling breeze,
Or cottage-chimney smoking through the trees.
The chilling night-dews fall: away, retire:
For see, the glow-worm lights her amorous fire!"

Incidentally, 'breath of kine' denotes the breath of cows, 'drowsy dor' is a drowsy bumble bee or beetle, and the 'churn owl' is a local name for the nightjar.

June 15th

At 7.30 this morning, local farmer David White, son of the country diarist Jim White, was wandering around Bilting Meadow in search three missing Sussex calves which were hidden in the metre-high grass of the meadow. We searched the two hectare field for an hour before David decided a more productive course of action would be to carefully mow the field, produce a crop of hay, and find the calves in the process. These fields consist of 'semi-improved' grassland which has been ploughed in the past, cut for for hay or silage and occasionally sprayed and fertilised, as opposed to 'unimproved' pasture which has developed directly from woodland clearance or drainage to create a species-rich grassland. Semi-improved grassland is, though, far from being devoid of wild flowers. Today we saw birds foot trefoil, common sorrel, sheep sorrel, oxeye daisies, buttercups, as well as a prolific range of meadow grasses in full flower. Most of the grasses are native and include coxfoot carrying tufts of flower heads, crested dogs tail, timothy, ryegrass, couch, sweet vernal grass, common bent with its loose fronds of widely spaced seed heads, and the violet plume of Yorkshire Fog. Identification of grasses is never straightforward but the job is easier when they are in flower. Across Trimworth and Bilting Meadows there is a pinky purple haze from flower heads en masse, in fact a healthy meadow is rarely green but a mosaic of colours. Where the meadow lies wetter, as in Kitchen Meadow, we find stubborn horsetail and soft rush growing in long, dark-green spikes from large tussocks.

There are 160 species of grass indigenous to, or naturalised in Britain, forming the most important family of flowering plants. In turn, they support a huge diversity of animal life. The Offwell Woodland and Wildlife Trust estimate that 2 hectares of grassland can contain a ton of insects, and an acre of hay meadow may contain 2.25 million spiders, each eating two insects a week for six months, i.e. 108 million insects! Long may these habitats, threatened by agricultural intensification and development, survive to produce food sources for birds, amphibians, reptiles and invertebrates as well as providing the kind of visual stimulus that we enjoy wandering around in search of lost calves. The richness of these meadow grasslands reminds me of Thoreau's observation that 'heaven is under our feet, as well as over our heads'.

June 16th

Cleaver, sticky willie, everlasting friendship, sticky weed, catch weed, robin-run-the-hedge are all common names for goose grass, one of the least attractive members of the rubiaceae family. I speak with feeling after trying to strim the dense tangled mass in long grass between the ponds, becoming covered in leaves, seeds, stalling the strimmer and choking up the cutting head with what seem like strips of Velcro. Its species name 'aparine' comes from the Greek meaning to seize, and it does so through being covered with small hooks that cling to fur and fabric. Each plant can produce over 3000 seeds which withstand the winter and get a head start on plant competitors in the spring, growing to the height of 2 metres and dragging down the plants into which it climbs. It's not all bad. It has medicinal and perfumery applications and the dye has been used to produce the scarlet of soldiers' uniforms and give certain cheeses a richer shade of red or orange. The fruits have been used on the tips of lace needles to protect the fingers of lace workers, and there are even accounts of the plant being used for making beer in Staffordshire. It also provides great amusement for my grandchildren who drape it on unsuspecting grandad and can hardly contain their glee when I 'unexpectedly' find it hours later. (I remember, as a child, putting a hard-boiled egg in my grandmother's hat as she dozed on the beach at Sea Palling. I chuckled for hours watching it roll backwards and forwards around the rim. Being the butt of childhood pranks has always been an obligation of grandparents!)

June 17th

We have our own rabbit warrens at Trimworth. I counted 28 rabbits in the corner of Great Tithe Field, basking in the evening sun, then hopping casually and contemptuously to the safety of their burrows in the dyke. In 1995, the year we moved to Trimworth, the house had been empty for five years and the fields around unused and overrun with rabbits. As we approached the deserted house from the drive they moved across the field towards the railway embankment like waves approaching a shore. Ted Hope, our shepherd neighbour, said he'd seen nothing like it since the 1950s. The rabbit, or coney, is one of the less acceptable Roman introductions, although for centuries the farming of rabbits on warrens was a profitable activity around large parts of the country, especially Norfolk. Kent was known for its black rabbits, the fur being used for hats and clothing. Warren Farm and Warren Wood are both places located within a few miles of us. Ted Hope's reference to the 1950s was significant because at that time rabbits in the wild were estimated at between 60 and 100 million, leading to the morally questionable introduction from France of the virus disease of myxamotosis. They now number about 40 million, still enough to cause widespread destruction of crops along field margins. We have netted the whole boundary of our garden, but these clever little creatures burrow, climb or scramble their way in. The problem is not helped by widespread culling of foxes by local gamekeepers, thereby removing one of the main natural predators of the rabbit. We will just have to live with them, and balance the destruction they bring to the garden with the positive contribution they make in grazing the surrounding downs to create and maintain the diversity of plant and wildlife habitats in which orchids and butterflies thrive.

June 18th

In the meadow grass of Six Acre Field are rafts of spiders' webs like fine-spun silken thread. These are not the orb webs built as a vertical plane in radiating lines, but dense tents or sheets about 10 cm². Lurking to the side of each one is a large grey-brown spider about 20 mm long. This is the nursery web spider, not patrolling the web to catch prey, but standing guard over the large number of tiny spiderlings that could be seen moving within the webs. The female carries the eggs in a ball-shaped sac the size of a pea, and before they hatch, a silk tent is built to protect the eggs and the emerging spiderlings. The male

The nursery web spider standing guard over tiny spider-lings contained in its raft of fine-spun silken thread.

nursery web spider takes a great risk when mating and doesn't hang around after the act. In fact, he offers the female a food gift, such as a dead fly, in case he becomes the female's next meal.

On the stems of hedgerow and garden plants is a white frothy substance produced by the frog hopper or cuckoo spit insect in spring and early summer, coinciding with the first calls of the cuckoo. The frog hopper is related to the aphid and it can hop frog-like over considerable distances. They are no friend of the fruit grower because they extract sap and carry viruses harmful to crops. The excess undigested sap is mixed with a secretion from abdominal glands and frothed up to give the spittle.

As a scientist by training I have been firmly persuaded by the need to use scientific names for plants, guided by a single set of rules accepted throughout the world and constantly updated. It is a system which avoids duplication and confusion, for example the English bluebell in Scotland is known as the wild hyacinth, a completely unrelated plant. On the other hand I love the charmingly descriptive use of common names which contribute richly to our vocabulary. Over the generations vernacular names have been introduced which are descriptive, witty and evocative. The dandelion was described by Shakespeare as 'chimney sweepers' because of its brush-like seed clocks. But this is one of dozens of novel local names for the dandelion, including 'devils milk plant', 'lions teeth', 'clocks and watches', 'wet weed' and 'priests crown'. Richard Mabey celebrates these common names as, "a kind of time capsule, a record of the powers of observation and literary inventiveness of ordinary people." During the 19th century many moths and butterflies also acquired common names such as the 'red admiral', so-called because the patterns on its wings resembled a naval flag. The 'drinker' moth gets its name from its dew-drinking habits, a much more pleasing and memorable name then Piludoria potatoria. 'Old lady' was so called because its wing pattern was thought to resemble the dark shawls worn by elderly Victorian ladies. 'Mother Shipton' refers to the witch-like profile of a legendary prophetess who lived in a cave in Yorkshire. The use of such common names also enriches the study of fungi. Why would the highly poisonous 'destroying angel' be so described? Who was slippery Jack? Would the field guide name of Amanita phalloides have saved lives if it had been better known as death cap?

So the use of scientific names avoids confusion, duplication and ambiguity, but it is the common names which are memorable, fascinating and rich. "Here are wild organisms' hues, habits, habitats, histories and humans' histories and curiosity, too. It's not stretching meanings to say that the vernacular lexicon is part of the ecosystem, a living and growing web which links us with all other species." (Richard Mabey)

This evening we walked across the Wye Downs, an area of chalk grassland and woodland with spectacular views over Romney Marsh to the Kent coast and the Weald. Cut into the escarpment are steep valleys formed during the last Ice Age when freeze-thaw action on the chalk surface caused meltwater torrents to carry away chalk fragments to the bottom of the scarp. The Devil's Kneading Trough is the best example, its name referring to the deep bowl shape of the feature. The prefix 'devil' probably refers to land that was impossible to farm, let alone plough, because of its steepness.

June 20th

The downs here are an extremely rich grassland habitat of wild flowers and fine grasses. There are 19 different species of orchid, the pyramid orchid being most

In the rich grassland habitat are patches of white and red clover, the deep violet heads of self-heal and the yellow flower spikes of agrimony.

prolific on this walk. We saw patches of golden birds foot trefoil, each flower head made up of six flowers, some streaked with orange and red, (eggs and bacon). There are herbs of marjoram and wild thyme and sheep sorrel, not welcomed by farmers because the oxalic acid can reduce blood calcium levels and lead to milk fever. Elsewhere there are bedstraws and plantain; vetches abound, set in patches of white and red clover. White flower heads of the yarrow are now a common sight. Less common is the looser inflorescence of dropwort, like a small meadowsweet, with its deep rooting system reaching down into moisture. Its finely cut fern-like leaves form a rosette from which the spike rises to 30 cm, ending with a spray of creamy white scented flower. What a perfect accompaniment to the pyramid orchids, yellow flower spikes of agrimony and the deep violet heads of self-heal, all flowering profusely nearby. These wild flowers have attracted dozens of bird species and a wide range of butterflies such as the Adonis blue, a warmth loving species preferring sheltered South facing slopes on the chalk down land.

June 21st

It is the summer solstice, the longest day of the year. 'Barnaby bright, all day and no night'. Barnaby refers to St Barnabas, said to have given up all his possessions to raise funds for the Christian movement and considered to be the 13th Apostle. The rest of the phrase refers to the summer solstice when the axis of the earth is inclined towards the sun in the northern hemisphere, giving the longest period of daylight. How opportune that (supposedly) 5 billion years ago, a planet hit the Earth and tipped its axis to a 23.5° tilt. Less, and we would be colder and darker all year round; a little more, and we would have seasonal extremes; and no collision would have given us no seasonal variety at all. The solstice has led to festivals, gatherings and rituals all celebrating the incredible strength of the sun and the divine powers that create life. For pagans, it was a point in the wheel of the year when deities were at the height of their power, creating the fruits of the earth. At 4:52 am on this day a cheer will rise up from 20,000 people gathered overnight at Stonehenge to witness views of the sun rising over the Hele Stone, (Helios).

We are five nights from having a full moon, enough light on a cloudless evening to potter around the garden as the light falls around us, celebrating the fullness of the garden at this peak of the year; or to walk along the river through the tall grasses and rising mists to the owl box. It will not get properly dark, but the business of the day is done, the evening comes, and the fields are still.

June 22nd

My despondency and pessimism a few months ago, following days of hauling rubbish out of the river and clearing up after thoughtless campers, has been replaced by a more optimistic, upbeat mood following the visit of 20 brownies from the 1st Godmersham pack. They were bright-eyed and sharp-minded inquisitive little girls, full of wonder about the natural world. Together we saw newly fledged swallows playing 'follow the leader' on short hesitant flights from the barn, watched goldfinch bringing food to nestlings in the neatest of nests in an apple tree, saw trout moving gracefully above the river gravels of a crystal-clear stream, studied a kestrel hovering over the flowering meadow grasses, its head perfectly motionless as it fought to maintain height and position in a gusty wind, examined the jawbone of a rabbit, leapt at the sudden flight of a pheasant as it exploded out of a hedge, watched bees coming and going from a hole in a dry bank. . . and much more.

Children need this first-hand physical experience, this direct contact with the natural world rather than the sterile, remote, 'virtual' field experiences offered in the classroom. Only by first-hand experience will children learn to explore, question, discover and appreciate connections in the real world. This fantastic heritage of eager young enthusiasts is being supported by innovative science and nature programmes on radio and television, together with the work of wildlife trusts and other voluntary associations. We have to nurture this enthusiasm by providing good environmental education in schools which must not be squeezed out of the curriculum by the 'more important' demands of teaching targets in other subjects. The sense of wonder, imagination and creativity which these young brownies showed today has given me a sense of optimism that they will develop into adults who understand and care about environmental stewardship.

June 23rd.

The garden and countryside seem flattened with heat and the brightness of the sun. The air is hot, heavy and still, so we turn for the relative cool of Oxen Leas Wood. The only sound is the melancholy repetitive call of wood pigeons and the buzz of flies. Along the riverside, fluffy white seeds of willow are blowing from the trees, floating on the water surface and covering the paths. There is a rich, heavy fragrance descending down from the limes in the drive, produced by small nectar-rich flowers growing in clusters, each with a bract acting as a mechanism for seed dispersal. This lime is 'tilia cordata', the small-leaved lime, frequently used to line drives leading to houses, or seen in parkland settings and churchyards. They invariably sprout many twigs from the trunk bowl unlike the large- leaved lime and they also attract aphids, the source of the sticky honeydew droppings which are a problem in lime-lined urban streets under which cars are parked. But a richly flavoured honey is produced from the flowers. Try adding the flowers to your bath to quell hysteria or steep in hot water for a tea to relieve anxiety! The wood itself is easily worked and has acoustic properties which make it popular in the making of guitars and wooden instruments. Another tree displaying an interesting stage of its seasonal cycle is the horse chestnut, also frequently planted as an ornamental tree. The candelabras of white and pink flowers have given way to the small spiked fruits which contain the conkers that will soon be prized by young children.

It is Midsummer's Night and the eve of St John, born on 24 June, the patron saint of farriers, tailors and missionaries. We are halfway through a year which began with the same John appearing as one of the two faces on the image of Janus, chosen by the Romans as the God of the first calendar month. It is also the night of a Midsummer Night's Dream and the night when magical plants like St John's Wort were thrown into the purifying flames of Midsummer bonfires, watched over by witches and fairies. This prehistoric ritual was thought to protect crops and cattle from drought and pestilence.

It is 5.00am on a still morning with heavy dew on grasses and dripping from trees. Bodies of cows appear to be floating on the misty pastures of Bilting Meadow. Early sunlight filters through dew-laden flowery meadow grasses. It is a walk of sounds, as well as sights: anxious screeching from the nests of buzzards, geese calling as they fly high overhead, the rusty squawk of disturbed pheasants, the distant bellowing of a bull, the 'plop' of fish rising, a song thrush tuning up in the wood, warning chirps from wrens as Sam splashes along the edge of the dyke. And then the homecoming – Trimworth silhouetted in the rising sun, standing solidly on its river terrace as it has for centuries. The words of Tennyson in an extract from 'Palace of Art' make a perfect description of that moment.

> "An English home – grey twilight poured
> On dewy pastures, dewy trees
> Softer than sleep – all things in order stored,
> A haunt of ancient peace."

It is Midsummer's Day, one of the four 'quarter days' of the legal calendar, marking the important Christian festivals of St John's Day (June 25), Lady Day (March 25), Michaelmas (September 29), and Christmas Day. The quarter day was traditionally when accounts and rents were settled, and when magistrates would visit outlying districts to clear up debts and unresolved conflicts so they did not linger on after quarter sessions. They have been observed since at least the Middle Ages. These days also coincide with the solstices and equinoxes; the word solstice is from the

It is 5.00am on a still morning, with early sunlight filtering through dew-laden flowery meadow grasses.

Latin 'sol' or sun and 'sistere,' to stand still. Today, the summer solstice marks the apparent movement of the sun's path where it 'stands still' over the Tropic of Cancer before turning back towards the Equator. The word 'tropic' is from the Greek 'tropos', to turn.

In the white garden are tall spires of foxtail lilies in full flower. Bees, heavy with pollen and intoxicated by nectar are bouncing clumsily off the spires like furry balls in a pinball game. How they even fly is a mystery to me with their large round bodies and tiny flapping wings. It is a trundling, laboured, inelegant flight in appearance, described by Mark Cocker as being like a model- T Ford that has taken to the air. But the wing-beat of a bee is 200 beats a second. No wonder it is such a large insect; it must be a mass of muscle in order to power its flight. Slow motion filming reveals that at the end of each down beat, the wing twists over giving uplift on both up and down beat of the wing, so despite its lumbering appearance, it is one of the most sophisticated movers of our ecosystem, and furthermore it pollinates almost 75% of the world's food crops.

If bees and other pollinators such as hover flies, wasps, moths and butterflies were to disappear completely, the cost to the UK economy is estimated to be over £450 million a year, or 13% of the country's income from farming. In recognition of this threat, a £10 million initiative has been launched involving universities, the Food and Environmental Research Agency, the National Environment Research Council and the Centre for Food Ecology and Hydrology. The research will bring new skills in genetics and epidemiology to address the complex problem of the decline of pollinators. Reasons for the decline have been well reported by the media and include attacks by mites (the varroa destructor), viruses, bacterial species and fungi (nosema), and pesticides (neonicotinoids), leading to the collapse of colonies. Moth and butterfly declines could be explained by habitat decline, loss of flower sources and of course pesticides, leading to brain disorders. The problems seem so numerous and complex that the £10 million grant will require further substantial inputs. The results of this research will be followed closely because bees and the countryside are inseparable. We are dependent on these 'singing masons building roofs of gold.'

It had been a hot, oppressive night and by 10 .00 am the natural world seemed to have retreated to the cool of the hedge, wood and riverbank. In the hot, still air above the meadows, small buff-coloured moths drifted between the flowering heads of grasses. High above, the skylark poured out its exuberant song of trilling and babbling and cascading notes, and a heron slowly lifted off from the river edge to begin its silent, laboured flight across the meadow. The sultry stillness was abruptly disturbed by a sheep, crashing wildly out of the river, emerging into the field with a 'coat' of goosegrass and river weed around its shoulders. The rest of the flock were slumped in a heap in the shade of the willows and looked mildly bemused. In the dyke the long narrow leaves of curled dock reach nearly 2 metres in height and the vigorous spreading roots of rose bay willow herb have generated long shoots which will shortly produce attractive spires of pink flower, hence its alternative name of 'fireflower.' It is also known locally as 'bombweed', due to its rapid colonisation of soil disturbed by bombing in the Second World War. At three o'clock the temperature reached over 30°C and the dark blue/black wings of the male 'beautiful demoiselle' fluttered over the ponds. Warm temperatures will guarantee their continued spectacular presence well into August. Also prominent, was our most common dragonfly at Trimworth, the fat, blue and fast broad bodied chaser, a stark contrast to the gentle grace of the damselflies.

In the relative evening cool we made a return visit to Yockletts Bank a nearby area of ancient mixed woodland owned by the Kent Wildlife Trust and renowned for its rich collection of orchids. En route we passed along the top of Wye Downs and met Fran Thompson, employed by Butterfly Conservation as Project Officer. The previous night she had set up lights on the Wye Downs Nature Reserve to attract and collect moths. Moths are an essential part of the food chain for birds, bats and mammals and are crucial pollinators of plants. Despite their importance many species are declining through changing countryside and climate. This makes the work of Fran and Butterfly Conservation so valuable. The result of her overnight find was impressive and we inspected a number of species in large plastic containers, such as the clouded buff with its orange/red veins on the forward wing; the pink and green, fast-flying elephant hawk moth, which had been feeding on bedstraws at night; the delicate green of the light emerald with its feint white cross-lines; the chinese character, which at rest looks like a bird dropping; the very pretty peach blossom with its deep pink patches on brown wings. We also saw scorched wing, ghost moth, golden Y and longhorn, all of which were released into the hedge later in the evening to resume their night flights. The experience made us aware that moths are not the drab, brown and boring alternative to beautiful, coloured butterflies, but are strikingly varied and beautiful in their own right.

After this memorable encounter, we left for the SSSI at Yockletts Bank, which turned out to be equally rewarding. The sun was low in the sky, and a golden light filtered through the beech leaves of this ancient woodland, giving shifting patterns of light and shade on the forest floor. Our search revealed six orchids: twayblade, common spotted, white spotted, the vanilla scented greater butterfly, sweetly scented fragrant, and the foxy smelling pyramidal. In addition, we saw stinking iris foetidissima, the beetroot red flowers of hedge woundwort, hairy St John's wort and common cow- wheat. It had been a hot, tiring but stimulating day, ending with a drive through landscapes coolly lit by the pale pink full moon of June, traditionally known as the strawberry or mead moon.

June 27th

Flying in small groups over the fescue, bents and other meadow grasses, is the meadow brown butterfly. These pretty orange/ brown butterflies have a black eye-spot on their fore wingtip with a single white spot as the pupil. Since the early flush of tortoiseshell, peacocks, brimstone and orange-tips there have been strangely few sightings of butterflies. I would have expected skippers, fritillaries and more.

The delicate green of the light emerald moth with its faint white cross-lines.

Flying in small groups over the meadow grasses is the meadow brown butterfly.

Butterflies are very sensitive to environmental change and I hope their lack of appearance is a reflection on my observation skills rather than adverse changes in grazing and woodland habitats. One little moth which cannot escape attention at the moment is the cinnabar. There is no other species like it with its unmistakable red forewings, the same colour as the mineral cinnabar, the ore from which mercury is refined. They can be seen feeding on the leaves of ragwort and are most frequent on rabbit-grazed grassland, a habitat which dominates the field margins around Trimworth. The distinctive larvae with yellow and black hoops will soon be feeding gregariously and greedily on the ragwort, but avoided by birds because, like the ragwort itself, the caterpillars are poisonous. An equally imposing caterpillar is feeding on the verbascum or mullein plant, reducing it to tatters during June and July. When fully fed, the fat caterpillar can reach up to 5 cm long with striking yellow and black markings. They will go into the soil and may take up to 4 years to pupate inside silk cocoons. The adult moth, the mullion moth, emerges in April as a very ordinary-looking brown, nocturnal moth in contrast to its striking caterpillar stage.

Kent has virtually a complete coverage of Tithe maps, usually at a scale of 20 inches to 1 mile, providing a fascinating picture of the rural landscape in the 1840s. Tithes were 'payments in kind' of a 10th of the annual produce of land, paid to the parson of the parish. Under the 1836 Tithe Commutation Act, payments became monetary, based on a seven-year average of crop prices taken across the country. These tithes were apportioned among the landowners according to their acreage and land quality, hence the process required the drawing of accurate maps to show land ownership and land-use, giving a detailed picture of the agricultural economy of the parish. The Tithe Map for Crundale parish was drawn in 1839, and one of the most interesting features is the field names, giving evidence of former landowners, land-use, prominent features of geology, soil and landscape. Close to Trimworth is Kitchen Meadow; the names Little Tithe and Great Tithe Fields are clearly relevant to the purpose of the survey; Tye Wood suggests, 'an outlying common', frequently used in southern England. There are names indicating the former use of land, such as Strawberry Fields, Oast Garden, Hop Garden field. Sometimes family names are used; others indicate the importance of the church or local trades and industries which have left their mark on the landscape. Animals feature here as well, such as Oxen Leas Wood or Hog Spot. Bridge Meadow (formerly Trimworth Meadow on the 1720s estate maps) indicates a once important crossing point on the Stour, linking the parishes of Wye and Crundale. Occasionally you will find the use of local humour, as in the case of the name Thousand Acre Field for a very small field in Cholesbury in the Chilterns or the whimsical use of faraway places like World's End or Zululand. One is left in no doubt about land quality of the field, Starvation Hill! The tithe map is one of the most complete records ever made of agriculture and gives us a valuable snapshot of the community and its social history over 150 years ago.

June 28th

Today the Kentish Stour Countryside Project began checking the contents of about 40 barn owl boxes spread along the River Stour. There is one close to us on the river which we watched late in the evening in early June and saw owls regularly arriving with food. Since then we have seen or heard little to suggest this box was still in active use, and assumed it had been abandoned. Today I watched the team as the 'dolly' was placed over the owl entrance, then the ladder was climbed and the door opened carefully. We were amazed and delighted to find five chicks and a freshly killed field vole in the box. The eggs of these chicks had been laid at intervals of 2 to 3 days, with the young hatching at two to three-day intervals (asynchronous hatching). This explains why the chicks are at different stages of development. The female does all the incubation and can sit continuously for nine weeks, becoming heavily soiled in the process. Sadly, this explains why many have been found drowned in steep-sided cattle troughs in an attempt to clean themselves.

Each fluffy white chick was gently lowered in a soft bag and placed on the grass. They were then weighed, measured and ringed. Weight ranged from 280g to 450g,

Each fluffy-white barn owl chick was gently lowered onto the grass to be weighed, measured and ringed.

suggesting ages of between 30 and 40 days. Weight on its own is not a good indicator of age, and is used in conjunction with the length of emerging feather quill. Three of these chicks had 25 mm of feather vane emerging, suggesting an age of 33 days. At this stage it is possible to sex the nestlings by the presence of spotting on the underside of the wing. All chicks had remarkably long legs and large talons, enabling them to catch prey at the base of deep vegetation soon after they have fledged. We were able to see the ear openings situated in the facial disc just behind the eyes, one higher than the other. This allows sound to reach the ears at slightly different times, giving an accurate fix on the sound source. The nest box also contained five dark grey owl pellets about the size of a golf ball and dark grey in colour. Prey is normally swallowed whole, with the fur, bones, teeth and feathers being regurgitated. In this case they are likely to contain remains of field voles, bank voles and mice. The field vole found in the box had bloodstains on its under-body suggesting the result of foot clenching with very sharp talons rather than pecking.

The young birds will fly clumsily at 54 days and more competently at 65 days. They will all leave the nest together, but survival rates are not good; it is likely that 75% of the young will die in the first year, with survivors living on for another 1 to 3 years. The smallest member of this brood was the most aggressive. Perhaps this explains the survival of this little fighter; the rest lay placidly in the grass with eyes half closed, enjoying the relative cool and freshness of the air before being put back carefully into the hot and foul smelling box.

The Barn Owl Trust reports experiments which confirms that the owl can locate and capture prey in total darkness using their hearing alone. Rough grassland of the river meadow, together with hedged field boundaries and dykes form an ideal habitat. A pair of owls will require up to 25 km of field edges and hedges containing suitable roosting sites. Trimworth and Bilting Meadows can supply this, so hopefully we will be able to see progress in these five chicks to the point when they leave the box together. Another owl box about half a kilometre downstream at Olantigh was found to be abandoned, the most likely reason being underweight of the female through food shortage.

We have heard the nightingale sing only twice this year, most recently at Yockletts Bank three days ago. The song is incomparable: a loud, rapid outburst of whistles, gurgles, and trills performed by the male only. There is sadness in the plaintive notes and deep passion in the rich liquid phrases, ending in a wonderful crescendo. Today, we heard birdsong which in my view comes close to the nightingale in its splendour. The sound belonged to the so-called 'northern nightingale' or blackcap, which is generally found in the margins of woodland settings containing both tall trees and bush shrubs, as in Tye Wood. Its song begins with a few chattering sounds, exploding into flute-like melodies with deep and beautiful notes. In 1774, Gilbert White described the performance of the blackcap in a letter to Thomas Pennant, "The blackcap has in common a full, sweet, deep, loud and wild pipe; yet that strain is of short continuance, and his motions are desultory; but when the bird sits calmly and engages in song in earnest, he pours forth very sweet, but inward melody, and

June 29th

expresses great variety of soft and gentle modulations, superior, perhaps, to those of any of our warblers, the nightingale excepted."

We may continue to hear both the nightingale and blackcap for a few weeks more, and then their songs will live on only in the memory until late spring next year. Soon the blackbird will fall silent until next January, except for their rattling alarm cries, and with the nesting season over, chaffinches will also stop singing soon, resuming their song next year at about the same time as the blackbird begins to sing. Robins are already quieter now, but will be heard again in September when they begin to establish their territorial claims for winter.

June 30th

The hedges around our garden are full of the noise of hungry nestlings, particularly blackbirds, dunnock, robin, wren and song thrush. Goldfinch have a neat, well-disguised nest in an apple tree, but the bright red face and yellow patch of the adult bird is difficult to conceal fully. The cup- shaped nest contains horsehair from Coco, dog hair from Sam, and plenty of wool lining from nearby sheep; perfect for the two-week incubation period undertaken by the female only. Now both parents are busy feeding young, and in another two weeks we hope to see the fledged chicks, less distinctive than the adults, without the red face. Our hedges contain five or six native species and are growing fast. We have to resist cutting with power tools between March and August, although, light pruning is acceptable. For some birds it is a long breeding season. Blackbirds can start breeding as early as February, having three broods lasting well into late summer or autumn.

House martins have been nesting on buildings around Trimworth, flying frequent trips between pond edge and eaves where the birds cling to the wall and plaster the mud into the face of the brick. Most of the nest building activity occurs in the morning, leaving the mud to harden off in the afternoon before applying another layer next day. The little hemispherical nests will be completed in about 10 days, during which we will hear the constant twittering calls between partners. They have a 'high altitude lifestyle', feeding on the wing and towering high in the air well above the level at which swallows feed. They are superb fliers, gliding, spiralling and diving in graceful arcs, distinguished from swallows by their white rumps and much shorter forked tail.

July

The second half of the year begins with July, the name chosen by Augustus to honour Julius Caesar who was born in this month. The Anglo-Saxons called it 'moed monad', or mead month, because the meadows were likely to be in full bloom. For the Greeks, the month was associated with 'dog days', to signify the hottest, most sultry days of the year. The labours of the month depicted in the illuminated manuscripts of the Books of Hours feature activities of harvesting using sickles, and sheep shearing with hand clippers, both tools almost unchanged in design since ancient times.

Two days after writing how seldom we hear the nightingale, it performed for us from the top of the field maple in Moat Field as we sat in the summerhouse on a still warm evening at about 10.00pm. It is a sublime song, almost painfully moving, a theme taken up by Keats in his famous poem, 'Ode to a Nightingale', in which he praises the bird, but links it with the transient nature of human experience. Our thoughts on hearing the song were closer to dreamy romanticism and peaceful contentment at the sheer joy of it. We felt highly favoured to be part of this virtuoso performance of liquid trills, aware of the declining numbers and contracting range of the nightingale, with surveys putting the number of singing males at no more than 6000. Descriptions of the song abound in music and literature, and most note how the power of the whole song is emphasised by dramatic pauses and periods of silence. Edward Thomas writes of the "full brimmed expectant silence....a downpour of rapidly repeated notes and the succeeding silence." H.E.Bates describes a tuning up of sounds, then "a flaring out in a moment into a crescendo of fire and honey, and then, abruptly, cut off again in the very middle of the phrase. And then comes the long, suspended wait for the phrase to be taken up again, the breathless hushed interval that is so beautiful." Whenever we've heard the nightingale, it becomes the unforgettable song of a particular place in a particular moment, when we seem remote from our surroundings and become 'free citizens of eternity.'

Did they fall or were they pushed? At this time of year, sparrow and starling nestlings frequently fall from nests under gutters and eaves around the house. Some are fortunate to land in soft shrubs and are found crawling around the borders. Others are killed or injured in the fall. In some cases the nestlings may be ill, deformed or dead, the parents letting nature take its course. Today, two young sparrows had fallen or been ejected from a nest, and were found sitting in a large pot of summer bedding plants. They seemed in a poor shape and were given rest and recuperation in a quiet, well ventilated, warm, darkened room and offered food from tweezers every few hours. After 3 or 4 days they had recovered well and could be handed over to the Wildlife Rehabilitation for eventual release.

Unless injured, the RSPCA advice is that very young animals are better cared for by their natural parents. The RSPB advice is also to leave young fledglings alone and let them hop into low branches or undergrowth and wait for parents to find and feed them. Quite often, by the time you return, they will have moved away. Some injuries often do merit intervention, for example, a young green woodpecker was found

The labours of the month illustrated in the Books of Hours feature activities of harvesting and sheep shearing, using tools almost unchanged since ancient times.

The garden has reached a peak of form and colour.

semiconscious on the grass beneath a French window, which it had obviously 'head-butted' in an attempt to 'fly' through the reflection of trees in the window. It was unable to support itself and we gave it a warm temporary home in a large cardboard box lined with soft tissue and offered it food and water. The following morning, it was more aware and was taken to the Wildlife Sanctuary and later released. Moorhen chicks frequently find their way into the sunken garden and are unable to escape. They are usually caught, released into the rushes around the bottom pond, where they scuttle off across the algae into more dense growth. Whether these vulnerable little creatures will survive in the wild world after their frightening experience is questionable, but at least they stand a chance

July 3rd

With the passing of the summer solstice, the garden temporarily moves into a slower gear, and so do I! The garden has reached a peak of form and colour which I have rarely seen before. I am astonished at the colour combinations and the fullness of flower in roses, peonies, poppies, delphiniums and fox-tail lilies. It makes me acutely aware of the hard-won progression from a weed-rich, flint-ridden field into a beautiful garden. But as we pass the summer solstice and move into the second half of the year, the garden begins to look a little tired. The foxtail lilies and peonies are finished; every morning I dead-head roses and collect buckets of limp, brown, faded petals; the lawns are bare and brown from drought; the soil cracked and baked dry; gaps appear in borders; seed heads of oriental poppies and delphiniums droop over their supports. In Katherine Swift's wonderful book, 'The Morville Hours', which I consider to be one of the great explorations of the gardening year, she talks about the garden in July "… sliding from juvenility to senescence without passing through maturity." I know this is only the end of an act and the rest of the play will continue with another cast of performers, including grasses, dahlias, achillea, mullein, fuchsias, roses, penstemon and verbena. In our garden planning we have worked hard to achieve a continuous thread of succession planting, but like any show there are highlights, and at Trimworth, one of these is June.

As the day progresses, the mood of garden and countryside is affected by changes in light. In the early midsummer morning of dew and mist, colours are fresh, subdued, diffuse, and the scents are damp and earthy. By noon, in the glaring brightness of a hot sun, the colours and scents are strong and vigorous. Shadows are sharper, "sharp as a sickle is the edge of shade and shine", in the words of the Victorian poet George Meredith; but this sharp contrast is softened when clouds pass the sun to give changing patterns of light and shadow. Evening brings coolness and a glorious golden light contrasting with lengthening shadows. It is when the countryside and garden look their most alluring; but the mood shifts again as the light drains out of the sky and dusk arrives with its seductive cool charms and mysteries.

July 4th

The day begins with the unwelcome sound of trail bikes roaring along the A28 en route for the byways and footpaths of Crundale Downs above Trimworth. The ridge walk from the church and the tracks through Warren Wood becomes hazardous, and the summer sounds of birdsong are drowned out. The quick wit and discerning observations of Roger Deakin sum up a similar situation in his native Suffolk. "We have sunsets worthy of Turner to a soundtrack of sterile adolescent testosterone." I wish I had known this enigmatic character whose sharp-eyed, perceptive thoughts, feelings and impressions about the natural world make his little book 'Notes From Walnut Tree Farm' such a charming, eloquent and amusing read. The originality of his writing is the result of a closeness to, and a curiosity about the natural world which few writers have been able to replicate.

There are over 250 species of native bee, and 200 of them are described as solitary bees: that is, they do not live in colonies like the 'social' honey bees and bumblebees. In the spring, the earth path between the wood and river was dotted with mini –volcanoes, little mounds of soft brown earth with a hole in the middle. They represent the home of the miner bee, resembling the honeybee in appearance but with bright orange-brown pollen brushes under their abdomen. They are very effective and useful pollinators. The female will dig the nest, usually in soft soil along paths or in lawns, then collect nectar and pollen to store at the bottom of the tunnels several centimetres below the ground. The nest is sealed, leaving the young to fend for themselves.

The rose garden reveals evidence of activity by another solitary bee. Many leaves have a smooth semi-circular cut about three-quarters of an inch in diameter from the edge of the leaves: the work of the leaf cutter bee. Gardeners should not consider this bee as a threat, but as a minor curiosity. The nibbled plant will not become defoliated or die, neither are the bees aggressive. They are extremely important pollinators. As with the miner bee, it is the female which does all the rearing, including creating nests in soft rotted wood or pithy stems, providing food and laying 35 to 40 eggs. The following spring the larvae pupate and become adult bees. A different kind of nest, but with a very similar life cycle is built by the red mason bee, usually in old, soft mortar such as the lime mortar. Some solitary bees, however, do not build their own nests, but like cuckoos will lay their eggs in the nests of bumblebees. Having killed the bumblebee queen, the larvae eat from the pollen and nectar food store provided by the host worker bees.

'Ratty' is back in the news again today with the release of 600 captive-bred water voles on the River Dore in Herefordshire. The Game and Wildlife Conservation Trust confirmed that the charismatic 'ratty' is in deep trouble as the fastest declining mammal in the UK, disappearing from 85% of sites in just seven years. Predation by American mink has had an overwhelming impact together with degradation of riverside habitats. The release of these water voles is part of a programme costing £1.5 million. Should we question the cost of restoring this native species at a time of unprecedented cuts in public services? The Project Officer, Dr Jonathan Reynols is convinced that the current threat to water voles is so critical that it could lead to their extinction, and once they are gone, they will be gone forever. The loss is most effectively expressed by an

American botanist, in an analogy reported in the Independent by Michael McCarthy. Living animal and plant species could be considered as resembling parts of a dismantled Boeing 737, laid out on the ground. If 10% of the parts were removed, would we still be happy to fly in the plane? Is planet Earth safe with 10% of its parts missing? The media seem preoccupied with concerns over the loss of big beast icons like whales, tigers, gorillas, polar bears, but we are in danger of becoming indifferent to the smaller, but equally important, elements of our natural world such as wild flowers, birds, butterflies, bees- and water voles, all of which I hope our grandchildren will continue to observe first-hand in these meadows by the river.

July 7th

A strong warm wind sends wave-like motions sweeping through the meadow grasses, gently swaying the supple willow trees on the woodland margins. This is an opportunity for the buzzard to demonstrate its aerial dominance by hovering, not as steadily as a kestrel, over the tallest pines or lazily drifting in wide circles around the woodland perimeters, ignoring the incessant 'cawing' and frantic wing beats of crows vainly trying to contest the buzzard's territorial claims. In contrast, a flock of long-tailed tits bounces merrily between the willows with a chorus of piping notes. Unlike other tits they form family flocks, consisting of the pair which bred together last summer and their surviving offspring. It is the whole family which helps to feed the nestlings, giving greater survival chances and allowing parents to concentrate on rearing the family. Nest building will have been an exhaustive process; it is estimated that the long-tailed tits will fly hundreds of kilometres to build and insulate the vulnerable bag-shaped nests of moss and lichen lined with feathers. Their charming companionship is much appreciated by us as they stream from tree to tree in search of insects. I wonder wistfully whether they appreciate my company as much as I enjoy theirs. Later in the morning I heard the sound of roaring chainsaws working in Tye Wood. I hope that the operators are sympathetic to the well-being of the inhabitants of the trees and the forest floor.

July 8th

Jack and I have been turning log piles under the garden hedge near the pond looking for beetles. We were rewarded by the intimidating sight of a stag beetle with its large mandibles or jaws, impressively serrated with projecting spurs which it uses to wrestle other males in protecting its territory. It is the largest and heaviest of Britain's beetles, up to 75 mm long, and despite its ungainly appearance the male stag beetle can actually fly, often at dusk, on warm, humid, thundery summer evenings. In Medieval times, the stag beetle was thought to be able to summon thunder and lightning. In Germany, it is associated with Thor, God of Thunder, and if placed on your head it would act as protection from the storm. Jack was not prepared to put this theory to the test. The stag beetle is actually a gentle giant, entirely harmless and great for gardens because they eat lots of rotting wood and return minerals to the soil. Their life cycle is long, approximately 7 years from egg to adult, but after emerging as adults, most live only a few weeks, and few will survive the winter. During their short adult life, males will 'sun' themselves to gain strength for the main evening event of flying in search of a mate. Their future is under threat from reduction of woodland habitats and the removal of rotting wood to 'tidy up'

We watched sticklebacks dart over the stony bed in shallow water.

woodlands. They are also affected by predators such as cats, foxes, kestrel and magpies. The People's Trust for Endangered Species conducts stag beetle hunts on a national scale, recording and mapping distributions, mostly in south-east England. (www.ptes.org). Chalk is not generally favoured by the stag beetle, except along riverbanks and damp areas. Its future has recently been given a welcome boost by being declared a priority species in the UK Biodiversity Action Plan.

July 9th

It is the hottest day of the year so far and so we made for the river to take pleasure in three very different experiences during the day. Several weeks without rain has left the river level very low, making it possible to wade from Kitchen Meadow, under the railway bridge and into Bridge Meadow. This is a very rare opportunity, the water was only 25cms deep, but shelving suddenly and dangerously to over 2m around the bridge piers, where the floodwaters of winter had deeply scoured the riverbed. Shallow water riffled and rippled over beds of rounded flint pebbles, except in places where generations of railway workers had disposed of stone, broken bricks and iron bars under the bridge to save carting them off-site. Moorhens and ducks were startled into flight by our unfamiliar presence, blackbirds sounded the alarm and pigeons clattered out of riverside bushes and perches under the bridge. Along the banks were the attractive pink flowers of the highly invasive Himalayan balsam, dotted against the towering dark-green banks of nettles and hemlock.

Two hours later, and another river experience as little Edward stood further downstream in the middle of the river with water up to his knees, holding his father's hand and watching the antics of Sam in the water. This was his first venture into river water and I will remember the moment as long as I live. We watched sticklebacks dart over the stony bed in shallow water. The usual silver-grey colour of the males has become transformed into golds and emeralds, the spawning livery of early summer. They are barometers of river quality, their presence being a good indicator of the healthy state of the water. Bright-green weeds were in effortless motion, wispy cirrus clouds in a deep blue sky were reflected on the water, and yolk-yellow buds of water-lilies lined the river bank.

At 10 o'clock in the evening, the river at the same spot gave us our third river experience of the day. We heard the sound of fish jumping and saw the river boiling with their movement. The barn owls glided low over the water meadows to their clamouring chicks in the owl box, and below, two swans with their four new cygnets ghosted quietly by. This field by the river is in many respects ordinary; there are thousands like it in Britain, but today, it became a very special, precious place providing unforgettable memories.

July 10th

I spent an hour lying in the meadow to watch the layers of life in the calcareous grassland habitat of Six Acre Meadow. Most of the grasses are perennials, sprouting new shoots from underground rhizomes each year and staying green all year round. The top layer consisted of the seed heads and flowers of grasses providing seeds and nectar for birds, bees, butterflies, moths, hoverflies and drone flies. I then became painfully aware of another visitor to this habitat-the dreaded horsefly. It is also a nectar feeder but unlike other insects which emit a buzz or hum, the horsefly is silent and arrives unnoticed to do its nasty business, administering a bite from piercing mouthparts, and leaving a small hole in the skin and a large swelling to follow. They manage to find the most tender spot on humans as well as horses and it is the female which does the damage, while the male collects the nectar. Little goldfinches arrive in a swarm to sway around on the seed heads of thistles, knapweeds and grasses, but it is the moths, butterflies and damselflies, which are most numerous at this level, dancing and fluttering in delicate spirals. Our movement through the grass sends up little puffs of buff coloured moths- meadow brown, small heath and peacock butterflies flop and flutter by in the warm sun, putting in mind the words of the French poet, Le Brun, that "the butterfly is a flying flower; the flower a tethered butterfly."

At a slightly lower layer, meadow grasshoppers and bush crickets are active in the hot sun. The grasshopper is a herbivore, feeding on stalks of grasses, voracious eaters consuming an average 16 times their own weight. They catapult themselves around at speed, leaping 20 times their body length (using the same ratio, I could manage a leap of 40 yards!). The sight and sound of grasshoppers is a summer delight. Their 'voices' are generated by rubbing their hind legs against their fore-wings, and they are easier to hear than see because their colour blends so effectively into their environment. At the lowest layer in the grassland is the grass litter occupied by ants, ground beetles, dung beetles, flies and spiders all breaking down and recycling plant and animal materials and providing food for creatures at a higher level in the food chain.

These unimproved calcareous grasslands bordering the river are part of a low-input/low-output system which is being put at risk by the introduction of higher stocking levels of sheep and cattle. This increasing intensification is often accompanied by the introduction of special cultivated grass varieties rather than native species, giving lower levels of diversity in flora and fauna. Over 95% of the meadows present in 1940 have now disappeared, replaced by improved grassland which covers over 5 million hectares in Britain. There are some encouraging signs through agricultural subsidy schemes like Environmental Stewardship, delivered by Natural England. For example on our lowland pastures grazing must be regulated to achieve an average sward height in the growing season and avoid under- and over- grazing. Other conditions relate to the timing of hedge cutting, and the use of pesticides and machines to ensure grassland is managed in a way that benefits wildlife and landscape in these treasured environments.

July 11th

The movement of wind through the riverbank willows produces a similar gentle, wistful, dream-like motion in the branches of the trees, to that of the water eddies through the submerged weeds of the river. Yesterday I wrote about life below the level of flowering grasses. Today, sitting on the streambed, I examined life below the water level, focusing particularly on submerged vegetation. We are in the middle reach of the River Stour, an unspoilt lowland chalk stream flowing in broad meander loops over beds of flinty gravel, sand or silt. The lush vegetation is dominated by various types of water crowfoot, all members of the buttercup family with variable leaves, depending on whether the plant is floating or submerged. Water starwort is another aquatic perennial with slender branching stems, forming a dense mat of green, slowly moving in the water. The tiny star-like white flowers have just finished but the plant continues to provide a home for small aquatic invertebrates and their larvae, all food for the water vole. The milfoils, another lime-loving water weed, have feathery bright green leaves with small pinkish flowers, rather like hornworts or the flowerless stoneworts. Parrots feather is a milfoil with a bad reputation; it is native to South America and very invasive, but has an important role in providing a good habitat for nymphs of dragonflies and damselflies, as well as snails and water spiders. Two swans appear with only one cygnet (where are the other four?). The adult swans are constantly dredging the bottom for water plants and snails. Mallards and tufted ducks drift slowly downstream in the still shallows of the water's edge guzzling duckweed. With the air temperature at 31°, I'm reluctant to leave this cool green environment, but I think the anglers who pay substantial sums for the privilege of catching trout would be less than enthralled to see this large half-submerged form in their trout-rich chalk stream.

When World Population Day was declared by the United Nations in 1987, the world population had grown to 5 billion. In 2011, the figure reached 7 billion, and is projected to reach 9 billion by 2050, bringing further questions about the sustainability of global life-support systems upon which we and the natural world all depend. Is it perverse and far-fetched to suggest that the global trend of burgeoning population has relevance to the river meadows at Trimworth? We have all become more aware of development pressures reducing the amount of countryside and wildlife habitats: the intensification of agriculture which has reduced biodiversity in the countryside: problems of waste disposal leading to pollution of air and water; and there is evidence that global warming is having an impact on the timing of naturally occurring events. These changes inevitably have an impact on all ecosystems whatever their scale, but the subject is extremely complex and multifaceted. There is clearly a need to consider material consumption as well as population growth; they cannot be seen as separate issues. As Paul Ehrlich, a figurehead of the debate, concluded "In one sense, it is the consumption that damages our life-support system, as opposed to the actual number of people expanding. But both multiply together."

Whatever the strength of the relationship between global trends and local impacts, I am reassured to hear that the Royal Society has announced the launch of a major study into human population growth and how it may affect social, environmental and economic development in the coming decades. The working group will be multidisciplinary and multicultural. The subject is hugely controversial from religious, cultural, economic and political points of view, with the questioners often being accused of racialism and colonialism. But the case for objective, scientific analysis is needed if policymakers are to be guided in making effective choices, which in the end may have repercussions on the environmental sustainability of these meadows by the river. Population growth and the environment should not be considered as two separate issues.

July 13th

Heavy overnight rain, after weeks of almost unbroken sunshine, has transformed the mood and colour of the countryside. Sharpness, radiance and clarity in both colour and light have been replaced by subdued and softer tones of greys and greens. Smoke from a dampened bonfire hangs on the trees; the tall pines in the wood are shrouded in low cloud; water drops heavily as leaves shed the rain; the river flows full and fast, and ducklings struggle to keep up with their unconcerned and impassive parents. The soft, refreshing rain, so welcomed by gardeners, is less welcome to farmers in the middle of cutting hay. They must be hoping that 'rain before seven is followed by sun after eleven.'

Removing blackbirds from the raspberry cage is a daily task. They hurtle around the cage bouncing off the netting and clucking with alarm. I'm happy to give them a few raspberries in return for the prolific song they bring to the garden. They have become one of our most numerous garden birds, partly because food sources are plentiful, and once established, a pair can raise between 3 to 4 clutches of up to 5 eggs a year. Fledglings appear brown and speckled, looking like young thrushes or even robins and follow their parents in search of food, rustling and scuttling along the hedge line. At this stage they are most vulnerable to predators such as cats. Soon the males will establish a territory which they will hold throughout their lives and defend aggressively against other blackbirds. The rainfall today will be very welcome because insects and worms, which for weeks have had to burrow deeper to find damper soil, will be brought within easy pecking reach. Softer soil has also encouraged mole activity with fresh, brown soil being heaved up into mounds across freshly mown lawns. It is not at all surprising to read they can shift up to 12 kg of soil in an hour!

Baby bird schooling is a common sight in fields and gardens. We have a family of four young green woodpeckers, being instructed by a parent in food-finding lessons. They follow the parent around the lawns scuffing up grass, making a small hole and sticking their long beak and tongues deep into the ants' nests, extracting ants with the barbed tip of their tongues which in an adult can be 10 cm long and has to be retracted and curled around its skull. We have also seen feeding lessons taking place on a nearby telegraph pole, each fledgling taking turns to drill the pole to develop the technique that will soon be used on insect-rich, soft and rotting wood from dead alder trees along the dyke.

Blackbirds and thrushes are also out and about with fledged young, fluttering along the base of hedges. The instruction is usually undertaken by the male, while the female prepares for the next nesting attempt. Robins are looking distinctly ragged and lean; parenting is an exhausting business, especially with three broods of up to 6 eggs and lasting well into late July. Robins have very strong parenting instincts and have even been known to feed the chicks of thrushes and blackbirds. Groups of recently fledged sparrows are seen flying together between the house and the edge of nearby meadows and fields in search of grass seed. Young starlings are also communal feeders, and great survivors too, because their nests in roof spaces and holes in walls are usually safe from predators. As a result, at least 10% of eggs laid will produce fledgling young.

Last night about 20 swallows were demonstrating their flying skills high above the barn which contains their nests. The air is full of their excited twittering as they catch insects in the air and feed the young in-flight. This activity supports the weather lore 'when swallows fly high, the weather will be dry', because on warm summer days, thermal activity will sweep insects high into the sky. Tomorrow coincides with another piece of weather lore, which has been a part of our culture for centuries.

It is St Swithin's day, named after a prominent character in ninth century Wessex, who was born of noble parentage in about 805. He acted as a tutor to the children of King Egbert, and was ordained Bishop of Winchester, living a humble life, never riding, always travelling on foot. History gives no indication of whether Swithin had any aptitude for weather forecasting, but his name is associated with a weather lore which states that if it rains on Swithin's Day, it will carry on raining until 23rd August: 40 days of rain. (Less familiar is the equally important tradition that if it is dry on this day, the next 40 days will also be dry.) An 18th-century writer, John Gay expresses this event in a poem:

"Now if, on St Swithin's feast of the welkin lours,
And every penthouse streams with hasty showers,
Twice twenty days shall clouds their fleeces drain
And wash the pavement with incessant rain."

Why should Swithin be associated with this meteorological event? The story goes that, in keeping with his humble nature, his deathbed request was to be buried in a simple grave, 'where the sweet rain of heaven may fall upon my grave'. Over 100 years after his death, his body was moved to a magnificent shrine in the cathedral, felt to be more in keeping with his worthiness. This translation of the body took place on 15th July, 971 and was ruined by torrential rain following a period of drought. The rain continued for 40 days and was seen as an indication of divine disapproval at the removal of his bones.

Although there is no statistical evidence to support the veracity of this weather fable, it is true that at this time of the year the weather becomes locked into a particular pattern, changing only when autumnal influences appear in late August. In fact, the path of our weather systems is controlled by the jet-stream, and if this shifts further south the fronts may bring cooler, wetter weather. If it shifts north, the Azores High will bring dry, warm weather and these patterns can last several weeks. We are not alone in having weather lore relating to this meteorological stability. In France, 19th June is St Gervais Day "Quand il pleut á la St Gervais, il pleut quarante jours après." In Germany, July 7th is known as Siebenschlafer, or 'seven sleeper's day,' when the weather is supposed to remain unchanged for seven weeks.

July 17th

Dykes cutting through the meadows are displaying attractive flowers from plants which are sometimes described as invasive. For example, purple

Dykes cutting through the meadows are full of purple loosestrife with its magnificent spikes of magenta flower.

Another striking feature of dyke margins is the biennial teasel displaying a delicate lilac nectar-laden flower around the egg-shaped flower head.

loosestrife with its magnificent spikes of magenta flower has been particularly problematical in North America. It is European in origin and was introduced to the USA in the early 19th century as a medicinal herb in the treatment of diarrhoea and dysentery. By the 1830s it had colonised much of New England and spread quickly along developing transport routes, especially canals. Now it impedes water flow and suppresses native wetland plants. I value its striking, small, purple-red, starry flowers which are so popular with butterflies and bees. There are also fine specimens of reed mace or bulrush. The flowers are like velvet brown cigars with a long wick. Later in the year the flower heads will burst into a dense, fluffy head containing thousands of seeds each attached to a fine, down hair. Many will be dispersed along the dykes by the wind, some eaten by reed buntings and tits, and many will remain throughout the winter as ragged balls of fluff waving on stems over 2 metres high.

Another striking, erect feature of the dyke margins is the biennial teasel. They are now coming into flower, a delicate lilac colour making a circular band around the egg-shaped flower head. Butterflies frequently visit to sip the nectar. The first part of the teasel's scientific name is Dipsacus, derived from the Greek 'to thirst', because of the way rainwater collects where the base of the leaves join the stem. The Romans called it the basin of Venus. The second part of the name is 'fullonum' derived from fuller, which is the name given to a person who teases out wool. (The Irish name for the plant is 'fullers' herb.') Even today, a cultivated form of the teasel is used in the manufacture of cashmere and velour fabrics. After the seeds have formed in autumn, the plant begins to die, but we retain it for its architectural form throughout the winter, collecting snow and frost, and providing food for groups of goldfinches.

The evening barn owl watch continues. On 28th June when five chicks were taken from the box to be ringed and measured, we estimated their ages to be between 30 and 40 days. Twenty days later some are now taking their first, anxious, speculative forays into the wider world outside the box. A young owl was sitting unsteadily on top of the box; it slid down the apex of the roof, claws scratching on the wood then reluctantly launched or pitched itself into the night air. It was cutting the chord between itself and the mother ship, and performed two wavering, hesitant circles over the meadow before crash landing into a tree near the box, fighting for balance. Perching is clearly a skill it had yet to master. It is not uncommon for some to accidentally fall from a nest, be ignored, and starve to death. We watched the silent drift of adults arriving every 10 to 15 minutes, food in beaks, landing on the ledge to a chorus of raucous, rasping sounds of nestlings. The comings and goings continued until about 10.00pm, by which time the light had faded. Then the silence of the evening was broken by a fox vixen barking incessantly from Tye Wood; the eerie sound, almost like a human scream, echoing down the valley.

July 18th

The bank overlooking the bottom pond has six different varieties of buddleia all attracting bees, moths, butterflies, hover flies and soldier beetles, the level of activity

July 19th

On buddleia, the level of activity increases as the heat of the day builds, including soldier beetles and the comma butterfly with its ragged wing edges.

increasing as the heat of the day builds. The generic name of buddleia posthumously honours the Essex botanist, the Rev Adam Buddle who died in 1715. We are all very familiar with the common species, Davidii, originating from China, and seen along railway embankments, waste ground and derelict sites. Less effective in seed dispersal, but more popular as a garden plant, is Globosa, from Southern Chile, its strong honey-scented globular flower heads being a magnet for butterflies passing through gardens, justifying the common name of 'butterfly bush'. Commas, painted ladies, tortoiseshell and whites are all present at the moment, but we have yet to see the unmistakable red admiral with its velvet-black wings slashed with striking red bands. The population of this attractive butterfly is topped up each year with migrants coming to cooler regions from central Europe, so its numbers are always very variable.

One of our most conspicuous butterflies was spotted in long grass lining the stream course running to our top pond. This was the marbled white, displaying white and dark-brown, chequerboard markings. I have seen several flying together in the tall grass of the river meadow, as well as on downland grass, settling together on flower heads to feed on nectar. The marbled white is the subject of fascinating research between the University of Durham and Butterfly Conservation. With warming temperatures in Southern England, several species of butterfly have been trying to colonise territory further north, but are hampered by the lack of 'stepping stones' or 'green corridors'. Assisted colonisation, which in this case is the transport of marbled white and small skipper in soft cages to safe areas in Co Durham and Northumberland, has proved successful.

The work of Butterfly Conservation deserves recognition for attempts to halt the decline in species and in highlighting the sensitivity of butterflies and moths to environmental change. Butterfly Conservation has worked in broad partnerships to successfully reintroduce the large blue to the UK, having become extinct in 1979. In the 1980s, eggs for the large blue were collected from Sweden and successfully reintroduced into sites in Somerset, where it now flies in greater numbers than anywhere else in Europe. The plan is to extend its distribution into the Cotswolds and colonise neighbouring areas of suitable habitat at the regional scale, rather than protecting small, isolated pockets of land. This is very delicate, detailed and labour-intensive work for which Butterfly Conservation and its partners deserve to be fully supported.

A perfect summer morning with fair weather cumulus gradually evaporating in a cobalt-blue sky, lightening at the horizon to a pale, duck-egg blue. Grasses and trees were in gentle wave-like motion from a cooling breeze. A flock of Canada geese passed overhead in chevron formation, their resonant 'honking' echoing across the valley which they follow almost daily between the reservoirs above Ashford and the

Young buzzards perch on fence posts, carefully watching, then dropping into the field for a ground search.

lakes downstream at Chilham. Escorted flying lessons for young buzzards were in progress to the accompaniment of high-pitched plaintive calls of 'pee-oo' as they took off from the high pines, floating a little shakily in the thermals rising above the warm sunlit meadow. They perched on the fence posts along the dyke, carefully watching us before dropping into the field for a ground search. Two hundred metres above, mere dots in the sky, skylarks were pouring out a sustained, liquid stream of song. Sam swam silently downstream on the way back, wading through the shallows, and emerging through the thick reeds of the bank. Backlit by sunlight he shook himself vigorously from nose to tail, and for a moment became shrouded in a golden mist of sunlit water droplets.

Back in the garden, the invasive chattering of magpies seemed a world away from

River banks have taken on the pink/purple hue from flowers of rose-bay willow herb and the most successful coloniser of all, Himalayan balsam.

the heavenly sound of the skylarks. They have become the subject of vilification, the avian equivalent of football hooligans because of their reputation for stealing eggs and nestlings, and their aggressive antisocial behaviour. However, studies conducted by the RSPB and the BTO find no evidence that the increasing population of magpies has caused a decline in the number of songbirds, whose population is more determined by the availability of food than the actions of predators such as magpies and sparrowhawks. We should give them a break and celebrate this immaculate, intelligent bird of garden and countryside with its purple-blue iridescent wing feathers and a green sheen to its tail, a sentiment not yet shared by all British gamekeepers.

July 22nd

River banks and dykes have taken on a pink-purple hue from flowers of rosebay willow herb, purple loosestrife, and the most successful coloniser of all, Himalayan balsam. These are all considered to be 'invasive' or 'alien' plants, in some cases attracting feelings of hostility. Himalayan Balsam is a native of the Himalayas, introduced from Kashmir to the UK in 1839. Now native species of waterside plants are being shaded out and smothered in places, leading many local authorities to organise 'balsam-bashing' events. Today, Roz and I spent an hour clearing a small patch on the riverbank in Kitchen Meadow, tugging at two metre long, hollow, red-ribbed, juicy stems before they dispersed their seeds. Each plant can produce up to 800 seeds which explode from the ripe pods, sending seeds up to 7 metres, many floating away to colonise banks further downstream. It's a thankless task, and it has to be an annual piecemeal clearance by hand because we are reluctant to use chemical controls so close to the river. I'd like to see thousands of students employed in the long summer vacation, wading and boating down river courses clearing comprehensively as they go! I have to admit affection for this plant, having seen it growing in Monet's garden at Giverny. It is actually a relative of Busy Lizzie and produces clusters of very attractive, delicate pink, white or dark claret flowers, with a very high nectar content. I'm tempted to plant a small patch in a place where I can keep it under control; after all, any invasive plant can be tolerated in small numbers. Only when growth is excessive and uncontrolled does it become a nuisance.

Animals and plants which are introduced to locations where they do not naturally occur are known as non-native species, and many exist without creating problems. Occasionally, however, they can be invasive, upsetting the ecological balance by growing faster and more aggressively than native species, for example, parrots feather from South America which has been overwhelming ponds and slow-moving rivers. These alien invaders are attracting great publicity, leading some researchers to request European-wide legislation to protect indigenous species on the grounds of economic costs as well as ecological impact. Some species introductions have been intentional, for example the ruddy duck was introduced to Europe as an ornamental species, and has become invasive because of its aggressive courting behaviour and willingness to interbreed, encouraging Spain to persuade the EC to exterminate the ruddy duck throughout Europe. This directive has even been endorsed by British conservation agencies, including the RSPB. Some observers of the natural world, however, are critical of what they see as a rising tide of hostility towards introduced species. We will always have immigrant species arriving because we are not isolated from the rest of the planet. New species will inevitably arrive and adapt to their new habitat and may even become firm favourites such as the ivy leaved toadflax with its delicate lilac flowers. This is a native of Mediterranean Europe which has become naturalised over almost the whole of Europe and is now at home in England, having been introduced into the Chelsea Botanic Gardens from Italy. So which alien species do we accept, and are we playing God in making decisions to wipe out certain creatures or plants and allow others to naturalise? The grey squirrel, introduced from America in the 19th century has now driven out the native red squirrel from much of England. What should we do about this? Do we exterminate the grey squirrel? In reaching such decisions, I hope that we are being guided by carefully thought out practical considerations, rather than value judgements which may well change over time. 'Invasion biology' is not yet well developed and may in time provide a better evidence base to inform policy. We do not know yet, for example, how climate change will affect distribution of native and non-native species.

Sarah, the shepherd, called in to say she had seen two kingfishers along the river in Bridge Meadow. They passed by in a brilliant high-speed dash upstream, returning several minutes later, one cutting across the fields of the meander core near the owl box, the other settling on a branch overhanging the shallows and entering the water several times in an unsuccessful search for sticklebacks or water insects. Colin Tudge, in his 'Secret Life of Birds' considers the kingfisher to be one of the most romantic birds in the world, "– a flash of blue on a summer's day as it dives into the stream, like gannet from an overhanging branch, seizes its prey in its dagger-like beak, and zooms out again, all in one movement, to eat at leisure on its perch." Interestingly, he considers them to have evolved from a terrestrial bird, originating in tropical forests, and plunging to the forest floor from perches on the trees to grab insects. Somewhere along the evolutionary line, they began to fish in shallow water,

July 23rd

and from this evolved the bird that we know, in the location that we treasure.

Up on the Crundale Downs later in the day we found that hot sun of the last week had encouraged a wonderful floral display on the south facing bank below Warren Wood. There were 80 or more pyramidal orchids, their densely-packed pink flowers on tall unbranched stems were a glorious sight. Common rest harrow is present; creeping through the grass to form dense patches of pink pea-like flowers, its deep root structure reputedly causing problems in the past for harrows and ploughs. There are golden yellow bedstraws, massive purple knapweeds and thistles of many kinds, and pink common centuary. The oddly named squinancywort displayed its sweetly scented pink and white flowers, the suffix 'wort' often referring to medicinal properties- in this case, the treatment of quinsy, often called squinancy.

July 24th

The Big Butterfly Count has been launched today, by Butterfly Conservation. This national observation and recording event takes place over a period of a week during which people are encouraged to spend 15 minutes in gardens, parks, fields and woodlands, recording the number and species of butterflies and day-flying moths. The aim is to get a better understanding on a national scale, of which species, in which habitats, have become sensitive to changes in the environment. The survey provides a good picture of the fortunes, not only of the country's butterflies and moths, but also the wider health of the countryside. "Butterflies in profusion tell us that all is well with nature. When they decline, it is a warning that other wildlife will be soon heading the same way." (Sir David Attenborough, President of Butterfly Conservation.)

The tranquillity of our early morning walk was interrupted by a pair of cormorants noisily taking off from a dark stretch of water shaded by alders, wings slapping the water, the birds rising slowly but powerfully through the trees and out into the meadow, necks stretched out, heads held up. Like most underwater fishers, the cormorant has evolved as a bird made heavier by the lack of waterproofing on its wings thereby floating low in the water. To dry out their iridescent wings they often perch with them held outstretched like a pair of umbrellas. It is mainly a marine bird, but is a regular visitor to the lakes and rivers nearby, much to the annoyance of anglers who regard them as 'sinister, black and greedy', as did John Milton in 'Paradise Lost', who portrayed them sitting in the tree of life disguised as Satan!

July 25th

The countryside and garden reveal varying elements of beauty, birth, love, amusement-and death. Early today I came across the gruesome sight of a young hedgehog in three widely scattered pieces of purple flesh and prickles. The greatest predator of the hedgehog is the badger with its good sense of smell and ability to uncurl a hedgehog by digging its strong claws into the underside and pulling it open. Excessive summer heat can be a factor in this carnage, because hedgehogs can only perspire and lose heat through parts of the body not covered by spines. In hot summer weather they may lie on their back to allow as much heat loss as possible, making them susceptible to predators like badgers or, most likely in this case, a fox on its nocturnal wanderings. The hedgehog is nocturnal because its food sources of beetles, slugs and spiders are particularly active at night. They can consume 100 invertebrate in a single night as they snuffle and snort about making pig-like noises, hence the traditional name, 'hedge-pig'.

Shortly after this macabre experience I was intrigued to find a grey partridge crouched at the end of the drive with four very young chicks. Usually we see partridge, with wings whirring, gliding across the arable fields. The adult appears to be a rather drab, dumpy bird, but on this occasion it stayed with its young and, close-up, revealed its grey-brown back, rusty red tail and orange face and throat. The precocial nestlings, (relatively mature and mobile from the moment of hatching) were clearly able to feed themselves, pecking in the grass for insects, the only food they can digest for the first ten days. As I drew closer the adult moved quickly away, leaving the chicks to scatter across the road. I herded them into the relative safety of the cornfield edge and hoped they would be reunited with parents and survive the vulnerable 25 fledgling days ahead. The grey partridge is on the red list, vulnerable because of changes in farming practice, (as well as poor road sense), but surprisingly, their numbers remain stable in this locality, probably because the managed shooting estates employ gamekeepers to maintain and manage stocking levels.

July 26th

By the light of the full 'hay moon,' we observed further developments in the barn owl life cycle. By now the nestlings are 9 to 10 weeks old and flying quite well. They appear to have moved into the nearby trees, returning to the box occasionally. There are no sounds of hungry chicks inside the box, suggesting that all have left their home range and are roosting in nearby trees or in other dry roost sites. The amount of food provided by the adult will gradually be reduced and in three of four weeks' time, the young will disperse from the home range in a series of moves, often temporary, until a permanent home is found. Those owls which have not dispersed by late November will be forced out by adults. The ringing of nestling barn owls, coordinated by the Barn Owl Trust provides some indication of the movement of birds and how long they live. The average dispersal distance of newly fledged owls is 12 kilometres, and they hardly ever return to the parent's home range. The survival rate of these juvenile owls is sadly very poor. Dispersal brings them into contact with man-made hazards such as roads, railways and overhead cables. They are also relatively inexperienced in finding food and some will inevitably starve to death. Will our nest box be re-inhabited? Perhaps the adults will stay in the area, or young juveniles arriving from other locations in their post-fledge dispersal will choose the box. We will know by the end of September or early November.

July 27th

Along field margins, the hedges display a variety of white flowers, usually weeds of cultivation but still attractive as in the case of bindweed, providing large, pure-white trumpet-shaped flowers, sometimes with a pale yellow centre. In a garden it throttles plants as it climbs anticlockwise through shrubs, but in a hedge it climbs to 3 metres or more, and can be an attractive combination with the white flowers of brambles

Along field margins, the hedges display a variety of white flowers such as pure white trumpet-shaped bindweed and the equally vigorous old man's beard or traveller's joy with its creamy fragrant flower.

which are rich in nectar. Equally vigorous is the clematis known as old man's beard or traveller's joy, displaying beautiful clusters of small creamy fragrant flowers which will become the downy fruits of September. The field margins are full of chamomile, another plant of arable and waste land. The white petals surround golden-yellow centres, but the plant comes scentless or in the case of stinking chamomile, with a strong, unpleasant smell. Mayweeds are very similar in appearance and all are members of the daisy family. The white heads of achillea and white clover also line the verges.

The common blue rests on a thistle head displaying its iridescent violet blue upper-side with narrow black margin.

As the eighth month approaches, there are signs of the emergence of nuts and berries in woods and hedges. Woody nightshade has clusters of berries, some still green, others deep crimson, while other parts of the plant are still in flower. On spindle bushes the dark-green leaves highlight the light sap-green berries shaped in four lobes, soon to be a shocking pink in colour. It seems like yesterday that blackthorn was heralding the arrival of spring with clouds of white flower; now it displays dark-green berries or sloes, and the elder hangs heavy with huge clusters of lime-green berries. The green fruits of the ash also hang in large bunches, next to the dry brown 'keys' from last year. Winged fruits of sycamore and field maple are all developing, but most attractive of all are the young hazelnuts in the hedgerows: pure-white, soft nuts sheathed in light-green frilly bracts.

July 28th

Under cloudless skies the temperature had reached 24 degrees by 8.30am, a perfect morning to observe and record butterflies and day-flying moths in the meadows and the garden. Where the railway crosses the river in Bridge Meadow there was a bank of creeping thistles in full flower and the fragrance was overwhelming. The scene resembled a butterfly house open to the skies, and the most astounding sight of these winged creatures I have ever experienced. I have passed this spot in many previous summers, but my interest and awareness is now sharper and my discoveries so much richer. From this fixed position I counted the maximum number of each species seen at a single time, and the results were: large white (four), common blue (two), gatekeeper (four), meadow brown (three), large skipper (one), marbled white (one), comma (two), and hundreds of silvery brown micro-moths rising from the grasses. These species are all widespread and commonplace, but their abundance made this a sublime summer experience.

The garden count took place amongst the flowering buddleia overlooking the bottom pond. There were honeybees, bumblebees with pollen baskets bulging with pollen, red tailed bumblebees bouncing off flower heads unaware of my close gaze, hornets hunting for grubs and many bee-like hover flies. The butterfly count here was: large white (two), small white (one), comma (three), gatekeeper (one), peacock (three), small tortoiseshell (three). The count in field and garden gave me reassurance that not only are good nectar sources available, but that the butterfly habitats are able to support large numbers of butterflies and moths at each stage of their life-cycle in these meadows by the river. The butterfly count has given me the chance to 'take the pulse of nature' and become even more aware of the charm of these heart-lifting creatures.

We have many water tanks in the garden, fed by rainwater falling on summerhouse, bothy, barns and greenhouse. Rainwater falling on the barn roof feeds the top pond, from which there is an overflow to the bottom pond, and a rain-fed Victorian water tank supplies the house. But any system of rainwater harvesting needs rain. At the moment I'm spending up to 2 hours a day watering, using a well to water plants near the house and dragging long lines of hosepipe to borders and beds. We've had less than 10cms of rain in three months and only one rain event in July.

I walked Sam over Wye Downs on this hot, sultry and still afternoon. Over the Central Weald and along the crest of the downs to the west, clouds were building from rapidly rising convection currents. Walls of dark-grey cumulus were developing into portentous towers of cumulonimbus- the godfather of all clouds- and moving towards us on a south-west wind. Thunder rolled around in the distance and flickers of lightning lit up the base of clouds. It was an exciting and slightly awesome sight. We made for the car as trees began to sway violently in the strengthening wind and the sky darkened and lowered. Still no rain as the storm passed overhead, but then came the first heavy drops resonating on the car roof, then a downpour. We splashed down the steep slope of the Downs, which had become a milky torrent of suspended chalk. At Olantigh the sky was lightening, the rain softer, the storm had passed as suddenly as it came and the sun shone 'through gulfs of calm and glittering air'.

At Trimworth the road was as dry as a bone. Not a drop had fallen on the fields or gardens of 'torrid Trimworth' and all the water tanks were still empty.

The roar of combine harvesters heralds the beginning of the grain harvest. The air is thick with flying chaff. Huge grain trucks squeeze through small country lanes fit only for horse and cart. Technology, noise and disruption come to the countryside as farmers, blessed by a good spell of dry weather, begin to 'raise the song of harvest home'. All is yet far from safely gathered in; our local farmer Peter Francesconi has over 2000 acres of rapeseed, linseed, oats, wheat and barley to harvest. The first crop will be winter barley, sown last autumn, followed by oilseed rape, winter wheat then other crops such as peas, beans and oats. Recent warm sunshine has ensured acceptable moisture content in the grain, but this can fluctuate throughout the day with variable cloud cover. Anything above 15% moisture content will adversely affect grain storage, or incur drying costs; too dry and yields suffer. Several readings may be taken in a day because hot sunshine can take 2 or 3% of moisture out of grain in a day. Added to this uncertainty of 'when to go' is the fluctuating price level for crops. Today, Peter is harvesting oilseed rape, which, over the last few months, has risen to £280 a tonne. Grains are more volatile and depend on fluctuating world stocks, influenced by variable weather conditions, export bans, regional variations and disease outbreaks. It is a precarious, speculative business, which would overwhelm me with anxiety and apprehension. Peter appears resigned to the unpredictability of farming and adopts a cheerful, buoyant resolve.

One of the most enduring images of harvest in the art world is the picture by Brueghel which exudes the late afternoon heat of a July day. Several groups of peasants are scattered around on the stubble, eating, sleeping and resting. The golden wall of uncut corn behind them stands as high as the farm workers harvesting with scythes or tying grain into shocks and taking them to the barns for threshing. The picture has its antecedents in the labour depicted in the Book of Hours, which associates July with reaping and threshing using small rounded sickles for harvesting, and leather flails studded with nails for threshing. The shape of the sickles and the way the blade was fixed to the handle can date these implements back to the Bronze Age. The blade was only about 7 inches long, compared to the longer medieval sickle with its tanged end, the precursor of modern tools. The sickle was used to cut about two hand-widths below the ears of corn, leaving long stubble in the field. Scythes were also used, the corn falling in rows behind the shearer to be collected up and set into stooks to dry. The process left behind heads of corn on the ground, which were collected or gleaned by the poorest peasants. Geese or poultry were then fattened on any loose grain before cows and sheep entered the field to graze on cornfield weeds and stubble. Pictures always showed the fields full of labourers and families, unlike the mechanised, depopulated farms of today.

Such bucolic images belie the harsh realities of drudgery, toil and primitive lifestyle. There were wide fluctuations in harvest yields which had a strong bearing on disease, mortality, social unrest and economic decline. Agricultural historians such as WG Hoskins have identified the frequency of disastrous crop yields in the 16th and 17th centuries, suggesting that one in every four harvests was a failure, with a tendency for good and bad harvests to run in a series. The subsequent shortages were a far cry from the romantic, bucolic scenes of rural contentment often depicted by artists.

August

It is Lammas Day, named after the Old English 'hlaf-maesse' or loaf mass, one of the great medieval religious festivals when the first baked loaves from the harvest were brought into the church, followed by parties and candlelight processions. The word first appears at the time of Alfred, but it is likely that the festival had pagan origins associated with the ancient Gaelic celebration of Lughnasa, begun by the god Lugh, son of the sun god. Celts celebrated the beginning of harvest with community gatherings, markets, horse races, reunions and trial marriages lasting a year and a day. The pagan origins of the festival are represented centuries later in the medieval ritual of the corn dolly, made from the first straw of the harvest which was stored during the winter and buried with the first planting of the new growing season. Labourers were also required, in most cases very reluctantly, to give a portion of their harvest to the landlord, which explains why Lammas became one of the Quarter Days on which rents and taxes were collected.

In Les Très Riches Heures, peasants are seen binding newly mown wheat into sheaves and loading the harvest onto an overloaded cart. In the foreground, a richly dressed horseman wearing a white hood and carrying a falcon on his fist leads two couples hawking. Leading on foot a falconer holds two birds on his left fist and drags a long pole in his right hand. The varied scene, which is emblematic of the Book of Hours, depicts the diversions of court life amid the seasonal work of the country in August.

It is a traditionally held view that snails have a homing instinct. This homing ability is now being tested in a series of experiments which have invited people to take part in a 'national snail swap', which will keep bored children entertained during long school holidays, whilst simultaneously contributing to scientific research. Garden snails will be collected in a bucket and labelled with coloured nail varnish. These will be swapped with the neighbours, who will have been persuaded to do the same thing, using a different colour for their snails. This could be a long process: snails are not the speediest of movers. If the experiment does confirm the homing instinct, ecologists will need to reassess the nature of the 'not so humble' garden snail, and gardeners will need to think again about throwing their snails over the garden fence to dispose of their pests.

Crundale church tower is made of flint with stone quoins and was built in the first half of the 13th century. From the battlemented top of the tower, weeds and small shrubs are flourishing, just as they probably have for the last 750 years and requiring, as ever, an ascent of the tower for a spot of weeding. The hazardous ascent from the vestry at the base of the tower uses a vertical metal ladder fixed to the wall, leading up to the belfry floor containing three bells. The oldest is the tenor bell recast in 1552 by Robert Mot at his foundry in Whitechapel, one of the most famous bell foundries in the world. This bell has two coats-of-arms of the Kempe family of Trimworth Manor, which held the patronage of the church at the time. The first features three wheat sheaves, the second a large bird on a wheatsheaf set on a wreath. Both of the coats-of-arms are represented on the Jacobean porch at Trimworth today, but we have never been sure about the identity of the bird, which we now know to be a pelican. From the floor of the belfry another ladder leads up to rafters 20 feet above the belfry floor. The entrance onto the tower roof is through a very small door reached by pivoting on the rafters, twisting and levering the body up to a ledge beneath the door and then squeezing through the opening onto the roof of the tower.

The view from the tower is worth the perilous ascent and must be one of the finest in the county. The church sits on a ridge running north to south separating two dry-valleys cut into the chalk of

Crundale church tower is made of flint with stone quoins and was built in the first half of the 13th century.

the downs. To the north, the valleys join and run down to the River Stour at Godmersham, passing close to the manors of Winchcombe and Trimworth. To the west, below the church, is Crundale House, another of the four ancient manors which exist today. To the right of Crundale house, tucked into the shelter of the valley slopes, is a scatter of houses forming the village of Crundale. To the south, the ridge line of Crundale Downs runs across the dip-slope to join the steep scarp-slope overlooking Wye, and to the east the land drops away from the church into another dry-valley containing the ancient manor of Cakes Yoke, now Hunt Street farm. My weeding experience had fortified my awareness of the delightful situation of this church in its downland setting and reconnected me with the landscape and its ancient manors.

Clear overnight skies, falling temperatures and ground left moist from previous evening showers has resulted in a morning of mist and shafts of breaking sunshine. The bowl-shaped dry-valley on the dip-slope of Trimworth downs was full of moist, cold air sinking down into the valley and bringing pulses of white vapour flooding into the meadows. The landscape changed by the second. Landforms and trees slowly emerged, and were then quickly engulfed under a milky white blanket. The crowns of trees stood out like islands, their trunks shrouded in mist. Only the river meadows were radiant with sunshine, reflected in water droplets outlining hundreds of cobwebs in the meadow grasses. I photographed two young buzzards taking off from an earth bank, beaks full, now accomplished fliers and becoming effective, independent foragers of field and forest. Now the tops of the downs become clear, except for rags of smoky mist hanging in the trees. The combine harvesters stand on the Downs like predatory green beasts, waiting for the heat of sun to crack the grain before they roar into life again. Back home, all the mist has wafted away in the warmth of the sun, leaving a sky banded in layers of pale-blue and wispy-white stratus.

August 3rd.

The bowl-shaped valley on the dip slope was full of moist cold air bringing pulses of white vapour flooding into the meadows.

In a late evening walk we made contact with our barn owl family to see how their nocturnal hunting skills were developing. We had a surprise. Owls were screeching from three groups of trees along the river and taking off in wavering flights across the meadow. As we drew closer, they became more intimidating and aggressive, following Sam, hovering and emitting piercing, drawn-out, rasping screeches. The sound was eerie, haunting and slightly sinister. Sam was clearly disturbed and hung close, tail tightly tucked in. At one moment an owl chased a small bird which we realised was a bat, whose quick change of direction easily out-manoeuvred the young owls.

August 4th

We are fortunate to have three generations of swallows performing song and flight for us. Their mud nests are now in three locations, all of which have been used in previous years. Adults are distinguished by their long tails and rapid flight, almost too quick for the eye to follow. They twist and turn and bank in rapid succession, soaring up, plunging down and skimming the water and grasses to catch their prey. Together with house-martins and warblers, they are spending a lot of time feeding, stocking up and turning food into layers of fat in preparation for the journey ahead, which may involve covering over 300km a day. They have become a defining feature of summer and we regard them with great affection. Gilbert White was similarly charmed with their behaviour, describing how the young in successive broods are introduced to life, and expressing his admiration for their 'unwearied industry and affection'.

Regular late-summer visitors from the Atlas Mountains of North Africa have arrived on our buddleia bank. Painted lady and its near cousin, the strong-flying red admiral are probably offspring of butterflies breeding in North Africa or Southern Europe earlier this year and have completed their thousand mile migration to our shores. There are sometimes mass migrations of these butterflies, as in 2009, when millions of painted ladies swept across the nation. An estimated 18,000 were spotted sailing on the breeze over the North Norfolk coast looking for open habitats with thistles, mallow and nettles, all serving as larval food plants or nectar sources for adults.

August 5th

Frequently on my daily walks in the local countryside, I have an experience that is difficult to put into words. Somehow the language is inadequate to convey the wonder of the event. It is not necessarily an earth-shattering or momentous event, but the encounter takes one beyond the ability to express it in words. Rather than resort to worn descriptions or platitudes, I would rather store it away as a treasured memory. This afternoon, for example, as we walked upstream through the meadow, a kingfisher flew towards us, banked, turned, climbed steeply and was gone. When I close my eyes, the image is still there, as if imprinted on the retina. Many people will have had similar experiences every day. This is a measure of the amazing capacity of the natural world to provide us with a sense of wonder, astonishment and happiness.

August 6th

As summer progresses, the winged creatures of our ponds become more prolific and entertaining, and I have come to regard the Calopteryx splendens, or the banded demoiselle, as one of the most radiant and beautiful. As I was trying to photograph one on the reeds around the bottom pond, I became aware of at least five fluttering together over the water. Iridescent blue males were performing a showy display in front of the green-bronze females. Sunlight was reflecting off their glistening gauzy wings and metallic-like abdomen and huge, bulging, compound eyes. They are such precious, fragile, transient creatures, with the flying males having a life span of only a few weeks.

Earlier this summer, the British Dragonfly Society (BDS), reported the return of a damselfly after a 57 year absence in the United Kingdom. The 'dainty damselfly' had been declared extinct after being washed out of an East Anglian pond in the floods of 1952/3. Now sightings have been reported from the Isle-of-Sheppey and other locations in North Kent. The damselfly is likely to have been blown in on a southerly breeze from the continent, probably Belgium or France, their advance northwards from central and southern Europe probably being associated with climate change. Whether the dainty damselfly will form a stable population is not yet clear. The BDC will be looking for discarded exuviae, or larval cases, which could indicate successful breeding. Identification of the adult is difficult because it is incredibly like the common blue, the most common damselfly which we see almost daily, with its turquoise and black banding.

Other similar invasions from mainland Europe have occurred as a consequence of warming temperatures. The small 'red-eyed damselfly' first appeared in 1999 and is now breeding across south-east England. European birds, bees, wasps, and butterflies are also appearing, such as the carder bee, the lesser emperor dragonfly, the Queen of Spain fritillary and the great white egret which has been sighted here in East Kent and is now resting in reed beds in Somerset. The most recent, and very exciting, success in Kent is the emergence from a nest of what is thought to be the first ever pair of purple herons bred in the United Kingdom from colonies in France and the Netherlands. They have been struggling in Europe over the past few decades and climate change has pushed them into the south of England. It is a migratory bird, overwintering in Africa and is closely related to our larger, more widespread, grey heron with its aristocratic stance.

August 7th

As Winston Churchill wittily observed, "We are all worms, but I do believe I am a glow-worm." Seeing glow-worms comes close to the top of the list of exciting moments in the annual observations of the river meadow. It was 11:30pm and the evening was warm and damp with an overcast sky as we crossed the open grassland of Bridge Meadow. Near the river in long grass was a yellow-green glow close to where we had previously seen glow-worms, (actually they are beetles, called Lampyris noctiluca). They prefer the unimproved grassland of chalk downland where there is a good supply of small snails on which the beetle feeds by paralysing them before sucking them empty. It is the female which produces the glow by mixing two chemicals, luciferan and luciferase. The purpose of the glow is to attract males which can detect the light from 50 metres away if there is no other light source to distract them. If mating is successful the female will lay 35 to 200 eggs and then immediately die. If no male is attracted she will retreat from the grass stems to lower levels and switch off her 'pilot lights' until the next night. Since they are unable to feed, the female can only repeat this activity for about 10 consecutive nights before she dies. For 90% of their lives the glow-worm exists as larvae, which can also produce light, hibernating through two winters for about 18 months before they pupate and transform into adults. Very few survive this process through to breeding.

Much of the information about the distribution of the glow-worm and its growth or decline is collected by Robin Scagell, who has no official status, funding or affiliation. Online recordings of sightings by the general public have allowed him to produce annual survey reports for the media and other conservation groups. (www. glowworms.org.uk) It is through such amateur enthusiasm and dedication that we are kept informed of the health the countryside and its inhabitants. Is it a peculiarly British characteristic to be so concerned about the welfare of small things in small places?

The water level in the upper pond is extremely low, but I'm resisting topping it up with tap water because this will deliver nutrients to pollute the pond and encourage growth of filamentous algae or blanket weed. Most natural ponds will normally experience a drop in water level of up to 5 metres, which creates one of the most biologically rich areas of the pond – the 'drawdown zone'. Here seeds of marginal plants such as water mint, sage, and water iris will germinate. Dragonflies are also attracted to this edge to lay eggs, together with semi-terrestrial insects such as beetles and flies. A pond drying out is not a wildlife disaster because most ponds have been created through natural processes and will have experienced periods of drought and silting up over time.

We survey the content of our ponds at different times of the year. During a brief inspection today we noted dragonflies, (broad bodied chaser, common hawker, emperor, common darter) damselflies, (banded demoiselle, common blue). We netted common newts, pond snails, greater and lesser water boatmen, water beetles, pond skaters, whirligig beetles, water mites, nymphs of dragonflies, damselfly and mosquito, leech, water mites and a frog. We have in the recent past seen caddis fly larva living in their built structures composed of reeds, twigs, bark and stones which they have bound together. It is in this sealed structure that the larvae develop before emerging as adults. All this suggests a biologically rich and healthy pond, which would achieve an excellent rating in recent surveys by Pond Conservation. Their criteria for excellence require a pond to have three of the following four groups of wildlife: damselfly, dragonfly, caddis fly, alderfly.

In a recent national survey by Pond Conservation, the charity dedicated to protecting wildlife in fresh waters, half of the 3 million garden ponds surveyed were classed as poor, although they still supported a limited range of wildlife. To address the problem, Pond Conservation launched a major project in 2008 to increase the number of clean ponds across the UK, and reverse a century of pond loss. The aim is to create 5000 clean water ponds in England and Wales, a quarter of which will be targeted to support some of the pond species which have become a national priority. The project, called the Million Ponds Project, in reference to the number of ponds which existed a century ago, is a collaboration between landowners, the Environment Agency, RSPB and other major wildlife organisations. It deserves success if only to increase the opportunity for young people to experience the excitement of pond dipping, often their first and most memorable physical contact with the natural world.

Crundale church is set on a remote hillside between two dry-valleys cut into the dip-slope of the North Downs. A ridge separates the dry-valleys and runs south from the church with far-reaching views of old farms and ancient woodland. It is one of my favourite walks and I have spent many hours trying to capture the essence of this landscape in paintings and drawings. Walking this ridge at the moment is like walking through an aromatic herb garden. Marjoram or oregano, wild thyme and wild basil are all in flower and on a hot day, the scent is pungent. This is a herb-rich

A ridge separates the dry-valleys and runs south from the church with far-reaching views of old farms and ancient woodland.

Marjoram or oregano is in flower, together with wild thyme and wild basil. On hot days the scent is pungent.

plant community, adapted to compete effectively in the shallow, impoverished, well-drained chalk soils. The marjoram stands upright as a bushy plant with dense collections of rose-purple flowers held in clusters. It is aptly known as 'the joy of the mountains' and stands as a symbol of happiness and felicity for newly married couples. Since medieval times it has had a reputation for warding off harm and is unarguably a great bee flower. Thyme also has happy associations with good fortune. The Romans used it to purify rooms and flavour cheese and liqueurs. The Crusaders wore it to give courage and it has long been regarded for its medicinal properties.

August 10th

A morning of steady, soft, gentle and refreshing rain bringing a welcome smell of damp earth and the sound of rain splashing on vegetation and drumming on rooftops. Farmers in the middle of grain harvest will be frustrated; gardeners will be delighted to be released from the daily task of watering. Chain saws in Tye Wood

Olantigh, Winchcombe, Crundale, Ripple Farm, Purr Wood and Godmersham; all local place names which remain as a 'word map' of the distant past. Place names are often signposts of earlier settlement colonisation. Sometimes they refer to the names of individuals or families, or to topographical features in the landscape, such as forests, rivers, marshes, or open fields which have long since been engulfed by settlement growth. Crundale is probably derived from the Old English 'crundel', meaning chalk pit or quarry, and 'dell' (hollow, valley, dale). Nearby Berton Wood derives from the Old English 'beretun', meaning barley farm. Purr Wood is an ancient woodland close to Trimworth, the word purr probably being a derivation of 'clean, pure, undisturbed'. Ripple Farm a few hundred metres away, comes from the Old English 'ripple', meaning a strip of land, and Winchcombe Manor is from 'wincel', meaning corner or angle of a combe or valley. Marriage Farm lies on a ridge on the boundary between Wye and Crundale. The name comes from the Old English 'gemaere,' meaning border or boundary and 'hryg', meaning ridge. Trimworth itself was first recorded in an Anglo-Saxon charter of 824 as 'dreamen wyrthe', from dreama (joy, delight) and wyrthe (enclosure). Unravelling how place names originated and what they mean provides fascinating stories of landscapes and local history.

have fallen temporarily silent; a good moment to examine the result. Management of woodland is essential, but the change is initially hard to accept and my main concern is that the removal of spruce and Douglas fir will disturb or even destroy the nests of buzzards which have become well established. I cannot say if the nests have been destroyed, but I doubt if they will continue to stay in such a disturbed environment of broken branches, loss of cover, rutted tracks and log piles, all of which will affect the small mammal life and major food source of this bird, surviving at the top of the food chain, despite a long history of persecution by man. Fortunately, there is now a more enlightened attitude and a greater willingness to accept this striking, impressive bird which soars and wind-hovers daily over the pine tops of Tye Wood.

Despite the lack of rain, the dykes running across the meadow are overflowing with lush green vegetation. Gypsywort looks like a large mint with deeply cut leaf

August 12th

The flower of the golden-yellow water lily stands on stalks well clear of the water surface and the large oval-shaped leaves.

Clusters of fragrant violet flower heads of creeping thistles are attracting the warmth-loving brown argus butterfly, frequently found on open chalk grassland.

margins, but it is unscented. The name comes from its use as a dye by gypsies who were also reputed to stain their skin with the juice of the plant so they would look like Africans or Indians while performing their 'magic'. The flowers are small and white and have been used as a sedative, reducing heart rates in people with overactive thyroid problems. Water mint is displaying its distinctive flower-head of mauve, purple and blue, forming in clusters at the end of square-shaped stems, which root at the nodes and spread rapidly. The distinctive and refreshing minty aroma is released when leaves are rubbed or crushed underfoot. Watercress is sprawling out of ditches, sending out stems at right angles to the main stem, with white flowers or umbels appearing in the axils. In still or slow flowing water, the largest and showiest of all water plants, the white water lily is in full flower. The huge, floating white flowers are about 20 cm across, and have up to 20 petals. Equally striking is the smaller golden yellow water lily, the flower standing on stalks well clear of the water surface. Eventually they will form into bottle-shaped fruit capsules above large oval-shaped floating leaves.

Along the dry chalky footpaths leading up to the downs is the outstanding purple flower of knapweed below which are green-brown phillaries with bristles. Clusters of fragrant, lilac flower-heads of creeping thistle were attracting butterflies including the warmth-loving brown argus frequently found on open chalk grassland. The blue-violet flower of the tufted vetch is scrambling through hedges and contrasts beautifully with the large golden yellow flower of the perennial sow thistles and the small purple-white umbels of bur parsley. Blowing and rattling in the breeze is the bladder-shaped flowerless calyx of the seed-filled bladder campion, gradually turning brown and opening to release the seeds. The scientific name of this plant, Silene, probably refers to Silenius, the drunken, merry god of the woodlands.

August 13th

A quick movement in the meadow as we walked across the wet grass. Grass moths flitted between stalks, grasshoppers pinged about in the turf, but this was a quick little mammal concealing its tiny body in the tufts of grass. Another movement and we recognised the long, twitching snout and long tail of the shrew, one of the most common mammals in Northern Europe, and living at densities of over 20 per hectare in grasslands, and often over 50 per hectare in woodlands. They are about 5 to 7 cm long with velvety dark-brown fur and a paler underside. This one was smaller and lighter in colour, probably a juvenile which had become separated from its mother and yet to have its first moult. When the nests are disturbed, young shrews are sometimes seen following their mother in a 'caravan', with each shrew grasping the tail of the one in front. The shrew has an insatiable appetite for insects and worms, eating every two or three hours. Survival requires them to eat the equivalent of their own body weight in a single day. They are frequently seen foraging through the damp grass in the day and night, becoming less active and smaller in winter, but never hibernating during their short 12 to 24 month life. This little shrew's greatest threat will come from one

The shrew is one of our most common mammals, living at densities of over 20 per hectare in grasslands.

of our five young barn owls, now becoming proficient hunters and gliding low and ghostlike over the meadows in the twilight hours. Foxes, stoats and kestrels will also target the shrew as a food source, but not cats which are deterred by the foul taste produced by liquid secreted from the glands. Why should this little creature be associated with the loud, bad tempered and unmanageable character in the play, The Taming of the Shrew? Shakespeare was evidently aware of the ferocious, territorial nature of the shrew, which communicates by a series of high-pitched shrieks and chattering, the volume of which increases when the shrew is angry, much like Shakespeare's Katarina!

The loud 'caw,caaaw' of rooks fills the early-morning air, the sound echoing across the valley. There were probably 150 or more in the lime trees lining the drive, dropping onto the recently harvested fields of Little Tithe and Great Tithe fields to feed. When disturbed, they rose in a noisy black cloud and began playing their games of soaring, swooping, diving, tumbling and other aerobatic manoeuvres before settling back on another part of the field. They will move from field to field throughout the day before streaming back to their regular roost at Godmersham in the late evening. The scene is captured by Coleridge, who frequently used nature to represent human feelings, such as being reunited in a homecoming.

> "… when the last rook
> Beat its straight path along the dusky air
> Homewards, I blest it!"

At this point in 1940, a damaged Spitfire returning from the Channel hit the ash tree and crashed into the river, an event commemorated today with an inspirational aerial display by a Spitfire from Biggin Hill.

With harvesting now complete around Trimworth, I walked into the middle of fields of stubble to appreciate views of the local landscape from viewpoints which we rarely use. I returned with pieces of brick and tile, strange shaped flints, and belemnites. These finger-like fossils of calcite represent the back parts of shells of sea creatures like squid, which occupied warm seas of the Jurassic and Cretaceous period, becoming extinct along with ammonites over 65 million years ago. They have been called 'thunderbolts' or 'devil's fingers' by country folk who believed they fell from the sky during thunderstorms.

August 15th

I often play mind games in the twilight, as the hills overlooking the valley darken and the light drains from the sky. Looking back across Six Acre Meadow towards Trimworth, I imagine how this scene may have looked to the Iron Age farmer ploughing fields with ox-drawn ploughs and grazing livestock on the slopes of the downs; or the medieval tenant working the fields of the lord's demesne. My imagination becomes completely liberated when I try to see this ancient landscape through the eyes of a succession of inhabitants, particularly those who saw it in its primeval freshness. Of course, most of the present landscape is almost entirely the product of the last 1500 years; the direct prehistoric elements of the landscape are very small, but nevertheless, I continue to be drawn back to a landscape which was the product of the forces of nature, waiting for the first human inhabitants.

August 16th

At 10:30am, standing under a huge ash tree at the point where the river path runs in front of Tye Wood, I watched a small dot in the grey-blue sky to the west grow larger and larger, and heard the sound of engine noise grow louder. It passed over Bilting Meadow heading for Trimworth at a height of about 100 feet. The Merlin engine roared overhead on full throttle and for five minutes the Spitfire performed a series of aerobatic manoeuvres and passes over Six Acre Meadow and Trimworth before heading back to Biggin Hill, leaving me deafened by the silence. This emotional and inspirational event was part of a small, intimate ceremony to honour a Belgian fighter pilot who lost his life at this exact location on 4th September 1940. The pilot, Albert van-den Hove d'Erstenrijck had been fighting over the Kent coast and was attempting to force land his damaged aircraft in Six Acre Meadow, but he stalled as he was turning and hit the ash tree. He was killed outright. Nearby, 14-year-old Donald Kay was fishing and saw the aircraft trailing smoke as it hit the tree and crashed into the river. He jumped in and attempted to free the pilot, but he was dead from massive head injuries. Today, Donald Kay and the two daughters of the pilot gathered on the bank for a touching ceremony to unveil a small commemorative plaque and witness this amazing display by one of the classic fighter aircraft of all time.

August 17th

Low growing, arching canes of brambles are half concealed in the dog's mercury, making progress through Tye Wood difficult. The bramble is a plant of ancient and recent woodland, going back to prehistoric times, as well as thriving in recently cleared woodland. Brambles in hedges can be an indication of the extent of former woodland, the 'ghost' edge of a grubbed out wood; they can also mark the spot where a blackbird deposited seeds after a good blackberry feed. There is a whole world of life in the bramble bush. It is the haunt of many insects and the common resting place for thrushes, robins and blackbirds. Bees feed on the nectar-rich flowers and wasps enjoy the sugar of ripening berries. After the skin of the fruit has been pierced, other insects such as flies are attracted, many of which get caught up in spiders webs spun in the bush. Commas and Red Admiral feed on the overripe fruits, sucking up the juices of mushy berries.

Our brambles grow vigorously along the fence line of the railway, and in the hedge surrounding Great Tithe field. They appear to be following the trend of ripening a little later than usual, according to national observations from the Woodland Trust's Nature Calendar Survey, which studies the timing of common seasonal events (known as phenology). Over the past five years, the average dates for the first observed ripe berries were around the 4th August, but today only a few berries are ripe. Kate Lewthwaite, the project manager for the Woodland Trust, suggests that flowering of blackberries was delayed by a very cold winter, and this has had a knock-on effect on fruiting. Perhaps the same weather phenomenon will cause a delayed autumn for trees, with autumn colours not appearing until October. However, nature has its way of adjusting. My feeling is that the long period of drought in East Kent this summer will lead to earlier, not later autumn colouring of leaves. As with all predictions of the natural world, only time will tell.

The natural world is grabbing the headlines at the moment. There is outrage over plans to sell off nature reserves, rivers and forests. Leading conservation groups are appalled at the proposed plan to cut the budget of DEFRA by 40% and substantially reduce staffing levels at Natural England and the Environment Agency. Their fear is that short-term savings would translate into huge long-term costs for the economy and natural well-being. In the face of declining biodiversity, the government has commissioned a report to put an economic value on parks, lakes, forests and wildlife, which will be used to re-shape planning policy. The National Ecosystem Assessment is a 20,000 word report which takes account of the true value of the economic benefits of nature. Some figures emerge with precision, such as the £430 million that pollinating insects are calculated to be worth, but most aspects of wildlife and biodiversity are impossible to quantify. The value of nature comes from the sense of wonder and enjoyment it provokes, and this cannot be reduced to a balance sheet.

As well as this inherent problem of placing a value on nature in a commercially driven world, the National Assessment has another shortcoming. It is somewhat preoccupied with placing a value on the living elements of the natural world. In common with other geographers, I feel we also need to consider the value of the non-living, physical basis of the planet such as rock structures, fossil beds, landscape features, soils and geology. In other words, we need to value and manage geo-diversity as well as biodiversity, placing physical and ecological attributes of our planet alongside wildlife species and habitats to get a fuller appreciation of our natural environment.

It has been a week since we have seen or heard buzzards over Tye Wood. Perhaps the fully fledged family has moved on, hastened by the noise and destruction of the woodland clearance. I have no problem with woodland management if the main purpose of the wood is to produce an economic product such as timber or game species, as in the case of some of Tye Wood. Selective clearance of trees and undergrowth is necessary to remove competing species, control disease and ensure good nutrition for the economic species to thrive. If such a wood is not managed it will not produce an economically viable product. Already the work has increased light levels under the main tree canopy and created glades which will encourage a greater variety of plants and food sources for birds, mammals and invertebrates. In such cases the woodland produces gains in biodiversity.

We may have (temporarily) lost the buzzards, but today there were other visitors to compensate for the loss. Crossing the footbridge at Olantigh we disturbed a little egret resting in a hunched up position at the edge of the river before taking off across the meadow with its bright, white plumage visible well into the distance. The attractive plumage of this bird was in great demand for centuries for decorating costumes, especially hats, creating a huge import industry, particularly from India. A significant response to this large-scale slaughter of millions of birds was the foundation of the Society for the Protection of Birds in 1889, which attracted royal patronage to become the Royal Society for the Protection of Birds in 1904. Little egret began to arrive in this country in the 1980s and first bred on Brownsea Island in Poole Harbour, Dorset, in the 1990s. Within 12 years, their numbers had rapidly increased to several hundred resident breeding pairs. It is an amusing and effective feeder, using its yellow feet to shuffle in the mud, stir up fish, and then accurately stab them with its dagger-like bill.

In the reeds and thistle beds along the river was a non-descript brown bird flitting between stalks and holding onto vertical stems very expertly. The upper body was warm brown with a pale underside, not much different from other warblers, but it did not have the eye stripe of the sedge warbler, or the white throat of the rarer marsh warbler. I was sure it was a reed warbler, and its chirping churring song more or less confirmed it. There was no uncertainty in the identity of the next sighting: the heart-stopping, mind-blowing, breath-catching sight of the kingfisher flying at full speed in full sun, under the railway bridge.

The greenfinch is one of the colourful characters of the bird world with its twittering song and flash of yellow and green as it flies, often in a group, through garden and countryside. We have become used to this frequent visitor to bird tables and feeders, often remaining for several minutes. But since 2005 it has been in trouble, declining by about 35%. The British Trust for Ornithology blames its demise on a fatal infection caused by the parasite Trichomonas gallinae, which can also affect other finches and house sparrows. The parasite lives in the upper respiratory tract of the bird, leading to congestion and eventual starvation, and can be transmitted through saliva of infected birds. They will display lethargy, fluffed up plumage, wetness around the bill and other signs of general illness. The disease is normally associated with pigeons, and appears to have jumped the species barrier, giving a higher level of mortality than researchers have seen before. The greater susceptibility of finches and sparrows is due to their sociability, gathering together for roosting and feeding, giving higher rates of transmission. Researchers are urging bird lovers to keep birdfeeders and baths clean and to stop putting out food when the disease is suspected until sick and diseased birds are no longer found. Outbreaks are most likely seen between August and October. The findings are another great example of 'citizen science' at work with several hundred observers recording numbers of garden birds since 2003. It highlights the valuable work that volunteers can play in monitoring new and emerging health threats to British wildlife.

It's been a wild night with heavy rain and strong winds continuing into the morning. The bird world has taken cover, except for rooks which are using the gusty wind to perform even more dramatic aerial displays. Seagulls, blown inland to shelter from coastal gales are foraging in the harvested fields and the odd pigeon races across the sky in the following wind with barely a wing beat. Deadwood has fallen from the tops of old ash trees and branches of young willows lie scattered along the river bank. It feels as if October has temporarily stepped forward into August and written off all future plans for late summer picnics and barbecues. Concerns about drought have suddenly been replaced by warnings of local flooding and damage from fallen trees.

August 23rd

It's been a great year for wasps. Hot, dry weather means improved breeding conditions and better survival rates for the insects on which they feed. Some neat, round holes of field voles in the meadow have been taken over by wasps and there is a steady stream of workers (infertile females) gathering insects to feed wasp larvae in nests. With plentiful supplies of food, the queen will keep laying eggs and the nests will grow bigger. Soon, males and new queens will be looking to consume ripe fruit and will mate, following which all the males, workers and the founding queen will die. The surviving queens will hibernate and begin a new colony next spring. Wasps in the vicinity of the nest are now getting aggressive, releasing pheromones with each sting which alarms other wasps nearby, causing them to swarm around invaders. Yet they do not deserve the bad press. They are essentially pest control insects and although more queens will go into hibernation carrying thousands of fertilised eggs, over 99% will die of natural causes in the winter.

A newly emerged migrant hawker dragonfly was seen resting on a grass stalk in the wild flower bank above the pond and was still there ten minutes later, so we picked the stalk and took it to the house to examine and photograph it more closely. The most distinctive characteristic is the prominent yellow triangle or 'tee peg' on the second abdominal segment. The abdomen is dark overall, making the pairs of blue spots on each segment stand out clearly. Holding it against a white background we

August 24th

A migrant hawker dragonfly showing the intricate geometrical patterns of the strong transparent wings.

studied the intricate geometrical patterns of the strong transparent wings. In contrast to other four-winged insects the fore and hind wings operate independently, explaining the incredible flight manoeuvres of the dragonfly. It had now been resting long enough for its wings to dry out, so the smallest of our hawkers, which flies late into the autumn, took off towards the pond, none the worse for being subjected to a close, critical human gaze.

As the early evening skies clear, a full moon comes into view over Trimworth Down. It appears clear and large, but this is actually the smallest full moon of the year. Thirty hours after being officially full, this August moon will be at its furthest point from the earth in its orbit, a point called the apogee 252,518 miles from the earth.

Even though the difference in size is 12.3% from the largest full moon in January, which is the closest point in the moon's orbit of the earth, (the perigee), it would be difficult to spot the difference. Whatever the calculation, it is a beautiful, romantic sight hovering above Warren Wood, on the crest of the downs, just as John Milton described it in Paradise Lost:

> "Rising in clouded majesty, at length
> Apparent queen, unveiled her peerless light,
> And o'er the dark her silver mantle threw."

From the wooded slopes of Marriage Hill, the view East towards the River Stour takes in the perfect circular brick walls of the kitchen garden near Olantigh House. A little further downstream is the walled garden in the grounds of Godmersham Park, and similar features exist in several nearby country houses, such as Belmont and Godinton Park. Walled kitchen gardens of country houses were at their height of productivity throughout the 19th century, declining in importance with the availability of cheap fruit and vegetable imports and the rising cost of labour. At their height they provided all-year-round produce for the family and estate staff with the walls used for training fruit trees and glasshouses for the tender, exotic products. These beautiful walled gardens at Olantigh still contain period glasshouses, plant houses, potting sheds and probably employed between 5 to 10 garden staff. The garden is located over 500 m away from the main house probably because it was felt that the high walled kitchen garden would be detrimental to the view of the landscaped gardens and parkland surrounding the house. Their location 40 m higher than the house also takes them away from the frost pockets and flooding problems of the valley into well-drained soils and a sunny aspect. The location also moves problems associated with smoke from hot-house chimneys and smells from decaying compost away from the main house and its occupants. The high walls created a micro-climate in the garden and a structure on which to train a great variety of fruit trees. The unusual circular walls of Olantigh were laid out in four quadrants separated by wide paths, unlike many kitchen gardens which were square or rectangular in shape. Sheds on the north side of the garden contained boiler houses, fuel bunkers, potting sheds with benches running the length of windows and workrooms for the staff. It must have been a busy place as gardeners created noise and bustle with the activities of digging, sowing, weeding, picking and packing. In more recent years the gardens have been occupied by a husband and wife team as a nursery and are currently being worked by a local farm producing organic fruit and vegetables.

At nearby Godmersham the walled gardens have been restored to their original layout whilst others in the area have become abandoned, or converted to other uses, but their story as a production unit and source of local employment over a long period is a fascinating one, told in detail by the garden historian Susan Campbell in her little book on 'Walled Kitchen Gardens.'

The circular brick walls of the Olantigh walled kitchen garden, for many years a great production unit and source of local employment.

A late evening walk around the garden between showers was rewarded by sights and sounds of busy birds. First, the plaintive song of the robin, one of the few birds which will sing all year long, singing now to defend its territories against intruders. Wrens are darting between the ivy and the cotoneasters, collecting berries, sounding their 'teck-teck-teck' alarm call. Scuttling through the dry leaves at the base of the hedgerows are young blackbirds, giving an alarm call which sounds like a rattle. But as darkness falls, the real stars of the warm night emerge from the bat boxes and yew trees. These are pipistrelle, circling the house hunting for moths, gnats, and other small insects, consuming up to 3000 insects in one night. I watch their darting, fluttering, agile flight as they flick their wings in pursuit of prey. Their jerky flight has given the pipistrelle the name of 'flutter mouse' (fledermaus in German). Using a system of echolocation similar to radar scanners they emit high-pitched squeaks which rebound off objects back to their ears, allowing the bat to 'see' its surroundings. We build up a mental map of an area through sight; bats build their mental maps through sound as they commute through familiar territory. The pipistrelle is the smallest and most common European bat. Recently, another species of pipistrelle has been recognised: the soprano pipistrelle, only distinguished from the more common species by the frequency of their echolocation sound, which is 55 kHz rather than 45 kHz. During August young bats will catch food for themselves. In September, mating begins and bats will swarm around roosts, but the females do not become pregnant until after hibernation, when the weather begins to warm in spring or early summer. We have resident bats in our roof-space: their droppings are dry and crumbly and glisten with the shiny, transparent wings of insects which they have consumed.

Medical science has once again confirmed what we already knew. There are therapeutic powers in listening to birdsong. An art project at Alder Hey Hospital in Liverpool uses birdsong recordings made by children to calm young patients as they receive injections and other treatments. The idea is the brainchild of Chris Watson, one of the world's leading recorders of natural phenomena, such as the unearthly groan of an Icelandic glacier; the vibration of sand in response to movement of waves and water; the sound of monsoon downpours; the sound of activity inside termite nests. Birdsong is his passion, and in this he is not alone. Recently, a digital radio station, 'Oneword', closed down, but the frequency was used to transmit birdsong. This proved far more popular than the programmes previously transmitted from the station. Our love of hearing birdsong is an example of what is known as 'biophilia,' our deep human need to connect with nature.

Blackberries are now fully ripe along the hedgerows and railway line, bringing back personal memories of journeys along Norfolk lanes sitting on the back of my mother's bicycle and watching her use a walking stick to pull down the arching branches laden with fruit- the end product of which was bramble jelly. Less genial is the very painful memory of getting my foot caught in the spokes of the cycle wheel on one of these blackberry days.

We met an early-morning, elderly walker slowly crossing the meadow in Bilting, welcomed by Sam with the customary sniffing and frantic tail wagging. The usual exchanges on weather took place opening with, ' It's like a hop pickers morning today.' He was referring to the cool, damp and often misty start to late August and September days when in the past, the hop fields of Kent filled with local families and migrant workers from the East End of London to pick hops. They returned for several generations, the scene in 1889 being described in John Bickerdyke's 'Curiosities of Ale and Beer.'

"The high road from London to the hop fields of Kent presents a curious appearance immediately before the hop picking season. A stranger might imagine that the poorer classes of a big city are flying before an invading army. Grey-haired, decrepit old men and women are to be seen painfully crawling along, their stronger sons and daughters pressing on impatiently."

By 1934, the first hop picking machines had arrived to replace most of the pickers. Village pubs could take down the signs reading 'No dogs, no gypsies and no hoppers'. In the late '60s over 20,000 acres of land were used to grow hops in Kent; there are now only 2500 acres with pickers coming from Eastern Europe, rather than the East End. Despite East Kent being home to one of the oldest working breweries (Shepherd Neame of Faversham was founded in 1698), little remains of this vibrant, colourful economy apart from map evidence (Kiln Field, Hop Garden), oast houses converted to chic residences and elegant offices, and redolent displays of rural life in Kent museums.

The fast flowing river is now full of duckweed, which has been flushed out of sheltered bays, and weed-congested stretches of the river upstream. We have duck weeds of all sorts: lesser, greater, fat, ivy leaved, all making green carpets on the inner banks of meanders where the water is still. Through this green carpet comes the coot, announcing itself with a surprisingly loud monosyllabic call of 'kruke-kruke', its head nodding as it swims, occasionally diving through the weed in search of insect larvae. We frequently see its smaller cousin, the moorhen so it is good to see the comparatively rare sight of the coot and its distinctive bare, white, shield above the white beak, earning it the title of 'bald.' They are extremely territorial birds, fighting violently like hooligans: the bullyboys of the riverbank, but today, placid and unruffled.

Upstream from the bridge we were disturbed by frantic splashing beneath the riverbank, followed by the appearance of an irritated cormorant trying to swallow a very large dead fish. At every attempt the fish became stuck and was regurgitated, before eventually the cormorant gave up and flapped off, laboriously, towards Godmersham.

Several days of damp weather have changed the appearance of our lawns. Everywhere, small patches of fine, soft soil form little mounds in the grass. Nothing moves on the surface, but brush away a little soil and the earth becomes a teeming mass of ants and exposed eggs which hundreds of workers are carrying off to safety. I am fascinated to see that their instinct is clearly to look after the next generation of ants, rather than their own. Each white egg will hatch into a larva, then a pupa, before becoming one of the worker ants who take on the nest building and food carrying for the colony. They search for sugary fluids such as the honeydew exuded by aphids. In the meadows a different species, the yellow 'lasius flavus', is building much larger mounds with colonies of many thousands of worker ants carrying soil to the top of the mound. These large mounds are an especially conspicuous feature on un-ploughed calcareous grassland and give the colony greater protection, more food storage space and a range of microclimates in the many chambered mounds. They are often orientated in an east-west direction to create maximum warmth from the sunshine and providing a useful, but not infallible, direction guide for lost shepherds and walkers. The biggest of the British ants are to be seen in the woodland and can often be heard rustling through dry leaves. They build nests of pine needles, leaves and twigs, and will administer a hearty bite or a squirt of formic acid as a defence against intruders. The ant has colonised almost every landmass on earth and thrives in most ecosystems. This success is attributed to their social organisation, and their ability to modify habitats, defend themselves and obtain resources- all important aspects of human society to which they are frequently compared.

A gang of Irish workers has arrived to strengthen the pillars of the railway bridge over the river in Bridge Meadow. A year ago, a fallen tree blocked an archway of the bridge, channelling the flow through the remaining arches and scouring the bed around the pillars. Despite many reminders, the Environment Agency failed to respond for at least six months by which time the damage was done. Today, eight men will begin work for at least 12 weeks, using heavy equipment to repair damage which could have been addressed earlier by two men in half a day and with a great deal less disruption and inconvenience. I'll be interested to assess the environmental impact of their activities in these meadows by the river.

September

Until 153 BC the Roman year began on 1st March, making September the seventh month (Septimus). The Anglo-Saxons called it 'gerst monath' or barley month, and in the Book of Hours for September, harvesting and treading grapes are the illustrated rural activities. In 'Les Très Riches Heures' we can see the gathering of grapes in the famous Angevin vineyard. Aproned women and young men pick the purple-coloured clusters of grapes and fill baskets to be loaded into hampers hanging from the mules, or into vats on the wagons. In the middle foreground a man displays his backside in a deliberately grotesque contrast to the extraordinary 10th century Chateaux de Saumur, which appears in the background in all its fresh newness. Chimneys, pinnacles and weathervanes thrust skyward, crowned with golden fleurs-de-lys. It was built as a fortress against the Norman predations and stands to this day, although the crowning crenulations have long since disappeared.

The result of the Big Butterfly Count for 2011 has been announced, revealing that over 10,000 observers conducted over 15,800 counts and clocked up nearly a quarter of a million butterflies and moths. This is another example of 'citizen science', richly contributing to our knowledge of changes in biodiversity. Counts took place in gardens, fields and other rural habitats. Nationally, highest counts were for the small and large white, but the outstanding result was that the gatekeeper was in third place, an encouraging result for a butterfly which has suffered a run of extremely bad years. In the 1980's the gatekeeper was only found around the fringes of London but has now spread across the urban area, helped by more wildlife-friendly management of parks and gardens. Nationally, the gatekeeper was closely followed by meadow brown, common blue, peacock, green-veined white, red admiral, small tortoiseshell and ringlet in 10th place. It was a surprise to me that the comma missed out on the top 10 nationally, because it is frequently sighted here both in field and garden.

Regionally the most dramatic result was the north-south divide in the performance of the small tortoiseshell. Amazingly, it was the second most common butterfly in North-East England, and did well in the North-West, Yorkshire and Humberside. In stark contrast, the species was 18th place in South-East England, faring only a little better in the East of England and London. Although no day-flying moths made the top ten nationally, the silver 'Y' was seventh placed in Eastern England where it was often seen flying in large groups. It is a highly migratory species that sometimes arrives in huge numbers, so perhaps there had been an influx into East England around the time of the count. It will be fascinating to see how things change, region by region in the years ahead. We need to keep our finger on the pulse of these valuable indicators of the state of the countryside and gain a greater understanding of why some species will expand their range, whilst others may go into decline.

A few years ago whilst researching the history of Trimworth Manor, I came across an extraordinary document in the archives of the Centre for Kentish studies. It was a parchment-covered hand-written volume, which recorded the meetings of tenants with the Lord of the Manor at Trimworth over the period 1648 to 1920.

These were the Court Manor Rolls. In 1648, Sir Robert Filmer became Lord of the Manor and from that date through to 1910, when Sir Robert Marcus Filmer sold the estate, a Filmer presided over the Manor Court. Throughout this period of over years the court met to set the rents, name the tenants, allocate fines, settle disputes, record deaths and appoint successors. The record gives a fascinating insight into the organisation and management of a manorial estate and the everyday lives of a host of tenants through the years. We read of problems of overgrazing, neglect of hedges, damage caused by straying animals, flooding of roads, people found guilty of eavesdropping or spreading gossip or 'walking by night'.

In the record for 1733, the steward responsible for the administration of the Manor pleads as follows "Let it be remembered that one day is not sufficient to keep the Court for the Manors of Trimworth and Hinksell and receiving the rents and wood money. Therefore let the dinner be divided into two, the first day for the tenants and the Woodman and on the second day for keeping the two Courts viz the first Tuesday and Wednesday in July."

We even have the menu for the two meetings:
    "A clod of beef boyl'd with butter'd carrots
    A leg and shoulder of mutton roasted
    One SrLoyn of rump or beef roasted
    One Loyn of mutton bak'd in a Pye
    Two bak'd suit puddings with Raysons.
    Malt three bushels"

1920 was the last entry for Trimworth Manor, and a few years later, under the Law of Property Act enfranchisement saw the last pieces of copyhold land being turned into freehold. So ended the operation of a landholding system that dominated the social and economic life of England and Wales from the Saxon period to the early 20th century. The Court Manor Rolls for Trimworth have given us the possibility to reconstruct a long and colourful history of the house, its land, and, of course, its inhabitants.

September 4th

The appearance of fruiting buds of fungi is an indicator of the onset of autumn. The horse paddock is dotted with the white caps of edible mushrooms. In the meadows, fairy champignons make familiar arcs and rings. This mushroom is also edible but as with many fungi, can easily be confused with poisonous species, in this case the deadly Clitocybe rivulosa. Typically, the growth of the fairy ring will consist of a necrotic zone of dead brown grass, inside which the grass is dark green and luxuriant. The ring gradually increases in diameter. This mushroom is not an individual organism: below the soil to a depth of 20 to 40 cm are threadlike mycelia, which effectively starve the soil of nutrients, inhibit root growth and prevent water uptake.

More spectacular are rapidly growing, large forms of boletus under lime trees. Nearly all forms of boletus grow in association with trees and the majority are edible, except those with red or orange pores. I'm always reluctant to try a species which is described as, 'edible, but has been known to cause severe gastric upsets.' The specimen we found was Boletus luridus, which has small orange pores, yellowing at the edge of the cap. When touched the pores change colour almost instantly to dark blue or black. It has an attractive large, smooth olive-brown cap with rusty tints, a beautiful sight in the golden evening sunlight. In complete contrast, but equally plentiful, is the puffball whose distinguishing feature is that spores are produced internally. They are so called because a cloud of grey-brown spores is emitted when the fruiting body bursts. We saw Calvatia expuliformus, which is shaped like a brown pestle, with the texture of chamois. Surprisingly, it is edible when young, before the spores are formed. Some, such as the giant puffball, have a stalk from which the fruiting body can easily detach, leaving the ball free to roll around scattering millions of spores.

September 5th

Lots of early morning bird activity in the garden as cold overnight temperatures rise quickly in bright sunshine. Flocks of noisy sparrows fly excitedly into the tops of laburnum and swoop down to the pond in the sunken garden, where adults try to push food into beaks of young. Long-tailed tits roam between the various birdfeeders making high-pitched squeaks in their bouncy flight. In contrast, jackdaws tumble out of the nest box into the paddock. Colourful groups of chaffinches dart through the silver birches, magpies and green woodpeckers are foraging noisily on the windfalls or in ants' nests. It is a scene of great energy and excitement in a contented, convivial bird world, and it fills our eyes and ears with joy.

In the willow trees by the river, small olive-brown birds were flitting between branches, picking off insects or snapping them up in flight. These little birds, the size of blue tits, were chiff-chaff or leaf warblers looking for midges, flies and aphids on the underside of leaves and wagging their tails excitedly as they patrolled the woodland edge, (their name Phylloscopus means leaf-explorer).They can be confused with the willow warbler which has a song like a rippling cascade, rather than the repetitive but cheerful, 'chiff-chiff- chaff-chiff-chaff'. In the alder by the owl nest box we watched the antics of a small bird spiralling mouse-like up the trunk with occasional sideways hops, using its tail like a prop to steady itself. This was the tree creeper searching for beetles, insects and spiders. It has a streaked brown back, white underside and gives a high pitched 'tsee-tsee' call as it flies between trees. Its nest is usually well hidden behind loose bark, in tree crevices, behind ivy or even behind cladding of buildings.

September 6th

Along the footpath over the downs, great skeletons of cow parsley and hemlock stand erect, and will probably survive the winter until new shoots appear from their widely dispersed fruits. The prickly heads of burrs from burdock catch Sam's fur, dispersing seeds even more widely. Common toadflax is also abundant along the edges of corn fields. The erect stem has blue-green leaves and is topped by masses of bright yellow flowers with a splash of orange on the lower lip or palate, resembling snapdragons, or antirrhinum, in appearance. In the harvested fields, scarlet pimpernel, a member of the primrose family, reveals its star-like scarlet petals having been exposed to the light and sun. The alternative name for this little flower is 'poor man's weather glass,' or 'shepherds sundial'. It is supposed to tell the time by

The appearance of the fruiting buds of fungi, such as this boletus with its orange pores, is an indicator of the onset of autumn.

Common toad flax is abundant along the edges of corn fields, their bright yellow flowers resembling snapdragons.

opening at 7am and closing at 2pm, and its petals close when rain approaches. Gerard, the 16th century herbalist wrote, "No heart can think, no tongue can tell, the virtues of the pimpernel." Another flower of cultivated arable fields is the bright yellow charlock, resembling the flower of a cabbage.

The landscape colours are changing to deeper greens of vegetation and darker browns of ploughed soils. Into these mellow, more subdued colours, comes the refreshing sight of the delicate blue harebell. It is a campanula or bellflower (bluebell in Scotland), and grows in dry grassland from July to October, its bell-like flower nodding at the top of an upright stem. Everything about it is fragile, but its vibrant sky-blue colour is a joyful boost at a time of the year when the rich colours of summer are looking a little exhausted.

September 7th

Tye Wood is quiet, as if in shock, recovering from the assaults of woodland clearance. There is one persistent sound, that of the repetitive five-syllable cooing of the wood pigeon. It is our largest and most common pigeon and somewhat taken for granted in its wide habitat of gardens, fields and broad leaved woodlands. Their numbers are certainly increasing and they can cause considerable damage when flocks of several hundred birds alight on young crops. For this reason, the British Association for Shooting and Conservation regard it as the number one agricultural pest, so shooting is permitted all year round. Despite its tormented status, the wood pigeon has some fascinating features, such as the way it uses its beak as a straw, unlike other birds which scoop up water and throw their heads back to drink it. Their wobbling walk suggests a portly obesity, yet their feathers weigh more than the skeleton and their flight is fast and direct, often incorporating short, steep climbs, then long downward sloping glides with wings set and tail spread. Instead of feeding their young on insects, pigeons feed them milk from liquid-filled cells in the crop lining which is supposedly more nutritious than human or cows' milk. So as we continue to 'persecute the pigeon', we should also admire its qualities and its capacity to survive and thrive.

Turning into the drive late this evening, a large pigeon-sized bird emerged from the limes and swooped ahead of us in long glides under the canopy of trees down the drive. From its flight, size and reddish-brown upper body it was clearly a tawny owl, a non-migratory, highly territorial nocturnal bird, arousing feelings of mystery or danger and even evil. We have seen them frequently in this area, dropping down from a perch high in the lime trees looking for a rodent to swallow whole. Detection of prey is mainly accomplished through hearing. Just like the barn owl, the tawny's two ear openings are asymmetrically placed so there are minute differences in the arrival of sound, which enables the owl to pinpoint its prey. August and September are very active times vocally for the tawny owls as they set about reaffirming their territories for the next breeding season. The distinctive haunting call of the owl has a prominent place in literature. In fact, the call is actually a duet with a female sounding the shrill 'kew-wick' and the male responding with the mellow 'hoo-hoo-oo'. It is a wavering call which can raise hairs on the back of the neck, especially when accompanied by eerie shrieks. The call is frequently mimicked by children wrapping hands together and blowing through a small hole between the thumbs, as Wordsworth describes in his poem, 'There was a Boy.'

> "And there, with fingers interwoven, both hands
> Pressed closely palm to palm and to his mouth
> Uplifted, he, as through an instrument,
> Blew mimic hootings to the silent owls,
> That they might answer him. And they would shout
> Across the watery vale, and shout again,
> Responsive to his call, with quavering peals,
> And long halloos, and screams, and echoes loud."

The garden has been refreshed by heavy showers washing the dust of autumn away, stimulating new growth and colour, giving a fresher, more relaxed feel to the garden. I sense the seasonal change. There is a chilly, misty start to the mornings, but often followed by a warm, even hot, midday sun. As the angle of the sun gets lower the light becomes richer, especially in the evening sun, which enhances the colours of the rain-washed garden. I wander slowly through, taking notes and photographs of changes. Dahlias dominate with bursts of contrasting colour and form. Pom-pom and cactus flaunt garish pinks, brilliant reds, deep velvety tones of the night, lemon-yellow, audacious starbursts of golden red in one flower, all far from subtle, but full of fun and boldness, and vibrating against glossy-green foliage. Roses have responded to the rain with a resurgence of growth and recent flowering. Vegetation contrasts seem stronger in this low sunlight. Golden acacia glows against a dark-green conifer; the white trunks of Betula jacquemontii stand like goalposts against lush green grass; dark maroon acers are backed by deep green hedges of hawthorn; fresh clusters of white cyclamen are dotted closely across the dark brown soil; clusters of milky white hazelnuts are framed in sap green leaves. All these contrasts are intensified as the day progresses towards the rich, golden evening sunlight.

Fresh clusters of white cyclamen are dotted closely across the dark brown soil.

Hedgerows are displaying the classic colours of autumn such as the bizarre bright-pink spindleberry (above) and the deep purple fruiting sloes of blackthorn.

The garden is wrapped around by hedges, still uncut and displaying the classic colours of autumn, such as the deepening red of hawthorn berries, (the alizarin red of the hedgerow), brilliant red and orange rosehips, purple elderberries, bizarre bright pink berries of spindle berry, burgundy coloured bracts of pheasant berry, deep purple fruiting sloes of blackthorn, clusters of crimson berries on the guelder rose similar in colour to the berries of the woody nightshade which climbs through the hedge. All this colour justifies our initial choice of planting traditional English hedgerow plants when we moved here 15 years ago. As the year advances, different plants dominate the flower beds. Michaelmas daisies, named to mark the feast of St Michael on 29th September, add colour and attract butterflies as does the tall self-sown Verbena bonariensis with their shimmering blue purple flowers waving high above other plants: dominant, but not obscuring. Pale yellow flower spikes of mullein also rise 3 metres like tall candles and are surrounded by grasses like the golden oaten heads of Stipa gigantea and other hairy, feathery heads which hold the dew and reflect the early morning sunlight in a million water droplets.

September 10th

The old saying that weather in September 'can either dry up wells or break down bridges' sums up the uncertainty of the weather prospects for the month. Today, the whole country is dominated by a high-pressure system giving still, warm weather, so perhaps 'fair on September 1st, fair for the month' could follow, or more likely, 'September blows soft until fruits are in the loft'. The month is commonly regarded as being the beginning of autumn, but like most seasonal changes, it will be a transition during which it is difficult to know when summer has slipped away, leaving us fully in the season of mists and mellow fruitfulness.

Where have all the acorns gone? The familiar little fruits in their light-green leathery shells and protecting cups have taken on a new morphology on the oaks in our garden. Instead of the familiar acorn, strangely shaped galls have been produced by the activities of the gall wasp which lays its eggs in the acorn. Many of the oaks have developed chemically-induced distorted forms with lots of small, smooth green knobs often known as knopper galls. The insect responsible is a fairly recent introduction to Britain, first arriving in the 1960s. The abnormal acorns develop through the summer, completely replacing the original acorn. In the autumn they become woody and brown and fall from the trees and the adult female gall wasp emerges from the top of the gall in spring. Fortunately the trees survive and continue to produce acorns in later years. Another species of gall wasp causes some trees to produce spherical galls up to 5cms in diameter on the underside of leaves. This is the oak apple which turns reddish-brown in the autumn.

September 11th

Flat bottomed fair weather cumulus floated gently eastwards, like 'bodies without a surface,' in the words of Leonardo. These rising, brilliant, white mounds changed form as the day progressed, from 'humilis' (humble) to the broader 'mediocris', then the angry, towering 'congestus' at which point it could no could no longer be described as fair weather cumulus. The 'morning mountains' were soon to become the 'afternoon fountains,' but we were spared the final stage of growth to the godfather of all clouds, cumulo-nimbus. Nevertheless, there was sufficient internal churning of convection currents in the cloud to give a rash of beefy showers interspersed with periods of gin-clear visibility. Looking upwards into the dark base of the clouds I could see the black specks of swallows darting and veering and

The brilliant white mounds of 'fair weather' cumulus change as the day progresses from 'morning mountains' to 'afternoon fountains'.

drifting in their hundreds, like burnt paper fragments, carried upwards from the rising air of a bonfire. Each day I anxiously check the overhead wires and cables for the gathering of large roosts of swallows prior to their departure.

The onset of autumn has been a popular subject in English poetry, usually featuring the season's soft, rich light and colours, and the slow maturing of fruits and berries. In Ted Hughes's poem, 'Autumn Song' the imagery is one of anger, frustration and even violence, with the first stanza talking of autumn 'killing-off' summer. After the belligerent mood of the first stanza, time, in the form of 'the day', appears amazed at the question of what will happen to the trees, and in the third stanza questions whether the sun will ever return again. The negative imagery continues with reference to the birds being frightened away; seed being sown too deep; and people stuffing themselves with apple and blackberry pie. In the last stanza, autumn is revealed as a monster with a mouth as wide and red as a sunset. It is a dramatic, rather than a romantic poem, with nature, portrayed in a harsh, fearful manner, although there are suggestions of humour as well as sinister intent.

"There came a day that caught the summer. Wrung its neck
Plucked it
And ate it.

Now, what will I do with trees?
The day said, the day said.
Strip them bare, strip them bare.
Let's see what is really there.
And what shall I do with the sun?
The day said, the day said.
Roll him away till he's cold and small
He'll soon come back rested if he comes back at all.

And what shall I do with the birds?
The day said, the day said.
The birds I've frightened, let them flit,
I'll hang out pork for the brave tomtit.

And what shall I do with the seed?
The day said, the day said.
Bury it deep, see what it's worth.
See if it can stand the earth.

What shall I do with the people?
The day said the day said.
Stuff them with apple and blackberry pie –
They'll love me then till the day they die.

There came this day and he was autumn.
His mouth was wide.
And red as a sunset.
His tail was an icicle."

The village of Challock, located on the dip-slope of the chalk downs a few miles from Trimworth, is of Saxon origin and means 'enclosure of calves'. The manor was given by William the Conqueror to Battle Abbey and remained in its possession until the Dissolution. The early link with livestock remains to this day when the huge village green becomes the scene of an annual Goose Fair. The name comes from the time when geese were driven from surrounding farms to be sold for fattening and then roasted for the feast of St Michaelmas later in the month. In the case of the famous Nottingham Goose Fair, geese were driven on foot from the fens of Lincolnshire, or even Norfolk, their feet being coated with a mixture of tar and sand to protect them on their long journey. The Nottingham Fair was recorded in borough records as far back as 1541, although the origin is probably much older. At Challock today the focus was still on local trades and merrymaking. The air was full of the mixed pungent smells of burgers, curries, candy floss and toffee apples. Local traders sold cheeses, fruits and vegetables, handmade crafts of wood, glass and pottery. Traditional skills of sheepdog handling, fencing and wood-turning were all demonstrated and the excited faces of children shone with exhilaration from roundabouts of hobby horses and dodgems.

September 14th

Along the riverbank the pollinated female flowers of the alders have grown into neat ovoid fruits which hang in clusters of four or five green cones. They will ripen by October and release small flat brown seeds which will be dispersed in the spring by wind and water. Empty cones from last year are hanging next to this year's fruits. The alder leaf remains fresh green and will not change to autumn colour, instead it slowly darkens before being shed in October or November. Nearby ash trees on the riverbank have very different fruits. Like the alder, the ash is monoecious, (i.e. bearing male and female flowers), so flowers with female parts in this sexually mixed-up tree produce bunches of seeds known as keys, which will stay on the tree until the spring, when they will be dispersed long distances on the wind and germinate quickly on almost any soil.

Birds seem to be 'grouping up'. Jolly jackdaws are bouncing around under the apple trees sticking their big black beaks into windfalls; starlings are lining up on cables in large numbers, jostling for position; groups of young sparrows line the gutters, puffing out their feathers and chirping incessantly in their social singing; the aerial displays of raucous rooks are even more spectacular in these strong westerly winds. As yet, no signs of swifts and swallows gathering for departure.

September 15th

The cereal grain from fields has been an attractive food source for collared doves for weeks; now they are moving into gardens looking for food, and will forage for ripe hedgerow berries later in the autumn. It is a smaller bird than the wood pigeon with a quite elegant pale brown/grey plumage turning pinkish brown around the breast. Adults can be distinguished by the narrow black-and-white band around the back of the neck – the collar. This bird, boringly common to the point of being almost overlooked, lays claim to being one of the greatest colonisers of the bird world, spreading outwards in the 19th-century from Asia and expanding into Europe, arriving in Great Britain in 1953 and breeding for the first time in 1956. Since that date numbers have increased rapidly, largely because of the long breeding season from March to October. Four broods are common and six broods have been known. It is a gregarious bird, feeding in large flocks where grain has been spilled, and then taking off to display similar flight characteristics to the wood pigeon. Its song does little to attract interest, being a repetitive, 'coo,Coo,coo. Forty five years ago the sight of the collared dove would have sent 'twitchers' scampering across the countryside. Today there are over 200,000 breeding pairs in Britain, breeding close to human habitation where food sources are more abundant.

There was a sudden disturbance in the long grass around the bottom pond, followed by the movement of duckweed on the water, and then the bizarre sight of the erect head of a grass snake moving swiftly through the water, its olive green body partly concealed by the thick green weed. During pond dipping sessions in May, the children all observed this largest of our indigenous reptile in grass close to the water, a fruitful spring hunting ground where they wait for toads and tadpoles using their sense of smell to catch and swallow them whole. It is easy to overlook them, even though they can be more than a metre in length when fully grown. Although non-venomous, the grass snake can put up an impressive display of aggression by hissing and inflating the body, occasionally discharging a foul smelling fluid from the anal glands; they can also feign death as a form of defence. We have seen them soaking up the sun in spring after emerging from hibernation under logs and vegetation, and then moving off to find a mate in April or May. Our compost heaps are frequently used as a warm site for egg laying, and we have exposed several young snakes in June, when the compost is turned.

Before the children arrive for pond dipping, we place black plastic sheets on the long grass by the ponds to encourage reptiles. The most frequent find is the grey-brown slow worm, gathering under these collectors of heat. They look like snakes but are actually legless lizards, which like the lizards in the stream course, have eyelids, whilst snakes are 'lidless'. The slow worm is a burrowing creature, hiding under logs and rocks, feeding on slugs and worms. They have the ability to shed their tails by breaking a tail vertebra as an escape mechanism, just like other lizards. They can have exceptionally long lives, living up to 30 years in the wild.

In previous years, adders, our only native venomous snake, have been routinely present basking in the sun on piles of old chestnut logs by the field gate. I remember coming within inches of kneeling on one when I was clearing under a hedge. Its response from a comfortable coiled position was to leap away to the safety of long grass. Two summertime day-dreamers both brought quickly back to their senses, and hastily giving each other mutual respect.

We frequently have uninvited winged guests coming through our open kitchen door in summer. This morning, Roz announced the arrival of a small bird found scuttling around in the greasy dust on top of kitchen cupboards and making hesitant, fluttering flights towards closed windows, rather than the open door. Great clumps of dust had accumulated on its feet, like a child in adult 'wellies' making the body look even more diminutive. It was a goldcrest, the UK's smallest songbird, distinguished by its yellow crown stripe, dull olive-green and white feathers, and thin black bill. It is rare to be able to observe and photo a goldcrest at such close range. Normally they are detected in the wild only by their high-pitched calls, similar to some tits, and almost above the frequency which can be perceived by humans. Alternatively, they can be seen flitting restlessly through branches. Many goldcrests are resident in Britain, often joined by immigrants from North-West and Central Europe in autumn. In 2005, huge numbers arrived on the East Coast, and bushes of gorse were described as 'dripping with goldcrest'. For such a small bird, these lengthy migrations are truly impressive. Worn and spent by repeated exertions to escape, this little bird stayed still enough for Roz to enclose it carefully in her hands before releasing it gently back to freedom.

Our journey through the 'geological museum' of south-east England has brought us just over the West Sussex border into Selbourne, Hampshire to follow in the footsteps of Gilbert White and to stroll through ancient beech woods and pastures which inspired this pioneering 18th-century naturalist. We visited his home and gazed at his little study in which he recorded his accurate and perceptive observations of the natural world. Walking up the steep 'zig-zag' path constructed by Gilbert and his brother in 1753, you come to spectacular ancient beech woods

We left today for a short break to follow the rolling sweep of chalk downland through Kent, East and West Sussex and on into Hampshire. This landscape is dominated by prominent scarps, rolling downs cut by dry-valleys and coombes, pastoral, wooded and farmed countryside. The chalk downs are emblematic of south-east England: icons of Englishness. The ancient downland turf is rich in flowers and butterflies, prehistoric field patterns, barrows, forts, old roads, deserted villages and exquisite little churches, all providing evidence of the way the edge of cultivation has ebbed and flowed over time depending on economic conditions. It is my favourite landscape, and the Weald, the most fascinating of geological structures. This fondness dates back to my time as a student in London when the Weald was used as a training ground for successive generations of geography and geology students. Structurally, it is a great eroded anticyclone of folded rocks with the chalk at its crest. The chalk has been worn away to reveal sandstones and clays in an alternating sequence, giving a succession of inward facing ridges and valleys. This is the environment where I learned geography 'through the soles of my boots', walking north to south and noting the way land-use, soils, vegetation, settlement patterns and drainage changed as geological boundaries were crossed. I take pleasure in Gilbert White's description of the downs as being "peculiarly sweet and amusing in the shapely figured aspects of the chalk hills....as they swell and heave their broad backs into the sky." H.E.Bates, who lived most of his life in Kent, described the Weald as having "a friendly, tranquillising effect of a familiar room... I come back to it with renewed pleasure. The easy familiarity of it folds around me, and I am glad to be home."

The poet and author Edward Thomas also drew inspiration from the downs. His book "The South Country", written in 1908, reads like a prose poem. He was a compulsive walker, reserved and meditative: walking was an act of re-creation rather than recreation. He often walked without a map, tracing the courses of clear streams, circling beech woods, following curving slopes of grass, bushes of gorse, juniper and yew, and studying wild flower meadows. Of all the downland features, he loved best the coombes or dry-valleys of the chalk. "All year round, the coombes, dripping, green and still, are cauldrons for the making and unmaking of mists, mists that lie like solid level snow or float diaphanous and horizontal of airiest silk across the moon or the morning sun." His writings are lyrical, passionate and sensitive to the rhythms of the seasons. For me they bring to life the beauty and wonder of the downland landscapes of today, and give glimpses of the natural history, folklore and culture of a bygone age.

Edward Thomas volunteered to the Artists' Rifles in the First World War, and in 1917 was assigned to the Western Front. Even here his writings had an absorbing fascination. "...the morning, chill and clear hurts my skin while it delights my mind. Neuville in early morning with its flat straight crest with trees and houses – the beauty of this silent empty scene of no inhabitants and hid troops, but don't know why I could have cried and didn't." On the night of April 8, the first day of the battle of Arras, snow was falling heavily, and through the snowflakes fell the German shells, one of which killed Thomas a few minutes after dawn.

September 21st

overlooking the village. These are the 'hangers' from the Old English 'hangra', meaning wooded slope. Paths lead on into the High Wood, traditionally coppiced, but now containing tall stands of oak and beech around which rooks flopped and clamoured; and below is the sheep down of Selbourne. These hangers, high woods and commons are the landscape elements which were the outdoor laboratory for White, and in which he observed the rhythms of the seasons and the richness of the wildlife, recording each with detail, humour and accuracy.

At every turn on our walk we sensed the presence of the busy, diminutive form of Gilbert White meticulously recording data on local conditions in order to establish his calendar of the natural world. Selbourne was his inspiration. He was surrounded by beech forest, chalk downland, sandy heath and water meadows. Within half an hour walk of his house he had a microcosm of the landscape elements of south-east England, and through his writing he enriched the national consciousness about this natural world.

Today is the autumnal equinox when the passage of the sun crosses the Equator on its way south, giving day and night of equal length. In 2010, the date of the equinox coincided with the date of the full moon, an event which had not occurred since 1991. The September full moon is known as the 'harvest moon' because there is no long period of darkness between sunset and moonrise, allowing farmers to continue to harvest even after the sun has set. 'Cornfield by Moonlight' is captured by Samuel Palmer in an ethereal scene which shows a man walking his dog through a cornfield that has been cut and stacked into sheaves. In the dark sky is a large waxing sickle moon and an evening star, casting a glimmering light over the Shoreham landscape. Tonight we watched the moon at about 10pm, rising high above the trees studding the pastures. On this clear, still night the daytime warmth of the earth was quickly

September 23rd

lost by radiation, bringing moist waves of air into contact with the cold ground surface. The result was a deepening layer of condensation as the air reached saturation point, gradually submerging the trees in a rising tide of mist above which shone what appeared to be a bigger and brighter moon than normal. This, however, is only a moon illusion, the brain being tricked into thinking that a low hanging moon is larger than when it is high in the sky. Despite this cool scientific rationalisation, it was still an enchanting sight, so, 'shine on harvest moon'!

September 24th

Outside the kitchen window a garden spider slowly and methodically consumes a dead moth trapped at the centre of the spiders spiral wheel-shaped web. It is one of the orb weavers whose work is a feat of engineering. The web is begun by the female spider 'floating' a line of silk in the wind, which attaches itself to another surface. Another line is dropped from the centre and also attached, making a 'Y' shape around which the rest of the radial silks are laid. Some of these lines will be sticky so that an insect will be captured, stunned by a quick bite, and then wrapped around with silk. Orb spiders are said to eat their web, consuming any insect trapped within and then constructing a new web for the following day. The silk construction is finer than human hair, yet stronger by weight than steel. The garden spider is one of the largest British spiders, distinguished by the white cross mark on its abdomen. It is particularly active now with webs draped between branches or bushes, or across doorways, each with flies and insects wrapped up in their silk death beds. The moth we observed was still being slowly consumed several hours later, having been injected with a venom to liquefy the inside of the prey, which can then be sucked out. This explains the hollow carcasses of flies and beetles slowly turning in the wind on the end of broken webs.

With the arrival of autumn we are now seeing more house spiders scuttling around floors or vainly trying to climb up the inside of sinks and baths into which they have fallen. This is their mating season and they will be more noticeable as they move around the house in search of a female. After mating, the male dies and is eaten by the female, thus contributing to the well-being of his offspring even after death!

September 25th

Autumn brings some intriguing insects to the field and garden. The crane fly or 'daddy longlegs' is far from being 'top of the tree of life' in terms of its morphology; it would rank high as a misfit of the insect world with its small wings. They are poor fliers, drifting and fluttering awkwardly in large numbers between the grass stems or shambling around in an ungainly, feeble fashion. Their long fragile legs are weakly attached to the body and frequently break off. They are usually nocturnal and are attracted to house lights where they perish on hot light-bulbs or drift around aimlessly on the floor, getting caught in spiders' webs. They neither bite nor sting and do not even feed as adults, existing to mate and then die. It is during mating that the long legs serve some purpose, because the female inserts its ovipositor into the ground, supporting itself like a cradle on its six legs. The larvae, known as leather jackets can cause considerable damage to lawns, but they are targeted by starlings which probe the ground with their beaks to find these hard, leathery, brown larvae. The striking larvae of the elephant hawk moth are feeding on rose bay willow herb along stream edges. It is 75 mm long, grey brown in colour and has a backward curving spine or horn on the final abdominal segment. When startled, it draws its body into the foremost segment and looks like a snake with four eye patches - a sight likely to deter all predators.

Beneath tree bark on dead trees, in dark crevices, in nuts and rotting apples, on birdfeeders and dahlia flowers, earwigs can be found, feeding on decaying plant

The snake-like larvae of the elephant hawk moth with its four 'eye' patches is a sight likely to deter predators.

material and other insects. They are also mating at this time of year, and sometime between January and April the female will lay up to 80 eggs in shallow hollows or under stones. Their pincer-like appendages look dangerously aggressive and are used to scare off predators. Another fascinating insect making an autumnal appearance is the dock bug, common in the South of England and using knotweed, sorrel and dock as host plants, sucking the sap from the plant foliage with their needle-like proboscis in September. They are often attracted to blackberries and raspberries, where their feeding can cause the drupelets making up the fruit to deflate. They are brown bugs, like shield bugs, shedding their skin five times as they pass through the nymphal stages to adulthood.

September 26th

We returned from our recent visit to the South Downs to find that swallows in our barns had gathered and gone. Perhaps they were prompted by the sudden temperature drop from 25° to 15° in three days; or the shift in wind to the north giving them a good tailwind; or the shortening daylight hours; or difficulty in finding insect prey. Or did they know the average date of swallow departure in England is the 25th September? Whatever, I feel saddened that this symbol of summer has gone, and without a chance for me to say farewell. I shall miss their restless silhouettes in the sky, and the flurries of family activity around the nests in nearby barns. I had hoped for a vision similar to that recorded by Gilbert White on the 22nd September 1771, when he noted in his Naturalistic Journals: "Today, the beeches are tinged with yellow. Heavy clouds on the horizon. This morning the swallows rendezvoused in a neighbour's walnut tree. At the dawn of the day they associated altogether in infinite numbers, occasioning such a rushing with the strokes of their wings as might be heard a considerable distance." White was obsessed with the problem of whether swallows really did migrate to Africa or whether they overwintered in some small shelter for refuge. Despite searching for evidence in the field or through correspondence with other observers and scientists he was never able to resolve this big question. He wrote: "… after all our pains and enquiries, we are yet not quite certain to what regions they do migrate: and are still further embarrassed to find some do not actually migrate at all."

September 27th

We have collected a good harvest of nuts today: filberts, cobnuts, chestnuts and walnuts, some from our orchard and some from the hedges and woodland margins. The hazel was one of the first trees to colonise after the Ice Age, becoming less widespread as the climate warmed. Now we find them along woodland margins, or as understory in woods, especially in chalk and limestone areas. Several stems rise from a stool, often as a result of coppicing, giving the hazel a long history of economic importance. Stems are versatile and can be easily bent without breaking, thus finding uses in wattle and daub, weaving hurdles, or making spars for thatching. The nut has been a staple food from prehistoric times. Hazels belong to the 'corylus' genus from the Greek 'corys', meaning a helmet. The Old English for hazel is 'haesil', or headdress, referring to the bracts surrounding the nut. There are several species such as the filbert (Corylus maxima), and the cobnut (Corylus avellana). The filbert is named after St Philibert, an abbot of Normandy, whose feast day is the 20th August, about the time that nuts are becoming mature. The tree was imported from south-east Europe and the nut is larger, more elongated than the cob and almost completely enclosed by bracts. We have Corylus maxima purpurea, which has a deep purple leaf. The cobnut is our native species and there are many cultivars such as our own Kentish cob, introduced in the 19th century. In 1913 there were 7000 acres of Kentish cob in the south-east, mostly around Plaxtol in Kent. There are now only about 200 acres, but there is a resurgence with the formation of the Kentish Cobnut Association. In the past, plats around Plaxtol have recruited itinerant workers from the East End, now more likely from Eastern Europe, to help with harvests.

Our nut harvest continued with the sweet chestnut, whose spiky cases had fallen, revealing small, often hollow nuts full of earwigs and ladybirds- and the occasional plump one. The smooth green globes of walnuts had also fallen from the layered branches of the shapely, handsome tree, to which hungry rooks are now frequent visitors. After 30 minutes picking from the walnut by the dyke my hands were stained brown from opening the soft, green cases surrounding the nut.

It is St Michaelmas Day, the feast of St Michael and all Angels. As it falls near the equinox, it is usually associated with the beginning of autumn. In England it is one of the 'quarter days', when servants were hired, rents were due and leases begun. Celebrations were associated with the need for protection during the dark months ahead. Usually the harvest had been completed, so it marked the end of the productive season and the beginning of a new cycle in farming. It was also the day when reeves were appointed to manage the manorial estates and oversee the peasants. Traditionally a well fattened goose, fed on the stubble of harvested fields, was eaten and many goose fairs were held. Apparently the reason for goose being eaten was that when Elizabeth I heard of the defeat of the Armada, she was eating goose and decided that goose should continue to be eaten on Michaelmas Day also. The festival is also associated with the Michaelmas daisy flowering at this time and giving colour and warmth to a season when many flowers are fading, hence the old saying:

> "The Michaelmas daisies, among dede weeds.
> Bloom for St Michael's valorous deeds.
> And seems the last of flowers that stood
> Till the feast of St Simon and St Jude."

(The feast of St Simon and St Jude is 28th October).

Decreasing daylight and lower temperatures mark the end of flowering activity for most plants, although on a warm day, ivies continue to attract wasps, bees and flies to their nectar-rich flowers, and some daisies are still in flower. The daisy, or 'days eye', so called because the flower opens in the morning, can be seen flowering in almost every month. The new leaves and flower buds, now forming in tight rosettes, will have to withstand some harsh winter weather. It has had a place in our culture since Saxon times. Chaucer wrote, ".....of all the flowers in the mede, Thanne I love most the flowers are white and rede, Swyche as men call days eyes in our town". Along the banks of the swollen river there are pinks and purples of Himalayan balsam surviving amongst the brown willow herb. Spots of sky blue water forget-me-nots are showing at the water's edge, struggling to stay afloat in the fast moving brown water. Around the garden pond only mimulus is flowering, while nearby teasel and cardoon will produce the seeds for goldfinch, and then remain standing gauntly throughout the winter. In garden and hedgerows it is berries which grab the interest: spindle, elderberry, rose hips, sloes, hawthorn, and dogwood.

Pessimistic media headlines highlight the threat of species extinction: 'Biodiversity Nears Point of No Return', 'Global List Cut by 600,000', 'Creative Thinking to Save Species', 'UN Asks for Action on Nature Losses', 'Key Time to Save Nature Crisis'.These are reactions to an analysis from the Royal Botanic Gardens at Kew, the Natural History Museum and the International Union for Conservation of Nature, all of which agree that a fifth of the world's 380,000 plant species are at risk of extinction. Clearance of forests for agriculture poses one of the most significant threats. The study investigated mosses, ferns, orchids and legumes and found that species are being lost which have valuable medicinal properties. Plant-based remedies are often the only source of health care in the world's poorest countries, and have proved essential in combating such conditions as malaria and leukaemia. There is also concern that we are becoming dependent on a narrow range of plants with a limited genetic base. The report estimates that 80% of the calories consumed worldwide are derived from just 12 different species.

These findings highlight the urgency of the work of the Millennium Seed Bank of Kew, based at Wakehurst in Sussex which has gathered 2 billion seeds from around the world. These are catalogued and stored in cool underground rooms and include seeds from plants that have already been judged extinct. Working with partners across the world, Kew has now successfully banked 10% of the world's wild plant species with a focus on those parts of the world in which plant diversity is tightly bound to people's livelihoods. Growing problems of food security, natural disasters and climate change will all impact on plant diversity, making the work of this valuable partnership even more crucial.

October

October, from the Latin 'octo', was the eighth month in the Roman calendar. The rural occupations for October in the Book of Hours are ploughing, tilling and sowing. It is a busy month with the fields full of activity. In 'Les Très Riches Heures', a scarecrow with bow and arrows stands in the middle of freshly sown fields across which white twine has been strung between twigs. A wooden harrow, weighed down by a large stone, is being drawn across a ploughed field, and mournful looking peasants broadcast seed from bulging aprons of corn. In the foreground a flock of magpies and rooks scavenge expectantly for seed in the footsteps of the sower. All this is set against the amazing background of the Louvre Palace, in front of which elegant men strut along the riverbank of pollarded willows. The image gives us a fascinating picture of the characteristics of the inner suburbs of Paris at the beginning of the 15th century.

The rural occupations for this month in the Books of Hours are ploughing, tilling and sowing. The scene in Lès Tres Riches Heures shows a wooden harrow being drawn across the field, and a mournful-looking peasant broadcasting seed.

October has often been associated with the meteorological phenomenon of St Luke's Summer, a period of warm, fine, settled weather occurring around St Luke's day on 15 October. The American equivalent is the Indian summer, so-called because it was a period when North American Indians took this opportunity to increase their winter stores of corn and squash. But it is unwise to generalise in the name of a benign physician and gospeller, because October has a reputation for surprises, as the BBC weatherman Michael Fish knows only too well; and October 29th, 2008, brought a fall in temperature to -4°C and over 3cm of snow in London.

Ploughing is an ancient skill in which the ability to plough a straight furrow of even depth is highly praised and a cause for celebration. This was the purpose of ploughing matches taking place at six locations across the county, including Eastry Court Farm on the rolling chalk hills of East Kent. We joined the crowds to watch modern and vintage ploughing, together with all the subsidiary activities of tossing the sheaf of corn, sheepdog trials, horse judging and rural crafts. Some events are over 100 years old but the objective remains the same: to turn and bury the stubble, leaving a smooth, straight furrow. On show were 19th-century Kent ploughs pulled by teams of horses, the sharp wrought-iron ploughshare slicing through the sod and the mould board turning over the dark, moist soil to leave even furrows in fields looking like brown corduroy. Steam-driven ploughing machines filled the air with pulses of black smoke, steam and the smell of burning coal as they worked in pairs. A cable with plough attached spans the field and winding drums on each engine pull the plough backwards and forwards across the fields, ploughing up to 30 acres a day. Other traction engines, worked by proud owners, were being used as mobile power sources for thrashing, tree pulling and other general farm duties. Although production stopped in the1930s traction engines were still in use in the 1950s. This was a joyful community event, generously supported and ensuring the survival of a great rural tradition. Watching a master ploughman at work, whatever the technology, is a stirring, stimulating sight, which perpetuates the strong association between man, machine and natural resources.

October 3rd

The dark green spires of pine trees stand out in Tye Wood surrounded by deciduous trees which are now beginning to show autumn colour. Only the blue-grey willows and fresh dark green of alders remain unchanged. Field maple and hornbeam, sycamore and lime lead the autumn yellowing and bring a new colour to the landscape. Horse chestnut is the most advanced and most attractive with rusty yellow and brown leaves, many beginning to fall and already revealing large sticky buds. The horse chestnut was introduced into England by John Tradescant, responsible for introducing so many trees and shrubs that he could justifiably be considered as the father of English gardening. In 1621 he travelled as a 'Gentleman Volunteer' on an expedition to the Mediterranean, where he collected gladioli and lilac as well as the horse chestnut, bringing back six conkers, the forerunners of one of our most attractive features of the landscape.

Changing leaf colour is the result of the interaction between different pigments produced by plants. As the amount and type of pigment fluctuates, so does leaf colour. It is the abundance of chlorophyll produced in response to sunlight which gives green leaves, but as the amount of sunlight decreases in autumn, less chlorophyll is produced and so the green colour fades from the leaves. At the same time, other pigments appear, such as carotenoids, which produce a yellowing of the leaf. The addition of anthocyanins will produce orange colours, and in combination with flavanoids will give red, purple, or even magenta colours. About 10% of the world's trees in the Northern Hemisphere contain anthocyanins, but in New England, the proportion rises to about 70%, accounting for the extraordinary displays of colour in Maine, Vermont and New Hampshire. When these pigments are absent, other chemical pigments may be produced such as tannins, giving brown colours, as in many oaks.

I was probably a little hasty in my criticism of woodland thinning at Tye Wood earlier in the year. At the time it seemed an insensitive, callous and brutal activity in landscape change, but I recognise now how dark, dense and overcrowded the wood had become. Autumn sun now filters deep into the wood along open glades; birds are more visible; saplings are being given a chance and the remaining standards of pine, oak, and sycamore look more majestic and imposing.

It is thrilling to discover the names of people who used to live in your home, especially when their life stories are interesting and unusual and come from the distant past. How different was the house then? What did these former residents do for a living? These people regarded your house as their home too, and it is fascinating to confront these 'shadows of the past.' It makes us realise that we are merely the present custodians of a house with a long and colourful history of previous occupants.

The Filmer family were a prominent Kent family from the 16th century, owning Trimworth Manor and the surrounding farmland for over 260 years from 1648 until 1910. One of the most interesting Filmers was Sir Edward, who inherited the estate in 1720. He took a keen interest in running the estate and was preoccupied with agricultural methods and techniques as illustrated in copious and detailed records that he kept. He was a great pioneer of crop rotation and developed a flexible rotation of: 'turnips –barley and clover seed after a summer fallow – wheat upon the clover lay – beans, peas or tares – oats – summer fallow.' This was an extended version of the Norfolk rotation of : turnips –barley– clover – wheat. His farming notes contain some amusing reminders, such as, "February, May, June, dig hop gardens, but don't let boys dig them in." Labour payments were recorded for sowing, digging, weeding, harrowing, mowing, reaping, charcoal burning, clay burning and mole catching, all paid by piecework. A copy of a day labourer's contract for 1728 records pay of one shilling and two pence per day. The labourer was required to mow the Bowling Green and grass walks of the estate in the summertime and "in return, the said Edward Mercer shall have liberty that morning to have his breakfast with the said Sir Edward's servants in consideration thereof." Marling was an activity particularly important on the lighter soils of the Weald, where a mixture of clay and lime was applied to the land to improve the soil structure. It was a practice used in medieval times and proved popular through the 17th century, when one observer advocated the application of 500 cartloads of marl per acre. Imagine the labour requirements for that work! These documents all provide fascinating insights into the farming year in the early part of the 18th century and indicate the strong personal involvement of Sir Edward in the practice and management of farms and farming. It was an activity taken up by later Filmer descendants. Sir Edward's grandson, the Rev William Filmer was born in Crundale in 1762. He was an experimental farmer as well as a vicar and followed the family tradition of being associated with the law, the army or in his case, the church. Arthur Young commented on many of his inventions and improved techniques such as a new six course crop rotation, greater use of swedes, sanfoin, lentils, as well as the breeding of Leicester sheep and Berkshire pigs.

A comparison of estate maps spanning the long Filmer ownership shows that despite years of intensive cultivation, landscape changes were kept to a minimum. Some fields have been enlarged and hedgerows removed, but in general, it is a picture of landscape continuity rather than change. Contrary to much of southern England over this period, the extent of the woodland on the estate actually increased. It is a story of a rural landscape being efficiently managed in terms of agricultural productivity and landscape preservation, a successful story which I'm pleased to say, is still being followed under the present stewardship of Peter Francesconi.

October 5th

Leaf fall from those trees which survived the Network Rail clearance on the railway embankment has exposed us, and the surrounding fields, to bursts of artificial lighting. The source of light is security lighting from lamps along the Bilting Road which are set at too high an angle. It means our walks along the river meadows after dark are suddenly interrupted by light falling across the fields and even penetrating as far as Tye Wood. More importantly, the strong light affecting the heart of our rural landscape has an impact on birds, mammals and insects, as recent research shows. Until recently it had been seen as a problem only for star gazers, whose view of the night sky had been disturbed by the night-time glow from cities. Increasingly though, natural behaviour patterns in rural areas are being affected. In light polluted sites, birds often sing throughout the night in anticipation of a dawn which will not arrive for hours. This has been shown to affect the timing and productivity of breeding behaviour. Low levels of light can also affect bats by delaying their emergence from roosts and limiting their foraging time, especially along river corridors, woodland edges and hedgerows. Owl numbers are also affected by a reduction in the area of suitable hunting habitat and the large decline in sparrow population has been attributed to light pollution assisting birds of prey. Research shows that insects are also detrimentally affected by too much lighting, because the light attracts insects which are either killed on contact with the bulb or circle the light incessantly until too exhausted to feed or procreate. More generally, the ability of insects to use moonlight or stars as markers can be compromised. We have spent many happy evenings in search of glow-worms and fireflies on these meadows and are aware of a reduction in numbers in the light affected sites. Clearly, the ambient light and glare seriously affect their ability to find a mate using their much softer, dimmer bio-luminescence. Moth populations can be similarly affected. Whilst I recognise that the use of security lights in rural locations is often a sensible and reassuring precaution, greater consideration needs to be given to the levels of power, the duration of lighting and particularly the direction of the light. Using a steeper downward angle restricts the area being lit, so avoiding some of the ecological consequences for birds, insects and mammals.

To the east, an ominous darkening with the featureless base of nimbo-stratus cloud, seen against a rapidly disappearing yellow sky. The ragged cloud base marks the point of falling precipitation and the dark-green trees are slowly obscured by a blanket of grey. To the west, Godmersham Down has disappeared behind a dark cloud base and rain begins to fall steadily. In the words of Milton 'the low'ring element now scowls o'er the darken'd lantskip.' A flock of well over over 100 geese heads silently and steadily north. Starlings, oblivious to the steady rain, chatter, click and whistle in growing flocks high in the ash trees. Work to strengthen the piers under the railway bridge has stopped as water levels rise, leaving heavy plant stranded in a sea of mud and water. For the first time in months, Sam and I splash back across the river field in large patches of standing water which slowly link up to form little lakes. The heavy rain and strong winds have brought down small branches and twigs from oaks and ash.

October 6th

In the early evening the cloud layer lifts in the west to reveal an expanding light-blue strip of sky tinged with pink, the colours changing as the sun sets behind the downs, throwing a golden light across the meadow. Having set, the high-level clouds now reflect light from the sun with shades of pink and red in a sky turning to deep blue and then violet. The whole twilight spectacle has lasted only 10 minutes during which a whole spectrum of colours has been displayed, made even more powerful by the preceding hours of leaden grey skies and heavy rain.

A warm, wet and windy morning brings an early-morning encounter with a young swan. On the Bilting side of the Olantigh footbridge, one of the four cygnets was in the field trying to break through the sheep fencing in order to join its mates in the river. It was caught up and frightened, holding the fence taught and waving branches from the riverside I released the swan into the field. Further upstream was an overgrown cattle 'go-down' to the river which was gated off. I undid the gate, returned to the frightened and furious swan and began to drive it towards the opening. It was not a smooth advance; there were furious hissings and wing beatings. Sam wisely kept a safe distance as we gradually reached the opening through which the swan anxiously made its way to the river and paddled serenely downstream at speed in the fast moving floodwaters to join her three comrades. I returned less calmly, feeling a little overheated and shaken by the experience.

With many birds departing for warmer climes, the garden is now short of birdsong, except for the robin, which seems to be enjoying the space, the food and the cooler mornings. They have a sweetness of song which reaches points where joy and melancholy merge. Their autumn song is a more sad, and thinner version of the spring song, described by Chris Mead as being 'softer, more watery and generally a little suppressed and introverted.' With the robins also comes the smell of rotting leaves, rain and mist, and hedgerow fruits. It feels like autumn has arrived and 'summer has gone on swallows' wings.'

In Tye Wood, badgers have constructed fresh setts with enormous openings. Their footprints are clearly visible, especially the large claws on their front feet, which they use to excavate and move soil away from the opening. Traces of hay, leaves and moss lie outside the opening where the badger has dragged material in for winter warmth. The sows are probably already pregnant and cubs will be born early next year.

Passing quietly through the wood, we were jolted from our thoughts by loud screeches from jays, twisting through trees and across an opening in the forest. (Its Welsh name Y sgrech y coed means 'shrieker of the wood.') The sight of a jay is a rarity because until the recent woodland clearance we heard, but rarely saw jays. They are shy, wary birds, reluctant to break cover in a forest opening until the first jay has made it safely across, (rather at odds with the term 'jaywalker', which suggests reckless, careless behaviour). The screech is more common in autumn because they are busy collecting and burying acorns for retrieval later in the winter. The jay is one of the most natural planters of acorns, burying them in damp earth beneath the leaf litter. It is estimated that a single jay can plant up to 3000 acorns in a month, so the distribution and density of oak trees should not be a conservation concern! The jay has attractive plumage, easily distinguished by its white rump, black tail and the striking shades of blue on the wing. Numbers can fluctuate markedly because of the occasional arrival of continental birds, driven to our shores by poor acorn harvests in Europe.

We are under the canopy of a low, lumpy strato-cumulus cloud which commonly forms around large high pressure systems covering thousands of square miles. It is the forecaster's nightmare because the thick, oppressive, smothering cloud layer can quickly break to reveal glimpses of blue sky accompanied by sunshine between billowing peaks of cloud, before the gap closes and the heavy grey blanket returns. Strato-cumulus is actually made up of rolls of cloud formed from weak convection currents in a shallow zone of dry, stable air above which sheets of cloud prevent any further upward movement. The quickly changing nature of weather associated with strato-cumulus is a good reminder that clouds are always in transition. They are ephemeral and nebulous, making them difficult to classify. Even Luke Howard, who proposed the classification of clouds in 1802, appreciated the futility of considering clouds as fixed forms. He referred to them as passing moments in the constant transformation of shapes. His great contribution was to show how clouds were a reflection of what was going on in the atmosphere: they were a visible reminder of the state of the weather. John Constable understood the forces of nature which created clouds. He had a great meteorological understanding built from close observation of the skies while he worked on his father's mill in East Bergholt. It was a post mill which had to be turned into the wind to get maximum speed of rotation whilst avoiding damage to the sails from strong winds. Constant surveillance was required to forecast wind direction and speed, often using clouds as indicators of future weather conditions. Later, when living near Hampstead Heath, he sketched and painted hundreds of cloud studies. The skies in his pictures were a true reflection of changing weather conditions, unlike many painters of the Romantic period who painted clouds in any form simply as a kind of distant backcloth on a stage set.

The daily collection of horse muck from paddocks is one of my least engaging activities, but also one of the most fruitful in terms of contributing to our large and productive compost heaps. Today the task turned out to be a more enlightening experience because of the discovery of dozens of large, black dung beetles under the faeces on which they feed, although some also feed on decaying leaves and mushrooms. These are scarab beetles, relatives of the stag beetle, and enjoyed a sacred status in ancient Egypt, where its image appeared frequently in religious art and carved objects, often being placed on the chest of the deceased to ensure safe arrival into the next world. As we removed each pile of dung, beetles emerged from holes in which they had buried the dung, and where the female will lay its eggs. They are tough insects with strong front legs for tunnelling and elongated back legs for holding onto and moving the dung into their food larders. The shield is black and tough, providing a hard cover for long wings, and the underside of the shield displays attractive metallic green and blue colours. Not all dung beetles are tunnellers, some will collect dung into a ball and roll it away from the dung heap, even though it may weigh up to 50 times their body weight. The ball is then buried, mating occurs and the eggs are laid inside the dung ball and the larvae will feed on the dung ball surrounding them. This remarkable ecology and behaviour allows dung to be recycled, providing nutrients and improved soil structure. A small, humble creature, but playing a major ecological role, whether as a tunneller, roller or dung dweller, and operating in every continent except Antarctica.

October 11th

Roger Deakin, in his stimulating 'Notes from Walnut Tree Farm', encourages us to shake the branch of an English oak to see what tumbles out of the leaves, so I placed a white sheet under a young oak tree between the ponds and shook the trunk vigourously. Out tumbled earwigs, several startled spiders, click beetles, mites, carcasses of gall wasp, flies, acorns distorted by the gall wasp plus pieces of birds nest and hibernating moths. Deakin estimates that different small creatures subsist in the bosom of a large oak tree, not to mention birds and plants such as lichens, mosses and various fungi. All have a symbiotic relationship with the tree and with each other, forming a huge oak ecology. We are in awe of the oak and its domination of our landscape and culture, but we tend to ignore the little creatures which subsist with this magnificent tree; rather like history concentrates on the lives of the great and good rather than the lives of ordinary people whose joint contribution is much greater than the sum of their parts.

We are in awe of the oak and its domination of our landscape and culture.

Late in the afternoon, two unusual riverside sightings, both of which might be sad cases of abandoned birds. Swooping freely and unrestrained over the river was a single swallow, left behind fully two weeks after the others had departed. Did it leave and then decide to return? Is it lost? Has it decided to overwinter here? Gilbert White was troubled by similar questions in 1789, when he wrote in 'The Natural History of Selbourne,' "Two swallows were seen this morning at Newton vicarage house, hovering and settling on the roofs and outbuildings. None have been observed at Selbourne since October 11. It is very remarkable, that after the hirundines have disappeared for some weeks, a few are occasionally seen again sometimes, in the first week in November, and that for only one day. Do they withdraw and slumber in some hiding place during the interval? For we cannot suppose they had migrated to warmer climes, and so returned again for one day. Is it not more probable that they are awakened from sleep, and like the bats are come forth to collect a little food?"

The other sighting was the cygnet which I released from sheep netting by the river 10 days ago. It is still separated from the other three cygnets and the adults. Could it have been left behind after the rest had gone in search of overwintering areas, or has the bird been forced off its territory and left to fend for itself? When I returned across the meadow, evening sun broke through the rain clouds to create a double rainbow stretching from Line Cottages at one end to Tye Wood at the other, with Trimworth symmetrically placed beneath the arc. The colours, seen from the meadow against a dark grey-blue evening sky, were beautifully distinct. Gradually the skies cleared, the sun set, temperatures dropped to near freezing and mist swirled above the dykes in the meadow.

October 12th

A still, cold start to the day, in which muffled sounds carried eerily through the mists. Moorhen calls echoed along the river, sheep bleated from faraway fields and harrows rattled and chattered as they were dragged across distant flint-covered fields. As the day warms there are sightings in the garden which take us back to late summer days. The amber wings of a brown hawker whirred along the edge of the pond. Its season is generally June to September, so we are lucky to see it still patrolling its regular hunting territory of the pool margins well into October. A single bumblebee trundles around the garden collecting whatever pollen and nectar still remains on the Verbena bonariensis. With the first real drop in temperature to near freezing, the old queen will die, leaving newly mated queens to survive in hibernation, ready to begin the cycle again next spring. The remaining flowers of buddleia have attracted a solitary red admiral. Deprived of solar energy to charge its batteries the wing beats look laboured in the cool air. Unfortunately, this favourite butterfly with its velvety-black wings and striking red bands is unlikely to survive the winter unless it finds a sheltered spot where it can wait for migrants to arrive next May or June.

Returning to the kitchen mid-morning, we found a speckled brown butterfly trapped in the window trying to escape back to the sun. I encouraged it gently into a large glass jar and studied it carefully, sketching the brown wings with creamy yellow spots and the dark eye-spot near the top of the upper wing. Each lower wing was fringed with three small dark eye-spots. The undersides were beautifully patterned in mellow tones of orange, yellow and brown. Again we were fortunate to see it because its season is from March to late September. In addition to these single sightings, rooks and starlings are still gathering in large flocks and the delightful goldfinches feed playfully on lavender seed heads around the sunken garden. In the

A still, cold start to the day in which muffled calls of moorhens carry eerily through the mists.

late evening sun the soft, quivering calls of tawny owls are heard as they reaffirm their pair-bonds, strengthen their hold on territory and ward off any interlopers. The owl clearly rules the woods under an October night sky in which Jupiter clearly rules the heavens, climbing from low in the east to become brighter than any other star.

October 13th

The departure of birds for warmer climes in autumn seems to be a gradual disappearing act over a long period of time. Cuckoos are usually gone by mid-September, the nightingale by mid-August, and swallows and swifts often leave unnoticed by early October, although Migration Watch (BTO), confirms that departures are spread across a wide front, with some recorded as late as December. Our sadness at the departure of these birds is understandable, but why do we not get more excited by the arrival of our winter visitors? During springtime we greet the arrival of birds with enthusiasm and elation, so why not rejoice at the arrival of jack snipe, bewick and whooper swans and brambling, for example. Two attractive thrush-like birds have been arriving from Scandinavia since mid-September, although the numbers of these fieldfare and redwing, pouring into Britain after a 500 mile flight, will reach a peak during October. Like many species it is adults that will arrive first. Redwing generally arrive at night, making a thin 'tsep-tseep' call as they fly overhead on dark, clear, autumn nights. The redwing is very similar to the song thrush, but with a red flank, red under wing and distinctive buff stripes over its eye. They are not generally seen in gardens unless the weather becomes very harsh, preferring to gather in groups in fields or hedges, looking for worms and berries. Their numbers may reach over 650,000 in Britain. One of the most spectacular migration events of recent times was the arrival of several hundred thousand redwing across north-west England in early October 2004.

Fieldfares are usually seen in association with redwing, roaming in large flocks in open country, moving into parks and gardens if severe weather brings snow cover to the countryside. They resemble mistle thrush in their size and colouring. Like many other birds species, climate change may be having an impact on the breeding range of these birds. Fieldfares have already been begun expanding their breeding range in a south-westerly direction. It is through the recording of the arrival time of these birds by Bird Track (BTO) that we learn more about how bird movements are being influenced by climate change.

October 14th

The environmental consultant who undertook an ecological survey of the river before recent bridge repairs started here at Trimworth was delighted to catch several eels in nets left overnight. Eel stocks have been drastically reduced to the point where the Environmental Agency has imposed a temporary ban on all fishing for mature eels, declaring a six-month closed season in England and Wales. During my childhood in Norfolk, I spent many hours fishing on the Norfolk Broads, dreading the all-too-frequent moments when the sinuous, slimy, slightly sinister eel had to be released from tangled hooks and lines. There was certainly no shortage of eels then. I wonder if my grandchildren will be in a position to know and understand the expression 'as slippery as an eel' and see its grey-green and silver velvety skin.

Eels have been an important currency in the past. Here at Trimworth, the Domesday Book lists "a mill at nine shillings and 60 eels." In the early 20th century, an author describing the Thames wrote that 'they made a black margin to the river on either side of the banks.' Another recorded how the city, 'teems and steams with eels, alive and stewed'. Scientists now estimate that the number of elver, the young eels which migrate upstream during flood times, have dropped to 5% of their 1980s level. Reduction in numbers is thought to be related to water pollution of rivers and seas or the construction of barriers to freshwater migration, or overexploitation for commercial uses. The main reason, though, is likely to be a shift in the position of Gulf Stream currents carrying the small, leaf-like larvae from spawning grounds near the Sargasso Sea to the coast of Europe, where they penetrate inland on incoming tides. Those that make it will mature, change to a darker colour and then, one overcast night during September or October, migrate seawards and swim the 3000 miles back to the Sargasso Sea, where they spawn and die. (Incidentally, this amazing migration is largely scientific conjecture, first elaborated in 1922; no one has ever found an adult eel or eel egg in the Sargasso Sea.) It is good to know that the River Stour is sufficiently clean to encourage the humble eel. They are now regarded as indicators of the presence of good water quality, but are not, however, popular with the angling community, which accuses the eel of eating large supplies of salmonid egg and fry. However, like the Sargasso Sea as a source of European eel populations, there is no evidence to support this claim.

October 15th

This year the annual Fungi Foray of the Godmersham and Crundale Gardeners' Association took place on a perfect autumn day in Denge Wood, a semi-natural ancient wood complex on the North Downs. The wood is predominantly sweet chestnut coppice with oak standards, hornbeam, hazel, sycamore, and beech. The small deer population which exists within, or passes through the wood, is mainly fallow, but there are also some roe deer. We've had a mild September with damp, warm weather, which has been ideal for fruiting fungi, giving a huge diversity of ecologies, morphologies and colour. An early start was essential because mushrooms grow during the hours of darkness and the best specimens are found before temperatures rise.

Eighty per cent of mushrooms grow in association with trees and some can only grow with a particular type of tree, making the woodland variety in Denge Wood particularly productive. This close, symbiotic relationship with trees is important in the exchange of essential nutrients between fungi and the tree root system. Under birch trees we found Amanita muscaria, or fly-agaric, with its white flecks on a bright-red cap containing toxins which can produce hallucination. The Sami people of Lapland take advantage of the reindeer's fondness for this mushroom by scattering dried ones for the reindeer to eat, rendering them more placid and manageable. Various forms of boletus, such as the cep or penny bun, were seen in

Shaggy ink caps were widespread on grassy banks and will turn from white to a slimy, inky mess as they mature.

Strange bracket-forming polypores grow on the trunks of trees.

the mixed woodland, and in the mossy clearing were patches of the beautiful and tasty chanterelle with its yellow-orange flesh, smelling faintly of apricots. The egg-shaped, shaggy ink caps were widespread on grassy banks and will turn from white to a slimy, inky mess as they mature. In beech or oak litter, the horn-of-plenty, grows in large groups, but is well camouflaged and difficult to spot. It is a strange-shaped fungus with a trumpet horn and a wavy edge, but it is a favourite in restaurants, served stuffed or added to stews. Its alternative name, however, Trumpet of Death, makes its culinary appeal less attractive. Wood bluits, puffballs and parasols added to the prolific display of over 14 species collected, which included strange shelf-like fruit bodies growing on the trunks of old and dead trees.

The fashion for collecting wild mushrooms at popular sites in the New Forest, Epping Forest and the Chilterns is creating some problems for conservation managers. Small-scale collection for personal use is not the problem but increasingly, commercial operators are seen leaving woods with large collections destined for London markets. The City of London Corporation, which owns Epping, has issued formal warnings and prosecutions to commercial organisations picking illegally from SSSI's. Fungi are natural recyclers, breaking down organic material from plants and animals. Many creatures feed on fungi and they are hosts to some rare invertebrates that are unique to these ancient woodlands and should be protected. Maybe the environmental concern about large-scale collections is overstated, and ignores the rewards of a growing public becoming more aware of an abundant range of food sources provided in the wild; nevertheless future generations should be able to admire the fascinating shapes, forms and colours of this amazing organic kingdom.

On 16th October 1987, we woke to assess the damage caused by the Great Storm. Gusts of up to 200 kph were recorded along the south-east edge of the storm in Kent and Essex. At Toys Hill in Kent, one of the highest points of the county, 98% of all trees were lost in the 40-hectare woodland. Nearly all these trees were beech, vulnerable because they are shallow rooted and top-heavy. Since this Great Storm and its January 1990 sequel, a number of lessons have been learned, principally that over-hasty and insensitive clearing up can cause far more damage than the gale itself. Trees which had lost a few limbs were unnecessarily felled, and many self-grown trees were killed in the effort to clear away fallen wood. At Toys Hill it was observed that only a year after the storm, the forest floor was carpeted with seedlings of beech and birch which had responded quickly to increased levels of light and moisture. In his book, A Brush with Nature, Richard Mabey identifies four tentative rules for speeding the recovery of storm-struck woods. Firstly, fallen trees are not necessarily dead and many can resume their growth in their new horizontal mode. Secondly, dead wood isn't useless, it is part of the woodland ecosystem and a good habitat for fungi, birds, insects and mosses. Thirdly, natural regeneration is often quicker and cheaper than replanting. Finally, where planting is undertaken, it should be small un-staked saplings which can acclimatise to wind.

Coinciding with this concern for woodland destruction we have cause to celebrate (albeit cautiously) news from the Forestry Commission that the woodland cover in the UK has returned to the levels of the1750's when forests were replenished after the agricultural revolution and before they were reduced again by the demand for wooden ships ahead of the Napoleonic Wars. Woodland in the UK now stands at nearly three million hectares, or 11.8% of the total land area, an increase of nearly half a million hectares since 2003. So much new forest is being planted that some areas could soon reach the 15% woodland recorded in England by the Domesday Survey of 1086. The amount of woodland now owned by individuals' accounts for almost half of the tree cover. Buying woodland as an investment can out -perform shares, and once owned for two years is exempt from inheritance tax. Despite the optimism, Britain still has a long way to go to reach the European woodland cover average of 44%. The Woodland Trust campaign to plant 20 million trees in Britain over the next five decades is a step in the right direction towards closing in on the European average. What moderates my optimism, however, are reports about selling off some huge landholdings of the Forestry Commission. If this happens, my concern is that the forest will then be seen as a marketable commodity rather than a protected ecosystem.

Good and bad news comes recently from the RSPB, Europe's largest wildlife conservation charity. I am heartily encouraged by the news that the RSPB's youth membership, known as the Wildlife Explorers, has exceeded 200,000 members for the first time, making it the largest wildlife club for children in the UK. In the last 18 months, more than 27,000 children have joined, so that one in five of the RSPB membership is now in the junior section. Contact with nature is an important part of a child's health, learning and development, and they are the hope of the future in terms of environmental stewardship. 50,000 of the junior membership are now teenagers, and they will be voting at the next general election. In the meantime, they will further develop the natural curiosity about the world around them, and will hopefully be aware of adverse changes in the biodiversity of the environment, such as the disturbing revelation from the RSPB that some of the nation's bird species are facing an uncertain future. Mark Avery, the RSPB Conservation Director, has identified 40 birds for which immediate action is required to protect them from serious decline. Ten of these, including the kestrel, cuckoo and swift, are

October 17th

in a state of decline for which there is at present no explanation. It is possible that changes in farming practice, lack of woodland management, drainage of wetlands, habitat destruction, climate change, reduction in insect populations, or building development, or a combination of these, will explain the decline, but more research is needed.

October 19th

The poem, 'To Autumn' by John Keats is about the abundance of autumn, with its cornucopia of ripe fruits and late flowering plants. He depicts autumn as a goddess sitting casually on the granary floor, her hair 'winnowing' in the wind, or sleeping in the harvested fields or watching apple juice cider oozing from the cider press. Keats asks us not to question where the songs of spring are, but rather to enjoy the splendours of autumn, such as the song of the robin, bees gathering around late-blooming flowers, the twittering swallows gathering in the skies, the song of hedge crickets.

"Season of mists and mellow fruitfulness,
Close bosom-friend of the maturing sun;
Conspiring with him how to load and bless
With fruit the vines that round the thatch-eves run:
To bend with apples the moss'd cottage trees,
And fill all fruit with ripeness to the core:
To swell the gourd, and plump the hazel shells
With a sweet kernel: to set budding more,
And still more, later flowers for the bees,
Until they think warm days will never cease,
For summer has o'er brimm'd their clammy cells.

Who hath not seen thee oft amid thy store?
Sometimes whoever seeks abroad may find
Thee sitting careless on a granary floor,
Thy hair soft-lifted by the winnowing wind:
Or on a half reap'd furrow sound asleep,
Drows'd with the fume of poppies, while thy hook
Spares the next swath and all its twined flowers:
And sometimes like a gleaner thou dost keep
Steady thy laden head across a brook:
Or by a cider press, with patient look,
Though watchest the last oozings hours by hours.

Where are the songs of Spring? Ay where are they?
Think not of them, thou hast thy music too,
While barred clouds bloom, the soft-dying day,
And touch the stubble-plains with rosy hue:
Then in a wailful choir, the small gnats mourn

Among the river sallows, borne aloft
Or sinking as the light wind lives or dies:
And full-grown lambs loud bleat from hilly bourn,
Hedge-crickets sing: and now, with treble soft
The red-breast whistles from the garden-croft:
And gathering swallows twitter in the skies."

The poem is all about the appreciation of modest, unspectacular daily observations, beautifully expressed. And yet there is a melancholic sadness in the last stanza, which suggests the end of warmth and plenty as the prospect of the desolation of winter approaches. The harvest is gathered, the lambs are fully grown, and, most moving of all, the swallows gather for their winter migration. There is a suggestion that autumn symbolises maturity in the natural world, as well as in our lives, expressed in a moving, gentle and beautiful way.

October 20th

The garden shows signs of autumn. The first hard frost has blackened the dahlia foliage and collapsed the courgettes into translucent green heaps. There is a pattering sound as the last gold, terracotta and bronze leaves fall to the ground below the chestnuts. Leaf fall has opened up the garden to the mature glow of the wider countryside; we are seeing through spaces which once were solid; the garden reveals its structure. There are smells of apples, bare earth and wet leaves. Onions are on display in trays behind windows of the summerhouse and potatoes fill hessian sacks. Potted geraniums, bougainvillea and agapanthus are dragged into the shelter of the pump room. All summer outside, all winter inside: the tide of the seasons. Rose prunings and woody stems from shrubs are loaded onto bonfires and from the glowing embers, lazy smoke rises in the cold dusk and then levels out to form a grey-blue layer of mist across the valley. We leave the fire with the smell of wood smoke in clothes and hair, flush-faced, despite frost-fall. The frost brings changes to the garden and we sense the end of an era of growth, flowering and fruiting. But there are also signs of a new era as shrubs are cut back to reveal rosettes of new growth. There is a sense of sadness mixed with anticipation at the cycle of the seasons. There is also a moving panorama of varied autumn skies: the clear green-blue skies of a song thrush's egg, high, drifting cirrus, castles of cumulus, a low evening sun casting lavender-blue shadows, and days of mist when nimbo-stratus snags the wooded downland skyline.

October 21st

On the 21st October, 1990, the pressure group Common Ground took over the Piazza at Covent Garden for a demonstration of the importance of the apple to our culture, landscape and wildlife. And so Apple Day was initiated. Subsequently, the idea has grown to involve hundreds of groups organising local events as an annual celebration to link the fruit we eat with the people who grow it. The day has become a celebration of local distinctiveness, as opposed to the uniformity of global markets. It is interesting to consider why the apple was chosen as an emblem of this movement. Perhaps it is because the apple has been a powerful symbol of Britain, as illustrated in literature and poetry. Or because it is a fruit which has incredible diversity with over 2000 English varieties each one having a story and a flavour of its own in a specific location, thus linking a variety with local production and local social customs and traditions. Many varieties can be traced back to a specific orchard or garden. The apple has been grown in traditional orchards for hundreds of years and become associated with a rich countryside ecology, involving insects, flowers and birds. It is an illustration of how the wild and cultivated can exist in harmony. Whatever the reason, Apple Day has become a hugely successful event with a great message to project.

Despite the success of these celebrations, it is 'crunch time' for apples. The acreage of dessert apples in the UK decreased by 30% in the last decade, yet production rose by 20%. This is because older, less-productive orchards have been replaced by more intensive plantings with an increase in output, but a decline in wildlife diversity associated with traditionally managed orchards. The buying power of supermarkets is a concern because the emphasis is not on variety, but in taking advantage of economies of scale in bulk purchases of Granny Smith from Australia, Golden Delicious from France and Macintosh Red from Canada. With such concerns, resources and organisations that can support UK fruit production will be important. An example is the National Fruit Collection at Brogdale in Kent. Supported by DEFRA, it is a significant provider of research in genetics and the maintenance of the national collection. For example, cryo-preservation of dormant cuttings at minus 193°C is being used to secure living collections and ensure against losses from pests and disease. However, it is the small charity, Common Ground, that has been the greatest factor in the revival of interest in our native apples and orchards. They have led the fight against bland uniformity and reignited interest in local distinctiveness. We have celebrated the day at Trimworth by preserving Conference and Commice pears, gathering apple varieties from our trees and collecting crab-apples to make jelly. Long may fruit trees continue to flavour the locality and contribute to the diverse geographies and histories of rural Britain.

October 22nd

The Environment Day at Trimworth involving fifteen enthusiastic local children usually begins with a game. This year the children formed a large circle with two at the centre. A ball was then thrown randomly across the circle and the two children in the middle had to intercept it. It soon became clear that the 'safest' way to avoid the ball being intercepted was to pass it around, not across the circle. If the ball was seen to represent a small bird and the children in the middle a buzzard and sparrowhawk, the circle of children would represent a 'corridor' of relative safety through which the bird could pass without being attacked. The game is a useful way to illustrate the importance of wildlife corridors which physically link habitats and allow species to move between otherwise isolated areas. It is particularly useful to slow-moving species which are vulnerable to predation, or those which have to rove over large areas in search of food. Over-wintering and breeding sites are provided in these situations, and they also offer a range of foods and microclimates for wildlife.

We have been conscious of this concept as a vital habitat link in our own fields and gardens. Enrolling our land into the Countryside Stewardship scheme has allowed us to link with owners of fields upstream and downstream to form a river floodplain corridor. The river bank acts as both home and corridor for water voles, kingfishers and various dippers, and hopefully, in time, otters. We have planted 'shaws' which link the river with the water meadows and the railway embankment, which is a site secure from human disturbance. Construction of ponds in our garden has provided stepping stones of activity, separated by areas of wildlife-friendly grasses through which reptiles, amphibians and insects pass. The hedges we planted 15 years ago run from the railway embankment up a river terrace to the cultivated slopes of downland. Others connect poorly-drained water meadows with dry, chalky embankments. Butterflies move between and through these habitats, as do mice, hedgehogs and bank voles. All these corridors help species to move, feed, breed, and ultimately survive. It is a concept which can, and should be applied at all levels from individual gardens to large-scale ecological networks at the county level.

Tonight the Hunter's Moon lives up to its reputation by providing strong moonlight for hunters as it rises above lower cloud layers in the north-east. Although the full moon appears very bright, the moon is actually one of the darker objects in our solar system, reflecting 7% of the sunlight that strikes it, (the albedo effect), while the Earth reflects 37%, Venus 65% and Mars 15%. This day is traditionally associated with feasting, especially among the North American Indian groups. Some re-enactments still celebrate the feast of the Hunter's Moon but in Europe such feasts disappeared in 18th-century. As I watched the moon climb, I noticed the flickering flight of bats around the yew tree at the north-east corner of the house. About three-quarters of British bat species are known to roost in trees. Our huge yew provides adequate shelter and a diverse range of insect species. Bats cannot bore holes, but the inside of the yew, with its heartwood fallen away has many junctions of branches in which needles have collected to form convenient roosting sites. Different parts of the tree are used throughout the year: higher canopy sites in summer, but in winter, bats will go deeper and lower in the tree. They are still mating in October and building up fat reserves to survive the winter. The activity outside the window of the study was probably a combination of feeding and a search for suitable hibernation sites. During October, the bats will begin periods of torpor which will increase in length in November, when some begin hibernation. My brief encounter with pipistrelle on this night of the full moon was to have a surprising conclusion. As I looked towards the window from my desk, I saw a bat had attached itself to the outside of the window and was hanging there motionless. It was smaller than I expected, no more than 4 cm long. In flight, they appear so much bigger because of the wingspan, which can be well over 20 cm. In amazement I looked at its face with its insignificant eyes, small ears and pug-like nose. Then in a flash it had gone. I looked below the window for a damaged bat, but there was no sign. My temporary lodger had returned to its roost in the yew to contemplate this face-to-face contact.

Our yew has an ecology of its own, with birds and bats, spiders and insects, rabbits and mice. Traditionally the yew was planted on the north-east corner of the house to ward off evil spirits, and also in churchyards for the same purpose, as here at Waltham.

Our yew has a little ecology of its own. It is as high as the house, shaped like a huge balloon and is several hundred years old. It is full of bird and bat activity throughout the year; rabbits nest under it and so do mice; it is home to spiders and insects, and as a female tree provides loads of red berries, which this time of year form a slithery carpet underneath the tree. Traditionally these trees were planted in the north-east corner of the house to ward off evil spirits, and also in churchyards for the same purpose. In places they line important routes like the Pilgrims' Way, especially in chalk country. The berries are known as 'snottygogs' in the South of England, 'snodder gills' in Hampshire, 'snat berries' in the Midlands and 'snottle berries' in Yorkshire. Birds love the flesh of these berries and although the seed or kernel is full of poisonous alkaloids, it is tough enough to pass through the bird- a clever evolutionary compromise which ensures that seed dispersal is widespread. The tree has been a symbol of death and mourning through the ages, with needles strewn on graves. Today, the tree has also become associated with life because needles from the tree can be used in the treatment of breast, ovarian and prostate cancers.

Another hard frost following a night in which a huge, pale moon threw silvery light across the garden and into the house. At 5.00am it was high in the sky, and by 8.00am it hovered like a pale disc over Godmersham Downs to the North-West. At that time, the sun had risen above Trimworth Downs to the East, invading the fading realm of the moon. Hilaire Beloc describes the scene:

> "The Moon on the one hand, the Dawn on the other:
> The Moon is my sister, the Dawn is my brother.
> The Moon on my left, and the Dawn on my right:
> My Brother, good morning: my Sister, good night."

The crowns of the willows along the river are being visited by flocks of 6 to 10 long-tailed tits which sway from tree to tree in search of spiders and larvae within their winter feeding territory. They twitter and trill excitedly. Flocks are generally family parties of closely-related individuals and their constant twittering calls help to keep the flock together. Those birders who can imitate this call can attract a flock to within a few feet. As a small bird, they can suffer badly in harsh winters, but they are gregarious by nature and will roost together to prevent heat loss by packing themselves into old nest boxes and roosts.

The Irish bridge repairers have departed the field by the river after two months work, leaving a drastically altered environment. The riverbed is full of large limestone boulders, banks are bare and more steeply inclined, and in places the field is rutted and compacted badly with the passage of heavy machinery on wet fields. How long will this river meadow take to recover, and will it re-establish its former rich grass, and wild flower ecology? Restoration will require recreating the physical conditions necessary for the habitat to exist, such as improved soil structure and drainage, then waiting for recolonisation from adjacent habitats; or assisting the process through reseeding and nurturing growth. Hopefully small mammals and insects will gradually return, but this will depend upon whether the species-rich water meadow can be re-created and how grazing will be managed. Thankfully, the critical safety of rail travellers is now assured at the crossing point, but the long-term damage to this intimate and fragile ecosystem will be less readily assessed.

Pigeons are being picked on – literally. Along the river path by the wood, a pair of wings lay flat on the ground attached to delicate breast bones which had been carefully, accurately and completely stripped bare. This was probably the result of a buzzard kill, finished off by fine beaks and the teeth of small mammals. The young buzzards, at least three in number, are now proficient fliers and hunters, ranging over greater distances from their roost in Tye Wood and invading the territories of rooks and crows. Aerial battles ensue with the 'meowing' cries of the buzzard carried far and wide through the valley.

With leaf fall, ivy is exposed clinging to trunks of trees, in some cases as thick as a wrist and climbing up to 30 m. It clings tenaciously with its multitude of adhesive roots, hence the regional name of bindwood and the maxim that 'Doctors bury their mistakes, architects cover them with ivy'! Apart from competing for soil nutrients and water they do little harm, although thick coverings can cause damage in high winds. The ivy is an important source of nectar from the flowers, which are composed of short flower stalks or umbels. From September to November they are green with yellow anthers and continue to attract flies, wasps, bees, small tortoiseshell butterflies and insects. The second brood of holly blue butterflies lay their eggs in the flower head and the larvae will burrow into the

The yellow anthers of ivy continue to provide a nectar source for flies, wasps and bees.

buds causing them to wither. In early spring the ivy flower will be replaced by black five-celled fruits. Deadly nightshade is also seen sprawling across field edges and woods, the clusters of green berries gradually ripening to black. There are few other wild flowers apart from the ever-present daisy, groundsel and dandelion, and those which have spilled out of gardens, such as cyclamen, brightly displaying clusters of pink and white flowers on banks in the autumn sun.

October 27th

October is a time for turning compost heaps and in the process exposing many compost earth worms which thrive in the warm, moist environment. Some are bright red or reddy-brown, and these tend to live just below the surface of the compost, living and feeding on litter. All the 26 species of earth worms native to Britain could be described as 'ecosystem engineers', changing the structure of the environment by burrowing horizontally and vertically in the soil and creating pores through which oxygen and water can enter the soil and providing a vent for carbon dioxide. Earthworm casts are the faeces of worms and help to create a fine crumb structure in the soil. Worms are also important in the process of decomposition, releasing nutrients from dead plants and animals and making them available to growing plants. For Charles Darwin, the worm demonstrated the importance of 'small agencies and their accumulated effects'. The garden at Down House contained a staked stone to measure how much soil was moved by earthworms. His last book, published in 1881, was about earthworms and their collaborative generosity, as earth passed through their bodies time and time again to sustain the fertility of the planet. No wonder he regarded them as 'nature's little ploughs'.

It is not uncommon for us to see birds of prey tracking each other when one is carrying food. Kestrel will even steal from owls in flight, as will sparrowhawks. Buzzards are frequently seen carrying food and being trailed by a crow or rook from which it had grabbed food. In some cases a bird can be harassed to such an extent that it will regurgitate the food which will then be eaten by the attacker. The RSPB has reported a situation where a sparrowhawk was robbed by merlin, which was robbed by a buzzard, which then had food stolen by a peregrine. This was probably where the exchange stopped because the peregrine can clock up speeds of 300kph! The sorts of behaviour described here are common enough among birds of prey to be known as klepto-parasitism.

As an amateur painter, I am intrigued by the association between art and nature, and an exploration of the natural world provides many opportunities to be inspired by the relationship. A wonderful local example of this inspiration can be experienced by viewing 'art in the wild' at Kings Wood, a 700 hectare forest in a designated Area of Outstanding Natural Beauty which caps the porous lime-rich chalk downs between Godmersham and Challock. It is an ancient woodland in which beech predominates, the last in a post-glacial succession of birches, willows and pines. Sweet chestnut and larch are also present, and there is a huge diversity of flora and fauna including fallow deer, nightjars, adders, woodpeckers and wild flowers. The woodland is managed for conservation, recreation and timber production by Forest Enterprise. In 1994 Stour Valley Arts commissioned artists to make sculptures and other art works in the forest. Many artists spent long periods in the forest developing a close relationship with the forest. Work was required to echo the huge scale of the forest and make use of the natural materials available, such as chalk, flint and forest products.

The results of this collaboration between Forest Enterprise and Stour Valley Arts is a series of earthworks and woodland art reflecting aspects of death and decay, regeneration, erosion, movement and stillness. The exhibits gradually change over time, the speed of change being influenced by the natural materials used. Many have now been reclaimed by the forest – they have become 'ghosts' of previous sculptures. Time-of-day, weather and seasons all create visual changes in the exhibits, which include structures, carvings, textures, coppice work, earthworks inspired by ancient burial mounds and barrows, wind and water chimes. Richard Harris has defined the shapes created by mining flint, using hundreds of pieces of wood. These are now in a state of natural disintegration and will eventually return to the forest floor. Lucasz Shapski has created an avenue of yews planted by local people and aligned to the sunset of a Midsummer Day. The work will not come to fruition for a hundred years and will probably last a thousand years or more. All these art objects leave subtle and non-invasive traces of human activity, which slowly revert back to nature.

October 28th

Our pollinators are busy extracting the last traces of nectar from late-blooming flowers. But what is the source of the pollinator diversity in the UK? Is it in urban habitats, farmland or nature reserves? The answer to these questions is likely to be informed by researchers from the University of Bristol, who will be conducting the largest ever field study of pollinators in 12 British cities, 12 farmland habitats and 12 nature reserves. Traditionally, urban growth has been linked to biodiversity decline, but it is now recognised that cities contain a huge diversity of sites, particularly in our urban gardens where the flowering season is long. Gardeners invariably look for early and late-flowering plants, providing forage for insects over a longer period of time. In contrast, farmland habitats offer a feast of nectar sources when crops such as oilseed rape are in flower, but once the bloom is over, the feast becomes a famine. Over the next three years, researchers will do 10m counts to identify the number of flowers and pollinators found along a series of 1 km-long transects in the cities of Bristol, Edinburgh, Leeds and Reading.

Much has already been done to promote biodiversity in cities. We recently visited friends at a mooring just off the Grand Union Canal near King's Cross, and walked for two hours through the residential areas of Islington, the London Borough with the smallest amount of green space per person of any London Borough. We found an amazing network of parks, open spaces, gardens, railside lands and waterways which all form part of the borough's Biodiversity Action Plan involving local community gardens and wild spaces. Most impressive of all was King Henry's walk where a once derelict site has been transformed by volunteers into an organic garden of flowers and vegetables with the emphasis being nectar-rich plants. Over a short distance we could find sorrels, ladies' bed-straw, fat hen, water mint, yarrow, horny mustard, wild rocket, sow thistles and much more. The place is teeming with wildlife and this is one of eight similar community gardens in the borough, each with streetside planting, green roofs and green walls. Together they form what has been described variously as a 'green corridor', or a 'river of flowers' across north London. It is these 'pollinator streams' which will in the future lead to cities being a key factor in saving pollinating insects.

October 29th

Bees are still working the flowers of ivy, sedum, verbena and Michaelmas daisies: the master pollinators still hard at work well into autumn, helped by spells of milder weather. Honeybees will soon be going into a cluster in hives and will rarely leave as November approaches. This sophisticated insect is always in the news, often in relation to problems from bloodsucking mites (varroa), colony collapse disorder and other threats to its survival, but there is good news of the return of five rare bumblebees to Kent and Sussex. Environmental schemes in Dungeness, (Romney Marsh,) which introduced pollen and nectar-rich flowers into field margins, has produced far quicker results than anticipated. About 50 farms in the area have been working since January 2009 to restore habitats over an area of 800 ha. Four of the species were carder bees and the fifth, the large garden bumblebee. They have all returned after decades of decline. The success of the scheme illustrates the benefits of agri-environment schemes and the role farmers play in protecting and improving wildlife.

Another story illustrates the extraordinary behavioural qualities of the bee. Scientists at Royal Holloway, University of London have shown that bees can learn to fly the shortest route between flowers discovered in random order. The bee visits its flowers at multiple locations, and because they use such high amounts of energy to fly, they need to find a route which keeps flying to a minimum, thus conserving energy and saving time. Computers are required to solve this complex mathematical problem of comparing the length of all possible routes, then selecting the one which is shortest. Bees managed to reach the same solution using a brain the size of a grass seed.

October 30th

At 8.00am the valley was filled with mist under a clear pale blue sky. Only the pines of Tye Wood and the beeches of Kings Wood poked through the mist like dark crowns on white ermine. The sound of gunshot from the pheasant-filled woods punctuated our walk. Pheasants were everywhere, gliding into the meadow, skulking under hedges, strutting frantically across the forest floor, exploding into the air from under our feet and screeching in justifiable panic. The whirring wings of partridge also rose from the base of hedges and field edges. The pheasant, introduced here by the Romans , and commonly bred for game, is one of the world's most hunted birds, and almost semi-domesticated. The rich chestnut with emerald green and red face makes a beautiful complement to the autumn colours of the landscape. As game birds they bring an obvious economic benefit to rural areas, but also a beneficial impact on the landscape and wildlife because many farmland copses, hedgerows and tree belts were planted as a cover and shelter for pheasants.

A pair of cormorants flew upstream on the top of the mist; two pairs of mallards circled speedily around the meadow making the plodding flight of crows seem even more laboured; a heron's lazy wingbeat was seen along the water's edge. As the sun rose above the wooded skyline, the mist broke into wispy bands and within minutes was gone. Shafts of sunlight broke through the spray rising above the weir at Olantigh and the movement of water and light was reflected on the underside of the still-green leaves of alders. Now the full sun brought out the glorious autumn

Shafts of sunlight broke through the spray at Olantigh weir and the movement of water and light was reflected on the underside of alder leaves.

colours of burnished gold and terracotta, red and bronze, yellow and orange. Hedgerows were like waves of rich colour running across the rough grazing. From the deep brown newly ploughed fields seagulls rose and fell, competing aggressively and noisily for scraps. The bird world seems to be celebrating the fruits of the season; magpies chuckle, starlings click and whistle, the piping notes of tits rise from birdfeeders, goldfinch twitter on the seed heads of cardoon and teasel, and pied wagtails dash jerkily over the muddy ruts left by the movement of heavy machinery by the bridge. Occasionally they rise into the swarm of gnats which move en masse in the warm sunshine above.

I seem to have formed an affiliation with a wren. As I approach the path separating the wood from the river, I'm joined by a wren which flits from the stems of one nettle bank to the next, flying just ahead of me like a trail-leader before disappearing into the wood at the end of the path. This is a perfect habitat for the little bird, where the woodland edge and the riverbank run parallel only 10 m apart. The family name Troglidytidae suggests a link with cave dwelling, possibly because of their tendency to forage in dark crevices. The little bird is also referred to as a 'kinglet' in a German legend because it won the contest to see which bird could fly highest. The eagle won this flight, but concealed within its feathers was a wren which took the title 'king of the birds'.

We watched snipe rise from the exposed mud of the riverbank, their mottled brown feathers and long straight beak clearly visible despite the fast, erratic flight across the meadows. Shallow water-scrapes have been created in Bilting Meadow which will encourage this bird, faced with reduced distribution and falling numbers. Drainage of meadows and conversion to arable are the main causes of this because snipe feed by digging deep into mud and soil, and if the ground becomes hard, feeding will be affected and breeding will cease. The pungent smell of urine and faeces of the red fox is noticeable along the woodland edge as they mark off their territory. Around urban areas their territory may be about 20 ha, rising to several thousand hectares in more remote upland locations. In Tye Wood they have taken over underground dens vacated by rabbits and badgers. We find fox droppings in the garden where these night-time visitors search for fallen fruit or rodents and rabbits. The cessation of fox hunting with hounds has led to shooting becoming the main method to control fox numbers. I wonder if this cull will lead to a greater understanding of ecological balance, as rabbit populations rise and begin to decimate young crops. Or is the increasing game population on shooting estate a more important factor?

The distribution of many animals and plants is shifting in both latitude and altitude in response to changing climate. The results, reported in the journal Science in 2011, are based on the largest study of its kind to date, involving over 2000 species, and demonstrate a clear link between climate change and shifts in the distribution of species. It is estimated that species have shifted to higher elevations at a median rate of 11 metres per decade, and to higher latitudes at a median rate of 17 kilometres per decade, (although the British Comma butterfly has moved 220 kilometres northwards from central England to Southern Scotland in the last two decades). The distances moved by species are greatest in studies which show the highest levels of warming. The results are positive in the sense that species are showing they can respond to warming by seeking out cooler habitats, providing there are no obstructions in the way, like major roads or building developments. The bigger concern, though, is for those animals which are already near the poles or close to the tops of mountains. For example, the polar bear does most of its hunting on the ice, and that ice is melting. This July was the lowest ever recorded Arctic ice cover, so the options for the polar bear are running out. This fate will be faced by a far greater number of species that are threatened at higher elevations.

November

November 1st

November has sombre connotations, marking the end of harvest and the beginning of winter. The Anglo-Saxons called it 'Blot-monath' or blood month, alluding to the custom of slaughtering cattle for winter consumption. In medieval times the onset of winter meant a declining diet for animals and therefore poor eating for people, so cattle were slaughtered and salted down, but from the mid-17th century, livestock could be grazed on turnips sown on the stubble, allowing the stock to be over wintered.

A solemn peasant is about to hurl a stick into the burnished oaks to bring down the acorns for pigs.

In the Book of Hours, the rural activities depicted are slaughtering beasts, roasting meat and baking pies. Sometimes the scene is of pannage, the practice of turning out domestic pigs onto the forest floor for acorns, beech mast and chestnuts. Often it was a right granted to locals on common land or royal forests. The Domesday record for Trimworth refers to 30 pigs being fed in woodland pastures and in later years, manorial records for Trimworth contain frequent reference to pannage. In the splendidly illuminated medieval manuscript of Les Très Riches Heures, a solemn peasant stands holding a stick which he is about to hurl into the burnished oaks above and bring down the acorns. The forest floor is littered with acorns being hoovered up by pigs. A golden labrador looks on obediently.

November is also the month for memories and remembrance. Today is All Saints' Day, or All Hallows Day, the day after Hallows Eve (Hallowe'en). It is a feast day celebrated by Anglicans and Roman Catholics to remember all the saints, known and unknown, through Christian history, a Christian tradition since the fourth century. Tomorrow will be All Souls' Day to commemorate the departed, and is marked by visiting family graves and reflecting on lost ones. In Mexico it is known as the 'Day of the Dead' ('el dias de los muertos') when people take picnics to graves, celebrate, and leave food for dead relatives. Remembrance Day and Remembrance Sunday will follow later in the month, making the first few days of the month a time when boundaries between this world and the next are recognised and explored.

November 2nd

The mature riverside willows have now been marked for felling as part of the willow replenishment programme pioneered by Gray Nicholls, the well-known cricket bat manufacturer. Harvested trees are taken to their factory in Robertsbridge, East Sussex, where they are cut into roundels, then separated into splits, each of which will form a single cricket bat. Willow is a soft fibrous wood, which is naturally very moist and therefore has to be kiln-dried for six weeks before being pressed, at approximately 2000 pounds per square inch. Will the bats produced from wood grown in this field by the river be used to get to the pitch of a full-length ball and drive it swiftly through the covers to rattle the railings at Lords? Or edge a swinging ball into the safe hands of a slip catcher on the village green at Chartham?

Whichever, the willows in question are part of a very sensible and successful programme of timber management, which ensures the replacement of felled trees to maintain the stock of wood, as well as preserving the landscape features of the valley.

In 2004 the Kentish Stour Countryside Project installed an otter holt on our riverbank in Kitchen Meadow where the railway and river meet. There is no public access here and we rarely visit this remote and secluded location. It is like the secret place which John Clare described in his poem , 'To the Snipe'

> "From year to year,
> Places untrodden lye.
> Where man nor boy nor stock hath ventured near
> Nought gazed on, but the sky."

In the past five years we have occasionally checked the entrances to the otter holts looking for signs of activities, such as droppings or sprait, which are most frequently found on raised sites along the riverbank and left as territorial markers. We have seen no evidence yet of this elusive animal. In the 1970s, the otter, poisoned by toxic pesticides in rivers, was rarely seen anywhere, but today the Environmental Agency reveals that otter numbers are now the highest for several decades. Evidence comes from extensive fieldwork for the Fifth National Otter Survey (2009-2010), which has examined 3300 sites across the country. Footprints and sprait of otters were recorded at well over half the sites visited.

Recovery has been in response to 3 main factors: a ban on the pesticides that almost caused their extinction; legal protection for the otters since 1978; and a significant improvement in water quality. Re-introduction programmes of captive-bred otters has speeded up the recovery in East Anglia, Yorkshire and the Upper Thames, but there has been a natural expansion of remnant populations in all counties, with the exception of Kent, although the Environment Agency has reported recent sightings in the Eden and Medway Valleys. The south-west region and the River Wye, on the other hand, have almost reached carrying capacity for the otter. The Environment Agency is able to show that the target for otter populations set for 2015 has already been reached, and that full recovery across England should be achieved within 20 years. This is a major success story for pollution control, as well as the efforts of landowners and river managers to improve river and riparian habitat. The otter is at the top of the food chain, and therefore is an excellent indicator of the health the rivers. Credit must also go to the Environment Agency in demonstrating the value of long-term monitoring of species such as the otter, but there is no room for complacency. Continued recovery has brought a significant increase in reported otter road kills and also some concerns about predation by otter, particularly in still-water fisheries. Meanwhile, here at Trimworth we will continue to keep a lookout for this iconic species, hoping to see signs of the inquisitive, intelligent, playful and agile creature taking childlike enjoyment on the muddy banks of our river.

November 4th

November came in with mild temperatures and wild westerly winds which stripped leaves from trees and piled them up against field margins and sheltered lanes. Who better to illustrate this autumn scene than John Clare, England's finest nature poet, whose poems perfectly illustrate the commonplace features of his native landscape? John Clare was born in 1793, the son of humble almost illiterate parents. His biographer, Jonathan Bate, describes him as "the greatest labouring class poet that England has ever produced. No one has ever written more powerfully of nature…" He was writing of his native landscape at the time of massive change and was deeply affected by it leading him to write critically of the destruction of long established ways of rural life.

> " I love the fitful gust that shakes the casement all the day,
> And from the glossy elm tree takes the faded leaves away,
> Twirling them by the window pane
> With thousand others down the lane.
>
> I love to see the shaking twig dance till shut of eve,
> The sparrow on the cottage rig, whose chirp would make believe
> That spring was just now flirting by
> In Summer's lap with flowers to lie.
>
> I love to see the cottage smoke curl upwards through the trees;
> The pigeons nestled round the cote on November days like these:
> The cock upon the dunghill crowing,
> The mill sails on the heath a-going."

This is a poem I remember from junior school days. At the time I was puzzled why my friend and classmate, Roger Casement, should get a mention in the second line, or why he should be shaken by the wind all day. (As a child, Roz had a similar concern about the use and meaning of words when her father talked about the exhaust manifold on his tractor and was puzzled why it should be referred to in church as, 'manifold sins and wickedness!)

I have been saddened by the death of an artist whose work was inspired by the natural world. David Measures painted butterflies flying in their natural habitats rather than from photographs or dead specimens. He painted them hovering, fluttering, alighting against the surroundings of meadows and woods, capturing the movement and light with a darting pencil or flickering brush. Amazingly, many of his delicate, energetic paintings were captured using his fingertips, with fine details picked out with his nails. Each drawing is accompanied by unedited notes. He was not attempting to create saleable paintings, but to produce a personal field notebook of the free-flying daytime activities of butterflies in the wild. When an insect flew off, he stopped drawing immediately, unwilling to generalise from memory, leaving an unfinished sketch on the page. He often tried to stay with the same butterfly and continue making notes and sketches for as long as possible. To be mobile, he reduced his kit to a minimum, using a tiny watercolour box packed with bright primary colours so that he could quickly capture the butterfly's brilliance.

In his book, 'Butterfly Season, 1984' are the collected drawings, watercolours and field notes he made during the wonderful summer of 1984. It is an extraordinary book, full of beautiful paintings of butterflies, which seem to fly off the page. Every mark, line, smudge, colour tone is alive with movement and light, and the animated notes convey his observational skills of the beauty and behaviour of the butterflies. On April 26th, he notes, "A male Brimstone meets a female along the hedge line and engages in a very determined courtship. In column flight, they go up into the sky and down again, fluttering just above the grass tops as though about to settle. The male always keeps below the female, causing upward flight to take place again. Higher and higher they go until, eventually, they are lost from sight. Down in the bleached nettle stalks, keeping very still, is the Comma of yesterday evening. It gets up to chase away a Peacock. A second Comma finds the first where it sits on its nettle stalk, closed and inconspicuous. It must have known exactly where the resident was perching. It settles alongside it, then nudges it, causing both to fly up in a tight, column ascent."

November 6th

We have a deep relationship with garden birds; an almost obsessive bond which is peculiarly British and reveals a great deal about ourselves, as well as the birds. Urbanisation has led to a profound need to reconnect with nature through birds to the point where we now regard them as wild pets, an extension of our living space. The burgeoning market for bird feeders and bird food is an illustration of this, leading to many garden birds becoming dependent on us. We have projected human values onto birds, regarding some as evil and mean, such as sparrowhawks, and some as friends, such as robins and tits, with their convivial characteristics. Magpies are thought of as being vulgar, greedy, noisy and aggressive, all human characteristics. They are generally disliked because they are bold and eat eggs and kill birds. But they are also smart and clever. Moreover, careful, well-documented research provides no scientific evidence that the decrease in garden birds is being caused by magpies. Perhaps we use the magpie as a scapegoat because there are other factors which have been responsible for many of the bird killings in gardens; for example cats are estimated to kill 55 million birds a year.

November 7th

Not a good day. As an East Anglian I know what an east wind can bring in November, especially when blowing from a cold continent. It is a similar experience here in East Kent, but today it was near gale-force and full of driving rain and I felt winter had arrived. Nevertheless, the dog had to be walked, and we braved the elements early. Rooks were being scattered across the sky, regrouping, then thrown away again in the wind. Seagulls rode the winds from the south-east and settled in fields in flocks. Leaves had been stripped from trees, exposing dark-green ivy-clad trunks and great clumps of old man's beard or traveller's joy, still holding onto their seed heads. Alders and some sycamore retain their leaves, the ash clings on to clusters of brown keys and the oak leaves look like faded brown pages of old parchment. In previous weeks, we've had a wonderful boost from vibrant early autumn colours and several shades of gold, bronze, terracotta and red. This is now replaced by more sombre tones and the stark bareness of an 'exhausted landscape' which some writers have taken to represent our own mortality. It challenges our romantic views of nature and reminds me of an exhibition at Tate Britain on the 'Art of the Garden', in which the Scottish artist Anya Gallacio worked with natural materials to confront our sense of mortality. One exhibit consisted of 10,000 fresh red roses laid out in a neat rectangle covering the floor of the gallery. During the course of the exhibition, the roses dried, withered and faded, prompting us to consider not only our own mortality, but our romantic notions of nature especially at the onset of winter. I should have followed the swallows!

A calm day following yesterday's storms which left a clutter of old branches beneath the ageing ashes. The dead crowns of these trees are dotted with the black shapes of starlings and crows. The bird world seems to be enjoying the stillness of the morning. There are tits, starlings, woodpeckers, sparrows, greenfinch, and even ungainly jackdaws, swinging precariously from feeders. Under a seed feeder is a group of gregarious chaffinches and today I noticed their close relative, the brambling, described as the chaffinch of the North. They are migratory birds, arriving here from the coniferous forests of northern Europe from late October, and wintering in woodland, especially birch and beech, or in stubble fields where they can search for seed. They are similar in size and shape to chaffinches, but with orange on the shoulder and breast, blotchy grey- brown head and mantle which may later change to black. Another clear distinguishing feature is the dazzling white belly, most obvious in flight. So far we have seen only a few, but they can flock into gardens and fields in very large numbers, depending on sources of food supply. In mild winters they may not even arrive at all, such is their unpredictability.

Blue tits follow us along the dyke, flying from tree to tree. It's a comfortable feeling, as if they regard us as an unthreatening part of their habitat. They are a delight to watch in the garden, hopping between the windfalls under the apple trees, carefully examining the fruit, flicking and twitching their wings and flying up into branches in search of insects. Close inspection reveals just how attractive this little bird really is with its bright blue wings, tail and crown, greenish grey back, yellow body and white cheeks with a black eye stripe. On feeders they are incredibly agile, hanging upside down to peck at peanuts, which will be an important source of high energy food to ensure their survival through the harsh winter, when many will sadly perish.

Monday was a day of strong winds and heavy rain; Tuesday was still, clear and bright; today the wind and rain have returned. How can we explain these dramatic changes in weather over such short periods of time? The answer lies with fast-flowing 'rivers of air' found at around 35,000 feet which reaches speeds of up to 650 kilometres an hour. This is the jet-stream, typically thousands of miles long, hundreds of miles wide and a few miles deep. This polar air stream runs at the junction of warm subtropical air to the south and cold polar air to the north and is formed by temperature differences in the upper atmosphere which gives a large pressure gradient, and hence wind. Sometimes the jet-stream flows straight across the Atlantic in a narrow ribbon, providing a very useful tailwind for pilots flying between the USA and the UK, although navigating into and out of the stream can be tricky and turbulent, whatever the size of the plane. Sometimes the stream crosses the Atlantic in a wide meandering loop. Its speed, depth, and altitude vary enormously, and it is this variation which creates our weather contrasts. On Monday the stream flowed over the UK and dragged cloud and rain with it. Yesterday it skirted the UK giving us a quiet, still day. Today it has returned at high speed, bringing more gales and rain. Meteorologists study the movement of these winds to identify areas below which a depression or anticyclone is likely to form. An understanding of these upper air movements is also necessary for making long-range forecasts and in fuelling the debate over whether it will be a harsh or a mild winter. A fascinating dynamic picture of the jet-stream wind in the North Atlantic can be found of the 'stormsurf' website (www.stormsurfing.com), which shows six-hourly forecasts of the height, speed and direction of the jet-stream for the next 180 hours. Another factor which informs the forecaster is the flow of ocean currents, the most significant being the Gulf Stream which is a key influence on our climate. Will freezing water from melting ice caps disrupt the Gulf Stream flow and cool our climate? These ocean movements are being monitored by the National Oceanographic Centre in Southampton, which has placed sensors in rows at different depths across the Atlantic Ocean.

November 10th

Coming down to earth after a wild day of wind and rain, Sam and I stood on the slopes of Trimworth Down late in the afternoon and looked south across the bright green shoots of emerging winter wheat sloping down into the dry-valley, then rising a deeper green to the dark pines of Oxen Leas. The wood ran like a black freeze between the green fields and the pale blue sky, grading upwards to a deep blue in which a bright crescent moon radiantly dominated the evening sky. Looking west to Godmersham Down, towering banks of heavy grey cumulus raced towards us, their tops reflecting the pinks and ochres of the setting sun. Fragments of wispy grey filaments broke from the cloud base and were driven by gale-force winds into the darkening slopes of Trimworth Down.

November 11th

Huge flocks of pigeons circle the fields and settle on newly emerging winter wheat. Fieldfares ('the field traveller') have been sighted in harvested fields, a sure sign of the approach of winter. These visitors from Scandinavia usually arrive in October or November and stay until spring. They rarely breed in Britain, although the breeding grounds of the fieldfare have now spread from northern and central Europe into Holland, Belgium and France. The first known fieldfare to breed in Britain was in 1967, but very small numbers have continued nesting in Scotland. It is a nomadic bird and shows no allegiance to regular wintering areas. It is like a large thrush, often seen in association with redwing or blackbirds. They are an attractive part of the winter scene as they roam the countryside in 'chucking' flocks looking for berries and settling in the ploughed fields at dusk. We have seen them in the garden, feeding on windfall fruit or finding invertebrates in the ground when it is frost free. Small groups of yellowhammers can be seen feeding along the base of field hedges

Huge flocks of pigeons circle the fields and settle on newly emerging winter beet

in contrast to their summer singing perches at the tops of tall trees. The distinctive yellow feathers of the male birds are now tinged with brown, but this will gradually disappear over the winter so that by next year the males will have their wonderful primrose yellow heads again.

November 13th

Removal of hedges and greater pesticide use has led to many hedgehogs moving from open countryside and becoming garden residents. They are now busy building their hibernacula, or winter nests of leaves and brushwood. Some will overwinter in the compost heaps or under sheds and summerhouses. Warmer winters are confusing some hedgehogs which delay preparing for winter and will sometimes have a second or third litter too late in the year. This can lead to young which are too small to hibernate and too inexperienced to find food sources. Their survival will be helped if we put out water, meat-based pet food to feed young hedgehogs and prepare them for winter, otherwise their sugar levels will fall, they will become torpid, and dangerously exposed to predators such as crows, magpies or hawks.

Roger Deakin's fondness for hedgehogs is demonstrated in a November entry in 'Notes from Walnut Tree Farm. "There's something medieval about a hedgehog:

the scavenging peasant of the undergrowth, the hedge bottom. What we love about them is their vulnerability, which they share with human babies: the way they curl up in that foetal ball, shielding the soft furry underbelly."

It is Remembrance Day, a morning of melancholy, with the distant muffled bells of Wye Church rolling sorrowfully across the meadows. On the 27th January 1916, Sir Robert Marcus Filmer MC, Captain in the Grenadier Guards, was killed in action and was buried in Merville Communal Cemetery north of Béthune. He died, aged 37, without heirs, thus ending a 260-year period of Filmer ownership of Trimworth Manor. When the First World War came to an end in November 1918, fewer than half of the Western Front dead had been given a proper burial in a designated military ceremony. A quarter of the 150,000 British casualties at the battle of Arras were never recovered. In the battle of the Somme, 420,000 British troops were killed, of which 74,000 were never recovered. The battlefields were strewn with hastily made 'soldiers cemeteries', just clusters of graves in fields. Countless bodies still lay unburied in what had been 'No Man's Land'. The awful job of battlefield exhumation and reburial was undertaken by special units working methodically and meticulously across devastated battlefields. The work was deeply unpleasant and distressing. Many dead, like Robert Filmer, were later reinterred in purpose-built cemeteries often designed by Edward Lutyens. His friend and colleague, Gertrude Jekyll, was appointed to design the planting. Thus to the corners of foreign fields came broad grass paths and the familiar scents and colours of English cottage gardens. Lavender, white thrift (sent from her garden at Munsted Wood in Surrey), lilies and floribunda roses cluster around the uniform ranks of headstones, with low-growing plants to protect the lettering from being splattered with mud. A simplified revision of her planting remains today, enhancing the sentimental associations with the gardens of home. From their foundation in 1917, the Commonwealth War cemeteries were conceived as gardens, using the design principle that they should not be places of gloom; simple English gardens arose from what had been a scene of brutal horror. Creating these gardens has been described as the biggest landscape project ever undertaken, with more than 1 million dead. The work was begun in 1918 and completed in 1939, just one year before Europe went to war again, and opening a new chapter in the Commission's work to commemorate the 600,000 British and Commonwealth casualties of WW2. What a strange species we are.

The gales have gone and an anticyclone covers the country bringing still, frosty, misty mornings clearing to shimmering sunny days and amazing sunsets. At seven o'clock the river meadow was grey with frost and the lines of dykes were marked with swirling banks of mist. All the bird activity seemed to be in the garden, even moorhens had left the ice-covered ponds to strut around under birdfeeders on which hung hosts of tits and finches of all kinds. Flurries of sparrows raced noisily around the house and settled together in bushes. As the sun rose over Trimworth Downs, the mist disappeared and the meadow changed from grey to sparkling white, with grasses sugared with frost. The last leaves were released from trees onto the still-frozen leaf litter where they collected layer upon layer to form a deep leaf mould. As they fall, there is a constant pattering and rustling. The rate of fall is constant: thousands upon thousands each waiting their turn before floating, fluttering and zig-zagging to the ground. Smoke from an early-morning bonfire at Bilting rises 20 metres to the level of the temperature inversion, and then spreads out across the valley, remaining there for several hours. But it was the evening which left the strongest impression of the day. As the sun set, the rippling cloudlets

November 15th

At seven o'clock the river meadow was grey with frost and the lines of dykes were marked with swirling banks of mist.

of cirro-cumulus (known as 'mackerel sky' by mariners), and the ice crystals of wispy cirrus were changed to an implausible pink against the duck-egg blue sky. Minutes later the sky and the horizon had changed to a blend of yellow ochre and cadmium red. Mist rose from the field forming a 5-metre milky layer through which the bare canopy branches of willows and ash marked the meandering course of the river. The screech of pheasant from the wood disturbed the tranquillity, and then the loud 'kee-wick' call of the little owl, sounding from the woodland margins as it searched the riverbank for small mammals such as voles and shrews. In the early part of the 19th century these little owls were rare in Britain, but subsequent introductions have led to their success as a common species and the breeding population numbers between 6000 to 11,000 pairs. It has a dumpy appearance, frequently sitting on fence posts and easily observed before taking off to begin a bounding flight, rather like a woodpecker. We returned home across the dark meadows with the spectacular light display, like a bizarre painter's palette, still etched in our memories.

November 16th

I watched the actions of a pair of kestrels hovering effortlessly over Bilting Meadow. Both appeared to be males, less dark in colour than females or juveniles. Their rapid, quivering wing beats allowed them to acquire the act of stationery flight as they faced into a headwind and matched the oncoming wind speed perfectly. Occasionally they glided forward, circled a few times, then hovered again looking for voles or mice. On seeing their prey they dropped down with closed wings then checked their speed just above the ground before dropping with feet forward in a final plunge to grab their quarry. This time of year they tend to stay within their home territory, which is usually less than 2 km^2, but can be as large as 10 km^2, depending on the adequacy of the food supply. They often take over the nest of crows or other 'stick nesters' in the wood, or occupy deserted holes in trees. After about 10 minutes watching I realised that the chilling East wind had penetrated several layers of clothing and I moved on to the shelter of Tye Wood. Pheasants were everywhere. Yesterday I heard the shouts of beaters as they emerged from Oxen Leas into the open fields waving white flags, driving the pheasants towards the guns. The 20 or 30 pheasants I saw today were the escapees, seeking protection in the nettle beds along the river or in the dry leaves of the wood. They will live to enjoy another few weeks before the next one-sided confrontation begins.

Returning across Six Acre Meadow we were startled by a blood-curdling scream coming from the dyke separating the meadow from Great Tithe Field and found a dead rabbit on the opposite bank. There was no sign of a fox, although when we returned several hours later, the rabbit had gone, presumably carried off to a den in Oxen Leas. The action of predators in the countryside is all part of the countryside ecology, but it is something about which we cannot remain indifferent. Our feelings are affected by culture, politics and emotions, provoking strong reactions. I share the view of John Lister Kaye expressed in his book, 'At the Water's Edge.' "Whenever I look at nature, I find myself confronted by the paradox of sublime design and grim function, almost as though one is mocking the other – a deadly game, sometimes so violent and brutish that it takes my breath away….And then the beauty floods back in as though some grander plan than evolution fits it all together with added value… So I walk, and I watch, and listen, and slowly I learn." Undoubtedly our sanitised modern lifestyle has affected our predator-prey feelings, but in the end we have to acknowledge that the human being is the most prolific predator on the planet.

November is traditionally the month when farmers, having harvested, ploughed up and sown, now turn to hedge trimming prompting cries of 'vandalism' from naturalists who argue for the environmental benefits of cutting every two or three years. The strength of their argument is that shrubs and flowers are produced on year-old twigs, so annual cutting would remove flowers, berries and nuts. The impact of this on butterflies, birds and mammals would be damaging. Natural England estimate that every year a hedge is left uncut it will gain two species of breeding birds. Yet ornithologists argue that certain species such as yellowhammers, linnets and white throats prefer short hedges, whereas skylarks and lapwing prefer open landscapes. Clearly we have to recognise that the purpose of the hedge has changed over the years. Today the role of the hedges as wildlife habitats has to be considered along with the long-established functions of making boundaries, keeping stock out of fields, and as a source of firewood, etc. Consequently, less frequent cutting of hedges with more varied height and thickness becomes more appropriate as the environment achieves a higher priority on the public agenda. Agri-environment schemes of the 1990s and the Hedgerow Regulations of 1997 have all addressed the even more serious problem of hedgerow loss, the most significant factor in the decline of plant and animal species traditionally associated with farmland. In a six-year period up to 1990, the hedgerow length in England declined by 20%, and in Wales by 25%. Half of the loss was the result of poor management. Since that date, removal has lessened, and even been exceeded by planting so that the net length of hedges now remains stable, with perhaps a slight increase; but newly planted hedges will not have the same value in terms of wildlife, landscape or historical importance as the oldest hedges which have been lost.

The monitoring of historical maps of the area around Trimworth shows that good management of the estate has resulted in the survival of many old hedges. Some mark ancient boundaries between the parishes or manors and are several hundred years old. The dating of hedges derives from the work of Max Hooper in 1970, who, in his own words, "rushed around the country counting trees and shrubs in the 30 yard samples, on chalk soils, clay soils, sandy soils… In the old hedges, I was left with 10 or 12 species, and in the younger ones only a couple." Working with a great landscape historian WG Hoskins, he dated 227 hedges of known ages from 75 to 1100 years, and confirmed the 'one in 100' law over a 30 yard stretch as a good rule of thumb (ie the age of a hedge = the number of species x 100). Several of the hedges around us contain at least five species in 30 yards, taking them back to medieval times. In parts of Suffolk, hedges of seven or more species predominate in areas which appear to have an Iron Age field system. Obviously there will be exceptions; sometimes species will have a strong suckering system which will invade a mixed hedge and suppress existing species; newly planted hedges may be planted up with five native species. So it is a rule of thumb which should be confirmed with other evidence such as maps, documents and archaeology rather than being applied uncritically.

November 19th

Noisy, cheeky starlings with their iridescent plumage are gathering to roost in dense flocks, sometimes mobbing predator birds by circling them in tight flock formation. They sweep across the sky like a loaded paintbrush of dark grey being slowly swirled across the paper. With humour and close observation, H.E. Bates describes their roosting habits: "Meanwhile, each evening, starlings perform a strange drama of their own. They have begun to gather on the highest branches of a group of Spanish chestnuts which have died back at their tips, so that they are like ebony skeletons against the evening sky. On these dark, naked branches the starlings descend in thousands, and the trees seem to become laden with countless gigantic seeds. Suddenly it is as if the pods of these seeds are simultaneously split open. They break from the branches with a harsh explosion, and the seeding wings lift briefly and then disperse. They blacken the air for a moment and then spread and scatter, sowing themselves into the coloured acres of sunset." ('In the Heart of the Country.')

November 21st

The quiet, unassuming and unobtrusive dunnock, formerly known as the hedge sparrow, is a frequent visitor to a variety of habitats around here, but particularly noticeable fluttering through hedgerows or creeping nervously and mouse-like along the edge of flower beds, twitching and flicking its wings. It resembles the sparrow, but closer inspection shows it to be smarter, neater and sleeker and quite attractive with its light and dark-brown streaks and blue-grey head and breast. It is an insect eater rather than a seed feeder and consequently has a finer beak. From the top of the gazebo comes its tinkling high-pitched warble and persistent 'tseeep', similar to the wren and rather unkindly described as sounding like a squeaky trolley. Otherwise it is inconspicuous; there seems to be nothing extraordinary or bizarre about this bird – apart from its amazing, prodigious sex life. The females are polyandrous, breeding with more than two males at once, a characteristic which only 2% of the bird species share. It is the female which initiates sex and as soon as the deed is done, (taking about a second), she will approach him again or another male, and may copulate 30 times a day, probably having sex with every male dunnock in the territory – and all this going on in the shrubbery! We are also seeing increasing numbers around bird feeders, especially seed feeders but they are very timid and easily displaced by robins which see the dunnock as a serious competitor.

Our resident rogues the jackdaws continue to amuse us, tumbling around the skies, strutting the rooftops or perching on rotten tree stumps.

Our resident rogues, the colony of jackdaws, continue to amuse us, tumbling around in the skies, perching on hollow tree stumps, strutting along rooftops. Less welcome is their habit of poking around in chimney pots looking for nesting sites. We have had to remove sticks, straw, twigs and even dazed birds from our fireplaces, having tumbled down the chimney. Today they were trying to master the hanging birdfeeders under the birch trees. They are like a group of children competing for the use of the swing, initially taking turns until one over-stays its time and is 'attacked' by the others who try to drag him away. There is clearly a pecking order in the jackdaw flock and after disputes, the loser will show respect for the winner. We always enjoy their sociable, inquisitive, intelligent and fascinating behaviour. They are full of character and very welcome in the roof spaces of our old buildings.

November 22nd

Buds give hope to the prospect that leaf will burst again. Most deciduous trees are now bare and so the bud and bark become useful guides for identification as we pass through the winter. Clusters of buds will form at the tip of each twig on oaks; the twigs of limes become shiny and red with buds arranged alternately; beech develops long narrow brown buds on slender twigs, and the pale grey twigs of the ash are bearing black conical buds. Like nearly all river-side trees the alder retains its leaves much longer than other deciduous trees, often staying green with little or no autumn colour until January. All year we have enjoyed its mass of glossy, dark olive-green foliage hanging into the river, its roots visible in the banks. The limes in the avenue leading to the house are bare. No longer do we wade through a gilded passage; the fallen leaves have become a dark brown slippery slush. But over the year this tree has provided us with an annual spectacle from pink buds to fresh green leaves, followed by nectar-filled blossoms humming like a hive of bees, then sweet scents and now the autumn colours. At the end of our drive is the most common of the winter-bare conifers, the European larch, with elegant, down-sweeping branches turning upwards at the tips. It is essentially a mountain tree, at its most beautiful on old upland crags or in glens. It is one of the heralds of spring with its light emerald green needles. Now these needles are golden brown, glorious in the evening sun with egg-shaped cones discharging winged seeds. Wordsworth was less impressed in his 'Guide to the Lakes': "…in autumn, spiritless, unvarying yellow, and in winter it is still more lamentably distinguished from every other deciduous tree of the forest, for they seem only to sleep, but the larch appears absolutely dead."

November 24th

Since the 1950s, 60% of the old apple orchards in the cider country of Somerset, Gloucester, Herefordshire, and Worcestershire have disappeared, and the decline in Kent and Devon approaches 90%. Not only are we losing apple and cider production in these areas, but mistletoe, which thrives in long established orchards, is also under threat. This semi-parasitic plant is part of the Christmas heritage and has a special place in our winter landscape where it forms light green growths with white berries in the bare branches of apple trees and other species. The white sticky berries are often rubbed into the bark by birds and the single round seeds sprout into a pair of slender pale green leaves which eventually become woody. These branches divide, making bushes that can grow to a metre across with a lifespan of many years. Plants may be either male or female, but it is the female which has the white berries and attracts mistlethrush and other birds. All mistletoe is semi-parasitic, relying on the host plant for water and mineral nutrients, and in some cases of heavy infestation the host plant may be killed.

As well as a fascinating botanical phenomenon, the plant has a wealth of cultural and mythological associations with a strong link to local folklore. Its mysterious and magical importance has been appreciated since the Druids, especially if it was found growing on oak, where the pearly pulp of the berry was thought to represent the oak tree god's semen. Disaster would befall anyone who cut down a mistletoe-bearing oak. The preserved body of Lindow Man, who lived in the first century, had mistletoe berries in his body, but it is not known whether this was the cause of his death or the residue from a harmless herbal drink or remedy. In the past it has been used as a remedy for barrenness in animals, as well as an antidote to poison. Another use of this versatile plant is as an adhesive to trap small birds and mammals. The sticky juice or 'bird lime' has been used to produce sticky strands which are wound around a branch on which the bird is likely to perch.

More commonly, the plant is now associated with peace and hospitality and used since the 18th century as a decoration at Christmas. Kissing under the mistletoe is probably an ancient fertility rite which was popularised in the 19th century and given humorous and sometimes suggestive imagery, particularly in Britain, America and other English-speaking countries.

November 26th

We are entering a prolonged cold snap which could bring one of the earliest significant snowfalls since 1993 and persist for a week or two. The explanation is found once again in that high-level ribbon of air, the jet-stream. Instead of taking a direct west to east path across the Atlantic, the jet-stream is meandering north into the Arctic and returning across north-west Europe bringing bitterly cold winds. It is a phenomenon called the 'omega block', because the shape of the system resembles the Greek letter Omega. At the centre of the system is persistent high pressure which blocks off the direct west to east airflow. Omega blocks make forecasting predictable because they are stable systems that dominate the weather for several days, or even weeks. But they can frequently make life difficult for those in the path of this flow of Arctic air, which drags with it the heavy snow and blizzards which some parts of the country are now beginning to experience.

As winter approaches, we become preoccupied with making predictions about how harsh a winter we can expect. Some are guided by weather lore and remain optimistic by the saying that, 'If November ice will bear a duck, there'll be nothing after but sludge and muck.' In other words, if November produces a spell of severe weather, there is a good chance that the remaining winter days will be mild and rainy. Past statistics give little support for this optimism and show that a cold

November has no predictive significance at all. During the past 100 years there have been 11 very severe Novembers, the last being 1993. Of the subsequent winters, three were significantly warmer than average and five were about average. Statistics also show that milder winters in the past 100 years are frequently preceded by average temperatures in November. So, make sure that the book of sayings on weather lore is kept alongside the statistics records!

"Around the house the flakes fly faster,
And all the berries now are gone
From holly and cotoneaster
Around the house. The flakes fly! -- faster
Shutting indoors that crumb-outcaster
We used to see upon the lawn
Around the house. The flakes fly faster,
And all the berries now are gone!"

'Birds at Winter Nightfall', by Thomas Hardy

The intricate relationship between birds and berries has developed into a mutual dependence for survival. In harsh weather, berries become a vital source as the ground becomes frozen, making worms and snails inaccessible, and insects scarce. Blackbirds, redwings, fieldfares and thrushes become dependent on berries as their principal source of food. Apart from the native berry-bearing species of holly, whitebeam, spindle, guelder rose, hawthorn, ivy and honeysuckle, gardeners can provide other sources of food from shrubs such as rosehips, pyracantha (also known as 'fire storm' as it blazes in front of dark green leaves), cotoneaster, and berberis. And it is not just birds which benefit, because mice, hedgehogs and insects will also look for berry-fruiting shrubs.

The other side of the relationship between berries and birds is the way trees and shrubs with berries will entice birds to distribute their seeds. Seeds from berries are usually encased in juicy, fleshy pith, giving energy and vitamins. The undamaged seeds pass through the birds' gut and can be dispersed over wide areas. Every year we find shoots of hawthorn and elder growing under fence posts and rails in the paddock, or under rose arches, which birds frequently perch upon. Some berry seeds actually benefit from passing through a birds gut because it removes chemicals that would otherwise retard growth of the seed. Red berries on green foliage, black berries on leaves

The intricate relationship between birds and berries has developed into a mutual dependence for survival: a food source for birds and a means of seed dispersal for berries.

turning brown or yellow in autumn make the berries easier for the birds to find. Some will feed in flocks such as redwings and starlings, moving from one feed source to another often in very large numbers. The mistlethrush is a shrewd feeder, going around in flocks until holly berries appear then setting up in holly trees to defend their territory from other birds. In spring, the defended tree still often retains berries whilst unprotected trees will have been stripped bare.

Smaller birds like great and blue tits, goldcrest and chaffinch, also feed in flocks, improving their chances of survival by having more pairs of eyes to spot predators like the sparrowhawk. As the light fails, birds head for their night roosts and the timing is important. If an individual leaves too late it may be picked off by birds of prey- too early and they may not have fed sufficiently to survive the low night temperatures.

With the UK experiencing Arctic conditions which are forecast to last another two weeks, comes news from the Meteorological Office that the world is warming. This is illustrated by evidence across a wide range of indicators, such as increase in sea temperatures at the surface and at depth, shrinking glaciers and sea ice, and increases in humidity caused by warmer air holding more moisture etc. We are seeing observations that are consistent with increasing greenhouse gases. The decade since the millennium was the hottest on record. It is not a steady increase in temperatures, because natural variability within the climate system, such as solar variability, as well as variations in the atmospheric aerosols resulting from growing industrialisation in Asia, will produce fluctuations.

With the present icy conditions, and also bearing in mind that last November was the coldest for 30 years, it may be difficult for many to be convinced that the world really is warming. But what is happening now, and during last winter, is a vivid illustration of natural climatic variability. To understand global warming we have to look at the longer-term global picture, recorded by more than 20 institutions worldwide using satellites, weather balloons, weather stations, ships and ocean buoys. The layers of ice laid down each year in Antarctica and Greenland also store a record of the earth's climate. Bubbles of air, trapped in the ice as it froze, can be analysed to give details on temperature at the time it froze, as well as information on the atmospheric concentrations of gases. The European Project for Ice Coring in Antarctica (Epica), for example, has allowed scientists to look back over a period of 800,000 years.

November 29th

"The first fall of snow is not only an event, but it is a magical event. You go to bed in one kind of world and wake up to find yourself in another quite different, and if this is not enchantment, then where is to be found?" (JB Priestley, 'Apes and Angels: a book of essays'.)

We awoke this morning in another world; the air was thick with snowflakes and a 12 cm blanket of snow had fallen silently and beautifully overnight, leaving a series of white spaces and shapes. The leafless trees along the river were skeletons of snow, and the silent wood was piled deep. Birds were silent as if stunned by the transformation of the landscape. A great white froth sat on the hedges which ran like breakers across the countryside. There was no horizon, the sky and the distant fields were a continuum of grey. The wide, sweeping curves of the Downs

The wide sweeping curves of downs and valleys are draped in sombre mists as trees and fields fade into the same grey tones.

disappeared under thick sombre mists and distant lines of trees faded into the same grey tones. The deep snow had slowed the pulse of life. As the sun struggles to make an impact, animals settle in for the long dark sleep. I felt a slight unease of isolation. It is winter.

The writings of Henry David Thoreau in 1856 describe 'the creative genius' of the air in which snowflakes are generated, imaginatively comparing them to stars which fell and lodged in his coat. Back in 1611, Johannes Kepler, the German astronomer had a similar preoccupation with the snowflake, publishing the first scientific reference to snow crystals in which he recognised the hexagonal shape of snowflakes. More than 300 years later a Japanese nuclear physicist unaccountably shifted his studies to snowflakes and identified and catalogued all the major snow crystal types by growing artificial snow crystals under controlled conditions. He had built on the observations of 'Snowflake Bentley', the Vermont farmer who was the first to photograph a single snowflake crystal. Wilson A. Bentley took over 5,000 photographs and categorised snowflakes into a great variety of hexagonal forms. Meteorologists now know that snowflake shapes depend on variations in temperature and humidity. Thin plates and stars grow at around -2°C while columns and needles appear at -5°C; the greater the humidity, the more complex the shapes. The many states of temperature and humidity which the snowflake experiences in its fall to earth explain why it is very unlikely for any two snowflakes to appear exactly alike. Today Sam is unconcerned about the subtle mysteries of snowflakes; he simply rolls, runs and scoops up mouthfuls of the white stuff.

December

We are in the grip of a biting North East wind and temperatures barely rise above freezing even during the day. How do birds survive in this harsh environment? The answer is that many do not. Latest results from bird-ringing studies at 70 sites across the country, coordinated by the British Trust for Ornithology, show that many bird populations fall significantly. Robins and wrens seem to be most hard-hit. Records for 2009/10 show bird ringers counted 27% fewer robins and 20% fewer wrens compared to average counts over the previous five years. Dunnock and greenfinch numbers also fell. All these little birds lose body heat very quickly. Finding enough food to build and maintain adequate fat supplies to store in the body and 'burn' for energy is the biggest challenge, especially on frozen or snow-covered ground. The smallest birds like blue tits and goldfinch have to feed throughout the day to consume as much as 30% of their body weight to get them through the long, cold nights. Some will fluff out their feathers to increase insulation. Small birds can double their size and increase insulation by a third. Others will squat so feathers cover the legs and hide their heads under their wing. Hoarders of food, such as jays, can turn to the larders of acorns which they buried during the autumn and are now safely covered in snow. We see robins hunting through leaf litter under the bushes or around the house where the ground is not frozen. They have very large eyes in proportion to their body, allowing them to see well in dark places. This also explains why we often see robins on food searches in the half-light of dawn and dusk. I'm watching goldcrest flitting in and out of the cypresses, feeding on tiny insects and spiders. Blackbirds are not fussy and will eat a wide range of foods. So will the gulls which invade our compost heaps and fight over scraps of kitchen waste.

Harsh weather may result in a change of location for some birds, leading to sudden and dramatic changes of bird numbers in an area. Lapwings and plovers can fly in search of snow-free pasture; kingfishers and herons appear at the coast to fish in salty ice-free waters. Instead of a change in location many small birds change their behaviour and become more sociable to improve their survival chances, flocking together in a huddled heap to conserve body heat. Some roosts are used from year to year and attract large numbers, birds piling on top of each other with only beaks and tails showing. The naturalist Robert Burton records that flocks of wrens usually number about 10, but 61 have been recorded in one nest box and as many as 96 in a loft space! Long-tailed tits line up closely on branches, blackbirds roost together in thickets, robins make for our ivy-clad walls or conifers, rooks shelter together on the leeward side of trees in Tye Wood. In addition to all these energy-saving practices we will keep feeding stations well stocked so that our feathered friends avoid the perils of 'night starvation'.

The Environment Agency has highlighted dramatic improvements in water quality and the state of our rivers, with claims that water pollution incidents have halved in number since 2001; water voles and otters have returned to our rivers; sea trout have been recorded in the Thames; large numbers of migrating salmon have been witnessed in the Tyne. All this has led Ian Barker, the Environment Agency's Head of Water to state "The last decade shows how far we've come in reducing pollution and improving water quality and river habitats. Rivers in England and Wales are at their healthiest for over a century, with otters, salmon and other wildlife returning to many rivers in record numbers in locations across the country." On the other hand European legal standards show that nearly 75% of all rivers in England and Wales fall well below the highest European standards, with only 26% classed as 'good.' There is no doubt that the water quality of rivers such as the Thames, Mersey and Tyne and other major rivers flowing through urban areas has improved, to the point where the Thames has won international awards for its restoration from a situation of being 'biologically dead.' But this is not true for many streams in the catchment area of these rivers; or the lakes and ponds which make up two thirds of our water environment, and which also come under the Environment Agency directive. The explanation for these conflicting viewpoints is based partly on government spin, but also on the different measures used. The Environment Agency assesses water quality by measuring levels of ammonia and dissolved oxygen found in the water, whereas since 2000, the European water framework directive assesses a much broader range of pollutants and biological characteristics.

There are other areas where the general view of the government is at odds with environmental agencies. Natural England considers the turnaround in the biodiversity of Sites of Special Scientific Interest (SSSIs) to be one of the great conservation successes of recent decades, but a report by independent conservationists, commissioned by the government, shows only 30% of SSSIs are in 'favourable' condition; the rest were considered to be 'unfavourable recovering'. Measures of biodiversity by Natural England are similarly upbeat, but latest available statistics show that habitats and species are in need of conservation action with 125 species out of declining in quality and extent. It seems that the government's ecological advisors are concentrating on "…oases of high environmental quality but ignoring the ecological deserts which surround them" (John Vidal, 2011). In all these assessments of environmental quality the government appears to cherry-pick success stories and over-emphasise the positive, whilst ignoring other indicators which use more sophisticated methods. This is not good for the environment, or the people who are anxious to be accurately informed about the true state of the natural environment.

As grey, cold days follow one another, the urge to garden fades, even though there are hundreds of bulbs to plant, borders to tidy, lawns to scarify, leaves to collect, hedges to top. My eye glides over the list of jobs to be done but I'm comforted by the words of Monty Don: "Over the years I have wasted days braving the elements, trying to wheel barrows through mud lapping about the axle, digging soil when more was sticking to my boots than to the spade or, on one embarrassingly memorable weekend, bullying house guests to help me plant a long beech hedge in constant torrential icy rain. Total waste of time. Not one plant out of 200 survived six months. There is no need for heroics. Gardening can be grim enough." Thanks Monty! A similar lack of eagerness was shown by Philip Miller, the famous gardener at the Chelsea Physic Garden in London from 1722 to 1770, who wrote of December: "This month (the days being the shortest) is commonly the darkest of the whole year, and is subject to different sorts of weather: sometimes the ground is frozen up so that little can be done in the garden: and at other times there are hard rains and thick, stinking fogs, which render it very uncomfortable stirring abroad, but especially to persons of tender constitutions: and this weather is also very injurious to tender plants."

December 2nd

My temporary inactivity, however, does give me a sense of freedom and a chance to plan new structures and planting schemes. It is a period of settling back, of reflection, and perhaps a recognition that if this is winter, spring cannot be far behind. The season also provides the opportunity to see the structure of spaces in the garden. The lines and distances between one bulk and another, the silhouettes of trees rising above hedgerows engraved against a dark grey sky, the contrast between skeletons and profiles of the different shrubs and trees of garden and countryside especially in the muffled silence of fresh-fallen snow. Mirabel Osler, the garden writer, extols the alluring charms of the garden in winter: "And momentarily, corners, hollows and forgotten recesses would be lit by shafts of a bleak sunlight pale as primroses. The quietude of winter is beyond reproach. There are numberless gardeners with whom I share this season with a profound sense of undiminished contentment."

December 3rd

Sitting at the desk in my study I look due East across fields which rise to the crest of Trimworth Downs, now covered in deep snow. Running down towards me from the crest are the wide, smooth gentle slopes of a dry-valley which enters the main valley of the River Stour close to Trimworth. In a strong bitterly cold north-east wind the snow is being blown in drifts, reducing visibility, filling hollows and forming overhanging edges of snow on the leeward sides of slopes. Watching these extreme weather conditions from the warmth of the study caused me to reflect on the origin and formation of these dry-valleys or coombes, which are such a common feature of our chalk terrain.

About 2.5million years ago, ice sheets were spreading across the northerly latitudes, extending almost as far south as the River Thames, but retreating and advancing as the climate warmed and cooled. In the tundra-like, periglacial conditions around Trimworth and other downlands of Southern England, the chalk would have been frozen and impermeable to water. During summer thaw, meltwater would run across the land, unable to permeate through the frozen chalk thus eroding river valleys such as the one which runs down slope towards Trimworth. These meltwater torrents carried chalky rubble, flint and sediment, which was deposited where the gradient of the dry-valley levelled out. With the return to a more temperate climate, the chalk thawed and become permeable again. Rivers no longer flowed across the surface, the water table fell and the valley became dry.

December 5th

Roz and I headed east towards Trimworth Down, creaking and crunching through a foot of fresh, powdery snow. At the foot of the downs we turned south, heading for Oxen Leas Wood, a fragment of ancient woodland with recent planting of conifers, sycamore and chestnut. The smooth contours and slopes of the downs were made inconspicuous by the dazzling whiteness, and were only revealed when the low flight of pheasants disappeared behind the imperceptible slopes of snow, reappearing as they rose up to the woodland margins. In the deep silence of the wood, snow had

In the deep silence of the snow, the wood was austere but beautiful, enchanting yet menacing as the grey light faded from the sky.

drifted deep, concealing hollows and tracks, weighing down the branches of spruce and forming fantastic wind-blown snow sculptures against the base of trees. The wood was austere but beautiful, enchanting yet menacing in the fading grey light of day. Flocks of pigeons flew fast through the wood, and a large excitable group of long-tailed tits rose from the crown of the pines, our attention drawn to them by their high-pitched twittering calls. Dozens of pheasants scattered away from the seed feeders stocked daily by the gamekeeper. Rabbit tracks converged on almost invisible burrows deep under the snow and we saw a hare take off suddenly, swifter than the rabbit, driven by powerful hind legs to its simple nest above the ground. The presence of rabbits and hares was obvious from the tracks as well as tree damage. Deep and destructive gnawing by sharp incisors had resulted in some small trees being barked almost all round the trunk and the snow driven against the trees have made their job easier. Their incisors grow continually to keep pace with the wear caused by gnawing. Rats teeth grow 2.77 mm a week and wear at an equivalent rate. Grey squirrels inhabit this world. A nest, or drey, was clearly visible in a birch tree consisting of tightly constructed twigs about the size of a football. The grey squirrel does not hibernate, so a larger, thicker winter drey is usually built where they will lie-up all winter, coming out occasionally to sniff out their store of hidden nuts. In fading light we crossed the road into Tye Wood, and dropped steeply down the snowy terraced slope to the river. Buzzards were returning to their roosts. Robins scuttled along snow filled dykes and the distant excited cries of children came from the smooth, long sledging slopes of Godmersham Down.

Trimworth, like many houses and small villages along the Stour Valley, is located on a river terrace 30 m above sea level and 200 m from the river, giving a dry-site settlement yet with easy access of the river and its fertile meadows. Throughout its long history there is no record that Trimworth was ever affected by flooding, which is a testament to the foresight of Anglo-Saxon settlers who chose these sites for settlement. They were perceptive in another very important aspect concerning microclimates. For two weeks we have been enduring very cold weather with frequent outbreaks of snow during the day, then night-time temperatures falling to freezing under clear skies. The low night temperatures are the result of heat being radiated back into space, giving a temperature inversion in which temperatures actually increase with height on the sides of the downs and in the coombe valleys running up into the downs. The extremely cold air above the ground sinks down into the main floor of the valley, where temperatures become significantly lower than the surrounding higher land. This phenomenon gives rise to a 'frost hollow' or 'frost pocket' because the air in the bottom of the valley frequently falls to freezing point whereas the air on the side of the downs remains well above freezing. Temperature differences can be as much as 6 - 8°C between valley bottom and land located a hundred metres higher. Gilbert White observed similar differences near his home in Selbourne in 1784, and assumed that his thermometer was faulty. The explanation for the apparent anomaly was explained in 1814 when Dr William Wells demonstrated the nature of temperature inversions and the formation of frost hollows, where delicate plants and crops growing in gardens and fields could be severely damaged by such frosts. Even the fresh green leaves of trees in spring can become black as a result of sub-zero temperatures. Thanks to our Anglo-Saxon settlers, Trimworth and other settlements located on a terrace 30 m above sea level are usually left above the frost hollow. We frequently see evidence of accumulating layers of cold air in the moist valley, defined by the local topography as a cold pool or shallow lake of ground fog above which Trimworth sits in frost-free, fog-free air.

We walked up through freezing fog, gradually emerging onto the clear slopes of Trimworth Downs and looked back to the level surface of fog filling the valley below us. 'Winter wonderland' is a prosaic phrase but there was nothing mundane about a situation where every tree, fence and blade of grass was covered in a thick coat of dense ice crystals. In the gentle wind, the needles, feathers, and tails of ice crystals had formed on the side of objects facing the wind. We were observing the effect of freezing air from the Arctic, bringing temperatures down to -10°C or even lower. At this temperature, water droplets of the fog can stay liquid well below freezing, but as soon as these 'supercooled' droplets touch a cold object like a tree or hedge, they freeze instantly into ice crystals. This is called rime, which will build up gradually to form quite thick layers of ice. Hoar-frost is a similar feature, the name deriving from the Old English word meaning white-haired, old and vulnerable. It describes the nature of delicate ice crystals which form under clear skies in moist air, and in very cold temperatures. It looks like snow, but is composed of small interlocking ice crystals. Hoar-frost might form first as liquid dew that subsequently freezes when the temperature drops. It is also known as silver-frost or white-frost. Whatever its name, or method of formation, both rime and hoar-frost produce spectacular results, especially on this day when seen against a clear blue sky and brilliant sunshine.

December 9th

Stockyards and cattle yards are full of flocks of corn bunting, a rather non-descript stout little bird with a fluttering flight. They flew up to fence posts then swarmed across the stubble returning to forage in the farmyard, where tractors were shifting huge bales of barley straw. In January 2010 the village of Stotfold, in Bedfordshire, experienced the largest ever roost of corn bunting settling in one field. They normally flock together when food is scarce, foraging more effectively and being safer from predator attacks, but the exceptional size of this flock was over 700 birds, about 5% of the breed's entire UK population in one field. This little 'fat bird of the barley', the largest of the buntings, suffered a decline of over 86% between 1967 and 2003, placing it on the red list species. Once again, responsibility for the decline lies with intensive methods of agriculture, which have progressively removed suitable nesting habitats and reduced the availability of grain and weed seeds as key foods.

December 11th

Late in the day we returned again to Kings Wood overlooking Godmersham and Trimworth, to wander through the roaring woods where hornbeam has been planted with beech to encourage the smooth grey columns to grow straight and tall. The impressive beech has a subterranean root system which spreads as widely as its crown, the roots yearning for water, and the crown for light. The fruiting structures of bracket fungi were clearly visible on the lower trunks of the trees, although there was little sign of heartwood decay. Beech wood is highly prized for flooring and furniture making, and fungal infection can lead to irregular wavy black lines etched by the fungi into the creamy wood adding economic value to the appearance of turned beech wood. Oak infected by the common beefsteak fungus develops a darker, richer colour to the wood and this 'brown oak' is much in demand in the furniture industry. Various Ganoderma brackets (G.adspersum) were plentiful with their concentric rings of cream and ochre standing out clearly on a dark brown

Every tree, fence and blade of grass was covered in a thick coat of dense ice crystals as the supercooled water droplets touched a cold object.

Ganoderma bracket fungi were plentiful with their concentric rings of cream and ochre on dark brown knobbly crust.

knobbly crust. What will happen to the majestic beech woods as the climate continues to warm? Already studies are indicating a loss of vigour in some old beeches. Presumably they will follow the isotherms and search the cooler climates further north, just as other trees have migrated in the past.

No diarist has ever created a more vivid portrait of daily life in rural England than parson James Woodforde, writing a daily record for over 40 years. Coming from Norfolk I am particularly interested in his entries from 1776 to 1803 for Western Longville, near Norwich. The diaries represent a unique document of rural social history, full of humour, and introducing a host of country characters: farmers, squires, pedlars, priests, butchers and blacksmiths, doctors and dentists, who all appear to be unaware of the Industrial Revolution, or the emergence of America, or the French Revolution. Nothing disturbs the tranquillity of life in this Norfolk village and yet the uncomplicated entries represent comments of historical importance on the social scene and social development of village life, such as the payment of tithes by parishioners to support the church and its clergy. On December 3, 1782, Parson Woodforde rejoiced in the company of 27 farmers gathered at the vicarage. Over £265 of tithe money was collected before a sumptuous meal was consumed. "Wine drank 6 Bottles. Rum drank 5 bottles besides Quantities of strong Beer and Ale." No wonder he describes the company as being "in very high glee" and "much disguised by liquor". In general, though the tithe meal , invariably held early in December, was a happy affair in which "… all behaved remarkably well and were happy and well pleased with the frolic." The diaries contain frequent reference to generous allocations of money and food for the rural poor; the easy relationship between different classes and sections of society with no indication of snobbishness; the constant entertaining with heavy drinking and drunkenness; the purchase of wigs; the awful impact of smallpox; and the frequent long journeys undertaken by horseback, coach or post-chaise, despite the threat of highwaymen. All these and many other aspects of life in rural England over 200 years ago are described in detail and expressed with understanding, candour and humour. It is a classic in the art of diary writing.

December 13th

It is St Lucy's Day, when the sun begins to set a minute or two later each day. The name means 'light' derived from the Latin verb 'lucere' (to shine). There will be no net gain in daylight hours yet because the sun continues to rise a little later until the end of December. But for some, it feels as if we have reached a turning point. The mood of the country, however, is far from light as Arctic air returns to the UK. Airports are closed, cars abandoned, gritting supplies exhausted, trains cancelled, politicians accused of complacency. At 7.00am as we walked through the snow towards the river, the temperature was -9°C. There was certainly no lightness in the sky. The colours were lead-grey and white, with snowflakes falling from heavy grey skies. The natural world appeared to be sleeping. The river was flat, grey and still, the banks fringed with layers of ice. Patches of ice lay trapped in the flattened reeds. Gradually the heavy skies lightened to a pearly grey and pale blue, and the natural world responded. Blue tits approached more closely; wrens flitted along the water edge; hungry buzzards slowly circled the treetops scanning the ground for movement; a startled snipe took off on an erratic flight pattern, zig-zagging and then soaring upwards; indignant-sounding moorhens scuttled into the safety of the bank and a pair of mallards drifted silently downstream.

The fresh snow was marked with tracks of rabbits, pheasant and fox. The tracks

Gradually the heavy skies lightened to a pearly grey and blue, and the natural world responded with the appearance of wrens, tits, moorhens and snipe.

of a trotting fox in the snow form a straight line of single prints, with a hind foot placed exactly in the fore print. The tracks lead to banks of the dyke where rabbit droppings are concentrated around the entrance to burrows, now partly concealed by the deep snow. Dark brown molehills, some fresh, some frozen, mark the activity of busy forepaws and tough little snouts. In the garden, berries have been stripped from holly and cotoneaster and there is a frenzy of activity around birdfeeders, one of which is dominated by the greater spotted woodpecker. This bird has become very familiar around birdfeeders and is a resident in the fir trees in our drive where it obtains seeds from the cones. They have a habit of wedging cones in clefts in the tree and hammering out the seeds, often rotating the cones so that all the seeds can be collected. In a tray of bird seed and apples near the house, I counted 15 sparrows, joined occasionally by jackdaws, starlings, greenfinch, blackbirds, chaffinch, crows and feisty little robins, standing legs wide apart, chests puffed out, beaks up, their aggressive body language demanding of the bird world "What's your problem?"

I have just received an e-mail from Dan Salter, the Ashford Countryside Officer working with the Kentish Stour Countryside Partnership. He has been a regular visitor to Trimworth and helps with the children's nature walks around Trimworth and along the river.

December 15th

"Just a quick message. I was at the Bilting owl boxes on Monday to do the yearly cleanout and refresh. Just for your records we saw dab chick (little grebe), seven common buzzards circling overhead in Tye Wood and an adult owl flew out of box number 1228 which was the productive box that we visited in the summer together and found five baby owls. Today we also found the remains of what was probably baby number five, the youngest as I remember when we weighed and measured them together earlier in the year."

I'm amazed at the number of buzzards he saw circling; We have never seen more than three or four. I'm delighted that the adult barn owl continues to use the box by the river and not at all surprised the smallest chick failed to survive. The little grebe Dan refers to is not a common visitor along our stretch of river, although the slow-moving river with plenty of vegetation is a favourite habitat of this dumpy little bird, the smallest of the grebes. It has no tail; instead it has a fluffy end like a powder puff, giving it what Michael Sego calls 'a blunt stern'. It has a distinctive trilling call, dives frequently and for long periods coming up some distance away. Shakespeare referred to it as the 'dive dapper' in Venus and Adonis, 'peering through a wave, who, being looked on, ducks as quickly in.'

December 16th

It is dusk and we are leaning on the paddock fence watching the glowing embers of a bonfire and talking about birdsong and listening to robins singing from three or four different points in field and garden. We realised how attached we were to this convivial companion. The songs of nightingale, song thrush, skylarks and blackbird will be on everyone's shortlist for the best birdsong, but my favourite is the robin because it is very vocal at dawn and dusk, singing throughout the year, including autumn and winter. It is often melancholic and wistful in winter, mellow and moody, languid, plaintive and yet melodic, with fluted whistles, rippling notes and dramatic pauses. Sometimes it is the alarm call of 'tsee-tsee' or 'tick tick tick,' like the sound of an old clock being wound up .The little bird is a ground feeder, seen in shady undergrowth of garden and woodland. It is quick and active with a heart rate of more than 500 beats a minute. The robin is my companion, almost a pet in the garden, perching on spade or wheelbarrow and waiting for worms to be exposed in freshly-turned soil. This romantic attachment is contemptuously dismissed by Colin Tudge ('The Secret Life of Birds') whose explanation for their friendship lies in their evolutionary woodland habit of following wild boars as they dig with their snouts for roots and digging up worms in the process. At this time of year the robins are in a very territorial mood, aggressively evicting each other, singing insults to potential invaders of their territory. Disputes are generally settled by displays. The territorial owner perches higher than the newcomer, showing off its red breast by taking an almost horizontal position. If displays fail to settle the dispute an all-out attack may follow leading to injury or even death. In December male robins may grudgingly welcome the presence of the female. Usually the female takes the initiative, responding to the song. She visits for short periods only and is often rebuffed. After several visits there may be a 'song and follow' ceremony in which the female responds to the song by following the male around his territory. They will often be seen hopping around together and eventually foraging together, a sure sign that they have paired up and become engaged. Breeding will take place between March and July. Robins can be knocked back in harsh winters but they bounce back because of their ability to have 3, 4 or even 5 broods, allowing populations to recover from winter losses.

December 17th

We have been extending our vegetable patch on the terrace slope above the paddock, spending many backbreaking hours unearthing and removing tons of flint in the process. Shortly after this laborious task I was told about an experiment conducted by Arthur Young, the great agricultural improver and social observer of the 18th and early 19th century, which was carried out on the flints-ridden fields of Suffolk. The purpose was to decide whether corn yielded better on farmland cleared of stones, compared with fields which had not been stone-picked. The result was that yields were considerably higher on the untouched fields. And yet in the 19th century, stone picking from the fields was a common practice. Maybe it had more to do with providing stone for the upkeep of local roads, which was the duty of the parish councils before Rural District Councils were established under the Local Government Act of 1894. Around Crundale, the Rural District Council paid farmers for cartloads of flints to be deposited by roadsides for road making and mending. It was work for the rural poor; men, women and children employed all day by Parish Overseers. Rex Lancefield's 'Within Living Memory' refers to Thomas Sutton who, at the age of 70, took over the care of Crundale's roads at the turn-of-the-century. He retired from this work during the First World War at the age of 85! He was replaced by youthful 60-year-old called George Sexton, who, with handcart and a few tools, patched up holes in the roads, cut verges with a sickle, kept open the roadside ditches so that water flowed into farm ponds, and scattered chalk over the flint roads to bind them.

December 18th

Apparently it's 'not so grim up North' if you are a bird. A recent study commissioned by the RSPB from the British Trust for Ornithology shows that since 1994 many bird populations in the East, South East and South West have declined substantially, whilst in the North they have performed much better. The report is based on updated results of the Breeding Bird Survey for the period 1994 to 2009. (It does not include species with national bird populations less than 500 breeding pairs.) Trends in farmland birds show a decline of 28% in the South-East, but increasing by 3% in the North. For woodland birds the differential is much greater with a 19% decline in the South-East and a 31% increase in the North West. Individual species follow these trends, for example, the linnet declined by 48% in the South-East with much smaller declines in the North. The chiff-chaff has recorded gains everywhere, but the 25% increase in the South-East is dwarfed by a huge 144% increase in the North-West. How can these differences be explained? Farm intensification in the South is likely to be a factor, together with differences in land-use, extent of development, variations in topography, and water availability. Perhaps climate change may eventually be shown to encourage some birds to move north. This intriguing gradient of decline from North to South is an indication of the ability of birds to survive, and raises questions about the impact of changes to the quality of our countryside.

Winter roosting surveys by the BTO are also yielding encouraging results, with the wren piling into nest boxes and old nests to stay warm overnight. Over a quarter of the roosts contained 5 to 9 individual wrens, and one nest box in South Devon contained over 30. The house sparrow is also a gregarious nester but, in contrast, the blue tit usually sleeps alone, with 63% of roosts being for solitary individuals. We know the importance of nesting boxes during the spring, but this survey confirms how vital they are for roosting birds in winter.

Surrounded by these 'Arctic' conditions, which are forecast to persist for several days leads me to reflect on the relationship between weather and behaviour. There is plenty of research which demonstrates the link between rises in temperature and an increase in violent and property crimes, but temperature changes are not the only factor linking weather and behaviour. Pressure changes can affect mental activity causing changes in memory function. Sunny days can be stimulating, whilst the present succession of dull, grey days can lead to 'winter blues' or Seasonal Affective Disorder (SAD), a problem affecting about 7 - 10% of the population in the UK, who experience lethargy, lack of appetite, lower energy levels and mood changes. Persistent wind can also lead to mood changes, and many seasonal winds are described as' ill winds', linked to anxiety and stress.

The behaviour of animals is also closely linked to weather conditions. We observe bees remaining close to hives during summer rainstorms, while birds increase their foraging, or gather to roost before bad weather sets in. Norman Ellis has studied how weather affects bird behaviour, such as the decisions about where and how to migrate; timing and success of reproduction; flight style and physical comfort. Many animals which I have observed and written about during the year have developed strategies to cope with the extreme weather conditions which we are now experiencing. Some moths can overwinter, but many go into a dormant phase known as diapause in which the development of the moth or insect can be delayed until better environmental conditions return, at which time offspring will be born. Our ponds are covered in ice and several inches of snow, but beneath the ice life goes on, even in the coldest weather the larvae of mayflies, dragonflies, caddis flies and various water beetles all overwinter under the ice. Frogs and smooth newts will also overwinter at the bottom of the pond taking in oxygen through their skin. Many mammals begin to conserve energy by decreasing their physiological activity as food becomes scarce. In winter the dormouse ('dormir' to sleep) shuts down its body and goes into a period of torpor which may last six months. Some may spend three quarters of their lives asleep. Its body temperature drops to the temperature of the surrounding environment and the heartbeat falls to a 10th of the normal rate. It is the only British rodent which hibernates, eating as much food as it can to build up body-fat levels, and making a nest deep in a hedge or in the hollow of the tree where it prepares a food store. During warmer spells, the dormouse wakes briefly, eats a little then sleeps again when temperatures drop.

The most extraordinary piece of recent research into survival during harsh weather winters concerns the young brown trout, which reduces its body length by as much as a centimetre or 10% of their length, in order to conserve energy when food supply is short. This phenomenon has been observed in some small mammals such as shrews, where reduction in length is probably caused by reduction in the volume of jelly-like substance between vertebral discs of those creatures with spinal columns.

It is the December solstice, the beginning of winter, when the sun has reached its most southerly declamation, or downward track. It marks the day of the year with fewest hours of daylight for those living north of the Tropic of Cancer. (Within the Arctic Circle, the sun is not visible at all at this time of year.) The date of the December solstice ranges from the 20th to 23rd of December, most frequently being on the 21st. The variation is due to the calendar system. The Gregorian calendar, with which we are familiar, has 365 days (366 days in a Leap Year), but the length of time the sun takes to return to the same position in the seasonal cycle is 365.24 days, varying because of the 'wobble' of the Earth's axis.

The December solstice has always been widely associated with traditions and cultural events, often associated with rebirth and the coming of lighter days. Even in Neolithic times astronomical events such as the solstice determined the time for the sowing of crops, mating and slaughtering of animals. The physical layout of Stonehenge gives a primary axis aligned on winter solstice sunrise and winter-solstice sunset. Hannukah is known as the Festival of Lights, an eight-day Jewish celebration, observed between late November and late December by the kindling of lights. The word 'yule', derived from the Norse word 'jol', refers to pre-Christian festivals marked by the burning of yule logs to symbolise heat, light and the return of the sun. In other European countries, ash from the burning of Yule logs was scattered as fertiliser on the fields every night until 12th night. In ancient Rome, the solstice festivals, (Saturnalia) began on 17th December and lasted seven days, honouring Saturn, the king of the gods, by decorating houses in greenery, lighting candles and giving presents. The event eventually ended in debauchery, hence the dictionary definition of Saturnalia as unrestrained merrymaking, revelry and orgy!

For the first time in nearly 400 years, this winter solstice coincided with a total lunar eclipse and also a situation where the sun and eclipsed moon were briefly visible above the horizon. Unfortunately, the moon was only 3° above the horizon at the time of the eclipse and was not visible, but there was a distinctive redness to the morning sky as the moon moved into the shadow of the earth at 7.40 am. At this point the sun, earth, and moon were in exact alignment, with the moon and sun on opposite sides of the earth – just as it was in the winter solstice of 1638.

Rapid thaw has set in, and, where sheep have been lying overnight, patches of green are appearing in the snow-filled meadow. There is a constant drip from trees and mist hangs in the wood like puffs of smoke. It is a dismal, gloomy, raw scene. The silence was broken by high-pitched shrill cries, immediately recognisable as the peewit or lapwing, one of our most evocative farmland birds, which has suffered severe declines in recent years. Its fortunes have been closely linked to the intensification of farming since the 1950s. Such practices as the conversion of large areas of grass to arable, the drainage and improvement of marginal lands, and the use of fertilisers and chemical pest controls have brought a severe reduction in lapwing numbers. Sadly declines have not been significantly reduced since the introduction of agri-environment management schemes of the 1980s. The sight of large flocks of lapwing on winter pastures, ploughed fields or marshes was a common winter occurrence. Michael Seago records the scene in Norfolk in 1992: "Battalion upon battalion lifted from the flats before swirling like autumn leaves high into the darkening sky. Ranks closed as the birds swept over the estuary, rising and falling, packed together. Again they climbed, flickering silhouettes against a fiery afterglow and reminiscent of a Peter Scott painting. Finally, all turned, slowly glided and pitched down, posing with uplifted wings momentarily before merging into the dusk. The performance was unforgettable."

Recent research identifies poor breeding success up to, or just after, the time of fledging as a significant contributory factor in decline, because there appears to be little change in adult mortality. At the Elmley National Nature Reserve, research shows that each breeding pair of lapwing needs to produce 0.7 chicks to maintain a stable population. This is being achieved through careful management of livestock grazing, the provision of water in shallow pools or scrapes to ensure water bodies remain through the wader breeding season, provision of a mosaic of grass, and tillage to encourage a variety of food sources. With such environmentally sensitive management schemes we should see the peewit, 'the farmer's friend', returning in greater numbers to delight us with their wavering flight, tumbling aerobatic displays and characteristic plaintive call.

December 23rd

It is a dreadful day. Temperatures hovered just above freezing, but with a strong sleet-laden wind from the north-east, (from the mountains and tundra of Scandinavia and Russia) giving a wind- chill factor well below freezing. The wind-chill factor is calculated from charts for given temperatures and wind speeds. Today, a wind speed of 30 km/h and air temperatures of 0 degrees centigrade gives a wind-chill factor of -11°C. The action of the wind affects how quickly we lose heat from our bodies through convection, and it thus has a particular relevance to the formation of frostbite on exposed skin, especially in Arctic environments.

We sought the shelter of Oxen Leas Wood, but the sound of wind in the pines and beeches was frightening: roaring and straining, branches breaking off and littering the forest floor. Edward Thomas captures the moment perfectly: "… The sound of trees, and multitudinous frenzied sound, of rustling dead oak leaves still on the bough, or of others tripping along a path like mice, all winding up in sudden spirals and forming again, of dead boughs grating and grinding, of pliant young branches lashing, of finest twigs and fir needles sighing, of leaf and branch and trunk booming like one…"

I was not the only one sheltering – pheasant and partridge rustled around in the understory, rabbits bolted for cover, a rabble of rooks flew in followed by jabbering jackdaws, then the sudden snap of pigeons wings. Under sweet chestnut trees were piles of spiky dark brown husks, like miniature hedgehogs. The forest floor had a rich, damp, musty smell. On dead wood and tree stumps the tiny forms of candle snuff fungus could be seen, their flattened antler-shaped branches tipped with powder whiter than the snow and turning black as they mature to resemble the aptly named dead men's fingers. We scrambled down the terraces in Tye Wood, tripping over snow-covered branches and faced the full force of the stinging, penetrating wind across the river meadow. Never was an open fire more welcome with a mug of tea, toast and honey and Sam's warm body sprawled across my feet.

December 24th

With rapid snowmelt and prolonged periods of heavy rain the countryside is awash, and the sound of running water is everywhere, raising the possibility that the usually dry-valleys in the chalk will soon contain sloshing, babbling streams of water flooding the frost-bound valley and its silent meadows. A recognised feature of the chalk downland country surrounding us is the intermittent nature of many streams. These are locally known as nailbournes in Kent, lavants in Hampshire and gipseys in the Yorkshire Wolds. The irregular and unpredictable nature of these streams has generated much local interest and folklore. They were often referred to as 'woe waters' because of the distress they caused and the belief that their appearance would be followed by war and poor harvests. In former times these streams flowed more frequently and for longer periods than today, indicating that water levels in the chalk were once much higher. In the rapid thaw and sustained rainfall today, water will move downwards through fissures and pores in the chalk, reaching clay seams which prevent further downward movement of water. Then the saturated zone of chalk (the water table) rises closer to the surface, occasionally emerging at ground level through fissures to form a temporary stream or nailbourne. The changing levels of the water table in wells and boreholes in this area are recorded throughout the year by the Environment Agency. Results show that in general, water levels rise in autumn and stay high until the spring after which the amount of precipitation falls and more water is taken up by vegetation. The Elham nailbourne is our nearest, fed by springs which invariably flow from around the village of Lyminge, continuing north through a series of spring-fed lakes at Bishopsbourne. In times of persistent, heavy rain the nailbourne can flow throughout its course such as in 1981 when a 'Rapids Race' took place with 60 'craft' competing over a 4 mile stretch! Despite the infrequent appearance of the nailbourne, it continues to provide a fascinating diversion for the village communities along its course who cherish the legends and folklore – if not the floods.

It is 1794 and we are back with Parson Woodforde and 'The Diary of a Country Parson,' in the run-up to Christmas. On 13th December he had been "Busy all the morning almost, in bottling two tubs of gin that came by Moonshine this mourn' very early." Festive preparations continued on the 16th when he brewed a barrel of 'common beer.' On the 22nd he demonstrated his personal generosity by giving sixpence to each of the 57 poor people in the parish. His diary overflows with similar founts of charity and liberal relief to alleviate the sufferings of the poor in hard times, especially at Christmas. On Christmas Day he refers to the terrible winter which came and went, continuing through to March. During the preparation of the sacrament on Christmas Day he 'fainted away', feeling he could never escape from feeling the effect of the 'shuddering sharpness of air'. Nevertheless later in the day he was able to eat plum pudding and potatoes, then later entertained some of the poor parishioners with a dinner of sirloin beef, more plum pudding and plenty of strong beer. The piercing, severe weather continued for many days, "The coldest I have ever felt in my life." Milk pans in the dairy froze as did the chamber pots under the bed. Many birds were found dead. Rooks and crows were so tame and desperate that they came up to the kitchen door for food. The snow was as deep as the shoulders of a horse, bedrooms remained ice cold and the temperature in his study dropped to 40°F even with the fire alight. On Boxing Day he continued to feel languid and low and complained of poor appetite, but having paid the church ringers and given Christmas boxes he dined on calf's fry and roast rabbit. "I drank plentifully of port wine after dinner, instead of one glass drank seven or eight wine glasses and it seemed to do me much good, being better for it." This is another little taste of social history combined with humour which has entertained a growing 'congregation' of appreciation for the diaries of this likeable man in his Norfolk parsonage.

On Sunday, 17 October 1803, the diary reads: "Very weak this Morning, scarce able to put on my Cloaths and with great difficulty, get down stairs with help. Mr Dade read prayers and preached this morning at Weston Church – Nancy at Church. Mr and Mrs Custance and Lady Bacon at Church. Dinner today, Rost Beef etc. The rest of the page is blank. The diary has come to an end. On New Year's Day, 1803, Parson Woodford died, aged 63.

December 26th

Jeff Doel is a travelling performer who uses old musical instruments, poems and literature to keep alive the rural heritage and traditions of Kent. His book, "The Kent Christmas," is full of extracts, anecdotes, recipes, festivals and songs which chronicle the traditions of the Kent Christmas. The conviviality of Christmas has not always been well received in Kent. In 1647, the puritan Mayor of Canterbury proclaimed that Christmas days and all other superstitions and festivals should be "utterly abolished", on the grounds that the symbolism of Christmas was linked to pagan festivals. He announced the closure of shops and Christmas markets, a ban on church services, a ban on the use of rosemary, holly, plum pottage and nativity pies. Riots followed, with assaults and imprisonment. Not until the restoration of Charles II (the 'Merry Monarch') in 1660 was Christmas properly celebrated again in Kent.

A favourite traditional Kent Christmas custom was the ritual of dressing up as horses by crouching under a sacking and carrying a pole on which was held the carved wooden head of a horse (hoaden horse). The custom is rooted in a pagan festival recorded in Kent in the seventh century and has survived to this day in East Kent. The wooden horse, accompanied by musicians and several other strange characters, including a man dressed as a woman with blackened face and besom broom, visited farms, pubs and markets during the Christmas period. The performance is full of songs, strange and scary antics, beer drinking, bell ringing and laughter. Several revivals of this custom have taken place in recent years, often incorporating local characters and events. Of similar antiquity and eccentricity are the 'mummers plays' involving death and resurrection to simulate the death of the old year and the birth of the new. Again, many were performed in market squares, pubs and houses around Christmas time. The scripts varied regionally, but most included the key characters of St George and the dragon, a Turkish knight, a quack doctor, old Father Christmas, and a fool whose job was to take the hat round and appeal for generosity from the audience. The custom of mummers' plays has been revived by numerous active groups in the south-east, such as the Compton Tipteerers and Darren Valley Champions.

The final reference to the Kent Christmas tradition must go to a wonderful story about the Frittenden Band, consisting mainly of brass instruments, drums and flugelhorn, which toured the neighbourhood at Christmas time playing carols to outlying farms and houses. On one Christmas Eve they set out in high spirits, not bothered by the deteriorating visibility, because most were unable to read music anyhow. Morris man Alan Austen takes up the story: "The fog grew thicker and thicker and the musicians began to long for the roaring open fire of the Bell and Jorrocks. Around midnight they cautiously felt their way across the fields to their last port of call, an outlying farm house renowned for its hospitality and for that reason selected as the final visit. The shadowy outline of the old building seemed to loom through the mist as they played their carols. There they were in full swing, halfway through 'Hark the Herald Angels Sing' when all of a sudden, as if by magic, the fog lifted and to their surprise they found themselves playing – to a haystack!"

Aerial predators are casting menacing shadows over the garden, and nothing clears the garden of small birds quite like the threatening presence of the sparrowhawk. This morning it skimmed low over the garden without a wing beat before rising up into the birch trees frequented by tits and chaffinch. From there, it identifies and focuses on the bird from a flock and chases it, ignoring the frantic calls of the other birds. It is highly manoeuvrable in flight, gliding effortlessly one moment, and then veering sharply in pursuit. The usual flying speed of a sparrowhawk is 30 to 40 km an hour, but speeds of up to 50 km an hour have been recorded in short bursts. Michael Seago in his 'Birds of Britain' website notes how persistent is the flight of a sparrowhawk, blindly chasing its quarry and striking wires or walls or trees and even becoming fatally wounded. Earlier this year, we had to release a sparrowhawk from an outbuilding into which it had flown in pursuit of a sparrow. The sparrowhawk has no serious predators itself, although crows will make life difficult for them by chasing them off their territory with rasping, raucous calls and aggressive charges.

Yesterday a group of crows was circling the wood, then dropping down to land in the meadow, bouncing along on springy legs and looking furtive. We then saw the reason for their presence. A sheep which for days had been looking frail and wasted was lying dead in the field. The crows play the waiting game, dipping their heads, preening themselves with their long, thick, black bills – but mostly watching. We walked closer and they rose up into the wood and perched, looking innocent, waiting for a chance to raid and plunder the dead sheep's body and gouge out its eyes. There is nothing we can do except contemplate the paradox of the glories and terrors of nature. The crows don't care. And why should they be concerned about my sensitivities? It's all about competition and survival in a natural world, which is being made even more precarious by our activities.

Now the snow has gone, the kestrel is on the hunt for its main prey of small mammals such as shrews and voles or small birds. We know their regular perches along the roadside verges where they scan the ground from the tops of telegraph poles and overhead wires. With better hunting conditions they will narrow their territory to a square kilometre, extending it when food supplies once more become scarce.

December 31st

Since March 1904, the Guardian's idiosyncratic Country Diary has been a source of delight and inspiration, penned by some of the great essayists and naturalists who have helped to build a national institution over 100 years. This makes it the longest-running uninterrupted column in British newspapers. Bill Condry, living and working in West Wales was a regular contributor for over 40 years from 1957 to 1998, highlighting issues about farming practices, use of pesticides, the destruction of hedges and the erosion of high-quality soils. However, his entry in November, 1974, under the heading "What use old diaries" is an appropriate theme on which to end this journal. Like the man himself, it is a modest, humble, droll but very germane entry.

"For maybe 60 years a chap will write down a daily miscellany of what seem rather pointless observations about plants, birds, mammals, insects, fish or merely the weather, pointless because he hardly ever refers to them again. Never mind, diary keeping amuses him and does no harm. And it's always possible that when he dies his journals will get preserved in a library somewhere. There they may lie neglected for half a century but eventually somebody feels inquisitive enough to dip into them. The dross of fifty years ago, like old bottles, has acquired an unexpected value. These thoughts occurred to me because I am just now reading the lifelong diaries of a local journalist who flourished earlier this century. J.H. Salter, Professor of Botany at Aberystwyth, was a true all-rounder. Wandering the lanes and woods he identified birds, reptiles, mammals, moths and beetles just as easily as plants. For many of these species there has been little change since his day. But some have gone. The corn buntings, woodlarks, shrikes and some of the plants he mentioned are not of our time. The world of nature he knew already seems a little unreal and will be even more interesting to readers fifty years from now. So, gathering his little daily store of notes, our diarist, without realising it, was writing a quite unique kind of history."

So, it is the end of the year and the end of this diary. At midnight the bell ringers will clamber into their bell towers and the bells of Wye and Godmersham will ring out in the darkness over sleepy villages, farms, moonlit meadows, marshes and streams just as they always have; pealing down the years across these peaceful and beautiful 'meadows by the river.'

The References and Further Reading

Country Diaries, an annotated selection

Baker J.A (2010) *The Peregrine. The Hill of Summer Diaries. The Complete Works of J.A. Baker.* Collins.
A writer frequently compared to Gilbert White in the quality of his observations and the richness of his prose. He has an intimate knowledge of the Essex landscape and its wildlife, particularly birds. The Hill of Summer describes his wildlife encounters between the seasons of spring and autumn, whilst the Peregrine is a close focus on one species.

Bates H.E. (1987 reprint) *In the Heart of the Country.* Robinson Publishing.
First published by Country Life in 1942, this beautifully written work is full of sharp observations of seasonal changes in the English countryside.

Bates H.E. (2011 reprint) *Through the Woods.* Little TollerBooks
First published in 1936, an intensely observed literary study of the changing character of a woodland year, revealing what a precious habitat the woodland is for plants and animals and people. Illustrated throughout with engravings.

Burnettt K. (2008) *The Field by the River.* Portico.
An entertaining account of a year's observations in the meadows of the River Sarre in Brittany, which captures the rhythms of rural life.

Burton R. (1998) *Nature Notes.* Hodder and Stoughton.
A selection of entries from the Daily Telegraph's Nature Notes, accompanied by illustrations, and giving brief but illuminating observations on the natural world.

Condry W. (1993) *A Welsh Country Diary.* Gomer Press.
An insight into the intricacies of Welsh country life seen through the eyes of the longest serving contributor to the Guardian's Country Diary column.

Deakin R. (2008) *Notes from Walnut Tree Farm.* Penguin Books.
Amusing, highly original and very perceptive observations and thoughts about nature and the changing world set in rural Suffolk. Has been described as, 'this century's Walden.'

Elford C. (2011) *A Year in the Woods.* Penguin.
The diary of a forest ranger whose school report in 1966 reads, 'Colin would do well to keep his eyes on the blackboard rather than the squirrels outside the windows!' An enthralling journey deep into the heart of an English woodland.

Gower J. (1998) *A Year in a Small Country.* Gomer Press. The story of three diarists in different places in Wales: salt marshes of the Dyfi Estuary, a hill farm in Carmarthenshire, and a poet on Bardsey Island.

Hale J. (2007) *The Nature Diary of an Artist.* Herbert Press.
This ceramic artist who lives in Devon has produced an enchanting collection of entries and watercolour drawings from a nature diary. She has an enviable talent for fresh, spontaneous field painting and sketching.

Holden E. (1977 reprint) *The Country Diary of an Edwardian Lady.* Michael Joseph Ltd.
A facsimile reproduction of the naturalists diary for the year 1906, describing the flora and fauna of the English countryside throughout the year, recorded in words and paintings. Enchanting, unique – a classic.

Lister-Kay J. (2011) *At the Water's Edge: a walk in the wild.* Canongate.
Seasonal observations from daily walks through a Scottish Glen, containing wonderful wildlife encounters. Beautifully observed and richly described.

Marsh J. (1979) *Nature Diary.* Book Club Associates.
Set in the Itchen Valley in Hampshire, the diary is a study of the animals and flowers around this fine chalk stream, with concerns expressed about development pressures and the vanishing English countryside. Exquisitely illustrated with wonderful watercolours.

May D. (2004) *A Year in Nature Notes.* Harper Collins.
A yearbook containing daily entries on the changing sights and sounds of the countryside throughout the year, by the author of Nature Notes in the Times.

Petrie R., Wainwright M. (2008) *The Guardian Book of the Countryside.* Guardian Newspapers Limited.

A reminder of how the British countryside has endured over the last 200 years from the spread of railways to the impact of global warming, yet still remains our most versatile and beautiful resource.

Swift K. (2008) *The Morville Years*. Bloomsbury
This would be one of my Desert Island choices. The setting is The Dower House at Morville in Shropshire which Swift designed and developed from her arrival in1988. A monthly meditation on local history, plants, trees, wildlife. Beautifully written, evocative, magical and intimate.

Taylor A. (ed.) (2009) *The Country Diaries: a Year in the British Countryside*. Cannongate.
Arranged as a diary of the calendar year, the book brings together some of the finest nature writers to produce a rich portrait of our rural landscape.

Thoreau H.D. (1995 reprint) *Walden: or Life in the Woods*. Dover Thrift Editions.
First published in 1854, it has become one of the defining texts in nature writing and continues to inform debates on environmental and conservation issues. The book is a product of his two-year sojourn in a cabin on the shore of Walden Pond, Massachusetts. A classic of nature observation.

Wainwright M. (2008) *A Good Year for Blossom: A Century of the Guardian's Women Journalists*. Guardian Newspapers Limited.
Chroniclers of the countryside have traditionally been men. This book examines countryside themes through the eyes of 10 exceptional women with very different backgrounds.

Wainwright M.(ed.) (2009) *A Gleaming Landscape: 100 years of the Guardian's Country Diary*. Aurum Press.
Delightful entries by some of Britain's finest landscape essayists and naturalists.Described as, 'A pocket Thoreau.'

White G. (1977 reprint) *The Natural History of Selbourne*. Penguin Books.
Originally published in 1788, this collection of letters by a country clergyman has become a classic of local natural history and one of the most published books in the English language. It has shaped our understanding of the natural world with its accurate and perceptive observation. This edition has an introduction and notes by Richard Mabey.

White G. (2010) *The Illustrated Natural History of Selbourne*. Thames and Hudson.
Has an introduction by June Chatfield, former Director of the Gilbert White Museum. The beautiful illustrations more than make up for the lack of footnotes which the Penguin version contains.

White J.T. (1974) *A Country Diary: Kent*. Cassell.
Originally a contributor to the Guardian's Country Diary, these entries have been chosen from a three-year diary of Kent. He combines a poetic style with careful scientific observations.

White J. (1985) *A Countryman's Year in the North Downs of Kent*. Blue Cat Press.
Jim farmed and observed this wonderful landscape, tucked away in the North Downs, for over 50 years. This is a perceptive guide to the farming year by a lifelong naturalist, complemented by delightful sketches from John Ward.

Woodforde J. (1978) *The Diary of a Country Parson, 1758 to 1802*. Oxford University Press.
First published in 1925, the diaries are a vivid portrait of daily life in rural England over 200 years ago and comprise a unique document of social history. In this edition there is an excellent introduction by John Beresford who has also selected the entries.

The British Countryside

Burney R. (2011) *Amazing and Extraordinary Facts on the English Countryside*. David and Charles.

Carr S. (ed.) (2010) *Ode to the Countryside*. National Trust.

Clifford S., King A. (2006) *England in Particular: the commonplace, the local, the distinctive*. Common Ground

Dimbleby D. (2005) *A Picture of Britain*. Tate Publishing

Grigson G. (2010) *The Shell Country Alphabet: the Classic Guide to the British Countryside*. Penguin.

Hoskins W.G. (1978) *One Man's England*. BBC.

Hoskins W.G. (1991, new edition) *The Making of the English Landscape*. Penguin.

National Trust (2009) *The National Trust Book of the Countryside*. National Trust.

Pryor F . (2011) *The Making of the British Landscape: how we have transformed the land from prehistory to present*. Penguin

Rackham O. (1986) *The History of the Countryside: the classic history of Britain's landscape, flora and fauna.* Orion Books.

Rackham O. (1990) *Trees and Woodlands in the British Landscape: the complete history of Britain's trees, woods and hedgerows.* Phoenix.

Rackham O. (1994) *The Illustrated History of the Countryside.* Weidenfeld and Nicholson.

Short B. (2006) *England's Landscape: The South East.* Collins.

Struthers J. (2009) *Red Sky at Night: the book of lost country wisdom.* Ebury Press.

Tuson D. (2007) *The Kent Downs.* Tempus.

Reference

Bang P., Dahlstrom P. (2007) *Animal Tracks and Signs.* Oxford University Press.

Chinnery M. (2009) *Collins Complete Guide to British Insects.* Collins.

Cocker M., Mabey R. (2005) *Birds Britannica.* Chatto and Windus

Cope T., Gray A. (2009) *Grasses of the British Isles.* Kew Books.

Garnett A. Devlin P. (2007) *A Year in the Life of an English Meadow.* Frances Lincoln Limited.

Greenhalgh M. Ovenden D. (2007) *Freshwater Life of Britain and Northern Europe.* Collins

Hensel W. (2008) *Medicinal Plants of Britain and the Europe.* A&C Black.

Hume R. (2009) *Complete Birds of Britain and Europe.* Dorling Kindersley.

Lang D. (1983) *The Illustrated Wild Flower Finder's Catalogue.* Chancellor Press

Mabey R. (1997) *Flora Britannica.* Chatto and Windus.

Marren P. Mabey R. (2010) *Bugs Britannica.* Chatto and Windus.

Phillips R. (1981) *Mushrooms and other Fungi of Great Britain and Europe.* Macmillan.

Philp E.G. (2010) *The New Atlas of Kent Flora.* Kent Field Club

Preston C.D., Pearman D.A., Dines T.P.(2002) *New Atlas of the British and Irish Flora.* Oxford University Press.

Pretor-Pinney G. (2006) *The Cloud Spotters Guide.* Sceptre.

Rose F. (1989) *Colour Identification to the Grasses, Sedges, Rushes and Ferns of the British Isles and North West Europe.* Viking Books.

Stace C. (2010) *New Flora of the British Isles,* (third edition). Cambridge University Press.

Sterry P. (2005) Collins *Complete British Animals.* Collins.

Sterry P. (2008) Collins *Complete Guide to British Trees.* Collins.

Sterry P. (2008) Collins *Complete Guide to British Wildflowers.* Collins.

Sterry P. (2010) Collins *Complete Guide to British Garden Wildlife.* Collins.

Nature Writing

Benjamin A., McCullum B. (2008) *A World Without Bees.* Guardian Books.

Boulter M. (2008) *Darwin's Garden: Down House and the Origin of Species.* Constable.

Bunting M. (2009) *The Plot: A Biography of an English Acre.* Granta Publications.

Cocker M. (2006) *A Tiger in the Sand: Selected Writings on Nature.* Jonathan Cape.

Collis J.S. (2009) *The Worm Forgives the Plough.* Vintage Classics.

Deakin R. (1999) *Waterlog.* Vintage.

Grahame K. (1908) *The Wind in the Willows.* Methuen.

Jefferies R. (2011) *Wild Life in a Southern County.* Little Toller books.

Lewin A. (2010) *Plants and Places.* Merrell Publishers.

Lovegrove R. (2008) *Silent Fields: the long decline of a nation's wild life.* Oxford University Press.

Mabey R. (1973) *The Unofficial Countryside.* Little Toller Books.

Mabey R. (1980) *The Common Ground.* Phoenix.

Mabey R. (2008) *Beechcombings : the Narrative of Trees.* Vintage.

Mabey R. (2008) *Nature Cure.* Vintage.

Mabey R. (2010) *A Brush With Nature.* BBC Books.

Macfarlane R. (2000) *Call of the Wild.* The Guardian, Saturday, 6th September.

Macfarlane R. (2007) *The Wild Places.* Penguin.

Macfarlane R. (2012) *The Old Ways: a journey on foot.* Hamish Hamilton.

Maconie S. et al.(2011) *On Nature: unexpected ramblings on the British Countryside.* Collins.

McCarthy M. (2009) *Say Goodbye to the Cuckoo.* John Murray.

Measures D. (1996) *Butterfly Season, 1984.* Arlequin Press.

Perrin J. (1997) *Spirits of Place.* Gomer Press.

Perrin J. (2010) *West: a Journey Through Landscapes of Loss.* Atlantic Books.

Thomas E. (2009) *The South Country.* Little Toller Books. (1st published 1909.)

Tudge C. (2006) *The Secret Life of Trees.* Penguin.

Tudge C. (2009) *The Secret Life of Birds.* Penguin.

Tomkies M. (1988) *Out of the Wild.* Jonathan Cape.

Wilson B. (2005) *The Hive: the Story of the Honeybee and Us.* John Murray.

Glossary of Flora and Fauna referred to in text

Mammals

badger.....................................Meles meles
bat
      pipistrelle......................Pipistrellus pipistrellus
      pipistrelle soprano.........Pipistrelle pygmaeus
      horseshoe ....Rhinolophus hipposideros
      serotine.........................Eptesicus serotinus
deer
      muntjac ....Muntiacus muntjak
      fallow...........................Dama dama
dormouse..............................Muscardinus avellanarius
fox ....Vulpes vulpes
hare ....Lepus europaeus
hedgehog..............................Erinaceous europeus
mink ....Lutreola vison
mole Talpa europaeus
mouse
      field..............................Micromys minutus
      wood............................Apodemus sylvaticus
otter Lutra lutra
rabbit ....Oryctolagus cuninculus
shrew ....Sorex araneus
squirrel
      grey..............................Sciurus carolinensis
      red ....Sciurus vulgaris
stoat Mustela arminea
vole
      bank..............................Clethrionomys glareolus
      water.............................Arvicola terrestris
      field..............................Microtus agrestis
weasel ....Mustela nivalis

Birds

blackbird...............................Turdus merula
blackcap ....Sylvia atricapillag
brambling ....Fringilla montifringilla
bullfinch ....Pyrrhula pyrrhula
bunting
      reed ....Emberiza schoeniclus
      corn ....Milaria calandra
buzzard ....Buteo buteo
chaffinch ....Fringilla coelebs
chiff chaff ....Phylloscopus collybita
coot ....Fulica atraphala
cormorant..............................Phalacrocarax carbo
corncrake..............................Crex crex
crossbill................................Loxia curvirostra
crow Corvus corone
cuckoo..................................Cuculus canorus
duck
      little grebe ....Tachybaptus ruficollis
      mallard ....Anas platyrhynchos

      ruddy ....Oxyura jamaicensis
      teal ....Anas crecca
      tufted ....Aythya fuligula
      wigeon ....Anas Penelope
dunnock (hedge sparrow) .....Prunella modularis
eagle
      white tailed...................Haliaeetus albicilla
egret
      little ....Egretta garzetta
fieldfare...............................Turdus pilaris
goose, Canada ....Branta Canadensis
goldcrest ....Regulus regulus
goldfinch ....Carduelis carduelis
great bustard.........................Otis tarda
gull
      blackheaded ....Larus ridibundus
      common ....Larus canus
      herring ....Larus argentatus
hen harrier............................Circus cyaneus
heron ....Ardea cinerea
jackdaw ....Corvus monedula
kestrel...................................Falco tinnunculus
kingfisher..............................Alcedo atthis
lapwing (plover, peewit) ....Vanellus vanellus
linnet ....Carduelis cannabina
magpie ....Pica pica
martin
      house ....Delichon urbica
      sand.............................Riparia riparia
meadow pipit........................Anthus pratensis
merlin ....Falco colombarius
moorhen................................Gallinula chloropus
nightingale ....Luscinia megarhynchos
osprey ....Pandion haliaetus
owl
      barn ....Tyto alba
      little ....Athene noctua
      tawny ....Strix aluca
partridge ....Perdix perdix
peregrine...............................Falco peregrinus
pheasant................................Phasianus colchicus
pigeon
      collared dove ....Streptopelia decaocto
      rock dove ....Columba livia
      wood ....Columba palumbus
raven ....Corvus corax
red kite ....Milvus milvus
redwing.................................Turdus iliacus
robin ....Erithacus rubecula
rook ....Corvus frugilegus
skylark ....Alanda arvensis
snipe
      common ....Gallinago gallinago

jack ....Lymnocryptes minimus
sparrow ....Passer domesticus
sparrowhawk ....Accipiter nisus
starling...............................Sturnus vulgaris
swallow ....Hirundo rustica
swan
    bewick ....Cygnus bewickii
    mute ....Cygnus olor
    whooper ....Cygnus Cygnus
swift ....Apus apus
thrush
    mistle...........................Turdus viscivorus
    song ....Turdus philomelos
tit
    blue ....Parus caeruleus
    coal............................Parus ater
    great ....Parus major
    long tailed ....Aegithalos caudatus
tree creeper ....Certhia familiaris
turtledove...........................Streptopelia turtur
wagtail
    grey ....Motacilla cinerea
    pied ....Motacilla alba
    yellow ....Motacilla flava
warbler
    garden ....Sylvia borin
    reed ....Acrocephalus arundinaceus
    sedge.........................Acrocephalus schoenobaenus
    wood ....Phylloscopus sibilatrix
white throat.........................Sylvia communis
woodpecker
    greater spotted ....Dendrocopus major
    lesser spotted...............Dendrocopus minor
    green ....Picus viridis
wren ....Troglodytes troglodytes
yellow hammer.....................Emberiza citrinella

Plants

Aconite winter ....Eranthus hyemalis
agrimony.............................Agrimonia eupatoria
anemone wood ....Anemone nemerosa
archangel yellow.................Lamiastrum galeobdolo
arum lily (lords and ladies)....Arum maculatum
bedstraw
    crosswort ....Cruciate laevipes
    lady's...........................Gallium verum
betony.................................Stachys officinalis
bindweed............................Convolvulus arvensis
bittersweet (woody nightshade) Solanum dulcamara
bluebell
    English..........................Hyacinthoides non-scriptus
    Spanish........................Hyacinthoides hispanica
box ....Buxus sempervirens
bramble..............................Rubus fruticosus
buddleia
    butterfly bush ....Buddleia davidii

orange ball tree ....Buddleia globosa
bugle.................................Ajuga reptans
bulrush ....Typha latifolia
burdock ....Arctium minus
butcher's broom ....Ruscus aculeatus
buttercup............................Ranunculus acris
campion
    bladder ....Silene vulgaris
    red ....Silene dioica
    white...........................Silene latifolia
cardoon ....Cynara cardunculus
celandine............................Ranunculus ficaria
chamomile
    scented ....Matricaria recutita
    stinking........................Anthemis cotula
choisya...............................Choisya ternate
cleaver (goose grass) ....Gallium aparine
clover
    red ....Trifolium pratense
    white...........................Trifolium repens
common fumitory.................Fumaria officinalis
cotoneaster.........................Cotoneaster horizontalis
cowslip...............................Primula veris
crowfoot ....Ranunculus aquatilis
cuckoo flower (ladies smock)Cardamine pratensis
cyclamen ....Cyclamen purpurascens
daffodil (narcissus)
    Cedric Morris ....Narcissus Cedric Morris
daisy
    oxeye ....Leucanthemum vulgare
dandelion ....Taraxacum officinale
dead nettle red ....Lamium purpureum
deadly nightshade ....Atropa bella-donna
dock
    curled ....Rumex crispus
dog rose ....Rosa canina
dog's mercury ....Mercurialis perennis
dogwood.............................Cornus sanguinea
dropwort.............................Filipendula vulgaris
duckweed ....Lemna minor
eleagnus.............................Eleagnes pungens
fleabane
    common ....Pulicaria dysenterica
    Guernsey ....Conyza sumatrensis
forget-me-not.......................Myositis arvensis
garlic mustard......................Alliaria petiolata
grasses
    crested dogs tail............Cynosurus cristatus
    common bent ....Agrostis capillaris
    couch...........................Elymus repens
    cow wheat ....Melampyrum pratense
    horsetail.......................Equisetum arvense
    rye...............................Lolium perenne
    soft rush.......................Juncus effuses
    sweet vernal ....Anthoxanthum odoratum
    timothy ....Phleum pratense
    Yorkshire fog.................Holcus lanatus

ground ivy ....Glechoma hederacea
groundsel ....Senecio vulgaris
gipsywort ....Lycopus europaeus
harebell..............................Campanula rotundifolia
hemlock...............................Conium maculatum
herb Robert ....Geranium robertianum
Himalayan balsam ....Impatiens glandulifera
honeysuckle.........................Lonicera periclymenum
hornwort.............................Ceratophyllum demersum
iris
    stinking ....Iris pseudacorus
    yellow ....Iris foetidissima
knapweed ....Centaurea scabiosa
lady's mantle ....Alchemilla vulgaris
loosestrife purple ....Lythrum salicaria
mallow..................................Malva sylvestris
marjoram ....Origanum vulgare
marsh marigold.....................Caltha palustris
mayweed..............................Tripleurospermum inodorum
milfoil ....Ceratophyllum submersum
mistletoe ....Viscum album
monkey flower ....Mimulus guttatus
mullein ....Verbascum Thapsus
nettle- common or stinging...Urtica dioica
orchid
    common spotted............Dactylorhiza fuchsii
    bee ....Ophrys apifera
    early purple ....Orchis mascula
    fly....................................Ophrys insectifera
    fragrant.........................Gymnadenia conopsea
    greater butterfly ....Platanthera chlorantha
    lady...............................Orchis purpurea
    pyramidal ....Anacamptis pyramidalis
    twayblade ....Listera ovate
    white helleborine ....Cephalanthera damasonium
oxslip ....Primula elatior
parrots feather......................Myriophyllum aquaticum
parsley
    bur ....Turgenia latifalia
    cow ....Anthriscus sylvestris
    hedge ....Torilis japonica
plantain ....Plantago major
poppy-common.....................Papaver rhoeas
primrose...............................Primula vulgaris
ragged robin ....Lychnis flos-cuculi
ragwort ....Senecio jacbaea
ramsons (wild garlic) ....Allium ursinum
rest harrow ....Onomis repens
rosemary ....Rosmarinus officinalis
sage ....Salvia nemorosa
scabious ....Scabiosa columbaria
scarlet pimpernel..................Anagallis arvensis
scurvy grass.........................Cochlearia officinalis
self heal ....Prunella vulgaris
snowdrop ....Galanthus nivalis
sorrel
    common ....Rumex acetosa

sheep ....Rumex actosella
    wood.............................Oxalis acetosella
sow thistle ....Sonchus oleraceus
speedwell ....Veronica persica
spurge wood ....Euphorbia amygdaloides
squinancywort ....Asperula cynanchica
St Johns wort.......................Hypericum perforatum
stonewort..............................Charophyta chara sp
teasel ....   Dipsacus fullonum
thistle creeping.....................Cirsium arvense
toadflax ....Linaria vulgaris
toothwort ....Lathraea sqamaria
travellers joy ....Clematis vitalba
trefoil birds foot....................Lotus comiculatus
vetch tufted..........................Vicia cracca
violet
    dog ....Viola riviniana
    sweet.............................Viola odorata
water cress............................Rorippa nasturtium-aquaticum
water lily
    white..............................Nymphaea alba
    yellow ....Nuphar lutea
water mint............................Menthe aquatic
water starwort ....Callitriche stagnalis
wild clary ....Salvia verbenaca
wild thyme............................Thymus praecox
willow herb- rose bay ....Epilobium angustifolium
winter sweet ....Chimonanthus praecox
woundwort
    field...............................Stachys arvensis
    hedge ....Stachys sylvatica
    yarrow...........................Achillea millefolium

Funghi

Blewit wood...........................Lepistra nuda
boletus
    cep.................................Boletus edulis
    slippery jack ....Suillus luteus
bracket
    common ganoderma .....Ganoderma adspersum
    many-zoned polypore ....Coriolis versicolor
    beefsteak.......................Fistulina hepatica
candle snuff ....Xylaria hypoxylon
chanterelle ....Cantharellus cibarius
death cap..............................Amanita phalloides
dead man's fingers ....Xylaria polymorpha
destroying angel ....Amanita virosa
fairy champignon..................Marasmius oreades
fly agaric ....Amanita muscaria
horn of plenty......................Craterellus cornucopoides
ink cap
    shaggy...........................Coprinus cornatus
parasol
    shaggy...........................Macrolepiota rhacodes
    stinking.........................Lepiota cristata
puffball

giant ....Langermannia gigantean
pestle ....Calvatia excipuliformis
Saint George's mushroom .....Calocybe gambosa

Trees and Shrubs

alder.......................................Alnus glutinosa
ash ....malus
beech ....Fraxinus excelsior
birch ....Fagus sylvatica
     jacqmontii ....
     river ....Betula jacqmontii
     silver ....Betula nigra
blackthorn...............................Betula pendula
box ....Buxus sempervirens
cherry wild.............................Prunus avium
chestnut
     horse ....Aesculus hippocastanum
     sweet...........................Castanea sativa
dogwood ....Cornus sanguinea
elder   Sambucus nigra
elm ....Ulmus procera
fir
     Douglas ....Pseudotsuga menziesii
     ginkgo..........................Ginkgo biloba
hawthorn...............................Crataegus monogyna
hazel
     cobnut ....Corylus avellana
     filbert ....Corylus maxima
hollyIlex aquifolium
hornbeam ....Carpinus betulus
ivy ....Hedera helix
larch ....Larix decidua
lime ....Tilia cordata
maple
     field.............................Acer campestre
Oak
     pendunculate ....Quercus robur
     sessile..........................Quercus petraca
rowan.....................................Sorbus aucuparia
sequoia
     giganteum or wellintonia Sequoia giganteum
     redwood ....Sequoia sempervirens
service
     wild.............................Sorbus terminalis
spindle ....Euonymus eureopaeus
sycamore................................Acer pseudoplatanus
viburnum
     arrow wood 'dawn' ....Viburnum bodnatense
     guelder rose ....Viburnum opulus
     wayfaring......................Viburnum lantana
walnut ....Juglans regia
whitebeam.............................Sorbus aria
willow
     crack ....Salix fragilis
     pussy or sallow..............Salix caprea
     weeping ....Salix vitellina

yew ....Taxus baccata

Insects

alderfly..................................Sialis lutaria
ant
     common black ....Lasius niger
     yellow ....Lasius flavius
     wood............................Formica rufa
bee
     leaf cutter ....Megachile centuncularis
     mason ....Osmia rufa
     miner ....Andrena fulva
bee fly ....Bombylius major
bumblebee ....Bombus lapidaries
     red tailed ....Bombus terrestris
     buff tailed ....Bombus subterraneous
     short haired ....Limnephilus lunatus
caddis fly...............................Athous haemorrhoidalis
click beetle ....Melolontha melolontha
cockchafer or maybug ....Nephrotoma appendiculata
crane fly................................Gryllus campestris
cricket
damselfly ....Coenagrion puella
     azure ....Calopteryx virgo
     banded demoiselle ....Calopteryx splendens
     beautiful demoiselle .....Enallagma cyathigerium
     common blue ....Coenagrion scitulum
     dainty ....Erythromma najas
     red eyed ....Coreus marginatus
dock bug
dragonfly...............................Anax imperator
     Emperor ....Libellula depressa
     broad bodied chaser .....Aeshna grandis
     brown hawker...............Sympetrum striolatum
     common darter ....Aeshna juncea
     common hawker ....Anax parthenope
     lesser emperor
dung beetle...........................Geotrupes stercorarius
     dor beetle ....Scarabaeus variolosus
     scarab beetle.................Typhaeus typhaeus
     minotaur beetle ....Forficula auricularia
earwig....................................Luciola lusitanica
firefly ....Philaenus spumarius
frog hopper ....Lampyris noctiluca
glow worm
grasshopper...........................Omocestus viridulus
     common green ....Chorthippus brunneus
     field.............................Vespa crabro
hornet....................................Volucella pellucens
hoverfly ....Chrysopa perla
lacewing
ladybird.................................Coccinella septempunctata
     7 spot ....Harmonia axyridis
     Harlequin ....Ephemera danica
mayfly....................................Gerris lacustris
pond skater...........................Palomena prasina

shield bug green ....Rhagonycha fulva
soldier beetle ....Bibio marci
St Marks fly ....Lucanus cervus
stag beetle
waspVespa vulgaris
     common ....Biorhiza pallida
     gall...........................Sigara dorsalis
water boatman

Butterflies and Moths

Moths

Chinese character ....Cilix glaucata
cinnabar ....Tyria jacbaeae
clouded buff...........................Diacrisia sannio
drinker...................................Philudoria potatoria
elephant hawk......................Deilephila elpenor
ghost.......................................Hepialis humuli
golden Y ....Autographa pulchrina
light emerald ....Campaea margaritata
longhorn...............................Nemophora degeerella
mother shipton.....................Callistege mi
old lady.................................Mormo Maura
peach blossom ....Thyatira batis
scorched wing.......................Plagodis dolabraria
silver Y..................................Autographa gamma

Butterflies

blue
     adonis ....Lysandra bellargus
     common ....Polyommatus Icarus
     holly ....Celastrina argiolus
     large ....Maculinea arion
brimstone ....Gonepteryx rhamnii
brown hairstreak ....Thecula betulae
comma...................................Polygonia c-album
fritillary
     marsh ....Eurodryas aurinia
     Queen of Spain ....Issoria lathonia
gatekeeper ....Pyronia tithonus
marbled white.......................Melanargia galathea
meadow brown ....Maniola jurtina
orange tip ....Anthocharis cardamines
painted lady..........................Cynthia cardui
peacock ....Inachis io
red admiral ....Vanessa atalanta
ringlet....................................Aphantopus hyperantus
skipper large ....Ochlodes venata
small heath...........................Coenonympha pamphilus
speckled wood......................Parage aegeria
tortoiseshell
     large ....Nymphalis polychloros
     small ....Aglais urticae
white
     large..............................Pieris brassicae

     small ....Pieris rapae

Amphibians and Reptiles

frog common ....Rana temporaria
toad common ....Bufo bufo
newt common ....Trituris vulgaris
lizard common
snake
     adder ....Vipera beris
     grass ....Natrix natrix
     slow worm ....Anguis fragilis

Other

spider
     garden...........................Araneus diadematus
     house ....Tegenaria domestica
     nursery web ....Pisaura mirabilis
Earthworm
     chestnut ....Lumbricus castaneus
     compost.......................Eisenia veneta
     redhead ....Lumbricus rubellus
fish
     chub ....Leuciscus cephalus
     pike...............................Esox Lucius
     trout ....Salmo trutta
leech......................................Hemiclepsis marginata
stickleback............................Gasterosteus aculeatus
snail
     garden...........................Helix aspersa
     pond ....Lymnaea stagnalis
woodlouse.............................Oniscidea (family)

Index